At last we have before us a major assessment of some of the most important Black radical organizations of the 1960s by one of the major figures involved in all of them. Well known to serious students of the civil rights and Black liberation movements, Muhammad Ahmad (aka Maxwell Stanford, Jr.) has given us in *We Will Return in the Whirlwind* a study of SNCC, the Black Panther Party, the Revolutionary Action Movement, and the League of Revolutionary Black Workers that only he could have done.

Drawing upon his extensive network of personal and political contacts and his unique understanding of the connections between persons, organizations, and events (too often viewed in isolation), Ahmad makes a significant contribution toward deepening our understanding of a period whose complexities might otherwise be lost to future generations.

—From the Introduction by John Bracey

Books for a Better World
Charles H. Kerr Publishing Company
Established 1886

Some Foremothers & Forefathers of Black Liberation

Queen Mother
Audley Moore

Malcolm X

Ella Baker

Robert F. Williams

Rosa Parks

James Forman

Muhammad Ahmad
(Maxwell Stanford, Jr.)

WE WILL RETURN IN THE
WHIRLWIND

Black Radical Organizations
1960-1975

Introduction
by John Bracey

CHICAGO
Charles H. Kerr Publishing Company
2007

Cover Photo:
Maxwell Stanford, Jr., of RAM forced into police car.
(Page 1, Philadelphia Bulletin, May 27, 1963.)

*This book is dedicated to
all freedom and liberation fighters
of African descent,
past, present, and future,
and to all our friends and allies:
the freedom-loving people of the world.*

—Muhammad Ahmad—

NEW ISBN 978-0-88286-314-6 paper
Old 0-88286-314-2
NEW ISBN 978-0-88286-315-3 cloth
Old 0-886286-315-0

**Charles H. Kerr Publishing Company
1740 West Greenleaf Avenue
Chicago, IL 60626
www.charleshkerr.net**

TABLE OF CONTENTS

In 1960s Chicago, "Freedom Schools" contributed
to the struggle against official school segregation

This drawing by Dorothy Higginson was featured in a special issue
of the SDS journal *Radical America* (March-April 1971)
devoted to the League of Revolutionary Black Workers.

INTRODUCTION

At last we have before us a major assessment of some of the most important Black radical organizations of the 1960s by one of the major figures involved in all of them. Muhammad Ahmad (aka Maxwell Stanford) of course is known to serious students of the civil rights and Black liberation movements. However, few if any, of the younger groups of scholars of those movements have thought to invite him to offer his reflections and insights at their numerous gatherings where events and organizations of which he has an intimate knowledge are the subject.

No matter, Muhammad Ahmad has given us in *We Will Return in the Whirlwind* a study of the Student Non-violent Coordinating Committee (SNCC), the Black Panther Party (BPP), the Revolutionary Action Movement (RAM), and the League of Revolutionary Black Workers that only he could have done. Drawing upon his extensive network of personal and political contacts and his unique understanding of the connections between persons, organizations and events too often viewed in isolation, Ahmad has made a significant contribution toward deepening our understanding of a period whose complexities might otherwise be lost to future generations. Ahmad has managed to gather the insights of persons whose roles have been overlooked by scholars unfamiliar with the names of people not already part of the public consciousness of those years.

My own understanding of the people and events has been both confirmed and expanded by reading Ahmad's study. My own political life confirms the connections between the groups that I worked in and around during the years 1961 to 1971 when I lived in Chicago. I knew my corner of the struggle quite well; it is the activities and interactions at the level of national leadership that I have found most illuminated by Ahmad's data and reflections.

This is not the place for a full blown history of RAM in Chicago, but I would like to offer a few observations to suggest that the view from the head or the center of any national organizations looks different from that of the branches. Interestingly enough, many of the internal problems at the national level did not manifest themselves in any significant way in Chicago. Ahmad's concerns about "disunity" we in Chicago saw as flexibility and as one of the benefits of an organizational structure in which we were not burdened with excessive knowledge of, or responsibility for, what happened in other cities.

RAM in Chicago, which was made up of individuals with their own unique experiences and insights, relied on a strategy of working diligently on issues generated by existing groups and taking great care not to put ourselves in situations where we could be isolated and crushed by the authorities. We saw our tasks as fourfold: 1) to participate in ongoing struggles so as to win the confidence and understanding, if not support, of the masses of Black people by helping them achieve concrete reforms; 2) to engage in ongoing discussion and debate about the limitations of liberal reforms and to suggest alternative analysis as presented in RAM publications such as *Black America*, the *Crusader*, and Ahmad's writings, especially *World Black Revolution*; 3) to prepare for, and remain tactically open to circumstances that were favorable to moving the struggles as far to the left as possible; and 4) where the need existed, to assist in the formation of organizations that would advocate RAM's analysis and goals in a public way. It will be up to future students of our efforts, and those of other local chapters, to make a more definitive judgement as to our successes and failures.

My final observations address Ahmad's judgements about the shortcomings of the groups that he has discussed. I think that he is being too hard on himself and on his comrades. I do not think that the burden of the failure to achieve a movement that would transform all of American society and eliminate all of the oppressive conditions faced by African Americans can be placed on the backs of the quite small numbers of Black Radicals. We were in conflict with the most powerful economic and military power in the world with scant resources other than our brains, courage, energy, and belief that what we were fighting for was worth risking our lives. That, after all, was what SNCC took into the Black Belt, not much more. That is why their achievements were so remarkable, and why they were held in such high esteem all along the political spectrum. As far as we got and as hard as we pushed, we were up against the realities that first, the majority of African Americans were, and are, liberals in their politics, though they might take radical actions to achieve liberal ends.

In any event, we are only ten per cent of the nation's population, therefore the need to seek out allies internally and across the globe. Second, there has been no significant segment of the white population organized to fight for socialism since the 1930s. The white left of the 1960s at the pinnacle of its influence and popularity was anti-war, but not pro-socialist. The vast majority of white workers, in or out of organized labor, are hostile to the idea of socialism, and resistant to efforts to achieve meaningful social and economic equality for African Americans. Finally, the U.S. political and economic system demonstrated that it had sufficient strength and resiliency to absorb the impacts not only of the domestic anti-war and Black liberation struggles, but those of the more radical anti-colonial movements in the third world.

Our reading of other struggles throughout history shows that there were periods of rapid progress followed by periods of stasis or repression, and then later struggles that built on the previous gains. In every revolution we studied—the American, Haitian, Russian, Chinese, Algerian, Cuban—final success was achieved by older persons who had learned from their own earlier failures or those of their contemporaries. My recollection is that during the 1960s we thought that we would fight, win or die, but leave a legacy of struggle and experience for those that surely would follow. We were optimistic because the times were optimistic.

Our popular metaphor of living and fighting in "the belly of the beast" captures the mood. A large part of our enthusiasm was based on the youthful conceit that we were engaged in a struggle to transform the world in ways that our forebears could only dream of; to complete tasks which they had left undone. Muhammad Ahmad has dedicated his life to carrying forward those struggles. Mistakes were made. Gains have been rolled back. I thought that we did the best we could for our day. An excellent place to begin to grasp the nature of those struggles is to read Muhammad Ahmad's *We Will Return in the Whirlwind*.

John Bracey, Jr.
Amherst, Massachusetts
August, 2006

'OUR THING IS DRUM!'

In addition to newsletters, pamphlets, posters and flyers,
DRUM and other constituents of the
League of Revolutionary Black Workers
also made a documentary movie, "Finally Got the News."

PROLOGUE

From the age of five, I was exposed to political ideas by adult members of my family. Several of my uncles were pro-Nation of Islam. My father's mother (mom) had been in The Garvey Movement. My father was a consistent member of the Philadelphia NAACP. My uncle on my mother's side of the family, George Lewis, had a master's degree from Temple University in Negro history and was an advocate of democratic socialism. One of my first cousins, Ernest Peale, nicknamed Sonny, joined the Nation of Islam in the early 1950s. My racial and political consciousness began to sharpen as I began to enter my teens.

While still in elementary school one day, hanging out in Fairmount Park in Philadelphia with a group of young brothers my age, we encountered and began to rumble with a group of Italian boys our age. In order to get to that section of Fairmount Park, we had to go from the African-American community through the Italian community and vice versa to get home. At some point, a group of older Italian boys came along and sided with the younger Italian boys. It was at this point that we (African-American youth) left the park. We began to walk quickly down 52nd street, going toward Girard Avenue, which was the dividing line for the African-American and white communities. As we proceeded walking faster through the Italian community, one of the older Italian boys shouted, "Niggers." At this point, a butcher came out of his store chasing us with a meat cleaver (butcher knife). Women, young and old, were shouting, "Niggers, get the Niggers!" It seemed like the whole Italian neighborhood was chasing us down 52nd Street. This was the beginning of my rude awakening and this is when I learned how to run. We ran for our natural young lives. After our group got back to the African-American community, we told some of the older brothers what had happened. Later that summer, the older brothers went back across Girard Avenue and dealt with the racists. About this time, my cousin, Sonny, now a member of the Nation of Islam, taught me that the Honorable Elijah Muhammad said, "the white man is the devil," and that Minister Malcolm X was the "Messenger's" chief minister.

During my early teen years, my mother continuously taught me, "if you believe you are right, then stick with it, no matter what the odds." She would always say, "stand up for what you believe in, be your own man, don't always follow the crowd." My social consciousness did not develop immediately. As a young African-American in the mid-50s, I was aware of the struggle for racial equality, but it was still fuzzy in my mind. I became interested in expressing my artistic ability and hanging out.

When I became a junior in High School, I ran for senior class treasurer and, to my surprise, I won. In the process of motivating each section to pay their class dues, I had my first experiences at public speaking by "sounding" on the slowest paying class.

In the summer, I would go to work with my father. He worked the suburban route as an exterminator for Theodore Myers and Company. One day as we approached a million-dollar-plus split-level house, he said, "you exterminate the boys' room." I went up to the boys' room to spray around the baseboards and windowsills and began to look around. First of all, the room was twice the size of mine, and then I noticed a table diagonal to the desk with a chemistry lab larger than any I had seen in real life. The only time I had seen one that large was on TV on the monster shows. When we had finished our work in the house and were outside in the truck, my father said, "You see that boy's room? I can't afford to buy you what he has (but) that's who you will have to compete with, and you will have to be ten times better than him just to get in." I never forgot that experience and what my father told me; it has stuck with me throughout my life.

About the age of fourteen, I had become a confused, angry young teenager. The most important person in my life became my father, who was a race militant known in those days as a "race man." In my father's home was always the latest *Jet, Ebony,* and *Sepia* magazines, as well as novels by Richard Wright, which I would look at.

The turning point in my consciousness came at the time of the lynching of Emmett Till. Emmett Till was around my same age, and my mother stressed that Till's lynching could have been mine. I would spend every other weekend with my father. Starting in December of 1955, my father began watching with intensity the Montgomery bus boycott. Whenever I would stay with him, he would ask me to watch the news reports of the boycott with him. Dad would say, "this is important, because this is the first time a black community of this size has stuck together." I would read my father's *Jet* and *Ebony* magazines every other weekend. I watched the Montgomery bus boycott with interest, but I was still too underpoliticalized to understand is importance.

It was around this time my father began to emphasize the importance of my getting involved in a sport. He said, "getting involved in a sport often keeps you out of trouble." He was right. I was trouble bound. Between Jr. High and Sr. High School, I began hanging out with guys who later became known as the "Jr. Syndicate," part of a gang in "the Top" in West Philadelphia. My father had been from "the Top," a section west of 51st Street, which was the dividing line in West Philadelphia between "the Top" and "the Bottom." My mother's side of the family was from "the Bottom," I had grown up in "the Bottom," but because of cousins living all over Philly, I could travel through both sections of West Philadelphia freely.

In my adolescent years, I use to hang out around 51st and Brown Streets. Then my mother moved to "the Top," 117 North Robinson Street, west of 62nd Street. First, I hung around Dewey Street, hanging out with Bobby Morgan and crew. And then I went to high school (West Philadelphia High). When I went to high school, I met Rodel Dorsey and rehooked with George Baron, who I had gone to elementary school with. I began hanging on the corners of "Peach and Arch" and on the south side with Feamester and the brothers, which was called "the Barbary Coast." The reason I mention these corners (street clubs) is because this is where my racial and class-consciousness began to crystallize.

We use to box on the corner, drink, sometimes sing and talk. We would discuss how African-Americans were going to get freedom. Rodel (our warlord), who was about 6'5" and about 230 pounds, who nobody would mess with, one day took me through his neighborhood around 36th and Brown. He introduced me to some old brothers, whom he said had been in the Abraham Lincoln Brigade. I had no idea what the Abraham Lincoln Brigade had been. Well, these older brothers said that they thought African-Americans would go into hills or mountains in the south and would wage guerrilla warfare and would win our freedom. That was the first time I had heard that.

My future projected interests went from wanting to be an industrial designer, to an architect, to being an art teacher. I became more interested in politics and history as time went on. Without me knowing it, I became known as "Black Max," according to a former schoolmate, John Poole. Often I would hang out with Len Hansford, whom

I called my cousin. Len's brother was attending Temple University and was in the Nation of Islam. He and Len believed the answer was separation. I wasn't sure what the answer was, but after I moved with my father in 1957, I began to study periodically; trying to piece together a puzzle. When Robert F. Williams defended the African-American community with an armed defense guard, NAACP members across the country were divided about whether to support him or not. My father was among the faction of the Philadelphia NAACP that supported him and the position of armed self-defense. The Monroe story was reported in *Jet* magazine and my father discussed the racial situation with me. He also showed me where he kept one of his guns. My father also helped establish a rifle and gun club at Fairview Golf Club. I was in firm support of Williams' position even when I was a teenager.

Then came Little Rock. One morning my father was watching the news and I was preparing to go to school. The news showed a mob hollering at and taunting one of the "Little Rock Nine" at a bus stop. A white woman offered the student protection as she walked away from the mob. I was preparing to walk out the front door when my father turned toward me and in a harsh and angry voice said, "would you face a mob to go to school?" I said, "yeah," to get out the door and to have a peaceful day, but as I walked to school in Philadelphia where there were no howling mobs, I wondered what I would do if I had to face an angry mob of white racists.

Two major events affecting my development occurred in 1958. I made the track (mile relay) team at West Philadelphia High. The real turning point that sparked my desire to study African and African-American history occurred while I was attending summer school trying for a double promotion to make up for failing my book in tenth grade. I went to summer school at Bartrum High, a mainly white school in the better section of the white community. I enrolled in an American History class. The teacher, who was white, told me I had been mistakenly scheduled for an advanced history class, but that if I could keep up, I could stay in the class. I would sit on the last row and would hope the teacher wouldn't notice me. There was one other African-American student in class. He was a veteran returning to school to get his G.E.D. He would sit on the first or second row. One day, he and the teacher got into an argument about African-Americans. He told the teacher the problem was the teacher didn't know anything about black folks. The teacher responded, "the problem is that I am white and Jewish and I know more about black people than black people know about themselves."

I was sitting in the back of the room about to doze off when I heard the teacher say that. I sat straight up, and the brother who had been arguing with the teacher turned around and looked dead at me. We were both in shock. We both had a stare on our faces of "do you believe that? Did you hear that?" A light bulb lit up in my mind. I couldn't believe the teacher had said that. As far as I was concerned, the teacher had let the cat out of the bag.

I went straight home from school. I would usually work out on the track at Bartrum under the tutelage of Red (called that because of his red hair), an Italian coach for the Philadelphia Pioneer Track Club. I went to my grandmother's house (Mrs. Ruby Williams, my father's mother, who had been in the Garvey movement in the 1920s) to talk it over with her. When I told my grandmother what the teacher had said, she agreed saying, "that's right, they do know more about us than we know about ourselves." She then went into the basement and brought up two old books. One was about African-American soldiers in the Civil War and the other was about African-American soldiers in World War I. I went to my mother's mother, my other grandmother's house (Mrs. Nancy Miller), where my Aunt Jeanne Miller had a beauty shop and where my mother was once a week, to see if they had any books on "Negro History." My mother said that there were some books in the basement that taught ancient Egyptians were white but in face were black and that I could get a good idea of some of the past by reading them. This started my intellectual search for the truth. I went to the public library and took out E. Franklin Frazier's, *The Negro in the United States* and began to read it. William ("Windy") Holmes, a partner on the track team who became an outstanding middle distance and cross-country champion, loaned me a copy of *The Communist Manifesto* by Karl Marx and Frederick Engles to read. Needless to say, I did not grasp, at first, the political implications of the *Manifesto* and Windy had to break it down to me.

During this time, my father began to groom me for participation in the Civil Rights Movement, whether he realized it or not. That same summer, I walked around with a sign that said "modern radicals." Whenever anyone would ask me what he sign meant, I would talk about how it was radicals who had changed the world. My father stopped me one day as I was coming into the house and said, "You know, it's not too wise to call yourself radical." He went on to elaborate that in his day, it was prestigious to be called a communist or be in the Communist Party. Often Leon Higginbottom, then president of the Philadelphia NAACP, would come over to my father's house to discuss racial politics and the forthcoming strategy of the Civil Rights Movement. Most of the time these meetings were in the late afternoon, because my father would get off from work early. He would always ask me to sit in on the discussions, and I would just sit and listen and try to comprehend what was being said. One late night after pizza, my father and I were standing on the steps just looking up and down the street. My father said, "You see how our people live? In order for it to change, someone is going to sacrifice their life to change it. I made an instant decision and I said, "I will sacrifice to do it." I guess my father thought I was just his young, romantic son talking off the top of his head, but he didn't say anything and we went back into the house.

My second greatest influence during my late teens was my uncle, George Lewis, who had a master's degree from Temple University in Negro History. He told me that the University had wanted him to major in African history, because they felt at the time that the American Negro had little history. He won his fight, but couldn't find a job teaching "Negro" history in the Philadelphia area, because no one was interested in "Negro" history in the 1950s. So he worked at and eventually retired from the post office. In the late '60s, he taught college in New Jersey. One weekend, my Uncle George took me with him up to New York to visit his aunt. He drove both ways and he talked more than I had heard him talk in life. We visited his aunt and then went for a walk in the park. We talked about black people's plight and how he thought that the solution to eliminating discrimination and racial oppression would be found through socialism. I found out later that my uncle was a democratic socialist.

So what did I do? I started studying socialism or what I could find at the time on it. I took out a book from the library entitled, *Man in Contemporary Society*, which discussed socialism. I would also follow the Cuban revolution, what I could find of it. I would imagine myself in the hills with Fidel.

Then came 1960, I graduated from high school in January, a half year behind the class I had entered high school with. On February 1st, the Sit-in Movement started in the south. Soon there was a picket line at Woolworth's at 52nd and Markets in West Philadelphia. I joined the picket line boycotting Woolworth's. I went to my mother's church to hear some sit-in leaders speak. Also during this time, the young turks in Philadelphia Pioneer began to buck, including myself. We formed the Spartans Athletic and Social Club, which eventually became a citywide club of African-American track and football players. I was elected the first president. I didn't make a good president, because I was becoming more interested in participating in the Civil Rights Movement than my career as a track star, but I was improving in my running ability. Somehow the Pioneer coaches got me a partial track scholarship to Central State College in Wilberforce, Ohio. In the interlude, I began hanging out with J.P. Elam (the anchor man on the West Philly mile relay team and excellent cross-country man) and Donald Beaufort (one of the fastest quarter milers Philly had produced up to the '60s). We formed ourselves informally into the "Funky Soul Brothers" dancing to the music of Ray Charles, whom we called the "Prime Minister of Soul." We would get "high" drinking 151% proof rum, go to parties and dance the "twist" or the "chimney," and ravish the young women. But before I left for Central, two major things happened that impacted upon my consciousness.

First was going to see Max Roach and Abby Lincoln present their "Freedom Now" suite at the national convention of the NAACP, which was held in Philadelphia that year. I had been raised on Jazz and had done my homework with Eddie Collier while listening to John Coltrane's *Giant Steps*. I had gone to the Newport Jazz Festival and was an avid fan of both Miles Davis and Cannonball Aderly. But this was the first time I had heard "message music" so direct for my generation. The "Freedom Now" suite immediately raised my political/cultural consciousness. It wouldn't be until a year later that I would listen to John Coltrane's *My Favorite Things* and become a "Tranite" until "Trane" passed on in 1967.

The second event was going to see Dr. Martin Luther King, Jr. speak and shaking hands with him afterward. There was a young lady I was dating who knew I was studying Dr. King's book, *Stride Toward Freedom* and Gandhi's story of mass non-violent social change. One night she said, "Dr. King is coming to my mother's church. Why don't you come to hear him speak?" I did, and was very impressed with Dr. King's message. When I shook hands with Dr. King, he looked dead in my eyes and said, "Keep up the good work." I knew immediately that my friend's mother must have put the bug in Dr. King's ear to say that, because they both, her and her daughter, would say that I was going to do "something great one day."

Off to college I was and the rest I describe in the RAM (Revolutionary Action Movement) Chapter where RAM was founded in 1962. I dropped out of college to test the organizing skills we had learned at college to see if they would work in an urban African-American community. Before doing this, I went to New York to meet with Malcolm X to ask him what I should do. That encounter is described in "Working with Malcolm," which is in the appendix. My meeting of Grace and James Boggs, Queen Mother Audley Moore, and Robert F. Williams are discussed in the RAM chapter. Their relationships overlap. It is important to understand that there was a dialectical relationship between the southern and northern movements that produced a synthesis making a national democratic African-American movement.

Muhammad Ahmad

CONTEXT FOR CHANGE

To begin we concentrate on movement's elders, analyzing the dimensions of their lives that are critical for understanding four black radical organizations—SNCC, RAM, BPP and LRBW. These movement elders were not coordinated but were decentralized, and constituted an influential African-American left, who impacted on the next generation. The elder freedom fighters by their actions, ideology, and advice to the new emerging forces became a historical force in the sense that their activities nurtured the political consciousness and actions of thousands and hundreds of thousands of people.

These six are Ms. Ella Baker, Queen Mother Audley Moore, Robert F. Williams, Malcolm X, and James and Grace Boggs.

Among the six movement elders Ella Baker as an organizer stands out monumentally as someone who was both a catalyst and nurturer of the concept that "the masses make the revolution." A more extensive exploration may be found in Joanne Grant's Ella Baker: Freedom Bound [New York: John Wiley & Sons, Inc., 1998] and in Belinda Robnett's How Long? How Long?: African-American Women in the Struggle for Civil Rights [New York: Oxford University Press, 1997].

ELLA BAKER (1903–1986)

Ella Baker was born on December 13, 1903 in Norfolk, Virginia.[1] She did not consider a teaching career, because she considered it traditionally "women's work." Graduate studies in sociology at the University of Chicago were too expensive, so Baker moved to New York City where she lived with cousins. She obtained a job as a restaurant waitress and later as a factory worker to pay her bills.[2] Baker came in contact with radical politics for the first time when she arrived in New York in 1927. It was there, in New York, in the early days of the Great Depression at Washington Square Park in Harlem that she heard debates over ideas such as communism, socialism, and capitalism discussed. Baker participated in discussion groups and demonstrations that were concerning themselves with praxis. Often, Baker would be the only woman and the only African-American in attendance. Politically she was becoming increasingly class conscious. Baker also began attending graduate courses at the New School for Social Research.[3]

1

In 1932, Baker joined with George Schuyler, an African-American writer with the *Pittsburgh Courier*, to organize the Young Negro Cooperative League. The Young Negro Cooperative League (YNCL) was an attempt at community organizing for African-American economic self-sufficiency. It attempted to discourage consumers from patronizing businesses with racist hiring practices.[4] The YNCL initiated "Buy Black" campaigns seeking to get African-American customers to patronize African-American businesses and use economic boycotts as a labor strategy. The YNCL also critiqued structural unemployment and was critical of "black capitalism." Eventually working as national director of the YNCL, Baker organized stores and collective buying clubs throughout the country. During this time, the Harlem Labor Union was picketing for jobs for African-Americans on 125th street, as part of the "Don't Buy Where You Can't Work" movement. The YNCL collectively banked funds, donated services and resources to cooperatives, and collectively purchased goods. The group cooperated with the New Deal Program Administration to develop a consumer education project.[5] In 1935, Baker accepted a position as director of the Consumers Education Project in the Works Progress Administration.

In the times of the Depression, African-Americans established cooperative classes in settlement houses and African-American women's clubs. For much of the 1930s, many African-Americans' social relations were based on an extended communal socialist economic interdependence family basis. This began to break down in the 1940s as the economy recovered. Starting in 1929, Baker joined the editorial staff of the *American West Indian News* and later served as office manager and editorial assistant for the *Negro National News*.[6] In 1932, Miss Baker began to freelance for *The Crisis*, the NAACP's publication of which W.E.B. DuBois was editor.[7]

In 1935, as an experienced labor organizer, Ella Baker co-wrote with Marvel Cooke, "The Bronx Slave Market." The article, which was researched by both women posing as domestic workers, exposed the roles of white working class women as employers, many of which cheated African-American women domestics. These activities earned Baker renown for her organizing abilities. In 1938, Baker began working for the NAACP as an assistant field secretary, traveling throughout the South to recruit, collect money and publicize the inequalities of African-Americans in the region. Eventually, Ella Baker became national field secretary for the NAACP and traveled throughout the South to organize NAACP branches and developed membership drives. In two years, Miss Baker attended 362 meetings and traveled 16,244 miles. "Because of her impressive success in the field, Baker was named the National Director of Branches in 1943."[8]

In 1943, Baker returned to New York. Under her leadership, Baker emphasized the need for job training for African-Americans to gain equal rights. Baker held leadership conferences and recruited low-income members into the organization. The NAACP's agenda was geared towards the middle class, that is, the leadership was more concerned with recognition from white liberals and did not have the foresight of realizing the potential of mass-based confrontational politics, often neglecting economic issues. As a result of Baker's criticism, several regional leadership conferences took place and a youth program was introduced. Ella remained in a confrontational status with the conservative NAACP leadership until she resigned her national post in 1946. In 1946 Baker became guardian to her eight-year-old niece, which restricted her ability to travel and she resigned from the NAACP. Baker's resignation was due more to the NAACP's conservative national leadership and its inability to incorporate the African-American working class in its ranks and establish participatory democracy for its members. Baker also felt that the national leadership of the NAACP catered to white interests. In 1954, Baker became president of the New York City branch of the NAACP and chaired the education committee. Under Baker's leadership, the New York branch of the NAACP became the best organized and most active in the country. Baker assisted in the beginnings of community action against de facto segregation in New York public schools.[9]

Baker became disillusioned with the NAACP, because it was directed from the top down rather than by the branches. Baker wanted the branches to be more active and in complete control.[10] Baker also raised funds for the National Urban League and ran unsuccessfully for the New York State Assembly as the Liberal Party candidate in 1953.

When the bus boycott erupted in Montgomery, Alabama, Baker and Stanley Levison offered assistance to the boycott movement. Baker, who had worked with Rosa Parks during her NAACP fieldwork in Alabama in the mid-1950s, collaborated with civil rights activist Bayard Rustin to found a new organization in New York called "In Friendship," which provided financial and organizational support to African-Americans who were fighting discrimination in the South, including the participants in the Montgomery (Alabama) bus boycott. Supporting the boycott was consistent with Baker's belief in building strong mass movements in the South that would pursue a more confrontational course of direct action than had been pursued by the NAACP, which Baker felt had become increasingly "hung up in its legal successes."

It was Ella's and the In Friendship group's influence that convinced Rev. Dr. Martin Luther King, Jr. and other southern civil rights leaders that the Montgomery bus boycott mobilization should be used as a foundation to form a mass organization built on mass confrontation with Jim Crow and the racist capitalist system to advance democratic rights for the masses of African-Americans. Baker felt that there was a need for a new organization. Her consistent arguments with Dr. King contributed to the founding of the Southern Christian Leadership Conference (SCLC) in 1957, with Dr. King as its president and Ella Baker as its interim executive secretary.

Baker consequently exhorted the leadership of the Montgomery Improvement Association to continue its fight against widespread racial injustice, not for just the desegregation of buses. Through Baker's efforts, in 1957 the Southern Christian Leadership Conference (SCLC) was formed to fight all types of racial injustice.[11]

Baker built up the SCLC's organizational structure; set up office in Atlanta, hired staff, worked with the community to prepare voter registration drives, created the SCLC newsletter, "The Crusader," and organized the 1958 Citizenship Crusade, the massive campaign to educate African-Americans in the South on how to participate in the electoral process. She began to work closely with her co-worker, Septima Clark. Baker came into conflict with the chauvinist African-American preachers, who dominated the SCLC structure. She felt SCLC was too centered on the charisma of Dr. King (single leadership oriented) and that the movement should have group-centered leadership. Instead of trying to develop people around a leader, efforts should be made to develop leadership out of the group.

"Spread the leadership roles so you're organizing people to be self-sufficient rather than to be dependent upon… a charismatic leader."[12]

In 1960, the sit-in movement to desegregate lunch counter facilities in restaurants in the South broke out mobilizing 50,000 African-American students to participate in non-violent direct action protests against the Jim Crow system. Ella Baker realizing the movement's potential borrowed $500 from SCLC and asked Dr. King's permission to call a conference of the sit-in leaders. The conference was held at Ella Baker's alma mater, Shaw University on April 14–17, 1960 (Easter weekend). It drew two hundred and fifty leaders and their supporters. Upon Ella Baker's insistence that the students had something no one could match, they formed themselves into the Student Non-Violent Coordinating Committee (SNCC) and became an independent action oriented civil rights organization instead of affiliating with Dr. King's SCLC.

Ella Baker always believed in the concept of mobilizing the grass-roots, therefore, she would participate in workshops and projects.

Ella Baker's philosophy of participatory democracy:

She also organized workshops for civil rights activists at the Highlander Folk School with Septima P. Clark. Believing that leaders should empower others, Baker emphasized that the people, knowing what they needed and wanted should be taught how to resolve their problems and help themselves. Through citizenship, education, and decentralized local leadership, Baker projected that national civil rights goals could be met.[13]

Baker left SCLC to become a staff organizer/advisor for SNCC. It was through her guidance that SNCC operated in rural counties in the deep racist South and organized the "Mississippi Freedom Summer" project in Mississippi in 1964. SNCC conducted successful voter-registration drives and raised the political consciousness of poor African-Americans to the point where they formed the Mississippi Freedom Democratic Party and challenged the racist Mississippi democrats in Atlantic City. Baker never imposed her will on SNCC and advised those who sought her advice.

Ella Baker often said, "Hitting an individual with your fists is not enough to overcome racism and segregation. It takes organization, it takes dedication, it takes the willingness to stand and do what has to be done when it has to be done."

Ella Baker taught that participatory democracy had three themes:

1. the involvement of grassroots people in the decisions that affect their lives;

2. the minimization of hierarchy and professionalism in organizations working for social change; and

3. engagement of direct action to resolve social problems.[14]

Baker emphasized, "in organizing a community, you start with people where they are."[15] Meaning that the organizer does not go in a community and start a new organization or struggle over something the people are not concerned with. The organizer agitates over the issues that the community is concerned with.

Ella Baker asked the questions,

> On what basis do you seek to organize people? Do you start to try to organize them on the fact of what you think, or what they are first interested in? You start where the people are. Identify with people.[16]

Baker stressed that the role of the organizer in the community is to act as a catalyst in the process that would bring to the forefront indigenous (local) leadership that should not be dependent upon the organizer or organizers and should avoid the "charismatic" messianic leadership approach. Ella Baker stressed group-centered leadership in which she emphasized that the role of leadership is to act as a facilitator, who brings out the potential in others, rather than a person who commands respect and a following as a result of charisma or status. Baker believed in empowering people through their direct participation in the process of social change. So at that point in the struggle, most young organizers saw that key to the development of people's organizations was mobilization of the masses around the immediate issues that affected them, then the organizers would guide the people's movement, once mobilized, to the goal of socialism. Ella Baker believed political action should empower people to solve their own problems. She felt the movement should be organizing people to act on their own behalf.

Baker taught how to work with the local leadership in a community by first assisting their activities before proceeding in a different direction. Baker constantly repeated that the common working masses had the power to change the system, once they saw their power and were determined to use it.

Baker said,

> My sense of it has always been to get people to understand that in the long run they, themselves are the only protection they have against violence or injustice...People have to be made to understand that they cannot look for salvation anywhere but to themselves.[17]

Ella Baker summarized her philosophy that political activists should work to build a strong people, not strong leaders by saying, it is important to keep the movement democratic and to avoid struggle for personal leadership.[18] Baker taught this philosophy of organizing, of creating mass oriented movements and organizations to a generation of organizers. Baker's importance of passing lessons of a creative pedagogy of teaching through involvement-participation and critical analysis by doing; was invaluable for young organizers of the 1960s–70s. In 1972, when SNCC dissolved itself, Baker moved to Harlem and served as vice chair of the Mass Party Organizing Committee and as a national board member of the Puerto Rican Solidarity Committee. Baker lectured about human rights, especially for South Africans. Baker continued her spirit of organizing until her death, December 13, 1986.

Though they never publicly worked together Baker's contemporary in the black nationalist movement who also nurtured many of the 1960s African-American activists was Queen Mother Audley Moore.

QUEEN MOTHER AUDLEY MOORE (1898–1997)

Moore was the oldest of three daughters born to St. Cyr Moore and Ella Henry. Moore's father, St. Cyr Moore was born as a result of his mother's rape by a white man. He was a onetime sheriffs' deputy in Iberia parish and ran a livery stable. Moore's father had married three times and fathered eight children.[19]

> Moore's mother, Ella Henry, was raised in a middle-class French Creole household after her father was lynched by whites and her mother driven from their property. Both parents died by the time Moore was in the fourth grade, ending her formal schooling. Moore trained in the Poro hairdressing system and at age fifteen became the primary supporter of herself and her two younger sisters, Eloise and Lorita.[20]

Moore and her sisters lived in Anniston, Alabama where they organized support services for African-American soldiers that were denied African-Americans by the Red Cross during World War I. Moore supported her family primarily through hair dressing and sewing. Returning to New Orleans, Moore married and opened a small store with her husband. Moore joined the Universal Negro Improvement Association in New Orleans. As an organizer in the Garvey movement she enlisted the support of over 3,500 people to defend with guns Garvey's right to speak in New Orleans.

> Everybody came with a gun in Longshoreman's Hall to guarantee that Marcus Garvey would speak. I was there, and I had two guns. Everybody had a bag of ammunition. Thirty-five hundred people and the police were in the hall. When Garvey came in everybody stood up and applauded. Garvey said, "My friends, I wanted to apologize to you before, but the reason that I didn't speak to you was because the mayor was used as a stooge by the police to prevent me from speaking. The police jumped up and said, "I'll run you in," and everybody took their guns out, held them up in the air and jumped up on the benches and said, "Speak, Marcus, Speak." We had blue-steeled Smith and Wessons, Germany Lugers, .38 Specials. Everybody said, "Speak, Marcus, Speak." Garvey continued."..and as I was saying..." and the police filed out of there like little puppy dogs, their little tails behind them. They filed out of the hall, every policeman, and we had a meeting that night.[21]

Moore became a life member of the UNIA, becoming one of the first investors in Garvey's Black Star Shipping Line. Moore, her husband and sisters traveled to the West and Midwest (California and Chicago) seeking employment. They eventually moved east, settling in Harlem in 1922. There Moore organized African-American domestic workers in the Bronx labor market and helped African-American tenants to defy evictions by white landlords. Moore founded the Harriet Tubman Association to address these issues. Moore was arrested repeatedly for her activities and used her jail sentences to organize fellow inmates.

Moore initially joined the International Labor Defense, thinking it was the Communist party because of its large number of Communist members. She officially joined the party in 1933, encouraged by its involvement with the Scottsboro Case (1931–1933) and its advocacy of voter's rights and civil rights. The party helped her to hone her organizational skills among working-class people and gave her an in-depth understanding of capitalism. While active in the party, she fought racial segregation on a number of fronts, helping to integrate major league baseball and the Coast Guard, fighting evictions, and organizing early rent strikes in Harlem.[22]

She actively, through street agitation and other methods, campaigned for aid to Ethiopia when racist Italy declared war and bombed million of Africans. In November 1938, she was a candidate for the State Assembly 21st District, on the Communist Party ticket. In 1940, she was the Communist Party candidate for alderman from the 19th Assembly District. An active organizer, Queen Mother took up able leadership in the Harlem section of the Communist Party. In March 1941, she was elected executive secretary of the 21st Assembly District, Harlem section of the Communist Party.[23]

In 1942, Queen Mother was chosen to be campaign manager of the Citizens Nonpartisan Committee to Elect Benjamin Davis, Jr. (African-American communist) to City Council of New York in 1943. She said she was given $40 and a $40-a-week salary and was told to raise the rest of the money herself. This she did by putting together a broad coalition soliciting the cultural support of Lena Horne and Duke Ellington. She said she organized a gala affair in Harlem in support of Ben and white communists were surprised when Ben Davis won.[24] Benjamin Davis served two successive terms on the New York City Council in the 1940s.

Queen Mother was elected chairwoman of The Young Communist League in Harlem in August 1942, and elected to the New York State Committee of the Communist Party. In December 1942, she became a member of the New York County Committee of the Communist Party, and in May 1944, promoted to the resolutions committee of the New York State Convention of the New York Communist Party. In February 1948, Queen Mother was speaker at the Women's State Committee Convention of the Communist Party.[25]

Queen Mother agitated in support of the Mau Mau and came to the defense of Charles Mack Parker.* She and her sisters, Eloisie and Mother Langley, were active in agitation during the "Don't Buy Where You Can't Work" rebellion in Harlem during the 1940s. Queen Mother consistently taught how Jews, who were secretly Zionists, had infiltrated the American Communist Party. She said the first wave of real communists were killed off or exiled and that the Zionists arose in positions of power within the party. The Zionists used the concept of integration and racial equality to open up avenues of upward mobility in American society in which they skillfully used to advance in. Once they began to develop educational, economic and political clout they used their resources to seize Palestine as their colonial base to make the Zionist state of Israel possible.[26] She was adamant about how Zionist Jews had infiltrated the Communist Party, using the concept of integration as a battering ram against the Anglo-Saxon bourgeoisie in order to secure Palestine as their colonial base to make the Zionist state of Israel possible. She said many Jewish comrades whom she had worked with and were neighbors with left for Israel in 1948, after its declaration of independence. In the late '40s, Queen Mother attempted to raise the question of African liberation inside the Communist Party.[27] She was instructed to wait in an alley in Harlem where someone would meet her to take her to a meeting. She said she waited in that alley for eight hours and then she said she realized that the party wasn't serious about the question. She went back home; realizing the party had degenerated and that she had misled the African-American people, and threw up all over the walls of her apartment. Eloisie, who had refused to join the party, came and found her and nursed her back to health.[28] In 1950, Moore resigned from the American Communist Party. Queen Mother, Eloisie Moore, Mother Langley, Dara Collins, and others soon founded the Universal Association of Ethiopian Women which protested throughout the '50s and '60s the legal injustice of African-Americans, particularly African-American men in the South. Moore became an advocate of poor people in the South, returning to the state of Louisiana to lead a successful campaign to restore twenty-three thousand African-American and white families to the welfare rolls after they were cut off by state authorities.

Moore also joined conventional groups such as Mary McLeod Bethune's National Council Of Negro Women (NCNW). She was encouraged to become a public speaker by Bethune and historian, Lawrence Reddick. Moore said she tried to apply dialectical and historical materialism, or a race, class and gender analysis in her presentations.

In the 1950s, as an independent organizer, Moore began her campaign for reparations* along with Richard B. Moore, previously of the African Blood Brotherhood and Communist Party. Richard B. Moore founded the African-American Cultural Foundation, which led the fight against the names "Negro" and "black."

Queen Mother was part of a group of nationalists who supported and raised funds for Robert F. Williams and the Monroe, North Carolina NAACP's war of self-defense against the KKK in the late '50s and early '60s.

Queen Mother and her sister Eloisie helped teach Malcolm X African history and helped him gain a more scientific understanding of the African-American experience. The two of them visited Elijah Muhammad and discussed the national question: the right to self-determination of the African-American oppressed nation in the black belt south. Elijah said that he would raise the question. Soon afterwards, Elijah Muhammad, in the early '60s, demanded a state or repatriation as an alternative to the solution of African-American people's plight in America. In 1962, Moore organized the Reparations Committee of the Descendants of United States Slaves, which filed a claim in California. She went to the White House in 1962 to meet with President John F. Kennedy. In 1963, at the time of the one hundred years of the signing of the Emancipation Proclamation, Queen Mother set up the Reparations Committee with a petition drive to get signatures to demand reparations for slavery and 100 years of economic, political inequality. She went all over the country getting signatures and organized the African-American Party of National Liberation in August 1963. It was based on "collective leadership" and its nucleus was essentially African-American Marxist-Leninist, and its political position was that African-Americans constituted a captive oppressed nation in the black belt South. Some members of the Revolutionary Action Movement in Philadelphia joined the African-American Party of National Liberation (AAPNL) and formed a joint study collective. Among the works assigned to study by Queen Mother was *Negro Liberation* by Harry Haywood, *The Negro Question in the United States and Reconstruction: The Battle for Democracy* by James Allen. Queen Mother sent Robert F. Williams (who was in exile in Cuba) a letter asking him to chair the AAPNL, and to become President of the provisional African-American government in exile. Williams accepted the offer and sent a telegram back to the States to Queen Mother. The AAPNL split in the late 1963 and became defunct. In 1964,

Queen Mother moved to New York where she worked closely with Malcolm X. She also helped educate many SNCC workers, some of whom would stay with her when they came to New York. Queen Mother was one of the founding members of the Black Panther Party in New York. It was at her forum, " The Black Nationalist Action Forum," held at the YWCA, 280 West 135th Street, on July 13, 1966, that the mass call for the Black Panther Party was launched.[29]

Queen Mother was the first signer of the Declaration of Independence of the Provisional Republic of New Africa (RNA) established in Detroit in 1968. In the 1970s, Queen Mother was an active organizer of African Liberation Day (ALD) and was a founding central committee member along with Abner Berry of the African People's Party.

Moore traveled to Africa in 1972 to attend Kwame Nkrumah's funeral. She spoke at the All-African Women's Conference in Dar es Salaam. Being inspired by tours of African farms and industries she founded the Queen Mother Moore Research Institute and the Eloisie Moore College of African Studies, and Vocational and Industrial School in Mount Addis Ababa in Catskills, New York that had been destroyed by fire in 1961.[30]

Moore was a member of the National Association of Colored Women and a founding member of the National Council of Negro Women. Queen Mother was a delegate to the 6th Pan African Conference in Tanzania, East Africa in 1974; an advisor to the National Black Student Association (NBSA) founded in 1976 and a president/founder of the World Federation of African People.[31] In 1973, traveling and speaking around the country for the release from incarceration of Muhammad Ahmad (Max Stanford, the author), Queen Mother contributed $4,000 of her personal funds to his bail. In the 1970s, Queen Mother went to Africa several times and raised the question of the right of African-Americans to self-determination at the Summit meeting of the Heads of the State of the Organization of African Unity in Kampala, Uganda. Moore also sought to establish a national monument in memory of the millions of Africans who died during the trans-Atlantic slave period. In the 1980s Queen Mother Moore was in the forefront of taking the question of reparations before the U.S. Congress.

During her long career of political activism Queen Mother Audley Moore fused black nationalism, socialism and Pan Africanism.

She has been a mentor to many of the sixties and seventies generation of activists. Queen Mother's last public recorded presentation was when she asked the participants of the Million Man March from the speaker's platform on October 15, 1995, not to forget about demanding Reparations. Queen Mother Audley Moore passed on May 2, 1997 in New York. There is no text that is a complete biography on Queen Mother Audley Moore.

The one African-American male leader who Queen Mother Audley Moore supported and felt could be the mass revolutionary leader of African-Americans was Robert F. Williams.

ROBERT "ROB" FRANKLIN WILLIAMS (1925–1996)

Robert F. Williams known as "Rob" was born February 26, 1925 in Monroe, North Carolina. His grandmother, Ellen, a former slave, told him stories as a child about his grandfather, Sikes Williams, who was also born into slavery. Grandfather Sikes Williams traveled up and down North Carolina for the Republican Party during Reconstruction. He also published a newspaper called "Free People's Voice." Grandmother Ellen Williams before she died gave young Robert the rifle his grandfather had wielded against the terrorist "Red Shirts" who attacked Southern African-Americans at the turn of the century.[32]

As a youth Rob Williams became radicalized by blatant racist Southern terror.

Williams came face to face with racism early on. As an 11-year old in 1936, he saw a white policeman, Jesse Helms, Sr. beat an African-American woman to the ground. Williams watched in terror as North Carolina Senator Jesse Helms' father hit the woman and "dragged her down the street to a nearby jailhouse, her dress over her head, the same way that a cave man would club and drag his prey."[33]

In his mid-teens, Rob Williams organized a group called X-32 to throw stones at white men who drove nightly into town trying to assault African-American women.[34] Later, Rob Williams was trained as a machinist in the National Youth Administration where he organized a strike of workers at the age of 16.[35] During World War II, Rob Williams went north to find work. Rob Williams moved to Michigan where he worked for a year at the Ford Motor Company as an automobile worker. Rob and his brother, John Williams fought in the Detroit 1943 riot when white mobs stormed through the streets and killed dozens of African-American citizens.[36]

Drafted in the army in 1944, Rob Williams served for 18 months, fighting for freedom in a segregated army. In the late 1940s Williams wrote a story in *The Daily Worker* entitled "Some Day I Am Going Back South."[37] Williams returned to Monroe and in 1947 married Mabel Ola Robinson, a beautiful and brilliant seventeen year old whom he had known for several years and shared his commitment to social justice, and African-American liberation. In the fall of 1949 he enrolled in West Virginia State College in Charleston, West Virginia taking creative writing. After his wife, Mabel gave birth to a second son, John Chalmers Williams, Williams moved back to North Carolina. In the summer of 1950 Williams enrolled at North Carolina College for Negroes in Durham, N.C. Moving back to Monroe, N.C., in the fall of 1950 Williams enrolled at Johnson C. Smith College in Charlotte, N.C. After a year at Johnson C. Smith Williams money and his G.I. bill ran out so Williams left school traveling around looking for a stable job. In 1954 in near destitution in Los Angeles, Williams joined the U.S. Marines.[38] In 1955 as a husband and father of two sons (Robert F. Williams Jr. and John C. Williams), he returned home with an honorable discharge from the U.S. Marine Corps. Keenly aware of social injustice, "Rob" Williams joined the local N.A.A.C.P. and became its president. As president of the Monroe North Carolina N.A.A.C.P. chapter, he went into the bars and pool rooms to recruit members of the African-American working class. He was also a member of the Monroe Unitarian Fellowship and the Union County Human Relations Council. Facing armed harassment and intimidation of African-American women by the KKK and denied justice in the courts Williams began to advocate armed self-defense of the Monroe N.C. African-American community. Members of the Monroe, N.C., N.A.A.C.P. chapter formed a rifle club, with a National Rifle Association charter, protected their homes with rifles, machine guns and sandbag fortifications.[39]

The Monroe, N.C., N.A.A.C.P. chapter fought the KKK on numerous occasions with rifles and Molotov cocktails. From 1957 to 1961 the armed defense units militarily fought the racists. Because of his militancy, Rob Williams was stripped of his presidency of the local N.A.A.C.P. by the national N.A.A.C.P. The Monroe, N.C., N.A.A.C.P. chapter had grown from a membership of fifty to two hundred and fifty through the leadership of Robert F. Williams.

Worldwide attraction came upon Monroe, N.C. in 1958 when Rob Williams took up the defense of two African-American Monroe boys accused of molesting a white girl—James "Hanover" Thomson, 10 and David "Fuzzy" Simpson, 8, were convicted of molesting a seven year old white girl after she kissed them on the cheek during a game. As the boys were pulling their wagon down Franklin Street later that day, police arrested them. They were thrown in jail and held for six days without seeing or speaking to their parents. As white racism inflamed the white community, a white mob surrounded the jail and shots were fired into Fuzzy and Hanover's homes. A court judge in a hearing six days later sentenced the children to reform school indefinitely.

Williams as head of the local NAACP came to the defense of the children and organized a massive media campaign that put the "Kissing Case" on the front pages of newspapers from the *New York Post* to the *London News Chronicle*. Williams called major newspapers, sent out news releases and went on a national speaking tour on the case. The result of Williams' efforts was that there were worldwide protests and North Carolina Governor Luther Hodges received tens of thousands of letters asking him to release the boys. Hodges eventually released them. Three months after they had been arrested, Fuzzy and Hanover came home and Williams was a hometown hero among African-Americans.[40]

Between 1960 and 1961 Williams organized demonstrations (peaceful pickets) to desegregate the city owned, whites-only swimming pool. The African-American community engaged in a struggle to use the local swimming pool that had been constructed with federal funds. Local white authorities would not allow integrated use nor would they consent to separate use. When the African-American community refused to give up and did not accept promises of construction of a pool at some undefined date in the future, the town government filled the pool with concrete rather than let the African-American community use it.[41] When the sit-in movement began among southern African-American students, Rob Williams staged sit-ins at lunch counters, organized boycotts of department stores and desegregated the local library. Rob Williams was a candidate for mayor of the city of Monroe, N.C., in 1960, running as an independent. Also in 1960,

Williams visited Cuba, met Fidel Castro and became a member of the Fair Play for Cuba committee. Rob Williams would even fly a Cuban flag in his backyard.[42] Rob Williams was a forerunner in the motion toward black political empowerment.

Rob Williams' physical and political stance on armed self defense impacted upon Malcolm X, who then was a minister of the Nation of Islam. Minister Malcolm X on one occasion let Williams speak at Mosque No. 7 in New York to raise money for arms. When the Freedom Rides began in 1961, Dr. Martin Luther King Jr. and Rob Williams, who had debated non-violence as a tactic or philosophy and self-defense, agreed to test non-violence in Monroe. Williams believed in peaceful demonstrations but using them in tactical flexibility with self-defense. He invited "Freedom Riders" to come to Monroe, North Carolina in 1961 to test non-violence. But when the Freedom Riders came to Monroe, white mobs numbering in the thousands attacked them.

The final confrontation came when the black community came to the aid of non-violent freedom riders who were demonstrating in front of city hall. The demonstrators had been attacked by a vicious mob who had beaten Student Non-Violent Coordinating Committee (SNCC) activist James Forman with a shotgun, splitting his head open. Unsuccessful efforts were made to rescue them and get them back to the black community. Armed black people set up defenses at the border between the white section of town and the black community of Newton.[43]

A racial riot broke out as shots were fired. During the race riot a white couple wandered into the angry African-American community. African-Americans from enjoining communities who had come to Newton for a showdown with the Klan surrounded their car. Rob Williams allowed the couple to take shelter in his home. Although the couple left unharmed, the local authorities pressed kidnapping charges against Williams.

Receiving word that he would be held accountable for all the violence that was taking place and knowing the racists were preparing to kill him; Robert F. Williams along with his wife Mabel and two sons, Robert Jr. and John left town; escaping a nationwide manhunt of at least 500 FBI agents Rob Williams and his family were forced out of the country and into exile.

Rob Williams' successful escape from "legal" racism was one

of the early victories of the civil rights movement. Rob Williams' example of courageous struggle stimulated a young generation of activists to emulate his actions. Williams went to Cuba where he was given political exile by Fidel Castro and welcomed by the Cuban people. He was a personal friend of Ernest "Che" Guevera. While living in Cuba for five years Rob and Mabel Williams organized a radio program called "Radio Free Dixie." Radio Free Dixie brought the message of collective armed self-defense to the African-American masses that were battling the racists in America's streets. Williams from exile in Havana, Cuba wrote the book, Negroes With Guns published in 1962 about his experiences from 1957 to 1961. Rob Williams continued to publish his newsletter The Crusader that called upon African-Americans to unite with their allies in Africa, Asia and Latin America (the Third World) and with progressive whites in the United States and throughout the world. Appealing to all heads of state to make a call in support of the civil rights movement, Robert F. Williams was influential in the issuance by Chairman Mao Tse Tung of the People's Republic of China in his declaration of support to the cause of African-American liberation.

As international chairman of the Revolutionary Action Movement (RAM 1964), Rob Williams traveled in Asia representing the African-American freedom struggle. Rob Williams moved to the People's Republic of China in 1966 and resided there during the height of the Proletarian Cultural Revolution. While there he met and talked with the Chinese leaders and toured the country. He visited North Vietnam and met and talked with President Ho Chi Minh. He also broadcasted anti-war propaganda to African-American soldiers in South Vietnam from North Vietnam. From the example Rob Williams set in the African-American freedom movement he inspired the formation in the south of groups such as the Deacons for Defense (1965); the development of the Student Non-Violent Coordinating Committee (SNCC) which changed its policy from non-violence to armed self defense in 1966. The Black Panther Party (BPP-1966) and the League of Revolutionary Black Workers (LRBW-1969) considered Rob Williams the godfather of the armed self-defense movement.

While in China "Rob" Williams was elected president in exile of the Detroit based self-determinationist organization, the Republic of New Africa. Rob Williams visited Africa and was imprisoned in

Britain while trying to return to this country. In 1969 he returned to the U.S.A., and fought extradition from Michigan to North Carolina, finally returning with all charges against him being dropped in 1976. After returning to the United States he continued his political relations with the People's Republic of China, helping establish an import-export trade agreement with China and paving the way for President's Nixon's historic trip to China in 1972. Rob Williams was a fellow at the University of Michigan's Center for Chinese Studies. Williams also published an article on the Proletarian Cultural Revolution. He served as director of the Detroit East Side Citizens Abuse Clinic where he was "too" successful in rehabilitating clients.

Williams often stated in private conversations that when a director of a substance abuse center successfully rehabilitates the overwhelming majority of the center's clients, he or she has worked himself or herself out of a job because the actual role is to service the clients and not to successfully rehabilitate them.[44] Rob Williams resided in Baldwin, Michigan remaining active in the People's Association for Human Rights. In the latter 1970s he traveled the country speaking for the U.S. China People's Friendship Association.[45] He also carried the message of African-American unity wherever he went and in the 1980s traveled again around the country fighting racial abuses wherever he found them. Robert Williams completed the first draft of his autobiography, *While God Lay Sleeping: The Autobiography of Robert F. Williams*. Up until his untimely death, October 15, 1996 due to Hodgkin's disease, Williams was planning to further escalate his leadership activities in the African-American liberation movement even at the age of 71.[46] His fighting spirit and leadership will be felt forever. The American press did not expose the African-American people to Williams as they did Martin Luther King. Williams' shining example as a courageous, sincere, scientific, spiritual, visionary and honest freedom fighter will be honored. Robert F. Williams' insight and foresight is an inspiration for those who cherish the establishment of a people's democracy based on humanitarian principles. One of Williams' supporters in Detroit, Michigan was James Boggs.*

JAMES BOGGS (1919–1993)

James Boggs was born May 28th in Marion Junction, Alabama in 1919. Boggs came to Detroit, Michigan in 1937 and was employed as a worker on the motor line at the Chrysler Corporation's Jefferson Avenue assembly plant from 1940 to 1968. He helped in the organizing of UAW Local 7.[47] Boggs began working with C.L.R. James in (1951) writing for the *Correspondence Newsletter* and chairing the editorial board from 1955 to 1964.

Though Boggs regarded C.L.R. James as his mentor, he clashed with C.L.R. in 1962 on Marxism and what was happening to the American workers. James Boggs was an "organic intellectual" developing his ideas from living struggles in the plant on the production line and in the community. He recognized that the developing changes in production had weakened the unions and, the next great movement was to come from African-Americans. Boggs began to discuss the effects of cybernation and automation on the American workers.

> On the other hand, C.L.R., was in Europe living by ideas that had come out of an earlier struggle, saw Jimmy's analysis and his proposal that the organization undertake a serious study of the development of American Capitalism as a threat and a repudiation of Marxism. Those who supported JB on the issue kept Correspondence. Those who supported C.L.R. formed a group called Facing Reality (which was led by Martin Glaberman).[48]

In 1963 Boggs wrote, *The American Revolution: Pages From a Negro Workers Notebook*, published by Monthly Review Press. This work was the first work published by an African-American worker in the 1960s on the past, present and future direction of the American Revolution. Boggs stated:

> The struggle for black political power is a revolutionary struggle, because unlike the struggle for white power, it is the climax of a ceaseless struggle on the part of 'African-Americans' for human rights.[49]

Boggs saw that every issue, whether local or domestic, had international repercussions inherent in it. In 1963, Boggs chaired the Grass-Roots Leadership Conference in Detroit, where Malcolm X made his famous speech, "A Message to the Grassroots."[50]

Boggs with his wife Grace Lee helped in forming the Michigan Freedom Now Party. The Boggs helped in the national formation of RAM (Revolutionary Action Movement), dialogued with and advised Malcolm X along with African-American journalist William Worthy and Patricia Robinson.[51]

When the Boggs felt that RAM was not pursuing a constructive path of development, they attempted to guide the civil rights movement towards independent political empowerment and self-defense. In April of 1965 on the initiative of James and Grace Boggs, a meeting was called that included Nahaz Rogers from Chicago, Julius Hobson from D.C., Jesse Gray (Harlem rent strike leader of 1960), and other activists such as Bill Davis from Philadelphia who formed the Organization for Black Power (OBP). Though short lived, OBP proposed to develop bases of black power through independent politics. OBP's development influenced SNCC's development.[52] SNCC (a year later, 1966) raised the cry of black power. The southern development of the Deacons for Defense in Louisiana and the 1965 Watts spontaneous rebellion in Los Angeles signaled a changing mood among African-Americans. Sensing there was ideological weakness in the emerging paradigm of the young African-American radicals, Boggs wrote a timely article titled, *"Black Revolutionary Power"* in the August 1970 issue of *Ebony* and authored another book titled, *Racism and the Class Struggle: Further Pages From a Black Workers Notebook* published by Monthly Review Press in 1970.[53]

Boggs and Malcolm saw eye-to-eye and he said,

> It is impossible for blacks to free or develop themselves without turning over every institution of this society, each of which has been structured with blacks at the bottom.[54]

Boggs felt the city was where most African-Americans were concentrated and it would be in those cities that African-Americans would constitute a majority of where the struggle for black power would occur. He emphasized that the struggle should be based on issues and terrain, which would enable the African-American community to create a form of liberated area out of what are occupied areas.

Boggs also wrote: *Manifesto for a Black Revolutionary Party*, February 21, 1969 (Pacesetters Publishing); *Awesome Responsibilities of Revolutionary Leadership, Uprooting Racism and Racists in the United States; But What About the Workers?*; and, *Liberation or Revolution*; *Black Power: A Scientific Concept Whose Time Has Come*; and *The City is The Black Man's Land*. While he was writing, he worked with Ken Cockrel and General Baker of the League of Revolutionary Black Workers until its split and demise.

In 1974, James and Grace Lee Boggs published the world

acclaimed *Revolution and Evolution in the Twentieth Century* (Monthly Review Press, 1974). They also contributed to the founding of the National Organization for an American Revolution (NOAR) from 1979–1987 and were primary theorists for NOAR from 1979–1987. NOAR was an attempt to give direction to the movement as it was floundering. Boggs helped form We The People Reclaim Our Streets (WEPROS) and Detroiters Uniting. In 1984 he helped form Save Our Sons and Daughters (SOASD) and Detroit Summer, a community-rebuilding effort that brought city and suburban youth together on beautification projects. These efforts, which are still continuing, are efforts to give youth a purpose in the period of post-industrialization. Boggs passed away July 22, 1993.

Kenneth Snodgrass in writing on Boggs stated:

> "Boggs use to say that since many of us probably won't see the transformation of the USA in our lifetime, it is imperative for committed people to transmit their knowledge, wisdom, and leadership skills to the next generation."[55]

There is no text that is a complete biography on James Boggs. Though James Boggs has passed, his widow Grace Lee Boggs continues his work.

GRACE LEE BOGGS (1915–)

Grace Lee Boggs was born June 27, 1915 in Providence, Rhode Island of Chinese immigrant parents. Ms. Grace Lee Boggs earned a Doctorate in Philosophy from Bryn Mawr College in 1940.

"There weren't jobs for Chinese women in Philosophy" so she headed to Chicago to join the March on Washington led by an early organizer of the AFL-CIO, A. Philip Randolph. Ms. Lee began working, with C.L.R. James in 1941. She also worked with a young African student (Kwame Nkrumah).

> I first met C.L.R. in Chicago where I had gone to live after completing my graduate studies. I had just discovered the power of the independent black struggle through my participation in the March on Washington Movement, which forced F.D.R. to issue Executive Order 8802 banning discrimination in defense plant hiring.[56]

Grace Lee joined the Johnson (C.L.R. James)/Forest (Raya Dunayevskaya) Tendency, a small collective of about seventy-five people inside the Workers Party and the Socialist Workers Party. The Tendency felt their special contribution would be its method of thought and conception of social development, which would make people's lives intelligible to them in rational and international terms.[57]

In 1951, the Johnson-Forest Tendency formed *Correspondence*, a loose collective centered in Detroit, after leaving the Socialist Workers party. In the fall of 1952, while he was still on Ellis Island, C.L.R. spearheaded the creation of the "Third Layer School," where rank-and-file workers, women and youth did the talking and intellectuals did the listening.[58]

At the Third Layer School Grace Lee met James Boggs, whom she would later marry. In 1961, James Boggs, who was chair of *Correspondence*, had a political split with C.L.R. James over the role of the working class in making the American Revolution.

Grace felt the same as James Boggs that

> ...any kind of revolutionary organization had to be built on cadres and that radicals ten to underestimate the critical role of class in building a movement. They swear that "without revolutionary theory, there is no revolutionary practice." But for their revolutionary theory, they tend to accept ideas that have come out of other traditions rather than undertake the more difficult task of deriving our revolutionary theories from our own historical conditions and experiences.[59]

Grace Lee Boggs felt political revolutionaries should always speak a language people understand and should be able to get to the root of things. She also believed that political revolutionaries should be conscious of the need to go beyond slogans and be able to create programs of struggle that transform and empower participants. Grace Lee Boggs has always thought that at the heart of movement building is the concept of *two-sided transformation*: one of ourselves and one of our institutions.

Grace Boggs co-authored *Revolution and Evolution in the Twentieth Century and Conversations in Maine*. In the fall 1993 issue of *Third World Viewpoint*, *Remembering James Boggs*, Grace Boggs stated:

> "The main weakness of the Black left has been its inability to focus on the youth, who are burdened by a very high unemployment rate and are targeted by the drug culture. Until the divorcement of the Black left from the youths is addressed, there is likely to be no real advance in Black radicalism."[60]

22

Grace always taught that cadre should never be content with merely interpreting American history, but must be engaged in the practice of struggling to change it; and our ideas, which should be an "organic" ideology, must come out of practice and the new contradictions which practice uncovers.

For a more extensive discussion of Grace Boggs' life, please refer to (*) below.

A person all of the forerunners of the 1960s; Ella Baker, Queen Mother Audley Moore, Robert F. Williams, James and Grace Lee Boggs, worked with either directly or indirectly was Malcolm X.

MALCOLM X: (1925–1965)

Malcolm X was a pivotal personality and catalyst for a transition from civil rights to black power. What made Malcolm X so pivotal to the black liberation movement (BLM) was that he followed the anti-imperialist tradition of Paul Robeson and W.E.B. DuBois, and was developing a mass following as a revolutionary democrat (not to be confused with the Democratic Party).

Just before his death, Malcolm had made an ideological leap, a leap that took many years to understand. I first met Malcolm X personally on Thanksgiving Day 1962 in New York. I stayed in touch with Malcolm until his break from the Nation of Islam, there upon traveling to New York to work with Malcolm from June 1964 until February 21, 1965.

During our last one on one meeting in 22 West Restaurant in Harlem, approximately the first of February 1965, Malcolm said, "I no longer call myself a black nationalist. The best way to describe myself is to say, "I am an Internationalist."

We can identify three periods in the development of the political thought of Malcolm X. The first period from 1952 through most of 1962, was characterized by the theology of the Nation of Islam in which Malcolm was the most articulate minister for the N.O.I. and its leader Elijah Muhammad. Black Nationalism's renewed popularity owed much to the Nation of Islam, which offered a scathing critique of white America. It was in the Nation of Islam that Malcolm X returned to aspects of the black nationalism of his childhood. Malcolm's father was an organizer for Marcus Garvey's U.N.I.A. and would take the young Malcolm Little with him to mass meetings. This left an imprint on Malcolm's thinking until the time of his death.[61]

Sometime in 1962, Malcolm X initiated the transition to secular black nationalism. This second period in his thinking reached its highest development with the creation of the Muslim Mosque, Inc. and his speeches in the spring of 1964. With his trip to the Middle East and Africa in late April and early May of 1964, Malcolm X ushered in the final period on the development of his thinking, the period of Pan Africanism and internationalism. It is important to know that by 1964 Malcolm was in rapid transition in search of the solution to the plight of African-Americans and persons of African descent the world over. Malcolm had become, at the time of his untimely death, a revolutionary international democrat or an anti-imperialist who stood against the oppression of people regardless of nationality, class, creed or color.[62]

One of Malcolm's brothers (Philbert) visited Malcolm in prison and introduced him to the Nation of Islam (N.O.I.) and Islam as taught by Elijah Muhammad.

Through religion (Islam), Malcolm began his self-transformation, gaining a sense of direction and commitment to the liberation of African-Americans. "Religion can either be an opium of the people or serve as an inspiration toward their liberation," so said Karl Marx. Malcolm learned through self-discipline how to educate himself.

During his time in prison, Malcolm was influenced by the activities of Paul Robeson, who had addressed the Civil Rights Congress at a meeting of (10,000) in Madison Square Garden and who had called on African-Americans to resist the draft and not to fight against their Asian brothers in the Korean War. Malcolm embraced Robeson's efforts and wrote a letter to President Truman stating his support of Robeson. Malcolm also embraced Robeson and William Patterson's (Chairman of the Civil Rights Congress) efforts to petition the United Nations denouncing the U. S. for genocide against African-Americans. These ideas were not new. Marcus Garvey, who Malcolm's father, Earl Little, organized around, had drafted a petition in 1928 to the League of Nations. Marcus Garvey had based his efforts on the earlier work of Bishop Henry McNeal Turner in the 1890s and 1900s.*

Also at this time C.L.R. James was so effective as a Socialist Workers Party organizer of African-Americans that he was detained at Ellis Island and later deported as an undesirable alien.[63] Malcolm studied intensely for six years while in prison until his release in 1952.

An emotional experience for Malcolm that transformed him into a religious fanatical true believer occurred when he was released from prison. Upon meeting Elijah Muhammad, known to him and others as the last messenger of Allah (God), Malcolm became an emotional disciple of the Nation of Islam. Malcolm was a hard working zealot organizing "fishing" (recruiting) campaigns for Temple Number One in Detroit and soon rose to be assistant minister there. He was soon assigned as minister to Temple Number Seven in New York. He helped found some thirty-five temples.

On June 20, 1963, Malcolm emerged as a national organizer when a Muslim was beaten by the police in Harlem. Malcolm and the Fruit of Islam (FOI) demonstrated in silent disciplined military order, consisting only of Malcolm's command of a hand signal; Malcolm dispersed the FOI only after securing medical treatment for the injured Muslim. Watching Malcolm's dynamics with the people of Harlem, the precinct police captain said, "No man should have that much power."[64]

To understand Malcolm's influence on the African-American student movement, we have to recollect where the student movement was in 1964. SNCC, the Student Non-Violent Coordinating Committee, which was formed out of sit-ins in 1960, was working on voter registration in the Delta South. In 1964, the majority of the membership of SNCC believed freedom could be achieved through non-violent, peaceful change within the capitalist system. They believed, as many African-Americans believe today, that reform of the system could be achieved by working through the Democratic Party. This is why SNCC formed with Mrs. Fannie Lou Hamer and other Mississippi Freedom Democratic Party (MFDP) members to challenge the racists at the Democratic Party convention held in Atlantic City in 1964.

Malcolm, however, put less faith in partisan politics. Malcolm said, "The Democratic Party, along with the Republican Party, is responsible for the racism that exists in this country."[65]

Malcolm taught that African-Americans were oppressed because African-Americans' oppression served the interest of the capitalist ruling class. He said liberation "freedom" could not be achieved through the capitalist system. Malcolm taught that it is foolish to limit yourself to one tactic when fighting for liberation. One should not just limit oneself to violent or non-violent tactics. You use whatever tactics are best for the situation you are in; you use any means.

Malcolm taught that the way to stop racial abuse was for the entire African-American community to arm for collective self-defense. Malcolm said every African-American household should have a shotgun. But he also said that African-Americans shouldn't use these guns against one another; they should be used mainly for stopping racial abuse, defending themselves.

Malcolm said African-Americans should love one another as brothers and sisters and never do to your brother or sister what you would not want done to yourself. But if a brother or sister did harm to the community, then it was up to the community to correct them.[66]

While Malcolm was in Africa, he met John Lewis, Chairman of SNCC, and other members of SNCC who were visiting the Republic of Guinea. John Lewis said that everywhere the young SNCC delegation went in Africa they were asked where they stood in relation to Malcolm. After the SNCC delegation met with Malcolm they decided to re-evaluate their program and place stronger emphasis on developing alliances with African liberation organizations that were fighting colonialism, and with progressive African states.[67]

Even while Malcolm was in the Nation of Islam, he was heavily influenced by the young students in the civil rights movement, and developing progressive forces in and around the NOI. The Nation of Islam was the center of black nationalism in the late 1950s and early 1960s. During 1962–63, several independent all African-American student formations developed in the North. All these organizations had a close association with the Nation of Islam.

In Detroit there was UHURU; in Chicago, NOA (National Organization of African-Americans); in Oakland, California, there was the African-American Association; in Cleveland, the African-American Institute; in New York, UMBRA; and in Philadelphia, the Revolutionary Action Movement. Malcolm, being the traveling representative for the NOI, was in contact with these organizations and others. Malcolm in a sense was a man in a physical pivotal position. He would constantly talk to the young activists as he traveled from city to city.[68]

Malcolm's break with the NOI began in 1962 when the Los Angeles police raided the Temple there, killing a Muslim and wounding others.[69]

By 1963 a group of young Muslims left the NOI and formed the National Liberation Front (NLF). The NLF group left the NOI before Malcolm left. Much of what Malcolm began to say in 1964 was the philosophy of this organization. The NLF was an armed self-defense Sunni Muslim formation that adhered to the ideology of revolutionary nationalism. When Malcolm left the Nation of Islam, the formation told Malcolm they were armed and in martial arts training and asked him if he wanted to be their leader. Malcolm agreed, and the NLF became the core of the Muslim Mosque, Inc.[70] On March 8, 1964, Malcolm announced his independence from the NOI. On March 12, 1964, Malcolm gave a press conference, introducing the formation of the Muslim Mosque, Inc. Malcolm's basic theme was unity with Africa, Pan Africanism, taking the United States before the United Nations for violation of the human rights charter, and uniting with other civil rights organizations. Between March and April 1964, Malcolm moved to form coalitions with civil rights leaders. He met with Lawrence Laundry (leader of the student/teacher walkouts in Chicago over quality education), Jessie Gray (Harlem, New York leader of mass rent strikes in New York City in 1960) and others who supported building a coalition of a new type.[71]

Malcolm's advocating of armed self-defense; the same as Robert F. Williams before him was a radical departure from traditional black nationalism. His position reflected the new mood among African-American youth. The left wing of SNCC (Student Non-Violent Coordinating Committee), particularly the Mississippi field staff, had become revolutionary nationalists, had armed and united with Malcolm's strategy. Before the end of 1964 several SNCC delegations met with Malcolm.[72]

On September 20, 1960, Malcolm met with Cuban premier, Fidel Castro, in the Hotel Theresa in Harlem. Malcolm had helped secure for the Cuban delegation the Hotel Theresa after the Cuban delegation left the midtown Shelburne Hotel refusing the accept unreasonable financial demands.[73]

In 1963, Elijah Muhammad named Malcolm the national representative of the Nation of Islam. Malcolm had also been representative in helping to build the Fruit of Islam (F.O.I.) into a powerful para-military wing of the N.O.I. and founded the N.O.I.'s national newspaper, *Muhammad Speaks*.

Another trauma for Malcolm and perhaps most devastating

for him was his learning of Elijah's extramarital affairs and Elijah having illegitimate children by his secretaries. Malcolm, not being one to believe rumors, went to the women to get the facts. He then went to Elijah Muhammad and Elijah confessed. Malcolm said Elijah's confessing made him realize that Elijah was just a man and from that point on "I will never believe in the divinity of a man."[74]

At the age of 38 Malcolm had to start his life anew and to renounce much of what he believed to be the truth for much of his adult life (18 years) and at the same time being thrust into national and international leadership. Malcolm had to build an organizational foundation from scratch. In less than a year, Malcolm laid the foundation to the Muslim Mosque, Inc. (M.M.I.) and the Organization of Afro-American Unity (O.A.A.U.). Between the summer of 1963 and 1964 Malcolm gave important speeches in cities such as Detroit, Cleveland, and New York City, which had militant and nationalistic activists in their African-American communities. These activists' cadres pushed Malcolm into a more radical stance as he attempted to clarify his own feelings about what was to be done.

In April 1964, Malcolm's theme became "The Ballot or the Bullet." If we listen carefully to these speeches we will be able to conclude Malcolm was responding to the political developments then occurring in the South, particularly with the Mississippi Freedom Democratic Party, and the rebellious mood simmering in the North.[75]

Malcolm called for a black nationalist congress or conference that was scheduled for August 1964, to form either a party or an army. While the congress/conference didn't occur mainly because Malcolm was in Africa, his envisioning of building a black nationalist party was later attempted in the form of the Black Panther Party (BPP) in 1966 and the National Black Independent Political Party (NBIPP) in 1980.[76]

The Chinese Ambassador to Ghana particularly impressed Malcolm. The Chinese Ambassador asked Malcolm if he knew a particular leader in Danville, Virginia. Malcolm was embarrassed because he had never heard of the brother. The Chinese Ambassador said the Danville struggle was one of the highest levels of struggle African-Americans had in 1963.

Malcolm was also impressed by an Algerian revolutionary who was a member of the FLN (National Liberation Front). He told Malcolm because of his press statement he thought he was a dark complexioned man and had assumed Malcolm was a racist.

These incidents and personalities, along with Muhammed Babu of Tanzania and the progressive African-American community in Ghana, helped Malcolm to see the nature of racial, class and gender exploitation in the world.

Malcolm was beginning to understand that U.S. capitalism made over 100 billion dollars due to racial determined wages of African-American workers. Taking the 200 billion which African-Americans circulate in wage power but return to the capitalists in high mortgages, rents, clothes, food and pleasure, African-Americans are the next best thing that the U. S. has except maybe trade with Canada.[77]

Malcolm was beginning to see this. Also taken with the racial division or stratification of labor worldwide through either outright imperialism and reaping more profit through neo-colonialism creates a race/class dichotomy.

In 1964 Malcolm X changed from viewing white people as devils to attacking the international capitalist system as the principle enemy of persons of African descent. Malcolm stated that the United States Federal Government was the cause and root of oppression being that the U. S. monopoly capitalist class controls the government. Malcolm changed from being a racial religious nationalist to a political internationalist.[78]

While Malcolm had become a political internationalist, he was also developing a practical day-to-day program. Essentially there were eight major points that Malcolm X was emphasizing.

Eight points of Malcolm

1. Malcolm said that persons of African descent couldn't get freedom under the capitalist system and had to struggle for "freedom" by any means necessary"

2. He said persons of African descent should arm for self-defense.

3. Malcolm believed that African Americans had not developed a national consciousness yet to struggle for self-determination even though he believed African-Americans constituted an oppressed nation. In this regard, he advocated revolutionaries to become involved in struggles, which the people were concerned about in order to raise their consciousness.

29

4. Malcolm advocated revolutionary internationalism, an internationalism that would change and overturn the world capitalist system.

5. Malcolm wanted to form a revolutionary political party independent of the Democratic and Republican parties.

6. Malcolm constantly spoke out against U. S. Imperialism, taking a revolutionary internationalist position. He condemned the war in Vietnam and U. S. Imperialist aggression in the Congo.

7. He appealed to African leaders to break off ties with the U. S.; Nasser of Egypt supported the move.

8. His move to bring the U. S. before the UN would have isolated the U. S. in the world and would have affected billions of dollars in international trade.

Before his untimely death, Malcolm, realized that non-equality of African women in African organizations hindered the liberation movement. He was practicing equality and consciously giving African-American women more responsibility and leadership in the OAAU.[79]

Since that time, African-American women revolutionaries have fought the male chauvinist positions and actions of men in the Student Non-Violent Coordinating Committee, Revolutionary Action Movement, Black Panther Party, Southern Christian Leadership Conference, League of Revolutionary Black Workers, African Liberation Support Committee and many other formations. Having been educated by the women's movement, all male revolutionaries should, by this time, uphold and fight for women's social, economic and political equality and the right to reproductive choice.

Travel broadens one's horizon was Malcolm's theme to explain his new understanding of the actual or real basis of race, class and gender oppression worldwide. Through travels in the Middle East, the Hajj (Muslim spiritual pilgrimage) and conversations with Algerian revolutionaries, Malcolm changed his views on race. He said he would never again judge a person on the basis of race but rather upon what they did in practice.[80]

Malcolm learned from his travels in Africa that in whatever country where the women were liberated, that country's liberation movement was strong. He therefore began to practice equality between men and women in the Organization of Afro-American Unity and received resistance to his equalitarian gender policies from many of the men who had previously been members of the Nation of Islam.[81]

Internationally, Malcolm spent 18 months in Africa and Middle East. Among the many dignitaries he met with, he was most impressed with Aziewkee of Nigeria, Sekou Toure of Guinea, Kwame Nkrumah of Ghana, Julius Nyerere of Tanzania, Muhammad Babu, representatives of Ahmed Ben Bella of Algeria and Ahmed Gamal Nasser of Egypt. Malcolm was first and foremost a Muslim. One of the purposes of his travels was to establish bridges or links with the Islamic world. In his understanding of the world economy and world politics he felt a great crime had been committed against the people of Palestine by the Zionist Jews stealing their land and establishing the colonial settler state of Israel with help of Britain and the United States in 1948. Malcolm felt the Zionist Jews served as client administrators in the world capitalist system. They are higher than middle men but in an administrative capacity that is needed to keep the system running. He therefore agreed when Nasser asked him to write an article on Zionism. The article titled "Zionist Logic" appeared in the Egyptian Gazette, September 17, 1964.

DOLLARISM

The number one weapon of 20th century imperialism is zionist-Dollarism and one of the main bases for this weapon is Zionist Israel. The ever-scheming European imperialists wisely place Israel where she could geographically divide the Arab world, infiltrate and sow the seed of dissension among African leaders and also divide the Africans against the Asians.

Zionist Israel's occupation of Arab Palestine has forced the Arab to waste billions of precious dollars on armaments making it impossible for these newly independent Arab Nations to concentrate on strengthening the economic standards of their country and elevate the living standard of their people.[82]

This article probably put Malcolm on the "hit list" for Masad, Israeli's intelligence forces.

In France, Malcolm united Africans from all over the African continent, who were previously at odds with one another along with persons of African descent from the Caribbean, and Latin America as well with those from the United States then living in France in exile. Malcolm gave them all a purpose to serve as a propaganda unit for the African-American liberation struggle by forming a branch of the OAAU in France. He also created similar developments in England, Ghana and the UAR.

Malcolm, in less than a year, became one of black America's most progressive spokesmen, which impacted on the young civil rights workers. Beginning to support the mass civil rights demonstrations taking place in the South, he called for taking the U. S. Government before the United Nations for its violation of human rights and the crime of genocide which Dr. King supported. Malcolm was in contact with Che Guevera (a leader of the Cuban Revolution) and had invited Che to speak at one of his weekly rallies. Guevera had to turn the invitation down after discovering anti-Castro Cubans planned to either disrupt the rally or murder him while in attendance.

Malcolm's philosophy was that African-Americans should control the economics and politics of the African-American community. Malcolm called for organizing independent political clubs. This was the essence of his "ballot or bullet" message. Malcolm called on all African people wherever they may be to build political "bridges," networks and organizations world-wide. Malcolm was about to introduce the OAAU program when he was assassinated.

MALCOLM'S POLITICAL SIGNIFICANCE

Malcolm was the first mass African-American leader to attack the U. S. government and the U. S. capitalist system in the 1960s as the cause of racism and the enslavement of the African captive nationality. Through his existence he formed a bridge between the 1940s, 1950s generation and the 1960s. He articulated the views of both generations and was going in the direction of developing a program that would have consolidated both generations towards African-American liberation.

It should be noted that Malcolm was really becoming a threat to the U. S. government's capitalist power structure because of his growing influence on African and Asiatic students in this country and throughout the world. Malcolm's trips to Africa had much to do with Nasser's repudiation of U. S. "dollarism" when Nasser told the U. S. to "go to hell" with regard to U. S. aid and also concerning its blatant, brutal, racist activities in the Congo. Malcolm's constant attacks on the U. S. Government, particularly the CIA, threatened U. S. foreign policy: particularly in Africa, and just about finished the "Peace Corps."

His influence in Africa was so strong that African leaders were not going to let James Farmer of CORE enter Africa unless Malcolm okayed it. Due to the efforts of Malcolm in Africa, coupled with those of Robert F. Williams in Asia and Latin America, the racist U. S. government was truly pictured as the citadel of world imperialism. This alone would give the CIA reason to assassinate Malcolm. Through his telegrams and speeches warning about the far right, he helped to expose the plan the far right was using to take over America. He interpreted the far right's (fascist's) plan and what it meant to African-Americans.

His efforts to organize the Organization of Afro-American Unity were very significant, for this was the first organization officially recognized by an African government since the UNIA of Marcus Garvey. It had the potential of becoming a national African-American liberation front.

Malcolm's example of attempting to build an all African-American coalition laid the basis for the direction that the African-American movement for empowerment took from his assassination until 1975 and created a pace of development for African-American radical organizations.

The aforementioned were some of the major organizers/theoreticians from earlier periods who influenced the emerging activist generation in the 1960s/70s. These transition forces prepared the way for black radical organizations 1960–1975 to flourish and develop.

1. Elizabeth D. Schafer, Dorothy C. Salem "Baker, Ella (1903–1986)," *African-American Women: A Biographical Dictionary* [New York: Garland Publishing, 1983], p. 25.

2. *Ibid.* (Schafer) p. 25.

3. *Op. Cit.* (Schafer) p. 25.

4. Joy James, Ella Baker: Black Women's Work and Activist Intellectuals," *The Black Scholar Volume 24, No. 4. Fall 1994* p. 10.

5. Britta W. Nelson, "Ella Baker—A Leader Behind the Scenes," *Focus Volume 21 No. 8, August 1983* p. 3.

6. *Op. Cit.*, p. 10.

7. Ibid. (James) p. 10.

8. Joan Corl Elliott, Ella Baker (1903–1986) in Jessie Carney Smith (ed.) Notable Black American Women [Detroit: Gale, 1992], p. 40.

9. *Op. Cit.* (Elliott) (Notable Black American Women), p. 40.

10. Ibid (Elliott) Notable Black American Women) p. 40.

10. *Op. Cit.* (Elliott) (Notable Black American Women), p. 41.

11. *Op. Cit.* (Nelson) (Notable Black American Women), p. 4.

12. *Op. Cit.* (Schafer), p. 17.

13. Carol Mueller, "Ella Baker and the Origins of Participatory Democracy" in Vicki L. Crawford, Jacqueline Anne Rouse, Barbara Woods (ed.) Women in Civil Rights Movement: Trailblazers and Torchbearers 1941–1965 [Bloomington and Indianapolis: Indiana University Press, 1990], p. 56.

14. Gerda Lerner, "Developing Community Leadership" in Black Women in White America [New York: Pantheon, 1972], p. 20.

15. Ella Cantarow and Susan Gushee O'Malley, "Ella Baker: Organizing for Civil Rights" in Moving the Mountain: Women Working for Social Change [New York: The Feminist Press, 1980], p. 16.

16. Charles Payne, "Strong People Don't Need Strong Leaders: Ella Baker, Models of Social Change," unpublished paper, Northeastern University, Department of African Studies, 1987, p. 5.

17. Carol Miller, "Ella Baker and the Origins of Participatory Democracy" in Darlene Clark Hime (ed.) Black Women in United States History, Volume 6. [Brooklyn, New York: Carlson Publishing, Inc., 1990], p. 57.

18. Interviews with Queen Mother Audley Moore, New York, NY, 1978.

19. Raymond R. Sommerville, Queen Mother Audley Moore (1898–) Jessie Carney (ed.) *Notable Black American Women* [Detroit: Gale, 1992], p. 764.

20. Barbara Bair, Moore, Audley (Queen Mother) (1898–) Darlene Clarke Hine, *Black Women in America Volume Two M-Z* [Bloomington and Indianapolis: Indiana University press, 1993] p. 812.

21. Raymond R. Sommerville, Queen Mother Audley Moore (1898–) Jessie Carney Smith, *Notable Black American Women* [Detroit: Gale, 1992], p. 765.

22. *Riots, Civil and Criminal Disorders*, Hearing before the Permanent Subcommittee on Investigations of the Committee on Group Operations, United State Senate, Part 0, June 6 and 30, 1969, pp. 437–438.

23. Interview with Queen Mother, Audley Moore, New York, New York,

1978.

24. Op. Cit., (Riots), pp. 437–438.

25. Conversation with Queen Mother Audley Moore, May, 1963–November, 1963, Philadelphia, Pa., September, 1964–October, 1966, New York, N.Y.

26. *Op. Cit.* (Interview Queen Mother, Audley Moore), New York, NY 1978.

*Charles Mack Parker, a resident of Poplarville, Mississippi, in 1959 was jailed for allegedly raping a white woman. A white mob abducted Mr. Parker from his jail cell, beat him, took him to Louisiana and then shot him.

27. Ibid

*Reparations, government administered funding and social programs intended to compensate African-Americans for the past injustices of slavery and discrimination.
Kwame Anthony Appiah, Henry Louis Gates, Jr. *Africana, The Encyclopedia of the African and African-American Experience* [New York: Basic Books, 1999], p. 1612.

28. Interviews with Queen Mother Audley Moore, New York, 1978 and Robert F. Williams, Cleveland, Ohio, 1994.

29. Black Scholar (Interview) 4 (March-April, 1973), p. 51.

30. Participant Observer at founding conference of the NBSA (National Black Student Association) at Tufts University, Boston, Mass., 1976.

31. Conversation with Robert F. Williams, Baldwin, Michigan, 1994.

32. Timothy B. Tyson, "Robert Franklin Williams: A Warrior for Freedom 1925–1996," *Southern Exposure Winter 1996* p. 5.

33. Ibid (Tyson) p. 5.

34. Darci McConnell, "The Father of Black Revolutionaries: While God Lay Sleeping, Robert F. Williams Changed Lives," *The Grand Rapid Press Sunday, February 19, 1995* p. E2.

35. Ibid (McConnell) p. E2.

36. Timothy B. Tyson "Robert Franklin Williams: A Warrior for Freedom 1925–1996, A Legacy of Resistance" (Detroit, Michigan: Robert Williams Tribute Committee, 1996) p. 47.

37. Timothy B. Tyson, *Radio Free Dixie: Robert F. Williams and the Roots of Black Power* [Chapel Hill & London: The University of North Carolina press, 1999] pp. 66–72.

38. Stephanie Banchero, "Hero or Renegade?" The Charlotte Observer Sunday, February 26, 1995, p. 10A.

39. Stephanie Banchero, "Hero or Renegade?" *The Charlotte Observer Sunday, February 26, 1995*, p. 10A.

40. Interview with Robert F. Williams, Cleveland, Ohio 1994.

41. Ibid. (Conversation)

42. Black Freedom Movement Loses Giant: Robert F. Williams of Monroe, N.C. Succumbs to Cancer, *Justice Speaks, Volume 14, No. 3*, p. 6.

43. Conversation with Robert F. Williams, Baldwin, Michigan, 1995.

44. "An Interview with Robert Williams" *Black News Volume 4, No. 7, May 1979*, p. 16.

45. Conversation with Robert F. Williams, Baldwin, Michigan, 1995.
*Timothy B. Tyson, *Radio Free Dixie: Robert F. Williams and the Roots of Black Power* [Chapel Hill: The University of North Carolina Press, 1999]; Robert Carl Cohen, *Black Crusader*: A Biography of Robert Franklin Williams [Secaucus, New Jersey: Lyle Stuart, Inc., 1972].

46. Leah Samuel, "A Life Lived for Justice: James Boggs worked hard for the equality he believed in, *Metro Times, October 13–19*, 1993, p. 14.

47. Grace Lee Boggs, Letter to Max Stanford, April 10, 1994.

48. James Boggs, *The American Revolution: Pages From a Negro Worker's Notebook* [Detroit, Michigan: Leftfoot Press, 2003], p. 87 The term 'African-Americans' has been used by author to replace the word, 'Negro.'

49. *Op. Cit.* (Leah Samuel) p. 14.

50. Grace Lee Boggs, Remember James Boggs (1919–1993), *Third World Viewpoint, Fall, 1993*, p. 12.

51. Conversation with James and Grace Boggs, Detroit, Michigan, 1983.

52. Ibid.

53. James Boggs, *Racism and the Class Struggle: Further pages from a Black Worker's Notebook* [New York and London: Modern Reader/Monthly Review Press], p.169

54. Kenneth Snodgrass, "James Boggs Lives," *Michigan Chronicle, August 4–10, 1993*, pp. 1–13.

55. Grace Lee Boggs "Thinking and Acting Dialectically: C.L.R. James, The American Years" *Monthly Review, October 1993*, p. 88.

56. Grace Lee Boggs, "Thinking and Acting Dialectically: C.L.R. James, The American Years," *Monthly Review, October 1993*, p. 88.

57. *Op. Cit.*, p. 42.

58. Grace Lee Boggs, "More on MLK and Movement Building," *The Michigan Citizen*, February 27th-March 5th, 2005, p. B8

59. Grace Lee Boggs, "Remembering James Boggs (1919–1993)" *Third World Viewpoint, Fall, 1993*, p. 3.

*Grace Lee Boggs, *Living for Change: An Autobiography* [Minneapolis: University of Minnesota Press, 1998].

60. Malcolm X, Alex Haley, *The Autobiography of Malcolm X* [New York: Grove Press, Inc., 1965], p. 6.

61. William Sales, Jr. *From Civil Rights to Black Liberation: Malcolm X and the Organization of Afro-American Unity* [Boston, Massachusetts: South End Press, 1994] pp. 60–61.

*Turner, Henry McNeal (b. February 1, 1834, Newberry Courthouse, S.C.; d. May 8, 1915, Windsor, Ontario, Canada), African Methodist Episcopal (AME) Church leader, Reconstruction-era Georgia politician, outspoken defender of African American rights, prominent leader of back-to-Africa movements, and supporter of the American Colonization Society. See *Encarta Africana* contributed by James Clyde Sellman.

*Karl Evanzz, *The Judas Factor: The Plot to Kill Malcolm*: [New York: Thunder's Mouth Press, 1992] pp. 15–16.

62. Kent Worcester, *C.L.R. James: A Political Biography* [New York: State University of New York Press, 1996], p. 91.

63. Spike Lee (Movie), Also, NYCPD Bureau of Special Services, *Malcolm X* [New York: AFRAM, 1993].

64. George Breitman, *By Any Means Necessary: Speeches, Interviews and a letter by Malcolm X* [New York: Pathfinder Press, 1970], p. 46.

65. Ibid. p. 54.

66. Telephone conversation with John Lewis and myself, Atlanta to New York, March 1965.

67. Conversation with Malcolm X, June 1965, New York, N.Y.

68. Conversation with Bill X White, (ex-member of the Newark, N.J. Nation of Islam), Atlanta, Georgia, May 1978.

69. Conversation with James Shabbaz, Malcolm X's Secretary, Hotel Theresa, Harlem, New York, March, 1965.

70. Conversation with Jesse Gray in May 1965, Harlem, New York.

71. Participant observer study: May, 1964 to September, 1964 being based in Greenwood, Mississippi and traveling the State of Mississippi meeting with African-American Mississippi field staff representatives and community activists. Engaging in various activities to inviting Mississippi SNCC activists to meetings to arranging meetings with SNCC activists and Malcolm X.

72. William W. Sales, Jr., *From Civil Rights to Black Liberation: Malcolm X and the Organization of Afro-American Unity* [Boston, Massachusetts:

37

South End Press, 1994] p. 103.

73. Conversation with Malcolm X, 22 West Restaurant, June 1964, New York, New York.

74. George Breitman (ed.) *Malcolm X Speaks*, "The Ballet or the Bullet," [New York: Grove Press, Inc., 1965], pp. 38–41.

75. George Breitman (ed.) *Malcolm X Speaks* [New York: Grove Press, Inc., 1965] pp. 38–41.

76. Conversation with Malcolm X, 22 West Restaurant, June 1964, New York, New York.

77. Conversation with Malcolm X, 22 West Restaurant, early February 1965, New York, New York.

78. William Sales, *From Civil Rights to Black Liberation: Malcolm X and the Organization of Afro-American Unity*, [Boston, Massachusetts: South End Press, 1994], p. 84.

79. Conversation with Malcolm X, in Harlem, New York while riding with him in his car, June 1964.

80. Conversation with James Shabbaz, March 1965, New York City.

81. Malcolm X, "On Zionism" *The Egyptian Gazette, September 17, 1964, World Wide African Anti-Zionist Front* (Reprint) [New York, A-APRP] p. 3.

The rise of Black Power included a surge
of lively periodicals and pamphlets.

THE STUDENT NON-VIOLENT
COORDINATING COMMITTEE (SNCC)

The Student Non-Violent Coordinating Committee (SNCC) grew from the black student movement. The black student movement of the 1960s began with the sit-ins.

On February 1, 1960, four students, Joseph McNeill, David Richmond, Franklin McCain, and Izell Blair from the North Carolina Agricultural and Technical College in Greensboro, North Carolina sat-in at a segregated lunch counter. This was the beginning of the sit-in movement. The center of focus was Woolworth's nationwide chain.

S.E. Anderson, in his article, "Black Students: Racial Consciousness and the Class Struggle 1960–1976," said:

> Their audacity, their non-violent defiance marked a turning point on black American history. Their militant action marked a qualitative change, not only among black people, but also within the general class struggle. Within a few months, thousands of black students and folk from the towns and rural areas were to join the numerous sit-in demonstrations at drug stores and national chain store lunch counters throughout the South.[1]

On Tuesday the four freshmen were joined by about 20 recruits from North Carolina A and T and returned to the same counter.[2]

On February 3rd, over 50 African-Americans and three white students participated in the demonstration. Demonstrations spread to Nashville, Tennessee, Charleston, South Carolina and Atlanta, Georgia. By February 11, the protests were already expanding their base of popular support when High Point, North Carolina, high school students sat-in. On the 12th, Rock Hill, South Carolina became the first sit-in city in a Deep South state. By the end of February, sit-ins had occurred in 30 cities in seven states (including, deep south Alabama and South Carolina) and the action focus had broadened with a sit-in at a library in Petersburg, Virginia.[3]

In less than a year more than 3,600 demonstrators spent time in jail and several hundred lunch counters had been desegregated in Southern cities. By spring of 1960 nearly 1,300 arrests had been made.

In Orangeburg (South Carolina) there were four hundred arrests, about one hundred and fifty in Nashville, Tennessee, nearly forty in Florence (South Carolina) and Tallahassee (Florida), about eight in Atlanta, Georgia, about sixty-five in Memphis, Tennessee and nearly eighty-five in Marshal, Texas.[4]

> Within six months after the sit-ins started, 28 cities had integrated their lunch counters; by the fall of 1960 the number had risen to almost 100, with protest movements active in at least 60 more.[5]

College students in the north, African-American and white staged supporting demonstrations and raised funds for arrested Southern students. Sit-ins began to broaden focus in the South to include libraries, museums and art galleries. Methods also expanded to include wade-ins on the beaches, stand-ins, kneel-ins and other forms of non-violent direct action.[6]

Activist Jim Lawson already was conducting non-violent direct action workshops for the students and local churches. He decided to target segregated lunch counters of downtown Nashville. The first three students to stage a sit-in were John Lewis, Diane Nash, and Angela Butler. These students and others who followed weren't seriously taken as threats at the outset of the endeavor. Most of the merchants of downtown Nashville looked at these students as outside "agitators" from the north. They felt they didn't have to worry about their "Southern Negroes." After two weeks without incident a gang of whites attacked and beat the students, who did not fight back. Eighty students were arrested while nothing was done to those who attacked. The African-American community united behind the students. The property owners put up their homes as collateral for the students bail. African-American business owners fed the students in jail. More and more jail, which had been a source of shame in the African-American community, became a badge of courage and honor to those associated with the movement. John Lewis and many other students went to jail for 33 days rather than pay a $50 fine after being found guilty.

Ms. Ella Baker, a veteran organizer and interim executive secretary of the Southern Christian Leadership Conference (SCLC), realizing the potential of the sit-in movement, borrowed $500 from SCLC and asked Dr. Martin Luther King for his permission to call a conference of the sit-in leaders. Ms. Baker went to Shaw University in Raleigh, North Carolina; her Alma Mater and got Shaw

University to provide facilities for a meeting of about a hundred students. The conference was held on April 14–17, 1960 (Easter Weekend). By this time there were sixty active centers of sit-in demonstrations. Over two hundred people came to the conference, one hundred and twenty-six student delegates from different communities in twelve states. Nineteen northern Colleges sent delegates.[7]

Ms. Baker who long had disagreements with Dr. King and the ministers of SCLC concerning the emphasis of single charismatic leadership as opposed to group centered leadership advised the students to strike on their own rather than become a youth affiliate of the SCLC. Ms. Baker also in her speech at the conference emphasized that the movement was about "more than a hamburger" (lunch counter desegregation).[8]

When SNCC (the Student Non-Violent Coordinating Committee) was formed it served as an ad hoc coordinating committee for local centers of action. In the early sixties SNCC provided the movement with a center for non-violent direct action against racial discrimination.

In the north, white students formed the Northern Student Movement (NSM) that raised funds for SNCC.

Some researchers have analyzed the sit-in movement as a movement of middle and upper class African-Americans under what has been termed relative deprivation.

> ...It is only when the subordinate group sees itself as being deprived (which implies a standard of comparison, a group relative to which the deprivation exists, or is perceived) that the type of situation arises in which a solution becomes desired.[9]

One effective cause of the spread of the 1960 sit-ins was a profound impatience over the rate of change in terms of desegregation among African-Americans and disillusionment over the progress of race relations in America.

SNCC met in Atlanta once a month from April to August 1960. On May 13 and 14, 1960, students from across the south came to Atlanta, Georgia, for the first official meeting of SNCC.[10] Brothers and sisters who founded SNCC were, for the most part, first generation college students with solid working class backgrounds.[11]

Ms. Baker offered SNCC an office in SCLC headquarters. Ms. Baker persuaded Jane Stembridge, a white female ministerial student to run the office. Later, Ms. Stembridge and others published *The Student Voice*, SNCC's first newspaper.[12] In October, there was a general meeting at which the name the Student Non-Violent Coordinating Committee (SNCC) was chosen and Marion Barry was retained as chairman.[13]

According to Ella Baker a basic goal of SNCC was to make it unnecessary for the people to depend on a leader. SNCC's hope was to develop leadership from among the people.[14] At the Highlander Folk School (1960) meeting the decision was made to go into hardcore rural areas under minority rule. During the meeting a split occurred between those who favored non-violent direct action mass demonstrations and those who favored voter registration. Those favoring non-violent direct action feared the movement would be corrupted and compromised if SNCC concentrated on voter registration. Diane Nash from the Nashville, Tennessee student movement and the freedom rides proposed that SNCC split into two separate organizations. Fearing that would weaken SNCC and serve the purpose of the enemy Ms. Baker opposed the split. Charles Jones was chosen as the director of voter registration and Diane Nash director of non-violent direct action. Charles Sherrod would later be proved correct when he said you couldn't possibly have voter registration without demonstrations.

Julian Bond said that tensions within SNCC were about an organizing approach. The debate was whether to proceed as a vanguard approach versus a pedagogic direction to organizing. He felt northerners were better able to articulate their ideas.

> This caused tensions in the organization between those who thought of themselves as organizing a faceless mass and those who thought you ought to let the faceless mass decide what to do.[15]

SNCC began to grow with the movement, as did its leaders. One of the main people involved with the state of Mississippi was Bob Moses. Bob Moses was a math teacher in New York who had graduated with a Masters degree from Harvard University. He met a SCLC worker who asked him to come to Mississippi for the summer. Moses did and was asked by Ella Baker to stay on and help recruit people for a SNCC conference.

Bob Moses went into Mississippi in early summer 1960 to recruit black students to come to the SNCC October 1960 meeting. While in Southwest Mississippi local people asked Moses to give them some help in trying to start a voter registration campaign. From there he also traveled to Alabama and Louisiana. This is what led to his involvement with SNCC. Moses would become a powerful leader in Mississippi. ""Moses established the pattern that SNCC followed for the next four years: involving local people in all phases of the movement, depending on them for support and protection.[16]

On October 14–16th the second conference of SNCC took place in Atlanta, Georgia. There were present ninety-five voting delegates, plus SNCC staff, which voted, plus thirteen alternates. There were probably about a dozen whites out of the ninety-five delegates and there were ninety-eight registered observers, twelve of whom represented eleven different groups or publications.

SNCC began a voter registration drive in McComb Mississippi. Several organizers were severely beaten and a crisis situation developed with mass arrests of students and SNCC activists.[17] After the October 14–16, 1960 SNCC conference in Atlanta, the students asked Dr. Martin Luther King, Jr. to join them in sit-in demonstrations.

On October 19, 1960, King and some fifty other African-Americans were arrested for sitting in at the Magnolia Room of Rich's Department Store in Atlanta. The others were released but King was sentenced to four months of hard labor in the Reidsville State Prison. On October 26, Kennedy called Mrs. King and expressed his sympathy and concern. His campaign manager and brother, Robert F. Kennedy telephoned the Georgia judge who had sentenced King and pleaded for his release. On the following day King was released. The news of the action of the Kennedy brothers swept through the African-American community, plus distribution of one million pamphlets telling of their deed.

In November 1960, the closest presidential election of the century occurred which African-Americans felt their vote was decisive in the election of Kennedy. Two hundred and fifty thousand African-Americans voted for Kennedy in Illinois, which he carried by 9,000 votes. In Michigan, Kennedy won by a margin of 67,000 votes; some 250,000 African-Americans supported him. He carried South Carolina by 10,000 votes including an estimated 40,000 African-American votes. Within two years, 70,000 persons had demonstrated and over 3,600 demonstrators spend time in jail.

In early 1961, the first group of SNCC activists experimented with the concept of going beyond their own community to challenge segregation.[18] Their decision was precipitated by the actions of Tom Gather, CORE field secretary. On January 31, 1961, he and nine African-American students sat in at a segregated lunch counter in Rock Hill, South Carolina. The following day a judge found all ten guilty of trespassing and sentenced each to thirty days in jail or a fine of $100. Gather and eight of the students chose to serve the sentence. CORE appealed for outside help.

> At a SNCC meeting in early February, the fifteen students present unanimously decided to support the Rock Hill protesters. Four black activists volunteered to travel to Rock Hill and join those in a jail. The four volunteers were Diane Nash, Charles Jones of John C. Smith University in Charlotte, NC, Ruby Doris Smith of Spelman College in Atlanta, and Charles Sherrod of Virginia Union in Richmond Virginia.[19]

The SNCC activists advocated "Jail, No Bail."

The SNCC contingent arrived in Rock Hill, was arrested and convicted for attempting to obtain service at a lunch counter and joined the group already imprisoned. There were some efforts at a jail instead of bail movement on Southern campuses, and at one point there were in various towns as many as 100 students serving sentences instead of appealing.

Although the jailed activists hoped that many others would join them in Rock Hill, few students were willing to leave school for extended jail terms. After a month in jail, the activists were forced to concede they had not achieved their objective. Despite the collapse of the Rock Hill jail-in movement, the decision of the four SNCC representatives to participate demonstrated the willingness of activists associated with SNCC to become involved whenever a confrontation with segregationists forces developed.[20]

Meanwhile student protest spread from Greensboro to San Antonio. A national campaign was organized and store chains that were boycotted in the South were picketed in the North. African-Americans controlled 10 million dollars of business in downtown Nashville alone. The local African-American community leaders and the students organized a boycott for all of the downtown area and also a picket line. After the home of Z. Alexander Lube, defense lawyer of the incarcerated students, was bombed, students came from campuses all around to form the first major march of the civil rights movement in Nashville. Mayor Ben West was asked whether he believed if it was morally permissible for a man or a woman to be discriminated on the basis of their color or race, and he responded, "no." Three weeks later, African-American customers were served at a lunch counter in downtown Nashville. African-American students had established themselves as a force to be reckoned with in the civil rights movement.

By April 1960, 50,000 African-American and white students had joined the sit-in movement.

DIRECT ACTION VS. VOTER REGISTRATION: FREEDOM RIDES

The turning point for SNCC came when CORE (Congress of Racial Equality) started the freedom rides in 1961 in order to put an end to segregation on buses and trains. In 1961, the movement took on national scope with mixed groups of Freedom Riders converging on cities in the Deep South from both the North and the South.

> African-American youth employed the non-violent tactics that had been evolved by Martin Luther King, Jr. in the Montgomery boycott. These tactics were extremely effective insofar as the enabled the youth to take initiative in a disciplined manner, achieve cooperation between white and African-American youth, and dramatize the realities of Southern justice.[21]

CORE decided to call off the Freedom rides, but SNCC, led by Diane Nash of the Nashville Student Movement, decided to continue them. On May 23rd, Dr. King, James Farmer, Ralph Abernathy, Diane Nash, and John Lewis held a press conference. They announced that the Freedom Rides would continue regardless of the cost.

> ...The White mob in the South responded with violence, and it was the mobs that were upheld by the Southern authorities as they restored order by hosing the students, throwing tear gas at them, arresting and jailing them, convicting them of breaking the law and fining or imprisoning them.[22]

> Other buses joined the Freedom Rides. Most of the Riders were professors and students from the North. On May 25th, Riders in Montgomery were arrested at a Trailways station while trying to eat, among them: Fred Shuttlesworth, James

Farmer, Ralph Abernathy and Reverend Wyatt T. Walker. Dr. King announced a "temporary lull but no cooling off" in the Freedom Rides. In Jackson, Mississippi, 27 Freedom Riders were convicted, fined $200 each and given 60 days' suspended sentences. Both Roy Wilkins of the NAACP, and the Americans for the Democratic Action urged Riders to disregard Dr. King's "cooling off" period. In order to organize the remaining attempts of the Freedom Riders, a Freedom Riders Coordinating Committee was formed in Atlanta. Representatives included members of CORE, SCLC, SNCC and the Nashville Movement. For the cause of the Rides these groups put aside their differences, to bond together for the impeding success of the Freedom Rides.[23]

By the end of May a few more non-violent arrests of Freedom Riders in Jackson had taken place. Several Riders were being put to work at a prison farm. More convictions were made and trials against the Montgomery and Birmingham police began. A ray of light appeared in May when Attorney General Robert Kennedy requested the ICC to ban, by regulation, segregation in interstate bus terminals (which had already been accomplished *in theory* by the earlier ICC rulings and the Supreme Courts—Boynton Decision). By June some Riders headed back North, but most would not be out of jail until CORE posted $500 bond 40-days after they were arrested.[24] CORE, SCLC, SNCC and the Nashville Movement were still organizing the Freedom Rides.

More Riders from the North and the West Coast were being sent into Jackson in order to keep the focus on the symbolic efforts for the Rides. All together, more than 400 Riders were arrested in Jackson under a cut and dried procedure, which allowed for no mob violence (and little exercise of constitutional rights on the part of the Riders). During June and July, more than 300 Riders spent from a week to two months in Parchman Prison and other Mississippi jails, experiencing beatings, torture and other mistreatment. For those who were released on bond, the City of Jackson informed CORE that if they don't appear in court on August 14th in Jackson they would forfeit their bond ($500). This was Mississippi's way to financially break the Freedom Rides. But the NAACP provided legal support and CORE got the majority of the defendants to Jackson.

On September 22, 1961, the ICC (after hearings requested by

Attorney General Robert Kennedy) issued the order banning segregation in interstate terminal facilities effective November 1, 1961.[25] Robert Kennedy petitioned the Interstate Commerce Commission to ban segregation during interstate travel. In September, the Commission complied:

> By the summer of 1961, SNCC had sixteen full-timers, fourteen of which were college dropouts and two young ex-school teachers: James Forman from Chicago, and Bob Moses from New York City. These two brothers became key figures in SNCC's ideological development s well as leaders in organizing and general practice. SNCC also had no funds and a tiny symbolic office in Atlanta.[26]

SNCC's Executive Secretary, James Forman, solidified SNCC's infrastructure. He recruited Norma Collins to become a full time secretary, Julian Bond as communications director, Casey Hayden (wife of SDS member Tom Hayden) and Mary King to handle publicity. Though the student representative committee was officially in charge of SNCC, field secretaries such as Bob Moses, who organized a voter registration drive in Pike County, Mississippi made most decisions.[27]

By the winter of 1961, SNCC members had begun to walk, talk, and dress like poor African-American farmers and sharecroppers of rural areas of Georgia and Mississippi. SNCC displayed a high level of self discipline and self-sacrifice and won respect of entire communities.

> One project report listed "five rules of staff decorum." The rules are indicative of the lengths to which SNCC members were willing to go in order to win respect and support from the people: "(1) There will be no consumption of alcoholic beverages, (2) Men will not be housed with women, (3) Romantic attachments on the level of 'girl-boy friend relations will not be encouraged within the group, (4) The staff will go to church regularly, (5) The group shall have the power to censure…when an organizer in southwest Georgia got a local teenager pregnant, he was given a small sum of money and told to "marry her!"[28]

President Kennedy was convinced he had to stop the Freedom Rides as he felt a crisis was being created. In his eyes, the Freedom Riders were acting as peaceful provocateurs and the white reaction was embarrassing to the administration.[29] President Kennedy was also worried about the political repercussions nationally and internationally. Requests were made to White House Assistant (for Civil Rights) Wofford by President Kennedy to "Stop them! Get your friends off those buses." The main reason for this request was the President's meeting with Soviet Union leader Khruschev. President Kennedy did not want to have an embarrassing situation damage any plans he had with the Soviet Union. Although President Kennedy admired the courage of the Freedom Riders and shared the goal of opening the Closed Society, he seemed reluctant to accept that you had to choose a side. The handling of the Freedom Rides set in motion a pattern for the next three years of the Kennedy Administration. They avoided direct involvement with movement activists and preferred behind the scenes contact with officials.[30] The President's objective was to prevent violence and he felt that if he stepped in federally another civil war would start in Mississippi. Assistant Attorney General Burke Marshall (an African-American man) tried to justify this by saying "the responsibility for the preservation of law and order, and the protection of citizens against unlawful contact on the part of others, is the responsibility of the local authorities." The Kennedy Administration was forced to abandon this when mob violence was so severe against the Riders that President Kennedy had to send federal marshals to Alabama to protect them. While President Kennedy seemed reluctant to support the Freedom Riders, he did support voting rights for African-Americans.[31]

There is not a question that the Freedom Rides marked an important turning point in the movement towards equal rights for African-Americans. More than any other attempt, the Freedom Rides represented a major move forward for the movement from the early spontaneous activities to a more organized "down to the nitty-gritty" movement style. The Rides went further than previous direct action movements in that the Rides attacked a broader problem and they involved more intense organizational support and participation. Important also was the challenge put to the federal government to uphold the laws they created. The Freedom Rides also brought together non-southerners and whites, clergy and academicians in greater than ever numbers, even groups who had previously not worked together. The Freedom Rides brought a halt to the fighting in major organizations such as CORE, SNCC, SCLC and NAACP in order to mobilize people, money, legal aid and publicity in a short period after the Alabama violence. The Rides created a deeper commitment than ever before. There were few participants, but those involved knew they faced almost certain physical or mental harassment. The deeper commitment is evidence early in the Rides when a "cooling off" period was requested after the Montgomery violence and the Riders rejected that request. The Rides provided a great stimulus for massive protests in the South, as well as a model for mass mobilizations of African-American communities.[32]

The national media coverage the Freedom Rides received was also instrumental in civil rights decisions to the Deep South. Before the Rides, the SNCC organization in the South was a mere dream, but that changed with each bus stop. The racist lifestyles revealed from the Rides were too brutal, too shocking, for any to keep quiet. Crisis forces people to take a stand. Only a few newspapers defended or took the side of people like Alabama Governor John Patterson and the police forces of Montgomery and Birmingham. Not until the Rides did the entire country pay attention to the grievances of the African-American community, but the nation was faced daily with pictures and news coverage that they could no longer ignore. CORE leader James Farmer said it best: "We were successful; we created a crisis situation. It was worldwide news headlines and everybody was watching it, people all over the world. The Attorney General had to act; and he did. He called upon the ICC to issue an order; a ruling with teeth in it which he could enforce."

While the sit-ins had made the movement look too easy, the Freedom Rides showed the defiance and determination of the African-American community.

> ...SNCC had three main foci of struggle in 1961: Southwest Georgia, where former divinity student, Charles Sherrod became project director in 1961; the Mississippi Delta, which was under Bob Moses, former Howard student and mathematics teacher; and the area around Selma, Alabama, where Bernard Lafayette asked his wife, Colia, and later, Norman, to run the voter registration projects. SNCC also had projects in Pine Bluffs, Arkansas; Danville, Virginia; and Cambridge, Maryland.[33]

1962–ALBANY, GA

During the early fall 1961; SNCC headquarters in Atlanta assigned a field secretary and two staff members to Albany, Ga. These men,

Charles Jones, Charles Sherrod and Cordell Reagan, set up a SNCC office in a run-down building in the African-American community. They began to recruit young African-Americans for instruction in the philosophy and tactics of non-violence.[34] Sherrod, a proponent of the voter registration action of SNCC soon found that one had to take direct action if the organization was going to lead in voter registration.[35]

The Interstate Commerce Commission on September 22, 1961 issued a ruling banning segregation on buses and in terminal facilities. The order was scheduled to go into effect November 1, 1961.

> SNCC representatives in Albany decided to test the ruling on November 1, 1961. Their efforts led to a sit-in at a bus station by nine students to test compliance with the Interstate Commerce ruling, which became effective that day, barring segregation in transportation terminals.[36]

Through SNCC's efforts a coalition of African-American community groups and civil rights organizations formed after the bus terminal demonstrations. The coalition came together on November 17th and was called the Albany Movement, which consisted of the NAACP, the Ministerial Alliance, the Federation of Women's Clubs, the Negro Voters League and other groups.

> William G. Anderson, a black osteopath, was elected president and Slater King, a black realtor, became vice-president.[37]

Over 700 people were arrested in a demonstration held in Albany, Georgia in December of 1961 to protest the segregation of the city's public facilities. Demonstrations continued into the spring and summer of 1962. Slater King, the brother of C. B. King and Vice President of the Albany Movement became more militant as the Albany movement preceded. After his wife was beaten and lost a child as a result of it, King began to advocate armed self-defense and became a supporter of Robert F. Williams.[38]

In July of 1962, Martin Luther King and three other African-American leaders were convicted of failing to get a permit. Police Chief Prichett arranged that an anonymous donor bail Dr. King out of jail taking the steam out of a publicized confrontation. Mass protests continued throughout the summer and at the height of the protest, 1,500 were arrested. The Albany movement was considered a set back for Dr. King but a mass breakthrough for SNCC.

In the winter of 1962, NAG, the Non-Violet Action Group in Washington, D.C., had about twenty-five to thirty students who belonged to it. Among the group, Courtland Cox, Muriel Tillinghast, Stokely Carmichael, Stanley Wise, William (Bill) Mahoney, Ed Brown (H. Rap Brown's bother), Phil Hutchins, and Cleveland Sellers. While NAG sponsored dances, its primary task was demonstrating against racial discrimination.

Early in 1964, some of the members of NAG from Washington, D.C. working in Cambridge, Maryland with the Cambridge Non-Violent Action Committee (CNAC) to protest the speaking of Governor George Wallace witnessed their first experience with community self-defense when a demonstration of six hundred on the evening of May 11, 1964 were gassed, beaten, chased, and shot at by the Maryland National Guardsmen; shots were returned.

I'm certain that a lot of people would have been seriously injured if a small group of black men had not started shooting at the guardsmen in order to slow them down. It was like a scene from a Western movie. The men would run a few steps, crouch on one knee, and fire; run a few steps, crouch on one knee, and fire.[39]

1963–1964: THE MISSISSIPPI PROJECT

SNCC's voter registration projects were concentrated in small rural southern towns. The first was held in McComb, Mississippi in August 1961, organized by Bob Moses, who having moved to McComb, had requested the support of the African-American ministers and storekeepers. SNCC needed them to help secure places to live and transportation for ten students who would be working with the voter registration school.

On August 26, 1961 Hollis Watkins and Curtis Hayes held a sit-in at a Woolworth's store in McComb, Mississippi. The two men were arrested, along with some high school students that joined the sit-in.[40]

This was the first of non-violent direct action demonstrations in McComb. The town of McComb was in an uproar. Some of the high school students were kept in jail for five days. They were sentenced for thirty-four days but were released after the murder of Mr. Herbert Lee (a local African-American man):

McComb, Mississippi became the site of one of the biggest demonstrations. Mr. Herbert Lee, an African-American farmer who had been working with Bob Moses was found shot to death. He had been murdered by a white man who was against SNCC's registration efforts. After the individual suspected of Lee's murder was released, 100 McComb high school students marched to the City Hall to protest. They were arrested. McComb, with its bitter legacy, was a beginning for SNCC in Mississippi. "We had, to put it mildly, got out feet wet," Moses said.[41]

Upon their release, the students tried to return to school. When they arrived, school officials were telling them they had to sign a petition saying they wouldn't protest any longer greeted them. Anyone who didn't sign was not allowed to re-enter the school. Some of the students refused and decided to boycott the school.

Parents were upset with SNCC for encouraging the students. SNCC was not against the boycott but tried to be cautious with the African-American community. The parents were also upset with the school for keeping their children out. SNCC wanted the community to stay united so they decided to set up a freedom school. This is when SNCC realized how deep the "southern way" was embedded in African-American children's minds.

A student asked whether they were fighting for southern independence. The child had meant the Civil War.[42]

Whites had become angry. Violence against African-Americans during this time rose significantly. SNCC leaders were also attacked. McComb was one of the worst parts of the state. It was well known for its Klan involvement. Many churches and homes were bombed and set afire. This terrified the African-American community as well as the white. SNCC was to move elsewhere to help. Following McComb SNCC arrived in Greenwood. SNCC learned from its mistakes in McComb.

It understood that direct action protest conducted against an intransigent and lawless white establishment could be counter productive.[43]

Bob Moses became the director of voter registration for the Council of Federated Organizations (COFO). COFO was a coalition of civil rights organizations including the NAACP, SCLC, CORE and religious groups formed to prevent haggling over the distribution of funds and to coordinate voter registration in Mississippi.

> The project focused in western Mississippi. Moses gained a reputation among the local community and other workers for being gutsy and taking many harsh beatings. His reputation became almost legendary. The townspeople were for the most part too scared to participate in Moses' efforts. SNCC started a food drive for local residents drawing on its supporters. Moses sustained effort paid off. By 1963 groups of several hundred African-Americans were trying to register to vote in the Greenwood courthouse.[44]

African-American businesses were burned and some workers were shot. Moses and six of his workers filed suit against FBI Director J. Edgar Hoover and Attorney General Kennedy to prosecute southern officials responsible for acts of violence against civil rights workers. The suit failed. After meeting Harvard Law School student Allard Lowenstein, Moses started a "one man, one vote" campaign based on an old Mississippi law in which protest votes could be cast by those illegally restricted from voting. These votes would be set aside until the exclusion would be eliminated. Lowenstein contacted 100 white students at Yale and Stanford to come register the people in the county.

A SNCC method of organizing was for a field secretary to go into a community and find a place to live. He would begin to listen and talk to people who would talk to him. He would nurture their development to take up the leadership of the local movement. Through weeks of house-to-house organizing and holding mass church meetings a mass voter registration march of African-Americans in a county would cumulate with a "Freedom Day" with numbers of African-Americans marching to the courthouse to register to vote.

SNCC in Mississippi through COFO started an independent electoral challenge by first running a project "Freedom" election in 1963. They ran Dr. Aaron Henry for Governor of Mississippi and Ed King for Lieutenant Governor. More than 80,000 African-Americans cast symbolic votes for Henry and King.[45]

SNCC made other breakthroughs in leading mass voter registration efforts in Greenwood, Mississippi in 1963. Led by SNCC organizers Sam Block and Willie Peacock who had been recruited by Bob Moses; SNCC workers suffered beatings, jailings, and shootings in their efforts to register African-Americans.

It was also during this time that three SNCC workers, seated in a car were shot at and the Greenwood SNCC Mississippi office was set on fire. In protest, fellow SNCC workers marched to the Greenwood courthouse where they were arrested and jailed for a week. This became the first incident where SNCC workers refused bail (a tactic which was used many times) and helped people to see the seriousness of their cause and the firmness of their beliefs. The Justice Department responded to the situation by seeking a temporary restraining order to force the release of the jailed workers and to prevent the town officials from interfering in the voter registration campaign.[46]

> The SNCC activists had two immediate goals in Greenwood. To show they were not there simply to stir up trouble and then leave, and to help local blacks overcome the paralyzing fear that had stopped the registration drive.[47]

SNCC began another voter registration campaign. Again, they faced the same problems as in McComb. Whites all over Mississippi began to fear the movement. They reacted the only way they knew how, with violence. SNCC believed in what they were doing. They believed that voter registration was the most important way to empower African-Americans in the south. Although almost half of the state was African-American there were very few African-Americans registered. "Negroes of the voting age far outnumbered whites. Only 2% of African-Americans were registered while 95% of whites were on the roles."[48] This figure is very disturbing. For African-American voters it wasn't just an easy trip to city hall. It was a life or death situation. Many people were beaten and later found murdered because they attempted to vote. SNCC helped in many ways, but it was still a fairly small organization:

> According to Cleveland Sellers, SNCC had 130 members through the winter and spring of 1963–1964 preparing for the summer projects.[49]

It didn't have much money. Most of the staff wasn't getting paid. This is when SNCC called for a new plan involving more people and national attention. This was called the Mississippi Summer Project.

John Lewis, then chairman of SNCC put Roland Snellings and myself on the Mississippi field staff to test our ideas of building an all African-American black nationalist self-defense project. Greenwood, Mississippi became a base for revolutionary nationalist activity as the organizers from Mississippi notably Jessie Morris, Jesse

Morrison, McArthur Cotton, and Willie Peacock concentrated there. The purpose was to win them over to the position of all African-American independent political empowerment, rather than the goal of integration. A showdown occurred in Greenville, Mississippi in May 1964 at a Mississippi SNCC staff meeting. The majority of the African-American members of the SNCC Mississippi field staff revolted against the SNCC hierarchy represented by Bob Moses and most of the white radicals. The field staff didn't want the whites to be brought into Mississippi. The revolutionary nationalists position was that whites should organize in the white community to divide the white racist front.[50]

Meeting at Amize Moore's house (a Mississippi leader in the NAACP), in early summer of 1964 many of the African-American members of the Mississippi SNCC field staff discussed preparing for a shift to armed self defense and entering into an alliance with the Revolutionary Action Movement.

After SNCC had built up a statewide network through its voter registration drives SNCC decided to form the Mississippi Freedom Democratic Party, a challenge to the racist regular Mississippi Democratic Party. After they first tried to join the local Mississippi Democratic Party and being denied membership, a multi-racial coalition called a convention on April 24, 1964 in Jackson, Mississippi, and the Mississippi Freedom Democratic Party was formed. Its purpose was to register votes with the MFDP and challenge the Mississippi regular democrats at the National Democratic Party Convention. After the convention, Ms. Fannie Lou Hamer estimated the membership of the MFDP at 78,000. Sixty-three thousand people in Mississippi registered with the MFDP in 1964 prior to the August National Democratic Convention. The turning point of SNCC's road to radicalism was the Freedom Summer of 1964. COFO organized the Mississippi Freedom Democratic Party as a multi-racial party, printed its own ballots, and in October conducted its own poll. The Freedom Democratic nominee for governor, Aaron Henry, head of the state NAACP received 70,000 votes, which was a tremendous protest against the denial of equal political rights.

> "One reason for the success of the project was the presence in the state of 100 Yale and Stanford students, who worked for two weeks with SNCC on the election. SNCC was sufficiently impressed by the student contribution to consider inviting

hundreds more to spend an entire summer in Mississippi. Sponsors of this plan hoped not only for workers but for publicity that might at last focus national attention on Mississippi. By the winter of 1963–64, however, rising militancy in the SNCC had begun to take on overtones of Black Nationalism, and some members resisted the project on the grounds that most of the volunteers would be white."[51]

The Freedom Summer of 1964 was very important to SNCC. SNCC wanted national attention to focus on the conditions that African-Americans had to live under in the state of Mississippi. The basic idea was to bring people in from the north to help with the project. The project consisted of voter registration, Freedom schools and political awareness. SNCC did not lead the project alone, although they had been the main organizers.[52] Others involved were NAACP and CORE. James Forman was the executive director of the summer project. SNCC was organizing projects in four out of the five Mississippi districts. CORE would take the remaining district. The first priority was to recruit volunteers. SNCC was fairly particular about who got an application. They were looking for a certain type of activist. SNCC wanted, "students from the nation's highest public and private colleges and universities. This made up 57% of the total application pool. Less than 10% of the applicants were African-American."[53]

SNCC was looking "to focus national attention on Mississippi as a means of forcing federal intervention in the state. For the project to be successful it had to attract national media attention." This was true; in fact nothing attracted more attention than white liberals helping "the downtrodden Negroes of Mississippi."[54] Before picking just anyone to volunteer, SNCC looked at his or her background, characteristics and motives. They also considered funding. Since SNCC wasn't that big, the organization couldn't pay for everyone to stay in Mississippi for the summer. They wanted the volunteers to pay their own way. This was very smart because students that did come to the south did it because they wanted to. The students that applied also considered themselves political. Many were already involved in political organizations.[55]

Another concern was the parents. Most parents were afraid to send their children south. But the parents couldn't argue with their children because this is what their parents had taught them. The volunteers and their parents knew this was going to be difficult. When the project got underway in the summer of 1964, there were 1,000 people involved. Most of these were volunteers from the North. The students first attended an orientation session. Then they had role-playing sessions and lessons on how to protect oneself if attacked.[56] All the volunteers were trying to prepare for the violence that awaited them. No one could really prepare anyone for what was going to happen in the next three months. "Most of the Mississippi staff had been beaten at least once and also shot at." No one really knew what to expect after this. The plans still continued. After the first week, voter registration workers arrived and 300 Freedom schools were opened.[57]

There were many projects going on all over the state of Mississippi. SNCC was soon to learn of both the safest and most dangerous places in Mississippi. The safest was the fifth district that included the northeastern part of Mississippi, including Biloxi. The most dangerous place in the state was the southwest corner, McComb. This was the home of the Ku Klux Klan.

It was now time to get the plan into action. The main focus for SNCC was the voter registration campaign. SNCC assigned volunteers to go around door to door and ask people to register. SNCC had two jobs when they registered voters. First, "SNCC conducted a mock international election among the Mississippi black population."[58] Bob Moses was involved in getting this started. The "Freedom Vote" was the vote cast for the newly formed Mississippi Freedom Democratic Party. First the SNCC staff would ask people to vote in this "mock election." This way people could see the end results. Bob Moses planned a regular non-election. African-Americans were asked to vote not in a regular election but in a parallel 'Freedom Vote.' This was designed to minimize the potential of violence and insure maximum voter turnout.[59] This would show the community how they could change the system. Most voters found it much easier than expected. This was also the easier part of the two. The second part was to show people parts of the Mississippi Constitution. This would prime them for going to the courthouse to pass the test. For African-Americans this was a potentially dangerous act.[60] Even after this, very few of the voter registration applications were accepted. "Only 1,600 of the completed applications were accepted due to discrimination.[61] This was not an easy task. But despite the setbacks, there were few African-American volunteers.[62] Going to the courthouse wasn't just another day. It was another step toward liberation. This was happening all over the state of Mississippi. It was also taking its toll on whites. McAdam (1988) provides a day-to-day account of incidents of violence and harassment that occurred during the summer project.

> It was because the people trying to change Mississippi were asking themselves the real question about what is wrong with Mississippi that the summer project in effect touched every aspect of the lives of Negroes in Mississippi, and started to touch the lives of the whites as well.[63]

The next part of the project was the freedom school. The SNCC field secretary in charge of the schools was Charles Cobb, Jr. He stated that SNCC was going to, "provide an educational experience for students which make it possible for them to challenge the myths of our society, to perceive more clearly it's realities and find alternatives and ultimately new directions for actions."[64] The freedom schools teachers were some of the volunteers. The teachers and SNCC freedom schools had four basic curriculums. One was remedial education, two leadership development, three contemporary issues, and four non-academic curriculums.[65] Again, when listening to the students they saw how unequal the schooling was. Most children could not read or write. It was like starting from scratch. Some of the volunteers were touched when they saw progress in their students. They felt something was happening that was positive, while surrounding them was an evil embedded so deeply in the southern lifestyle.

COFO organized a grassroots political movement by holding precinct, county and state conventions that chose 68 integrated delegates to go to the Democratic Party convention in Atlantic City in 1964 to challenge the credentials of the regular Democrats and cast the states' vote for the party nominees. COFO developed the Mississippi Freedom Democratic Party (MFDP), which had 60,000 members. This was to be a high point of Freedom Summer.

The FDP went to Atlantic City to challenge Mississippi regulars. Northern liberals tried to work out a compromise that would appease the FDP and at the same time keep the bulk of Southern delegates in the convention. President Johnson's proposal and Johnson sent Senator Hubert Humphrey to draw a compromise. Humphrey offered to permit two FDP delegates to sit in the convention with full voting rights if he could choose the delegates. The Mississippi white regulars walked out and the FDP led by Mrs. Fannie Lou Hamer decided not to accept the compromise.[66]

The Mississippi Freedom Democratic Party's failure to be seated at the Democratic Party Convention in 1964 is what led to SNCC attempting to organize an all African-American political party in 1965:

> ...by 1965, SNCC had made certain fundamental qualitative changes. It was just about fed up with the futile non-violent struggles. It was being wrenched apart due to a lack of structure and discipline that its projects demanded. It was becoming more aware and more influenced by revolutionary black nationalism, and, to a lesser extent, Marxism-Leninism.[67]

The volunteers were beginning to feel like Mississippi was their home. This was a life-changing experience for most. The volunteers were seeing and feeling too much. They saw poverty like they had never imagined. They were unwarned of how Mississippi poverty affected African-American families. Many problems were created because of this. There was a lot of hostility towards those housing the volunteers.[68] The hostility was not from the African-American community but from the whites. Four project workers killed, four persons critically wounded, eighty workers beaten, one thousand arrests, thirty-seven churches bombed or burned and thirty black homes or businesses bombed or burned.[69] For the parents of the volunteers, this was astonishing. They awaited the end of the project.

The majority of the African-Americans on the field staff in Mississippi in SNCC by the summer of 1964 began to feel while there were progressive elements in the Federal government in Washington, D.C.; basically the national government was in opposition to the movement.

The SNCC African-American field workers also felt that the place white students should be working is in their home white communities to break down white resistance.

As the project came to a close, SNCC was realizing the reality and the success of the summer. They had managed to raise a lot of national media attention but "the press emphasized the white volunteers more than the local African-Americans and SNCC.[70]

Granted, the goal was to attract media attention. The attention was to be focused on the terrible conditions faced by the residents of Mississippi. Instead, the media focused on white students risking their lives. The freedom summer got lost in the background to all the other things going on in the sixties, which were the presidential campaign, the Viet Nam war, and other national interests. For the volunteers and SNCC staff, it was not easily forgotten. The Mississippi project was a success, although it was still not enough. There wasn't much apparent change. Out of the change that did occur, it mostly appeared in the black middle class. It had little or no effect on the poor African-American community, which was the majority. SNCC then tried to get the Mississippi Freedom Democratic Party a seat in the national elections. After the project, some members of SNCC went to Atlantic City for the Democratic National Convention.[71] They were offered two seats that SNCC turned down. They felt they had worked hard and two seats weren't enough. After the summer project, SNCC debated about non-violence because of all the violence they had endured. No federal protection was offered and in most cases, the acts of violence were against African-Americans. SNCC had hit its peak in the summer of '64. The organization was starting to become bitter towards the whites in the project. SNCC eventually started branching off into two different factions. The "freedom high" faction led by Bob Moses stressed that the individual is the organizer. The structural faction was more organized and worked from the top down. Eventually the structural faction would take over.[72]

1965 MARCH FROM SELMA, ALABAMA TO MONTGOMERY

SNCC began working in Selma, Alabama in early 1963. SNCC worked on voter registration clinics and mobilized local people to the local courthouse to become registered to vote. Soon voting rights movements began in Marion and Selma, Alabama. African-American youth played a great role in the movement. In and around Selma, the youth would be eager participators in the voting rights marches particularly while their parents were at work. Also it was around this time that SNCC organizers Bob Mants, Willie Vaughn and Stokely Carmichael all disillusioned with the failure of the MFDP challenge decided to attempt to build an all African-American political organization in Alabama.[73]

After laboring with a fledging movement with SNCC for three years Amelia Boyton and the Dallas County Voters League appealed to SCLC and Martin Luther King, Jr., in the fall of 1964 to help in securing voting rights. On January 2, 1963, the Dallas County Voters League held an "Emancipation Day" evening service violating a city injunction against demonstrations and meetings. This was the beginning of SCLC's and Dr. King's campaign in Selma.

> King moved from mass meetings to direct action in mid-January when he led four hundred marchers to the Dallas County Courthouse in Selma.[74]

Selma Sheriff Jim Clark met the demonstration. There was no violence at this demonstration. On January 19th, the second day of SCLC demonstrations, Sheriff Clark began mass arrests. Demonstrations increased in numbers daily. The turning point was when the African-American teachers marched on the courthouse. Soon after the teachers marched, the undertakers marched, the beauticians marched. On February 1, 1965, Martin Luther King, Jr., and two hundred and fifty marchers were arrested and jailed. In the next two days eight hundred school children marched and were taken into custody. A congressional delegation of fifteen from Washington, which included African-American Congressman Charles Diggs of Michigan, came to Selma to investigate. SNCC invited Malcolm X to speak in Selma on February 4th at a mass meeting held in Brown's Chapel.

Malcolm X in his speech supported Dr. King's efforts but warned of an alternative. Dr. Martin Luther King was released from jail in early February. Demonstrations continued. Three thousand more demonstrated and were arrested. In mid-February SCLC's C. T. Vivian, led another march to the courthouse and was viciously punched in the face by Sheriff Jim Clark.

> At the beginning of February 1965, James Orange from the SCLC went to Marion County Alabama to work in the voting rights movement there. Each day blacks would go down to the courthouse to register to vote. They would be arrested. In an effort to stop Blacks, the local sheriff arrested Orange on February 17th. In response, the local blacks decided to hold a night march. They would go to jail and sing songs to Orange.[75]

The Mayor of Marion, Alabama called Governor George Wallace and told him African-Americans were planning to break Orange out of jail and cause a riot. Wallace sent state troopers and deputized many white men in the area. Sheriff Jim Clark sealed off all roads to Marion and no one could get in or out. African-American women were beaten at the will of the racists that night. Voting rights demonstrators were viciously attacked. Jimmy Lee Jackson who was trying to protect his grandfather and his mother who was bleeding after being beaten, was murdered. After the three of them fled to a building with the police in hot pursuit, Jackson died in the hospital on February 26th, five days after Malcolm X was assassinated. The movement decided to carry Jimmy Lee Jackson's dead body to Montgomery and to drop it on the steps of the Capital, but Dr. King had a better suggestion; that was to lead to a mass march from Selma to Montgomery. SCLC scheduled the march from Selma to Montgomery for Sunday, March 7.[76]

SNCC thought the march was too dangerous and voted as an organization not to endorse the march but said any member of the organization could take part in the march if they wanted to. As the march proceeded on March 7th to cross the Edmund Pettus Bridge, it was stopped by a posse of a 100 men under the command of Selma's Jim Clark and a 100 state troopers sent by Alabama Governor George Wallace. The state troopers on horseback began to beat and tear gas the marchers. They also rode over the marchers as they were beaten. This was called "Bloody Sunday."

The march was forced to turn back. Dr. King issued a national appeal to come to Selma. The second attempted march was scheduled for March 1965. Dr. King led the march but was told the march did not have a permit. Dr. King led 1,500 marchers to the crest of the Edmund Pettus Bridge turned around unmolested by state troopers waiting there and marched back to Selma. SNCC called this "Turnaround Tuesday." SCLC secured a permit and on March 1, 1965, the March from Selma to Montgomery proceeded. The march took five days and covered 54 miles. Few marched the whole distance. Many only marched part of the way. By the march's end in Montgomery 25,000 people had joined. Dr. King gave a very militant speech, which signaled that the movement was shifting.

1965–1966 THE LOWNDES COUNTY FREEDOM ORGANIZATION: THE BLACK PANTHER PARTY

In late 1965 and early 1966, SNCC decided to go into Alabama and organize an independent black political party.

SNCC's plans were shaped in part by its experiences in the MFDP 1964 convention challenge and the 1965 seating challenge, both of which ended in failure. This new effort, SNCC decided would be a county political organization rather than a statewide organization such as MFDP. "We decided," said a SNCC field secretary, "after the Mississippi experience that it would be better for political organizations to be on the county level so they could be closer to the people.[77]

In January 1966 before launching the Lowndes County Freedom Organizations (LCFO), SNCC encouraged a group of African-American voters to sue in federal court for a special election in 1966 for all Lowndes County administrative, law enforcement, and judicial offices.

The suit contended that white officials were holding office illegally because they had been elected before the state's Negroes had acquired the right to vote. The suit stated that, although some county officials were up for election in 1966, the terms of others continued until 1968 and 1970. In essence, this challenge rested on the contention that the white minority, under sanction of the law and by threats, terror, and violence, had prevented Negroes from even attempting to exercise their suffrage rights, in violation not only of the Fourteenth Amendments to the U.S. Constitution, but of the 1965 Voting Rights Act as well.[78]

In March of 1965 SNCC field workers led by senior field secretary Stokely Carmichael went in Lowndes County to solicit the aid of local leaders in getting support for the idea of organizing an all African-American political party in a majority African-American southern black-belt area. Carmichael arrived in Lowndes County on March 26, 1965. The SNCC research staff found a state law that allowed for the establishment of independent county political parties, provided they had a membership equal to 20 percent of the county's eligible voters. By August 1965, Stokely Carmichael had managed to register 250 people.[79]

The Alabama Democratic Conference (ADC) and the Alabama Southern Christian Leadership Conference (SCLC) announced plans of running African-Americans in the Democratic Party May primary. SNCC proposed a statewide boycott of the primary and to run a concurrent mock primary. The Alabama SCLC felt this would hurt the chances of African-American candidates and called on Dr. Martin

Luther King for help. Dr. King came to Alabama and traveled the state for SCLC urging African-Americans to vote in the Democratic primary but stayed clear of Lowndes County, SNCC's proposed project.

On March 3, 1966, African-Americans in the process of developing local leadership founded the Lowndes County Freedom Organization led by John Hullet. In Lowndes County, African-Americans, 80% of the county, agreed to boycott the regular Democratic primary and support candidates of the newly found Lowndes County Freedom Organization (LCFO) in their own primary. LCFO as an all African-American political party choose a black panther as its symbol.[80]

SNCC also attempted to help build several other African-American freedom organizations in some of the other black belt counties (near or majority African-American) in Alabama. Problems of having lack of financial resources and with its key personnel focused on Lowndes County hindered the process. Though sporadic, non-coordinated and limited, SNCC did help to register some African-Americans, organized mass meetings, helped some African-American candidates obtain information on how to run for political office and gave some assistance in campaigning. In Lowndes County tax assessor, tax collector, coroner, sheriff, and district attorney were five offices that were at stake in the November, 1966 election. Nine hundred voters showed up to vote for the Black Panther (LCFO) in the primary. By Election Day SNCC had been able to register 2,000 African-Americans.[81]

On Election Day LCFO received less than 46 percent of the votes. Between the primary and election day in November, several events occurred which impacted upon the election and nation.[82]

1965–1966: THE ATLANTA PROJECT: BLACK CONSCIOUSNESS/ANTI-VIETNAM WAR

In the interview with Don Stone (Atlanta Project activist) he contradicted Julian Bond who said the Atlanta Project didn't accomplish much. According to Stone the Atlanta Project helped Bond get re-elected by doing house to house canvassing in the buttermilk bottom section of Atlanta, put out the *Nitty Gritty* local community newspaper, began Anti-War demonstrations and raised the question of black consciousness within SNCC and the community.[83]

The Atlanta Project began in February 1966 when Julian Bond

was dismissed from the Georgia State legislature for supporting SNCC's anti-Vietnam statement. In a special election Julian Bond was re-elected. Judy Richardson, office manager for Bond's campaign, in an interview October 15, 2000 felt that the Atlanta Project had not been involved in the Julian Bond campaign and did not see them in a favorable light at that point.[84]

The leadership of the Atlanta Project engaged in a two-line struggle. One consisted of urban organizing of maintaining door-to-door contact with grassroots people in Atlanta and two, consisted of an internal ideological struggle within SNCC over its direction. Between February and March of 1966 the Atlanta Project published two issues of their newspaper, the *Nitty Gritty*. The Atlanta Project also circulated their "Black Consciousness" paper. Mike Simmons in an interview said that members of the Alabama Project which eventually formed the Lowndes County Freedom Organization or the Black Panther Party, saw the ideological struggle raised by the Atlanta Project's, "black consciousness" paper in the spring of 1966 as a struggle to determine who was going to run the organization.[85] The Atlanta Project was not trying to seize power in the organization. Their only purpose was to influence the leaders and membership of the organization (SNCC) to become a black organization and to consider black nationalism as an option. The Atlanta Project concentrated on four areas of organizing. They were:

1. Working with workers in Atlanta. The Atlanta Project worked with dry cleaners trying to form a union.

2. Using the Vine City area of Atlanta as their base, the Atlanta Project worked with local tenants in Vine City and Dixie Hills area of the city in covering rent strikes.

3. Through electoral activity of getting Julian Bond re-elected to the Georgia legislature, the Atlanta Project began to see themselves as independents and began to advocate the development of a third political party through a petition for one.

4. The Atlanta Project held several rallies against police brutality. The Atlanta Project organized mass rallies in low-income housing projects having SNCC leaders speak while playing "James Brown" over loud speakers. The activity of the Atlanta Project began to polarize contradictions in

and among the SNCC leadership. Mike Simmons said that Bob Moses was beginning to side with the Atlanta Project at the confrontational meeting with the SNCC steering committee. At the time of the annual staff meeting held in Kingston, Tennessee in June of 1966, members which voted Stokely Carmichael in as chairman of SNCC, members of the Atlanta Project were attending a meeting organized by Bob Moses in New Orleans on Black Nationalism which featured Dr. John Henrik Clarke as guest speaker.

Members of SNCC began to receive draft notices. Mike Simmons of Atlanta Project was one of them. Simmons went through six months of evasion not to take a physical for the draft.

On August 16, 1966, the draft date for Mike Simmons, the Atlanta Project began picketing the draft office in Atlanta. On August 17, 1966, the Atlanta Project went in the draft office and had a sit-in in the draft office. The next day, August 18, 1966, the Atlanta Project continued and Mike Simmons tried to enter the draft office and was blocked by military police. The police grabbed a sister (African-American woman) in a headlock and a mass disturbance broke out. Ten men of the Atlanta Project and two women who were students were arrested, charged and convicted for disturbing the peace. After going to jail, the tension between the Atlanta Project and the SNCC leadership eased.

After their release from jail, Larry Fox and Mike Simmons began to move around the country to form an anti-war network, which included incorporating African-American women in anti-draft counseling and ministers to ordain people.[86]

One of the many events that may have caused SNCC to think about changing it's policy of having whites work within the pre-dominantly African-American communities in the south was the murders of Reverend Jon Daniels and Father Richard Morrisroe in the town of Haynesville in Lowndes County, Alabama on August 20, 1965. Rev. Daniels was arrested with a group of about thirty SNCC demonstrators who were picketing against Jim Crow policies at three local stores in Fort Deposit, the largest town in Lowndes County. The demonstrators were taken to jail in Hayneville. As SNCC supporters were attempting to raise bail, the demonstrators were set up according to Gloria House, "we were put out of jail."

> ...suddenly on Friday afternoon, without warning, and without prior notification to associates who would have picked them up, the civil rights prisoners were told they were free. No bail had been paid. The Chief Deputy ordered them out of jail and out of the county.[87]

Gloria House further recalls:

> We asked to go back to jail but weren't allowed in. As people went to make phone calls, and several of us went to the store, a man came up and shot the two white priests who were with us.[88]

Gloria went on to say:

> "We were standing around outside the jail and they forced us off the property on to the blacktop, one of the country roads, again at gunpoint.

> Since we had been in jail and really hadn't any food to eat or anything to drink—we had been eating pork rind and horrible biscuits and whatever, some of us thought, "Let's walk to the little store here and get a drink, have some ice cream." We headed to a corner store. Just as we turned onto the main street of Haynesville, gunfire broke out, and we realized the gunfire was coming in our direction. The youngsters, of course, started running everywhere, and some of us just fell on the ground. Ruby Sales and I had been walking with Jonathan Daniels, and we fell there on the ground. Jonathan was hit and we think he must have died immediately. Father Richard Morrisroe, the only other white member of the group, was also hit. He did not die, but he moaned and groaned and moaned and groaned in a horrible way that none of us who were there will ever forget. It seemed to me it was hours before anyone appeared on this road in Haynesville."[89]

Ms. House said that she felt everyone had been informed that something was going to happen and, of course, no one was around. SNCC later learned that the targets were Jonathan Daniels and Father Morrisroe, the two whites in the group, assassinated by a hired deputy marksman, who got off scot-free during a trial.

THE MEREDITH MARCH: BLACK POWER

SNCC members had great expectations for the May 1966 SNCC

retreat in Kingston Springs, Tennessee. There were concerns about the discussion of SNCC projects and the holding of election of SNCC officers. People had been aroused and polarized by the "black consciousness" paper circulated by the Atlanta Project and its call to turn SNCC into an all-African-American organization. There was a split in SNCC between the "old school" integrationist, SNCC members and the "new school," militant black nationalists. The black nationalists were advocates of non-violent direct action but combined with defensive self-defense (violence). The integrationists represented by John Lewis believed in non-violence both as a tactic and some as a philosophy and favored keeping SNCC as a multi-racial organization. Stokely Carmichael represented a successful all African-American project in Lowndes County, Alabama. As an organizer, Carmichael was known as one of SNCC's best. He ran against Lewis for chairman of SNCC.

> Early in the emotional conference, by a vote of 60 to 22, John Lewis, the gentle advocate of non-violence, retained the chairmanship of SNCC by defeating the challenge of the militant Stokely Carmichael. But as the conference went on, the arguments of the militants began to prevail. When the staff voted to boycott the coming White House Conference on Civil Rights, Lewis announced that he would attend anyway and the question of the chairmanship was reopened. This time SNCC workers chose Carmichael as their new leader by a vote of 60 to 12.[90]

The conference represented a major shift in political emphasis for SNCC. SNCC reemphasized its opposition to the Vietnam War around January 1966 and called for African-Americans to begin building independent political, economic and cultural institutions to be used as instruments for social change in the country. SNCC began to take one organizer's emphasis that SNCC should operate on three levels:

1. SNCC workers should use nationalism as a way to organize the black community;
2. They should begin to build community wide political movements; such as the LCFO; and,
3. White SNCC organizers should begin "to organize the white community around black needs, around black history, the relative importance of blackness in the world today." [91]

SNCC created a new central committee with Stokely Carmichael as chairman. SNCC proposed to go in a new direction.

On June 6, 1966, James Meredith, the African-American who had integrated the University of Mississippi in 1962 with the help of the United States Army, started on a 200 mile walk from Memphis to Jackson to show the African-Americans of Mississippi they could go to voting booths without fear. Twenty-eight miles out of Memphis while walking along U. S. Highway 51, South of Hernando, Mississippi, Meredith was shot three times by a white man with a shotgun. Though he was badly wounded, he wasn't killed. Immediately, civil rights leaders rushed to Mississippi to promise Meredith that they would continue his march. Carmichael of SNCC met with Roy Wilkins of NAACP, Floyd McKissick of CORE and Martin Luther King, Jr. of SCLC. Carmichael convinced the SNCC central committee to support the march but with qualifications. SNCC wanted to de-emphasize the role of whites in the March and not issue a call for the liberal army to come to Mississippi. SNCC through it's chairman Stokely Carmichael demanded that the march be protected and invited the self-defense Deacons for Defense and Justice to protect the march. Dr. King agreed only if the Deacons didn't march with guns that may lead to the march being attacked.[92]

As the march entered Philadelphia, Mississippi, Dr. King conducted a memorial service for Goodman, Chaney and Schwerner. When the whites attacked the march, demonstrators fought back. The SNCC central committee saw the march as a good opportunity to raise a new slogan for the movement representing its new direction. SNCC decided to raise the slogan of "Black Power" counter posed to "Freedom Now" when the march approached a SNCC stronghold in Greenwood, Mississippi. On June 17th, the march entered Greenwood, Mississippi. The marchers tried to set up tents on the grounds of a school.

> The police told the marchers the school grounds couldn't be used without the school board's permission. Carmichael tried to settle the dispute and ended up in jail for six hours for resisting the police order. That night a rally was held. About 600 people showed up. Carmichael was the last speaker.[93]

Carmichael said, "This is the twenty-seventh time I have been arrested. I ain't going to jail no more!" Carmichael began talking about the atrocities African-Americans had faced in the recent past and began to shout, "we want black power." Willie Ricks of SNCC who had been priming the march before Greenwood with the slogan of "Black Power" jumped on the stage and shouted, "What do you want?" The crowd shouted, "Black Power!" He did this five times until the audience drowned out all sound with "Black Power."

> "We had been going against 'Freedom Now' for four days [before the rally]. That's what SCLC (Southern Christian Leadership Conference) would be shouting: Freedom Now, Freedom Now. We'd say, 'That don't scare white folks'. The only thing that's gonna get us freedom is power." [94]

The cry of black power changed the movement. As the march proceeded 4,000 African-American registered to vote. [95] Through the march not only were there fights between the marchers and white mobs, but also on several occasions, gunfire was exchanged both ways between the white mobs and the marchers. James Meredith (recovering from his wounds) joined the march on its last day by car. By June 26, 1966 as 15,000 marchers entered Jackson, Mississippi in the "March Against Fear," the civil rights movement had died and the black power movement was born.

ALLIANCES IN THE NORTH

With the mass cry of black power SNCC became a catalyst for a black awakening of the mid-60s to early '70s. SNCC began to respond to this black awakening or consciousness by appealing to the nationalistic aspirations of many of the urban black under/working class.

When the Student Non-Violent Coordinating Committee (SNCC) raised the slogan of black power in 1966, it represented a transitional slogan within the civil rights movement. Black Power as articulated by the SNCC leadership still was a bourgeois democratic demand. It was a call in essence for portional representation of African-Americans in the capitalist political arena. SNCC failed to advance a program and organize the masses around black power. SNCC at first organized the Lowndes County Freedom Organization (Black Panther Party) around black electoral power, which was correct, but as the spontaneous rebellions increased SNCC's program was reduced to leftist rhetoric. Instead, SNCC only mobilized the masses around the slogan of Black Power and as a result the motion generated around

Black Power subsided after a couple of years.

The Black Panther Party ("BPP") also followed SNCC in mobilizing the masses in left adventurist actions and the motion for black political power fell to the initiative of the black middle class.

Many African-American radical groups in the '60s organized on the basis of the revolutionary mood of the African-American masses and failed to develop correct tactics. *Revolutionary tactics are not built upon revolutionary moods alone.* The failure of SNCC, RAM and the BPP to organize for revolutionary African-American electoral power during the high tide ('67–'69 period) of the Black Liberation Movement (BLM) liquidated the left wing of the BLM from having a solid mass base.

As SNCC speakers were invited to speak in urban communities and on college campuses, SNCC also ceased to do concrete day-to-day organizing in rural local communities.

> SNCC began to rely almost totally on speechmaking and its New York Office manned by professional fund-raisers and veteran staff members, to provide funds for payroll expenses.[96]

In January 1966 SNCC announced its opposition to the Vietnam War, with SCLC following that position four months later along with CORE.

SNCC concentrated on getting press attention but the more radical SNCC became publicly the less funds it received from liberal white, mainly Jewish liberals.

> Although some Jews cut off their support to SNCC during 1966, most did so because they like many former non-Jewish supporters disagreed with SNCC's anti-war stance and with Carmichael's inflammatory rhetoric.[97]

As SNCC's financial base was eroding, organizationally, it made alliances in the north that further alienated its liberal supporters. Responding to a letter from myself to Stokely Carmichael requesting permission to establish a chapter of the Black Panther Party, Carmichael came north to make the alliance with revolutionary black nationalists in New York.[98] From meetings in New York, a collective decision was made to build the Black Panther Party into a national organization. The revolutionary nationalists in New York were not alone in seeking to make an alliance with SNCC.

Kwame Ture (Stokely Carmichael) recalls:

> When a volunteer from Oakland, California, working in Lowndes County returned home, Huey P. Newton and Bobby Seale asked for permission to use the emblem for a party they were forming.[99]

Stokely Carmichael would also threaten to make an alliance with the Nation of Islam and spoke often to N.O.I. mosques audiences.

As SNCC made alliances with black nationalists and major street gangs in northern cities, it often came under a quasi-para-military pressure to adhere to one or another aspect of black nationalist rhetoric. According to John Bracey, Jr., this occurred on one occasion at a dance of the Blackstone Rangers in Chicago. According to another source, a similar situation occurred in Cleveland, Ohio. Often these instances made SNCC personnel leery of black nationalist forces providing an uneasy alliance. SNCC also was involved in an internal split, resulting from the Atlanta Project's continual demands that whites be purged from SNCC.

At a staff meeting held in upstate New York during December 1966, SNCC's veteran leaders came under strong attack from separatists in SNCC's recently established Atlanta Project.[100]

Several members of the Atlanta Project were from the North, and took their ideological direction from the writings of Franz Fanon and the speeches of Malcolm X and often refuted aspects of the Marxian paradigm. They insisted the organization (SNCC) engage in an internal ideological purification movement. The Atlanta Project against the Carmichael faction waged ideological battles until Carmichael fired all members of the Atlanta Project for insubordination in the winter of 1967.

Staff members elected H. Rap Brown as Chairman, believing that he could remove SNCC from public controversy.[101]

Due to the Atlanta Project's demand that SNCC break its umbilical cord to white supporters, SNCC gave a scathing denouncement of Israel settler colonialism and support for the Palestinians.

> Veteran staff member Cleveland Sellers later acknowledged that afterward many donations from white sources just stopped coming in.[102]

Kwame Ture recalls how his wife's (Miriam Makeba) concerts were cancelled overnight.[103] SNCC's international positions; its alliances with black nationalist organizations and SNCC's flirtation with urban guerrilla war lead to SNCC reaching the crisis point. Combined with the struggle of women in SNCC for equality and the rapid growth of the Black Panther Party for Self Defense lead to SNCC's twilight.

WOMEN IN SNCC

Women were treated more equally in SNCC as opposed to SCLC or the NAACP probably because of their active role in the spontaneous demonstrations that led to the development of SNCC (most notably Diane Nash from Fisk University in the Nashville movement) and Ms. Ella Baker, the convener of the April 14–17, 1960 conference, which led to SNCC's development. Despite the gallant role of women in SNCC's development and continuity in its leadership (Ms. Ruby Doris Smith Robinson); women, both African-American and European-American ("white") suffered from male chauvinism. Also there was a struggle within the gender between Euro-American women and African-American women in terms of sexual relations with African-American male activists within the SNCC organization.

Following the concept of integration, white and black together early in SNCC's development (1960–1965) took on sexual (politics') connotations between the races socially. SNCC's rhetoric of equality and personal dignity and respect was not always achieved. While women were more decisive on the front lines of organizing in the sit-ins and freedom rides (1960–1961) they became relegated to administrative and education (office, freedom schools) and fundraising as SNCC ventured off campus and into the rural south. Much of this sexual division of labor came from fear of male organizers of atrocities that may be carried out against African-American female organizers (1961–1963). There was also increased anxiety concerning European-American women being in the field in the state of Mississippi and having sexual relations with African-American men from the community.[104]

What has not been adequately recorded was the social motif of the American left from 1919 to the late '70s. Part of the cultural motif of the left represented by the Communist Party U.S.A. (C.P.) and the Trotskyites, Socialist Workers Party (S.W.P.) dominated by a radical Jewish culture, was the recruiting of African-American

73

male cadre through seduction by European-American females. There were some instances of radical African-American females socially connecting with radical European-American males but seldom.[105] So when the civil rights movement exploded in mass youth numbers, sexual politics practiced by most groups on the organized left became informal social etiquette. This produced a double standard regarding sexual behavior. While it was all right for an African-American male SNCC staff member to date and have sexual intercourse with European-American women in and around SNCC, sexual contact between an African-American female and a European-American male was considered taboo.[106]

African-American women in SNCC became estranged and alienated from the European-American women in SNCC because they resented willingness, eagerness of the African-American male SNCC staff members to sexually relate to the European-American women staff members and volunteers.[107] At the same time, the European-American women began to feel like sexual objects of exploitation. Led by Mary King and Casey Hayden, they articulated this concern in a paper prepared for a SNCC retreat in the fall of 1964.[108] At the same time, Casey Hayden had organized clandestinely a "Society for the Protection of White People's Rights Within SNCC." This was a reaction to the growing African-American nationalistic sentiment that had grown with the ranks of SNCC's African-American members in relation to its European-American SNCC workers.[109]

African-American SNCC women began to relate to more nationalistic minded SNCC staff members, often from the north or relate to African-American men on the outer fringes of the organizing circle of the SNCC staff.[110]

During the racial purges within SNCC, 1966–1967, SNCC consciously sought to upgrade some of its African-American female cadre who had been loyal, effective, charismatic and courageous organizers since SNCC's formation in 1960. While several African-American women had been SNCC project directors in the south, there were few African-American women on the central committee of SNCC. In May 1966, Ruby Doris Smith Robinson was elected Executive Secretary of SNCC. This represented an upgrading for Ms. Smith, since the position of Executive Secretary of SNCC had been just as powerful or more powerful than chairman of SNCC when James Forman held the position.[111]

Judy Richardson felt that males and females had more fluid relations in SNCC than those of SCLC, where women had rigid defined roles. Though sexism did exist in SNCC, the women would unite to fight the contradictions of sexism in SNCC. There were strong women leaders and some female project directors in SNCC. For instance, women in SNCC had a protest and decided not to continue to take the minutes at meetings in the winter of 1963 or 1964, so the men in SNCC had to begin taking the minutes.[112]

African-American women who had faced danger in the field, suffered beatings and imprisonment, fought a two-lined struggle within SNCC; one for gender representation within the leadership and, for a cultural "self-esteem" among the African-American males. At the same time, the feminism of the middle class European-American women in SNCC though having legitimate claims against sexual exploitation were not concentrated on the realities of the 1960s American south. African-American SNCC female workers were more inclined to unite with African-American SNCC male workers on the analysis of race and class exploitation. In an interview with Muriel Tillinghast said she loved the brothers in SNCC and had a lot of respect for those who were in the field organizing. Some of the white women felt they were being handled very sexistly. Muriel said she raised "a question with the white women in SNCC, who worked in the office that they wanted to confront. She said,

> "the people you were talking with are in the field and not only are you white and young and inexperienced, but you really wanted to go up against people who had been ducking bullets, who had been organizing people, living in the rough, haven't had a bath in a week, surviving off a half of baloney sandwich and some Vienna sausages and really you want to go to jaw to jaw with some in terms of what they should be doing in their rural areas.[113]

Muriel said to the white women this is where you take notes and this is where you learn. The question of gender tended to be a complex question related to the dialectics of sexual colonial exploitation and the politics of paternal dominance by the super ordinate race over the subordinated one. The question of eliminating sexism, as it became known was more of a perplexing question for SNCC because it was originally multi-racial organization. But as SNCC became a single ethnic organization, the question of women's equality was not resolved and this question remains a central issue in the African-American liberation movement.

In the 1966–67 period SNCC decided to raise the consciousness of African-American college students.

Organizing on Black College Campuses

George Ware, previous SNCC campus coordinator, describes his initial involvement in SNCC;

> SNCC had a very strong focus in Alabama and that is when I became involved with SNCC. It was really through an organization that we had created on our campus to help the civil rights movement called the Tuskegee Institute Advancement League. We called it TIAL.[114]

The students at Tuskegee Institute were aware of the conflict between SCLC and SNCC. They did not want to get involved in the competition between civil rights organizations. Rather than form a SNCC chapter, the students formed an independent organization. George Ware became co-chairman of TIAL and George Davis and others got involved in support groups giving financial and material backing to the various civil rights organizations. Members of TIAL went to all the demonstrations held in Selma in 64 and into 1965, including the march over Pettus Bridge in which demonstrators were beaten in March of 1965. TIAL also participated in the Selma to Montgomery march. TIAL also continued support of Mrs. Fannie Lou Hamer in Sunflower County, Mississippi. TIAL at the suggestions of Mrs. Hamer began picketing in Tuskegee, Alabama, demanding that the local A & P hire African-Americans for the summer.

> Fannie Lou Hamer came up with this idea. Let's go and ask the A&P to hire blacks for the summer. Most of the people who shop in the A&P are black and all the people that work in their stores are white. So, we went down and asked the persons if they would consider hiring college students for the summer. The guy told us that it was against policy for his own business and to get out of his store. So, we set up a picket and at first people went past it, the picket line, but very soon black people were no longer going past. There was this one white man who went past and he made the mistake of thinking that we were like Dr. King, he took a camera and a guy on the picket line took the camera and beat him up.[115]

The TIAL decided not to change from non-violent resistance or demonstrating for integration to black power as SNCC had done. The TIAL decided to integrate the churches in Tuskegee.

> On Sunday, the men of the church, who were there every Sunday, locked us out. One Sunday, we came there and all the men were across the street in their work clothes, all the white folk. That Sunday they attacked us with baseball bats, guns. They beat us up and drove us away from the church. The following Sunday, the black middle-class population turned out with guns to escort us to the church. We wanted to demonstrate things weren't so perfect in town.[116]

George Ware soon joined SNCC. He became campus coordinator for SNCC. George Ware's role as campus coordinator was to encourage students on college campuses (usually southern or African-American) to organize. Ware picked Fisk University and Tennessee State as his first projects. SNCC was actively involved in the black power project and rebellions (riots) that were occurring around the country. The SNCC project at college campuses was to challenge college students to make sure their education was relevant to the needs of the African-American people.

I would take kids from Fisk and take them to Lowndes County, Alabama during an election.[117]

From the African-American college students' participation in electoral politics in the black belt and facing armed intimidation from the KKK radicalized them. They began to take a closer look at the subject matter they were studying in school and how relevant it was to the conditions of the African-American community surrounding Fisk University. The young college students through efforts of SNCC created summer literacy programs using the Autobiography of Malcolm X to teach reading. In the north, SNCC's campus program targeted African-American students on white colleges to form black student unions and demand black studies departments in all major colleges in America. The height of the SNCC campus program came in the 1966–1967 school year at Central State College and Wilberforce University in Wilberforce, Ohio.

Michael Warren who was a student at Central State had gone to a feast that was being given by the Wilberforce president.[118]

When he got there, he attacked the president's political positions. He was expelled from school. Students of the campuses began marching in support of his reinstatement, took over a building on campus and held it until state troopers invaded the campus. The school was closed down for a couple of weeks. Ware and SNCC's campus program cadre came in the area to help the students work through the whole affair.

> We took the core of the revolutionary cadre to a retreat in upper Michigan for two weeks. When school started back, we sent some people off to places to talk to parents. When school started, all the parents and students came back with a solidified position. Central State became much more responsive. We brought Farrakhan in and they set up a Muslim Mosque on campus.[119]

Many of Central State's students were from New York and Philadelphia and were Muslims. One of the demands was that a Mosque be established on an equal basis with the Christian Chapel as an alternative religious experience.

The African-American student demonstrations escalated in 1967, reaching some urban communities. They continued into 1968 and by spring, had reached a peak along with white students either in support of African-American students or demanding the U.S. end its involvement in war against Vietnam. At Orangeburg, South Carolina, African-American student demonstrations against a segregated bowling alley ended with police shooting up the campus and shooting to death three student demonstrators.

The Orangeburg Massacre

In an interview with Cleveland Sellers, October 3, 2000, he described events that led up to the Orangeburg Massacre. In the fall of 1967 Cleveland Sellers decided to re-energize himself (rest and recuperate from previous organizing experiences throughout the south) and return to South Carolina. Sellers enrolled at South Carolina State University At Orangeburg, South Carolina. He said while continuing his education he wanted to share experiences and strategies he had learned in SNCC while organizing in other parts of the South. He also wanted to organize students to interact with the rich community base and indigenous leadership in and around the Beaufort, Johnson Island area, and the Penn center. Sellers said "there was just a richness in that area for African history, African-American history and culture." Sellers wanted to share with the students certain realities and historical pieces of information about the

Africans in the diaspora and their struggle, how they were successful in maintaining the faith and continuing the struggle.

At South Carolina State University and Clafin students organized the Black Awareness Coordinating Committee (BACC). Most of the students were involved in study of African and African-American history. The students had an appreciation for black power politically and the new nationalist kind of awakening that was emerging around the country. The youth chapter of the NAACP initiated demonstrations against racial discrimination at the bowling alley in Orangeburg. African-American students spent their money in Orangeburg, South Carolina but faced racial discrimination at the bowling alley.

Most of the students in BACC were not involved in the confrontational mood even though they were aware of what the youth chapter of the NAACP was doing. BACC was into the history and cultural aspects of the area during this time. BACC voted not to be part of confrontational efforts even though BACC supported the demonstrations planned by the youth chapter of the NAACP.

The first night of the demonstrations the students who went downtown were threatened with arrest but weren't arrested. That was on Monday, the 5th of February 1968. The second night, the students went back downtown to demonstrate at the bowling alley and thirteen or fourteen students were arrested. Word got out to about 200 students at South Carolina State University who were watching a movie that the arrested students wanted their support.

Students began to assemble in the parking lot of the bowling alley around 9:00 p.m. in the evening. A number of the South Carolina State University faculty and administrators came and began negotiating with the local police where the students would be released and that they would be responsible for getting everyone back on the campus and work through the night to decide what they would do the following day. It seemed that as though an agreement had been reached so one of the students was allowed to get on top of a car and tell the students that "we are released, we are not harmed and we all need to move back to the campus." When he was getting down from the car a fire truck mysteriously showed up.

The students confront members of the fire truck asking the firemen why they were there. Two or three of the students made an effort to get into the bowling alley not knowing there were police inside the bowling alley. There were no police in front of the bowling alley. The students pushed up against the door of the bowling alley to go in. The police were inside the bowling alley so they pushed back. The crowd saw the pushing going on and they all kind of pushed in the area the students were trying to get in. The bowling alley was in chaos. When the crowd shifted to the bowling alley, the pressure from all of them and the students pushing against the glass door, the glass door broke. When the glass door broke the South Carolina Highway Patrol issued out billy clubs to the local police and began beating the students indiscriminately. Thirteen students were admitted to the hospital that night with lacerations to the head and scalp and many had concussions. Many were young women.

The students ended up going back to the campus, which was about two and a half blocks away. Along the way they broke the windows of white businesses. The police classified it as riot. Later that night the student organizations came together to work out a strategy and the acting president of South Carolina State University suggested that the students not leave the campus. Most of the students did not leave the campus. The next day the campus was completely surrounded by national guardsmen. Entrance to and exit from the campus was denied in most instances. Some of the students felt the need to go off of campus on Wednesday night February 1st. A white homeowner who said he thought the students were going to burglarize his house shot them. The students were using the path behind his house as a way to get off campus since the front of the campus was sealed.

The FBI and local police were propagandizing Orangeburg residents that Sellers was a dangerous terrorist and that the students were violent and the community needed to be armed. Even though the campus was sealed a car with two white youth got access to the campus and rode down a campus street, which was a dead end. When the car approach the dead end, one of the white youth panicked and started firing indiscriminately at students.

The students threw bricks and bottles at the car. The car was allowed to leave the campus. The two white youth in the car were never arrested and were never prosecuted. Because this incident implied compliance by the National Guard and local police Sellers began to talk to the press. He called for State intervention in the crisis and called upon the African-American community to come forth to assist the students in the activities they wanted to be involved in. The adult chapters of the NAACP had stepped to the side. No intervention came. Wednesday night was spent with the students negotiating what types of activity they needed to consider, whether they wanted to march downtown or whether they wanted to march on the State capital. The students had few alternatives because they had been fairly isolated to the campus. The National Guard intensified its seizure by bringing in tanks and placing one of the tanks in front of the house Sellers was living in.

At this point, Sellers decided to stay within the interior of the campus. Sellers was trying to provide some information on experiences so they may have a better idea of what their options were. One exception was Sellers advice to the students not to have anymore night demonstrations. Many faculty members of South Carolina State University were also involved in trying to work out solutions with the students. On Thursday evening students approached Sellers and said he could use a student's room who had gone home. Sellers went to the room and went to bed about 7:00 p.m. because he had been up all day and the night before. Students who said they heard some gunfire on campus awakened sellers. Sellers went to the backside of the campus but it was quiet. Sellers then walked to the front side of the campus where he saw students standing in a circle in an open field. Sellers looked down to his right and saw white helmets of what appeared to be police. He was going to tell the students to move closer to the school's buildings because their location was not a safe place to be in. Sellers believes that when he crossed the street, the silhouette of his large Afro hairstyle caught the attention of the police. As he was calling out to a student leader, "Henry," the police open fire. The police had shotguns, rifles, pistols, plus their personal weapons, and fired indiscriminately at the students. All the students turned and tried to move away from the police gunfire. Sellers tried to drag as many wounded students as he could. He hid behind a trash can and along with other students carried the wounded to the infirmary. Thirty-six students were wounded including Sellers and three were killed. The campus police brought some of the students to the infirmary. The students were in shock.[120]

Police used tear gas to quell crowds of demonstrations at Alcorn A&M College. In March after a year of anti-war demonstrations,

Howard University students seized administration buildings demanding Black Studies. Before the month ended, students seized buildings at Bowie State College and state troopers crushed demonstrations at Cheyney State College. At Tuskegee, students demanding campus reforms took the school trustees hostage. At Boston University, students occupied administration buildings demanding increased African-American enrollment and changes in the curriculum. Trinity College officials had to deal with campus racial bias when students occupied the administration building there.

> At Columbia University, students seized five buildings throwing papers out windows and creating so much chaos that the school year ended early. These acts were repeated at Ohio State University, Northwestern, University of Michigan, and many other campuses seeking action from appointed officials.[121]

In 1970 the National Guard shooting of students at Kent State and in May Jackson State eventually quelled the mass student uprisings.

While many of the campus activities had been started by SNCC and SDS (Students for a Democratic Society) SNCC was simultaneously losing ground on campus from its off shoot, the Black Panther Party and various cultural nationalist groups such as the U.S. (United Slaves) led by Maulana Ron Karenga and the RNA (Republic of New Africa).

Demise/Alliance with the BPPSD

The period 1967–1971 was a period of SNCC's eclipse as a vanguard for the black liberation movement. Coming under attack organizationally with the dynamite plot in Philadelphia on August 13, 1966 and then again in 1967 with the arrest of its'[122] Chairman H. Rap Brown, SNCC became a target of government oppression.[123]

James Forman ex-Executive Secretary of SNCC describes reasons for the dynamite plot.

> "The frame-up took place because Philadelphia had become the first metropolitan area in which SNCC was developing the concept of a national freedom organization with the panther as it symbol. SNCC's work there was going well. Response in the ghettos had been good and relations with other organizations had been built."[124]

Forman goes on to describe:

In 1967 spontaneous urban rebellions occurred in fifty-nine cities as African-American college students led revolts on southern campuses. African-American high school students led revolts against the lack of teaching of African-American history in the school curriculum in Philadelphia, New Haven, Trenton and Los Angeles.[125]

Forman estimates the number of arrests of African-American revolutionaries in 1967 reached well into the thousands.

In October 1966 Bobby Seale and Huey Newton had formed the Black Panther Party for Self Defense. Throughout 1967 the Black Panther Party for Self Defense had several confrontations with police in Oakland, California. SNCC trying to develop northern alliances, periodically sent organizers to work with the young BPPSD. Eldridge Cleaver a recently released prisoner political writer had joined the BPPSD. On May 2, 1967 the BPPSD grabbed headlines when members mistakenly walked into the state senate chambers with arms. As the confrontations continued the Black Panther Party for Self Defense became the predominate black news item. SNCC organizer George Ware describes the growing dilemma that Panther organizer Huey P. Newton was having:

> My position was, once the law came down and said you could not longer carry a gun and if you carried a gun, if you said you were going to continue to go on, a policeman could assume you were Panther, if you were armed. So when I went back out to California and I got with Huey out there, formalized a meeting. I sat down with him and I questioned how safe it was going to be for the Panthers to come to operate that way...the way they had in the past. Huey asked me, what did I think? I said that I thought the Panthers should completely reorganize, that they couldn't have an above ground organization, any more, that if they continued to operate above ground and continued to say they were armed, the police would target them. I felt a shoot-out would occur in which the Panthers would be killed because a policeman could assume that you were a Panther and you had a gun. Huey felt, that if he didn't continue to do what he was doing, he would be like a sell out. I thought that it was futile at that point to actually force him to go underground.[126]

George Ware felt Newton should work above ground in SNCC's campus program and let the rest of the Panthers who were not so well known to move in a more discrete way. Ware said, "Huey resented that." A few weeks after the discussion Newton was involved in a shootout with the police in which a police officer was killed and another wounded. Within the next few years Newton was involved in fighting for his freedom. Ware felt when Eldridge Cleaver became the dominant figure in the Panther leadership; the Panthers took a direction that he wasn't sure they would have taken if Newton had been there.

As the "Free Huey" defense movement began to mushroom SNCC first in promoting the Panthers began to be overshadowed by them in the mass media. On February 1, 1968 three figures in SNCC's leadership, James Forman, Stokely Carmichael and H. Rap Brown spoke at a mass Free Huey rally in Oakland, California. Four Thousand people were in attendance. SNCC and Panthers announced having made an alliance with Eldridge Cleaver announcing that the two groups had merged. H. Rap Brown less than a month later had further entanglements with legal authorities, as a result of his breaking travel restrictions on an earlier conviction on riot charges stemming from urban rebellions in the summer of 1967. Brown was re-incarcerated in late February 1968 and released a week after Martin Luther King's assassination, which was on April 4, 1968. SNCC faced a dilemma with its Chairman H. Rap Brown having legal entanglements with the law.

SNCC workers attending the annual staff meeting that began on June 11, 1968 recognized that they had to select new leadership to rebuild SNCC. Rap Brown, too pre-occupied with his own legal problems to attend the meeting, was not a candidate to succeed himself as chairman.[127]

SNCC reorganized its structure and elected nine deputy chairmen to replace Brown. Phil Hutchings was elected program secretary, as acting spokesman for SNCC.

James Forman describes SNCC's alliance with the Black Panther Party for Self Defense:

> At the annual SNCC staff meeting in June, 1968, I introduced a resolution stating that SNCC would work to help build the Black Panther Party, of which Huey Newton is the minister of defense and Bobby Seale the chairman, as a national organization. The honest intent of this resolution, which passed, was to commit SNCC formally to make available whatever resources and skills that it had to help build the Black Panther Party. The references to Huey P. Newton and Bobby Seale were included to eliminate any confusion if

another Black Panther Party arose (there had been many in the past).[128]

By the end of July 1968 the leadership of SNCC began to question, the SNCC/Black Panther Alliance.[129] Also in July, contradictions within the SNCC leadership occurred. Under repression, having operational problems with the BPP, differences in the SNCC leadership turned inward. The alliance between the Oakland Black Panthers and SNCC had broken down in near violent confrontation. H. Rap Brown and James Forman announced their break from the BPP; but Stokely Carmichael of SNCC remained with the BPP. SNCC in return expelled Carmichael. SNCC continued to degenerate into internal bickering and personality struggles throughout 1968.

Forman, previously the strongest leader in SNCC, was on the verge of complete nervous collapse after the breakup of the alliance with the Black Panthers, and he spent much of the fall resting and traveling in the Caribbean.[130] After the December SNCC staff meeting, veteran staff members Cleveland Sellers and Willie Ricks were expelled for maintaining contact with the BPP.[131]

By April 1969, Forman was once again active taking control of the National Black Economic Development Conference in Detroit, Michigan. He drafted a Black Manifesto demanding reparations from religious organizations. SNCC in its June 1969 staff meeting refused to support the reparations motions.

In a political battle for control of SNCC, H. Rap Brown's faction won control of a dying organization. James Forman resigned from SNCC and moved to Detroit to join the League of Revolutionary Black Workers (LRBW). Under Brown's leadership, SNCC became the Student National Coordinating Committee. SNCC formed a revolutionary council, which soon broke up into factional personality and ideological disputes.

H. Rap Brown was to have a trial on his previous charges stemming from his 1967 Cambridge, Maryland demonstration:

> On March 9, 1970, the day before the trial was scheduled to start, two of his associates in SNCC, Ralph Featherstone and William H. (Che) Payne, were killed by an explosion that ripped apart their car as they drove away from Bel Air.[32]

Brown went into exile and underground after the incident and was wounded and captured in a shoot-out on October 16, 1971 in

New York. Brown was part of an effort to eradicate drugs from the African-American community. SNCC soon afterward dissolved with remaining individual members providing support for Brown who served a five to ten year prison term for armed robbery. The pressure brought upon SNCC by the state's repressive apparatus eventually led to SNCC's demise.

AFTERWORD

In building a mass base of support from the bottom up, it is necessary to include all in the community and to have a commitment to include an indigenous, bridge and local leadership. With the understanding of Sisters Ella Baker and Septima Clark, "resources, charismatic leaders, hierarchical structures (organizations, party's, etc.), mobilizations, demonstrations, and organizing and political opportunities are not sufficient to sustain or even mobilize a movement."[133]

Belinda Robnett, in *How Long? How Long?: African Women in the Struggle for Civil Rights*, goes on to explain:

> "SNCC's philosophy and organizational shift away from the teachings of Ella Baker and the methods developed by Septima Clark destroyed the foundations of the movement. And SNCC, which had been the grassroots mobilizing force for the movement, collapsed in the early seventies."[134]

While SNCC's chairmen traveled throughout the U.S. and around the world stimulating, arousing, and mobilizing the black consciousness of African-Americans, it was reduced to a mobile agit-prop committee with mass charismatic spokesmen from the period 1966 to 1971. As a result, SNCC's freedom organizations and other field organizations/projects suffered and/or deteriorated. SNCC became the opposite of what sister Ella Baker had previously advised. SNCC's greatest error, an honest error, was its decision to leave its base, which it had built in the south. Unconsciously it fell into a media trap, when it raised the call for Black Power. Kwame Ture, in recalling the period in self-criticism:

> Flying across the country speaking, meeting with community groups, meeting the press on national TV, on college campuses, in churches. It was constant motion. I could not spend the time I had expected with SNCC in the field...[135]

Kwame Ture, in hindsight, realized this error of SNCC's saying,

"Politically it makes no sense to abandon one base before developing a new one."[136] He further reiterates, stating, "you cannot conduct serious political organizing in the media. The revolution will not be televised."[137]

Robert Mants felt that SNCC went through four periods:

1. The early period, 1960–1962
2. The period of desegregation: 1963–1965
3. The Black Power Era: 1966–1968
4. After the Storm: 1969–1971[138]

The importance of SNCC cannot be underestimated and the lessons to be drawn from it. Diane Nash said, "I think history's most important function is to help us better cope with the present and the future.[139]

1. S.E. Anderson, "Black Students: Racial Consciousness and the Class Struggle, 1960–1976," *The Black Scholar, January/February 1977*, p. 35
2. Donald Mathews and James Prothro, "Negro Students and the Protest Movement" in James McEvoy and Abraham Miller (ed.) *Black Power and Student Rebellion* [Belmont, California: Wadsworth Publishing Company, Inc., 1969], p. 379.
3. James H. Lane, *Direct Action and Desegregation 1960–1962: Toward a Theory of the Rationalization of Protest* [Brooklyn, New York: Carlson Publishing, Inc., 1989], p. 76.
4. Martin Oppenheimer, *The Sit-In Movement of 1960* [Brooklyn, New York: Carlson Publishing, Inc., 1989], p. 43.
5. Anne Braden, "The Southern Freedom Movement in Perspective," *Monthly Review Magazine, July-August 1965*, pp. 26–27.
6. James H. Lane, *Direct Action and Desegregation 1960–1962: Toward a Theory of the Rationalization of Protest* [Brooklyn, New York: Carlson Publishing, Inc., 1989], p. 79.
7. Dallad Shyrlee, *Ella Baker* [Englewood Cliffs: Burdett Press, 1990], p. 70.
8. Anne Braden, "The Southern Freedom Movement in Perspective," *Monthly Review Magazine: Vol. 17, July-August 1965*, p. 28.
9. Jo Freeman (edited) *Social Movements of the Sixties and Seventies* [New York: Longman, 1983], p. 35.
10. Jacqueline Johnson, *Stokley Carmichael: The Story of Black Power*

[Engle Cliffs, N.J.: Silver Burdett Press, 1990], p. 27.

11. *Op. Cit.* (S.E. Anderson) p. 36

12. Ibid., p. 27.

13. Emily Stoper, *The Student Non-Violent Coordinator Committee* [Brooklyn, New York: Carlson Publishing, Inc., 1989], p. 266.

14. Ibid., p. 266.

15. *Op. Cit.* (Stoper), p. 275.

16. John Dittmer, *Local People: The Struggle for Civil Rights in Mississippi* [Urbana & Chicago: University of Illinois Press], p. 104.

17. *Op. Cit.* (Braden), p. 321.

18. Clayborne Carson, *In Struggle: SNCC and the Black Awakening of the* '60s [Cambridge, Mass: Harvard University Press, 1981], p. 32.

19. *Op. Cit.* (Braden), p. 32.

20. Ibid., p. 33.

21. James Boggs, *The American Revolution* (40th Anniversary edition) [Detroit, Michigan: Leadfoot Press, 2003] p. 82

22. Ibid., p.82

23. *Op. Cit.*, *Direct Action and Desegregation*, 1960–62, p. 104.

24. *Op. Cit.*, August Meier and Elliott Rudwick, *CORE*, p. 143.

25. *Op. Cit.*, Hampton and Foyer, *Voices of Freedom*, p. 94.

26. *Op. Cit.* (S.E. Anderson) p 37

27. *Op. Cit.* Meir and Rudwick, *CORE*, p. 140.

28. Cleveland Sellers with Robert Terrell, *The River of No Return: The Autobiography of a Black Militant and the Life and Death of SNCC* *[Jackson and London: University Press of Mississippi, 1990] p. 53–54*

29. *Op. Cit.*, Blumberg, *Civil Rights*, p. 84.

30. *Op. Cit.*, Branch, *Parting the Waters*, pp. 472–473.

31. James H. Lane, *Direct Action and Desegregation*, p. 106.

32. Ibid., p. 109.

33. Cheryl Lynn Greenberg, *A Circle of Trust: Remembering SNCC* [New Brunswick, New Jersey and London: Rutgers University Press, 1998] p. 5

34. Robert H. Brisbane, *Black Activism* [Valley Forge, Pa.: Judson Press, 1974] p. 59.

35. Fred Powledge, *Free at Last? The Civil Rights Movement and the People Who Made It* [New York Harper Perennal, 1991] p. 341.

36. Clayborne Carson, *In Struggle: SNCC and the Black Awakening of the* '60s [Cambridge, Mass: Harvard University Press, 1981], p. 58.

37. Ibid., (Carson), p. 58.

38. Interview/conversation with Slater King, Albany, Georgia, November

1962.

39. *Op.Cit.* (Cleveland Sellers with Robert Terrell) p. 60

40. Fred Powledge, *Free At Last?* [Boston: Little, Brown and company 1991] p. 325

41. Ibid., p.340

42. Howard Zinn, *SNCC-The New Abolitionists* [Boston: Beacon Press, 1964], p. 78.

43. John Dittmer, *Local People* [Urbana and Chicago: University of Illinois Press, 1994], p. 112.

44. Ibid., (Dittmer), p. 115.

45. Nicolaus Mills, "Forgotten Greenville: SNCC and the Lessons of 1963," *Dissent, Summer 1990*, p. 339.

46. *Op. Cit.* (Powledge) p. 474.

47. *Op. Cit.* (Dittmer) p. 135

48. Ibid., p. 136

49. *Op. Cit.* (Sellers) p.56

50. Participant-Observer report interview, Max Stanford 1996, from attendance at SNCC Field Staff retreat in Greenville, Mississippi, Spring 1964.

51. Bracey, Meier, Rudwick (ed.) *Conflict and Competition: Studies in the Recent Black Protest Movement* [Blemont, California: Wadsworth Publishing Company, 1971], p. 140.

52. Doug McAdam, *Freedom Summer* [New York and Oxford: Oxford University Press, 1988], p. 42.

53. Ibid., p. 39.

54. *Op. Cit.*, p. 40.

55. Ibid., (McAdam) p. 4.

56. Ibid., p. 71.

57. Mary Aickin Rothschild, *A Case of Black and White: Northern Volunteers and the Southern Freedom Summers, 1964–1965* [Westport, Connecticut: Greenwood Press, 1982], p. 118.

58. Emily Stoper, "The Student Non-Violent Coordinating Committee: Rise and Fall of a Redemptive Organization in Joe Freeman" (ed) *Social Movements of the Sixties and Seventies* [New York: Longman, 1983], p. 324.

59. Len Holt, *The Summer That Didn't End* [New York: William Morrow & Co., 1965], p. 35.

60. Howard Zinn, *SNCC: Student Non-Violent Coordinating Committee, The New Revolutionists* [Boston: Beacon Press, 1964], p. 251.

61. Doug McAdam, "Gender as a mediator of the Activist Experience: The Case of Freedom Summer," *American Journal of Sociology*, Vol. 97, Number 5 (March 1992), p. 1,212.

62. *Op. Cit.* (Doug McAdam, Freedom Summer), p. 82.

63. Peter B. Levy, *Let Freedom Ring: A Documentary History of the Modern Civil Rights Movement* [New York: Praeger, 1992], p. 143.

64. *Op. Cit.* (McAdam), p. 83.

65. *Op. Cit.* (Holt), p. 112.

66. *Op. Cit.* (Bracey, Meir, Rudwick), p. 142.

67. *Op. Cit.* (S.G. Anderson) p. 38

68. *Op. Cit.* (McAdam), p. 88.

69. Ibid. (McAdam), p. 89.

70. Ibid., (McAdam), p. 89.

71. Allen J. Matusaw "From Civil Rights to Black Power: The Case of SNCC, 1960–1966" in Bracey, Meier, Rudwick, *Conflict and Competition: Studies in the Recent Black Protest Movement* [Belmont, California: Wadsworth Publishing Company, 1971], p. 143.

72. *Op. Cit.* (Clayborne, Carson), pp. 139–140.

73. Jacqueline Johnson, *Stokely Carmichael: The Story of Black Power* [Englecliffs, N.J.: The Silver Burdett Press, 1994], p. 61.

74. Henry Hampton and Steve Fayer with Sarah Flynn, *Voices Of Freedom: An Oral History of the Civil Rights Movement from the 1950s through the 1980s* [New York: Bantam Books, 1990], p. 216.

75. *Op. Cit.* (Jacqueline Johnson), p. 62.

76. *Op. Cit.* (Henry Hampton, Steve Fayer with Sarah Flynn), p. 226.

77. Hanes Walton, Jr., *Black Political Parties: An Historical and Political Analysis* [New York: The Free Press; London Collier-McMillan Limited, 1972], p. 138.

78. Ibid. (Hanes Walton, Jr.), p. 139.

79. Charlie Cobb, "*Black Power*" *Emerge Magazine, June 1997, Volume 8, Number 8*, p. 43.

80. Jacqueline Johnson, *Stokely Carmichael: The Story of Black Power* [Englewood Cliffs, New Jersey: Silver Burdett Press, Inc.], p. 71.

81. *Op. Cit.* (Jacqueline Johnson), p. 74.

82. Ibid., p. 75.

83. Interview with Don Stone, Atlanta, Georgia, 1994.

84. Telephone Interview with Judy Richardson, October 15, 2000.

85. Telephone conversation with Mike Simmons (Philadelphia to Cleveland), February 5, 1998.

86. Ibid., (Interview Mike Simmons).

87. Jack Mendelsohn, *The Martyrs* [New York: Harper and Row Publishers, 1966], p. 209.

88. Interviews with Gloria House, Detroit, Michigan, March 2001. For a detailed account of the incident, read Jack Mendelsohn, *The Martyrs* [New York: Harper and Row Publishers, 1966] pp. 196–218.

89. Cheryl Lynn Greenberg, *A Circle of Trust: Remembering SNCC* [New Brunswick, New Jersey and London: Rutgers University Press, 1998] p. 105–106

90. Allen J. Matuson, "From Civil Rights to Black Power: The Case of SNCC, 1960–1966" in Bracey, Meier Rudwick, *Conflict and Competition: Studies in the Recent Black Protest Movement* [Belmont, California: Wadsworth Publishing, Inc., 1971], p. 148.

91. Jacqueline Johnson, *Stokely Carmichael: The Story of Black Power* [Englewood Cliffs, New Jersey: Silver Burdett Press, 1990], p. 78.

92. "Cleveland Sellers" in Henry Hampton and Steve Fayer with Sarah Flynn, *Voices of Freedom: An Oral History of The Civil Rights Movement from the 1950s through the 1980s* [New York: Bantam Books, 1995], p. 285.

93. *Op. Cit.* (Jacqueline Johnson), p. 84.

94. Charlie Cobb, Jr., "Black Power," *Emerge Magazine*, Volume 8, Number 8, June 1997, p. 41.

95. *Op. Cit.* (Henry Hampton with Steve Fayer with Sarah Flynn, *Voices of Freedom*, [New York: Bantam Books, 1990], p. 41.

96. Clayborne Carson, *In Struggle: SNCC and the Black Awakening of the 1960s* [Cambridge, Massachusetts: Harvard University press, 1981], p. 234.

97. Clayborne Carson, "Blacks and Jews in the Civil Rights Movement, The Case of SNCC," in Jack Salzman, Adina Back, Gretchen Sullivan Sorin (ed.) *Bridges and Boundaries: African-Americans and American Jews* [New York: George Brazidler, Inc. 1992], p. 41.

98. Max Stanford, Participant/Observer, Bronx, New York, June 1966.

99. Charlie Cobb, "Black Power" interview with Kwame Ture, *Emerge Magazine*, June 1997, p. 43.

100. *Op. Cit.* (Carson, "Blacks and Jews"), pp. 41–42.

101. *Op. Cit.* (Jack Salzman, Adina Back, Gretchen Sullivan Sorin), p. 42.

102. Ibid., p. 44.

103. Interview with Kwame Ture, Oberlin College, Oberlin, Ohio, 1996 (Max Stanford).

104. Doug McAdam, "Gender as a Mediator of the Activist Experience: The Case of Freedom Summer," *American Journal of Sociology*, Volume

97, Number 5 (March 1992), p. 1220.

105. Harold Cruse, *The Crisis of the Negro Intellectual* [New York: William Morrow & Company, Inc., 1967], pp. 147–171, Interview with Queen Mother Audrey Moore, Harlem, N.Y., 1980.

106. Interview with Ruby Doris Smith Robinson, Philadelphia, Pa., March, 1967.

107. Interview with Ruby Doris Smith Robinson, April 1964, SNCC National Office, Atlanta, Ga.

108. *Op. Cit.*, (McAdam) "Gender," p. 1232.

109. Interview with Ruby Doris Smith Robinson, March, 1967, Philadelphia, Pa.

110. Interview with four African-American female workers on the SNCC staff, May, 1964, Atlanta, Ga.

111. Cynthia Griggs Fleming, "Black Women Activists and The Student Non-Violent Coordinating Committee: The Case of Ruby Doris Smith Robinson," *Journal of Women's History, Volume 4, Number 3 (Winter)*, p. 74.

112. Telephone interview with Judy Richardson, October 15, 2000.

113. Interview with Muriel Tillinghast, New York to Cleveland, August 24, 2000.

114. Interview with George Ware, Philadelphia, Pa. 1994, p. 18.

115. Ibid., p. 18.

116. Ibid. (Interview with George Ware), p. 19.

117. *Op. Cit.*, p. 19.

118. Ibid., p. 19.

119. Ibid., p. 19.

120. Interview with Cleveland Sellers, Jr., September 7th, 2000 and October 3rd, 2000, Cleveland to Columbia, South Carolina. The interview is not singled spaced because I paraphrase Sellers words. The essence of Cleveland Sellers' interview is there. The reader should also refer to Jack Bass and Jack Nelson, The Orangeburg Massacre [Macon, Georgia: Mercer University Press, 1984].

121. Dorothy Salem, Long Journey: History of the African-American Experience [Dubuque, Iowa: Kendal/Hout Publishing Company, 1997] draft for Manuscript, p. 373.

122. James Forman, *The Making of Black Revolutionaries*, [Seattle, Washington: Open Hand Publishing, Inc., 1985], p. 460.

123. James Forman, High Tide of Black Resistance, [Seattle, Washington: Open Hand Publishing, Inc. 1994], p. 136.

124. Op. Cit., (Forman, *The Making of Black Revolutionaries*), p. 460.

125. Op. Cit., (Forman, *High Tide of Resistance*), p. 135.

126. Interview with George Ware, Philadelphia, Pennsylvania.

127. Clayborne Carson, *In Struggle: SNCC and the Black Awakening of the 1960s* [Cambridge, Massachusetts: Harvard University Press, 1981], p. 290.

128. James Forman, The Making of Black Revolutionaries [Seattle, Washington: Open Hand Publishing, Inc., 1990], p. 352.

129. Ibid., p. 538.

130. Clayborne Carson, *In Struggle, Op. Cit.*, p. 293.

131. *Op. Cit.*, Carson, *In Struggle*, p. 297.

132. Ibid., p. 297.

133. Belinda Robnett, *How Long? How Long?: African-American Women in the Struggle for Civil Rights* [New York: Oxford University Press, 1997] pp.202–204

134. *Op. Cit., pp. 187–188*

135. Stokely Carmichael [Kwame Ture] with Ekwame Michael Thelwell, *Ready for Revolution: The Life and Struggles of Stokely Carmichael* [Kwame Ture] [New York: Scribner, 2003] p. 52

136. *Op. Cit.*, p. 561

137. *Op. Cit.*, p. 546

138. *Op. Cit.*, (Circle of Trust) p. 216

139. *Op. Cit.*, (Circle of Trust) p. 18

The struggle for Black Studies in schools united
all black radical groups, as indicated in this 1960s
mimeo'd pamphlet by C. L. R. James

6 Injured at School Picket
NAACP Blocks ~~Mad~~ Riot

Black Power Riot

16 Arrested in Plot

Pickets Battle Police

AMSTERDAM NEWS, SEPTEMBER 3, 1966

BLACK PANTHERS OPEN HARLEM DRIVE

Black men must unite and overthrow their white "oppressors," but must do it "like panthers, smiling, cunning, scientifically— striking by night and sparing no one," Max Stanford, a member of

Pickets Battle Police
18 Hurt, 57 Arrested

Black Power Pickets

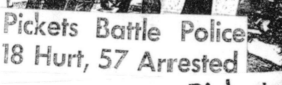

The young man in the lower middle is
Maxwell Stanford, Jr., of RAM (June 1967)

94

REVOLUTIONARY ACTION MOVEMENT
(RAM)

The Revolutionary Action Movement (RAM) evolved from the southern civil rights movement of the early 1960s and the black nationalist movement in northern cities. As a result of the sit-ins, students in northern cities organized solidarity demonstrations. Traditional civil rights organizations like the NAACP and CORE held mass rallies in northern African-American communities. African-American and white students demonstrated against Woolworth stores and along with progressive clergy led economic boycotts. Black students with more radical leanings in the north, while supporting SNCC, had a tendency to reject its non-violent philosophy. Some of these students joined CORE to participate in direct action activities.[1]

Don Freeman of Cleveland, Ohio, who was executive chairman of RAM in 1964–65,[2] said he became involved in the civil rights movement early in 1960. Freeman first became involved in the civil rights movement while a student at Western Reserve University in February in 1960. The Cleveland Chapter of the NAACP led a mass demonstration in downtown Cleveland in support of African-American students in the south who had begun non-violent sit-in demonstrations (February 1, 1960); sitting in at segregated lunch counters (Woolworth chain stores) and other public places to desegregate them. Pickets continued at the local Cleveland branches of Woolworth stores and an economic boycott convened. Freeman and a white female companion attended a socialist conference at the University of Michigan in Ann Arbor, Michigan, Thursday, April 28th to Sunday, May 1st, 1960. Freeman said his attendance at the conference was the turning point in his life. At the conference, Freeman met many of the leaders of the democratic socialist left (socialist party) and became a dedicated life long socialist.

In the summer of 1961, at the end of the freedom rides, Robert F. Williams, president of the Monroe, North Carolina chapter of the NAACP, issued a nation-wide call for African-Americans to arm for self-defense and come to Monroe for a showdown with the KKK.[3] Williams also called for freedom riders to come to Monroe to test non-violence.

Within the white left, the League for Industrial Democracy (LID), planned to form a student branch called Students for a Democratic Society (SDS). SDS was to hold a conference on the new left at the National Student Association (NSA) conference (summer, 1961) in Madison, Wisconsin. SNCC was also represented at the NSA conference.

During the conference, news of Williams' flight into exile reached movement circles. Discussions among African-American SNCC and CORE workers and independent African-American radicals took place as to what significance the events in Monroe, North Carolina, had for the movement. African-American cadres inside of SDS met and discussed developing an African-American radical movement that would create conditions to make it favorable to bring Williams' back into the country. This was a small meeting of four people. Freeman said he would correspond with everyone and would decide when to meet again. One of those present at the meeting was a student at Central State College in Wilberforce, Ohio.

During the fall of 1961, an off-campus chapter of SDS called Challenge was formed at Central State. Challenge was an African-American radical formation having no basic ideology.

Its membership was composed of students who had been expelled from southern schools for sit-in demonstrations; students who had taken freedom rides and students from the north, and some had been members of the Nation of Islam and African nationalist organizations.

At Central State College, Wilberforce, Ohio among others were Haskell Brewton, from Philadelphia, Pa., Scott Young from New York—who later set up a CSC, CORE chapter—Wanda Marshall from White Plains, NY, Donald Worthy from Cleveland, Ohio, and myself from Philadelphia, PA. They made up the core of Challenge, a chapter of the Students for Democratic Society (SDS). Donald Worthy from Cleveland, Ohio served with me as the political ideologists for Challenge. Donald Freeman, a school teacher in Cleveland, Ohio who had graduated from Case Western Reserve University was mentor for the group (1961–1962). Granville Reid who chaired the CSC chapter of the NAACP was passively critical of the group. Challenge's main emphasis was struggling for more student rights on campus and bringing a black political awareness to the student body. In a year-long battle with Central State's administration over student rights, members of Challenge became more radicalized. Challenge members attended student conferences in the south and participated in demonstrations in the north. Freeman sent letters to the Challenge cadre, discussing ideological aspects of the civil rights movement. Part of my initial activities the year before in 1960, was to subscribe to Robert F. Williams newsletter, *The Crusader*, which was published in Monroe, N. C. I also became a Freedom Rider recruiter for CORE. Heath Rush was one of the white students from Central State College that I recruited to go on the Freedom Rides to Monroe, N.C. I began to recruit whites on campus at the time, because there was a shortage of whites for the rides. One of the organizers who influenced me and the Challenge collective was John Friedman of CORE at Antioch College in Yellow Springs, Ohio. John Eiseman, editor of the *Activist* magazine at Oberlin College, was also a mentor.

In the spring of 1962, *Studies On The Left*, a radical quarterly, published Harold Cruse's article, "Revolutionary Nationalism and the Afro-American."[4] In the article Cruse described Afro-Americans as an oppressed nation within a nation. Freeman wrote a letter to the Challenge cadre telling them to seriously study the article. He also said African-American radicals elsewhere were studying the article and that a movement had to be created in the north similar to the Nation of Islam, using the tactics of SNCC but outside of the NAACP and CORE. The Challenge cadre studied Freeman's letter but did not know where to begin.

After much discussion and through the efforts of Kenny Adderly, a senior at CSC, the Challenge cadre decided to form a broad coalition party to take over student government. Meetings were held with representatives from each class, fraternity and sorority. A slate was drafted and a name for the party was selected. At the meeting of the coalition party, the name Revolutionary Action Movement was chosen. But it was felt by the members at the meeting that the word revolutionary would scare Central State's administration so they decided to use Reform Action Movement (RAM) for the purposes of the student election. Charles "Chuck" Reed was candidate for student body president on the RAM ticket in May 1962 at Central State College (later to become Central State University) in Wilberforce, Ohio. It was called RAM, later to be known as the Revolutionary Action Movement.

The Challenge cadre met and decided to dissolve itself into RAM and become the RAM leadership. RAM won all student government offices. After the election, the inner RAM core discussed what to do next. Some said that all that could be done at Central State had already occurred, while others disagreed. Some of the inner core decided to stay at Central State and run the student government. A few decided to return to their communities and attempt to organize around Freeman's basic outline. Freeman, in his letters, outlined a general perspective of creating a mass African-American working class nationalist movement in the north. He stressed this movement had to be political and more radical than the Nation of Islam. He emphasized that the movement should use direct action tactics but would not be non-violent. Two of the students who decided to return to their communities were Wanda Marshall and me.

Freeman wrote to me in Philadelphia, saying that he was coming to Philadelphia in the summer of 1962 and that he wanted me to organize a meeting. Freeman went to Philadelphia and met with a group of my high school friends. He discussed the movement and the direction it had to take. Later in discussions with me, Freeman gave instructions that Philadelphia should become a pilot project for the outline of the type of movement he described in his letters to the RAM cadre. He said the movement once started should be called the Revolutionary Action Movement (RAM). Freeman continued to travel from city to city. In September of 1962, I went to the National Student Association headquarters in Philadelphia. There I met Marion Barry from SNCC, who was in Philadelphia to help raise funds for SNCC. Wanda Marshall transferred to Temple University and began working with African-American students there. I began studying with Mr. Thomas Harvey, president of the Universal Negro Improvement Association (UNIA).[5]

In the process of working with SNCC, I met most of the African-American left in Philadelphia. One acquaintance was Bill Davis, a leader of an independent African-American Marxist cadre called Organization Alert (OA). During this time, I had discussions with Marion Barry about the direction of the civil rights movement. One night while listening to discussion in the NSA office, Miss Ella Baker encouraged me to continue to develop my ideas.

After Marion Barry left Philadelphia, Bill Davis asked me to join Organization Alert. I wrote Freeman about OA and Freeman decided to meet with Davis. Freeman came to Philadelphia in October of

1962 and after long discussions with Davis told me that OA was too bourgeois/intellectual and not sufficiently action-oriented. Freeman had organized the African-American Institute in Cleveland in 1962. He was also a school teacher in the Cleveland school system. He told me that I had to start something independent of OA. I was still not convinced. Freeman left and returned to Cleveland.

During a meeting of OA, Davis harshly criticized SNCC and said that SNCC would never change. I opposed that position, saying that SNCC was at the center of the movement and events would force SNCC to change. The discussion ended in a heated debate. I discussed the debate with Wanda Marshall of the original Central State campus RAM cadre.

Freeman returned to Philadelphia one week before the Thanksgiving holidays. At a social meeting, Marshall harangued me for not having organized. It was decided at that meeting to organize a study group in January of 1963.

During the Thanksgiving break, Marshall and I decided to visit Malcolm X. I wanted to seek Malcolm's advice about joining the Nation of Islam. Wanda and I met with Minister Malcolm at the NOI restaurant in New York. After a lengthy black history lesson by Minister Malcolm, I asked Malcolm if I should join the Nation of Islam. Malcolm, to my surprise, said no. He said, "you can do more for the honorable Elijah Muhammad by organizing outside of the Nation."[6]

Minister Malcolm's statements convinced Wanda and me to do independent organizing. I soon afterward drafted a position paper titled "Orientation to a Black Mass Movement, Part One" and circulated it among much of the African-American left in Philadelphia. The paper stated that:

> Organizers must be people who can help masses win victories around their immediate problems. Organizing should be centered on black youth with the objective of building a permanent organized structure...

> ...The organizing of the black working class youth should be the primary concern for the black revolutionist because the black working class has the sustained resentment, wrath and frustration toward the present social order, that if properly channeled can revolutionize black America and make black America the vanguard of the world's black revolution. Within the black working class, the youth constitute the most militant and radical element. Therefore, effective

mobilization and channeling of their energies will function as the catalyst for greater militancy among African-Americans.[7]

Through the NSA coordinator on civil rights, I secured Ethel Johnson's phone number and immediately after going home called her. Mrs. Johnson was receptive to talking to me and invited me to visit her.

I went to visit Mrs. Ethel Johnson (Azelle), who had been a co-worker with Robert Williams in Monroe, North Carolina and who was now residing in Philadelphia. Little has been written of Azelle (Ethel Johnson). All that I know is that Ethel Johnson was married and that she and her husband had agreed that she would do political work (civil rights) while he would maintain income for the family in Monroe, North Carolina, and that they had one son, Raymond Johnson. Johnson lived within the same block or next door to the Williamses (Robert F. and Mable Williams). They recruited Johnson as a co-worker in the Monroe, North Carolina branch of the NAACP. Johnson helped Williams with his newsletter, *The Crusader*, and also participated along with Mable Williams in the community self defense efforts of the African-American community against racist attacks from 1957 to 1961. Johnson had visited the Williamses in Cuba in 1962 and served as a barometer for the Williamses of what the masses of African-Americans were thinking in the early 1960s. Raymond Johnson, Ethel Johnson's son, died of mysterious circumstances and Johnson was advised by her family and friends to relocate for a while at her sister's house in Philadelphia, Pennsylvania. Ethel Johnson was also a student of Marxism-Leninism, sympathized with the Trotskyist tendency, was a member of Workers' World Party, maintained correspondence with James and Grace Boggs of Detroit, who were then publishing *Correspondence*, a monthly newsletter.

Johnson (Azelle), as she was affectionately called, was a good friend of Septima Clark; had worked with her on citizenship schools in the South and also knew Ella Baker and Queen Mother Audley Moore.

Mrs. Johnson read my position paper and later told me she would help me organize in Philadelphia. I continued to circulate my position paper getting various activists' opinion of it. But as time passed, I was still reluctant to start a group of my own.

Towards the end of 1962, Wanda and I called together a group of African-American activists to develop a study/action group. I notified Azelle (Mrs. Ethel Johnson) of our decision and she said she would help guide the group. Within a month's time, key African-American activists came into the study/action group that was guided by Azelle. The three central figures were Wanda Marshall, Stan Daniels and me. After a series of ideological discussions, the Philadelphia study/action group decided to call itself the Revolutionary Action Movement (RAM). It decided it would be a revolutionary black nationalist direct action organization. Its purpose would be to start a mass revolutionary black nationalist movement. By using mass direct action combined with the tactics of self-defense, it hoped to change the civil rights movement into a black revolution. RAM decided to work with the established civil rights leadership in Philadelphia and eventually build a base for mass support.

In 1959, four hundred black ministers in the city formed an organization that placed "economic injustice" at the top of its "agenda for change in Philadelphia." The organization was made up of preachers representing churches throughout the city, who were just as attuned to social issues as the early black preachers/community leaders.[7]

RAM contacted Rev. Leon Sullivan who had organized selective boycotts in the early '60s and volunteered to help with the selective boycotts, which the Philadelphia ministers were conducting against industries that discriminated in their hiring practices.

RAM distributed leaflets in the tens of thousands door to door throughout the community.

> With about 15 people, we distributed about 35,000 leaflets in 3 days. Brother Stan Daniels and I covered almost all of West Philadelphia, block by block; going in bars, candy stores, slipping leaflets under people's doors, working into the early hours of the morning.[8]

In the early months of 1963, a new Philadelphia NAACP president was elected named Cecil B. Moore, an attorney who was prone to direct action.[9]

Temple University initiated a pilot project called Philadelphia Community Action (PCA) composed of white liberals who had been given a grant of one million dollars to study African-American people in North Philadelphia. No African-American person from the community was included on the commission. The NAACP decided to hold a mass rally to protest the commission. Moore asked all community groups to help in organizing the project.

The RAM study/action group immediately became involved. RAM members circulated through North Philadelphia streets with homemade loud speakers, holding street meetings and handing out leaflets. RAM members went into the bars and poolrooms holding rap sessions.

The rally was a total success. But all that the petty-bourgeois community leadership did was give flowery speeches. The week following, the NAACP and RAM picketed the PCA offices. For some reason, the NAACP called off the picketing. RAM reacted with dismay, but we felt this was a NAACP protest and didn't want to conflict with the older, established leadership. RAM was just getting its feet wet in terms of engaging in direct social action and didn't want to cause conflict. Therefore, RAM also ceased picketing. Not too much came of the protest.

RAM members felt the movement needed a voice that was independent of the existing civil rights groups. RAM assessed that all of the civil rights groups—except SNCC—were bourgeois in orientation. RAM believed that full integration was impossible within the capitalist system. It believed that all of the civil rights groups were seeking upward mobility in capitalism and were not seeking a structural transformation of the system. On the other hand, RAM felt SNCC would move toward trying to change the system, because it was mobilizing the grassroots masses in the south.

RAM believed that the Nation of Islam, while placing emphasis on economic self-reliance, was also bourgeois in its orientation, because it was attempting to establish a black capitalist economy, which would only benefit a privileged few black capitalists and not the majority of the twenty-two million African-American people. It was thought that an African-American radical publication should be created. RAM began publishing a bi-monthly titled *Black America*. To begin to agitate the masses, RAM circulated a free one-page newsletter called *RAM Speaks*. *RAM Speaks* addressed itself to local issues that were constantly arising in the movement. *Black America* was more theoretical dealing with the ideology of RAM. Members of RAM went on radio and publicized their study group and programs.

As more community people joined the RAM study group, the

class and age composition of the study group changed from basically students in their early 20s to members of the African-American working class who were in their early 30s. RAM decided to begin mass recruitment. The organization began to hold mass street meetings in North Philadelphia. Free weekly African and African-American history classes were held, taught by Playthell Benjamin, a young self-educated historian, who was from the student movement in Florida and a student of Queen Mother Moore. Cadre meetings would discuss building RAM into a mass movement.[10]

In an interview on May 15, 2002, Barbara "Overton" Montague, who was 15 in 1963, said she remembered her mother, Barbara Overton, being a member of RAM. Her aunt Ethel Johnson, along with Barbara, had recruited Mrs. Montague's mother, Ruth Overton, a registered nurse, to join RAM. All were lifetime members of the neighborhood. RAM had decided to conduct door-to-door canvassing in the neighborhood to find out what were the central problems on people's minds. Using this information, RAM would build its program around the most pertinent needs of the community. Teams of two RAM members would canvas the community, one female member and one male member. The idea of the female/male teams were that two females would be vulnerable to harassment from neighborhood toughs and two male members would be "too strong" and would frighten many of the residents who were single heads of households. The female would approach the door and ask the resident questions, while the male would provide protection for the female. If invited into the house both members of the organization would enter.

Because Mrs. Overton's work schedule would sometimes occur in the evening, she was paired off to canvas the area immediately surrounding the RAM office at 2811 Diamond Street, not far from where she lived, with RAM member, Bill White. One day while canvassing on Diamond Street she was asked by a frantic resident, "Does anyone know how to deliver a baby?" Ruth responded that she was a registered nurse. A young lady in the house was in labor and her water had broken. Ruth delivered the baby on the front porch. The baby was well and healthy; so was the mother. The family and the community were in gratitude. RAM had provided a service. The North Philadelphia community became receptive to RAM.

Azelle, at central committee meetings of the RAM cadre (Wanda

Marshall, Stan Daniels, Jomo L.M.X, Paul Ellis, Mabel Holloway, Bill White, and Max Stanford), would tell us that she was in an organization with Queen Mother Audley Moore. She asked the RAM cadre to attend Queen Mother's periodic public meetings, which she held in her house in west Philadelphia.

Queen Mother Audley Moore, a former CP organizer, sponsored monthly black nationalist ideological training sessions at her house that RAM members would attend. Through its publication, *Black America*, RAM began to communicate with other new nationalist formations. Don Freeman of Cleveland had initially traveled city to city on holidays and vacations, establishing links among socialist-minded African-American activists. From the very beginning of RAM's efforts, the organization was aware of organizing in other cities.[11] In San Francisco, Donald Warden had started the Afro-American Association. In Detroit, Luke Tripp, John Williams, Charles (Mao) Johnson, General Baker, John Watson, and Gwen Kemp were the leadership of UHURU, a revolutionary nationalist student collective and in Cleveland, Freeman had organized the African-American Institute. Sterling Stuckey, Thomas Higginbottom and John Bracey, Jr., had formed the National Afro-American Organization (NAO) in Chicago, and there was a black literary group in New York called UMBRA.

While John Bracey, Jr., was a student at Roosevelt University in Chicago, he associated with a group of anarchists around the IWW.

> We got banned from campus when we invited Joffre Stewart who was a black anarchist to give a speech on anarchism. We had it in a class lecture hall and Joffre burned the U.N. flag, the American flag, the State of Illinois flag, the city of Chicago flag and the Roosevelt University flag.

> In the spring of 1963, we developed Negro history clubs. We had a Negro history club in Roosevelt University and the Amistad Society, which was a Chicago-wide black history club. We were doing a kind of educational work. Then we began to get involved in demonstrations around the schools. The Amistad Society was also supporters of the Monroe Defense Committee and the self-defense efforts of Robert F. Williams.[12]

I would travel on weekends in the south and across the north to keep in touch with new developments.

The year 1963 produced the second phase of the protest era. By spring, through the efforts of SNCC and SCLC organizers, various southern cities were seething with protest revolt. SNCC began mobilizing African-Americans in mass voter registration marches in Greenwood, Mississippi. Mississippi state troopers attacked the demonstrators and masses of people were being jailed.

The turning point of mass black consciousness and for the protest movement came during the spring non-violent offensive in Birmingham, Alabama. Dr. Martin Luther King, Jr., who had become the symbol of the direct action non-violent struggle through the efforts of SCLC and SNCC, pushed Birmingham to the brink.

The racists' tactics of using dogs, tanks, and water hoses on women and children was too much for African-Americans to stomach. Within months mass demonstrations had occurred all over the south. The movement seriously began to gel as the mood of African-American people in the north became angry.

In Philadelphia the NAACP called a mass demonstration in front of City Hall in which RAM participated, carrying signs calling for armed self-defense. NAACP president Cecil Moore decided to test mass direct action in Philadelphia by protesting against union discrimination on a construction site at 30th and Dauphin Streets in the heart of the African-American community in North Philadelphia.

Cecil B. Moore was born in Yokon, West Virginia on April 2, 1915 to Dr. Alexander M. Moore, a medical doctor, and Beulah Moore, a school teacher. Moore attended elementary and junior high school in West Virginia. He graduated from Paul Laurence Dunbar High School in Lexington, Kentucky. Moore did his undergraduate work at Bluefield College in Bluefield, West Virginia.

Upon completing his undergraduate studies, Cecil signed on as an insurance salesman for the Atlanta Life Insurance Company.[13]

Moore enlisted in the U.S. Marine Corps in Columbus, Georgia in 1942 and served as a Marine sergeant until 1951. Moore and his wife, Theresa Lee Moore, moved to Philadelphia during his later years in the Marine Corps where he was stationed at Fort Mifflin. During this time, he enrolled in Temple University's night law school graduating in 1951.

> After passing the state bar examination, Cecil started his law practice in 1953. The Moores were parents of three daughters, Cecily, Alexis, and Melba. While waiting to take the

state's bar examination, Moore made two other career moves. He got a job as a whiskey salesman and became active in Republican politics.[14]

Moore served as the GOP committeeman of the 89th division of the 4th ward from 1953 to 1963, when he changed his registration to Democratic.

Moore took the oath of office as president of the Philadelphia NAACP on January 3, 1963, giving a statement that he was dedicated to engaging in direct action in an effort to eliminate discrimination in Philadelphia. Mrs. Ethel Johnson (Azelle) visited Moore right after his election and committed our forces to helping his desegregation of Philadelphia if he was committed to direct action. Moore asked RAM to help in the mobilization.

> In picketing the school board's building site, Moore had two objectives: to secure better employment opportunities for blacks in the city, and to break down forever the barriers that limited opportunities to these jobs in the past.[15]

The construction site was in RAM territory, three blocks from its office.

> By the time Cecil made the decision to go into mass action, we sat down with him and told him that Philadelphia would be another Birmingham, Alabama. Cecil, seeing that we were young, not knowing we were organizers, just didn't believe it. He said, "Okay, go ahead."[16]

Moore made NAACP's equipment available to RAM. RAM immediately took a survey of the community, asking residents if they would support demonstrations in Philadelphia similar to the ones being held in the South.

> We found key contact people in doing the survey. Like we would drop leaflets on who was with us. People would tell you, if you are doing this, don't go somewhere because so and so works for so and so. That is what the survey provided us with. Then, we would just walk up and down North Philadelphia preparing the people. At the time, demonstrations were occurring in Jackson and Greenwood, Mississippi. We asked people, "if we had this kind of demonstration up here, would you come?"[17]

The overwhelming response was "Yes." RAM members circulated throughout the community with leaflets and bullhorns, going door to door and talking to street gangs.

The demonstration was scheduled to start at 6 a.m., May 27th, 1963. RAM leaders Stan Daniels and I joined the picket line, which blocked the workers, all whites, from entering the construction site. Within minutes the Philadelphia police formed a flying wedge and attacked the picket line. Singling out Daniels and myself, twenty police jumped us and we fought until unconscious.[18]

As word spread throughout the community, thousands of people went to the construction site. Daniels and I were arrested for inciting to riot. In the police station, I asked to make a phone call. I called Minister Malcolm X and told him what had happened. Malcolm promised to publicize what was happening in Philadelphia. Malcolm went on the radio that night in New York and traveled to Philadelphia two days later, speaking on radio again. Word spread about what was happening in Philadelphia not only throughout Philadelphia, but the entire east coast. Within a week, 50,000 to 100,000 people participated in demonstrations that often turned into violent clashes between the masses and the police.

> ...people from a cross section of the black population had been on the picket line supporting his (Cecil Moore's) militant stand against injustice. Those who had manned the lines included everyone from students and gang members to the clergy, from wild-eyed revolutionaries to professional members of the community to pimps and whores. All had ralled in the name of justice and equality...[19]

The pressure became too much for the NAACP and they called off the protests.

> CORE took an activist stance also against building trades' discrimination in Cleveland and New York City. Black nationalism grew in CORE as its membership became predominantly African-American for the first time.[20]

The name RAM became known among African-American radical circles in the North. The May demonstrations were the first breakthrough in the north that had mass involvement.

Grassroots organizations in various communities in the north began to use direct action tactics. Brooklyn CORE used the mass confrontation methods RAM had used at the Down State Medical Center demonstrations in New York.[21]

We went to block club meetings that Ethel Johnson set up through her sister, who was a longtime community resident of the Strawberry Mansion area. "Have direct daily contact with the masses; the ordinary brother and sister on the street" was Ethel Johnson's continuous message. RAM members walked the North Philadelphia community either communicating with homemade loud speakers or through ordinary discussions with people sitting on their steps. Queen Mother Audley Moore trained the RAM cadre in the philosophy of black nationalism and Marxism-Leninism. Queen Mother emphasized the importance of understanding the national question and the demand for reparations. She organized the African-American Party of National Liberation in 1963, which formed a provisional government with Robert F. Williams elected premier in exile. RAM cadres were members of the party.[22]

The national NAACP convention was being held in Chicago during the summer of 1963. Cecil B. Moore decided to take Stan Daniels and me "to keep them out of trouble while I'm gone."[23] Daniels and I stopped through Cleveland on the way to Chicago. There we conferred with Freeman, who decided to drive into Chicago and introduce the two of us to the cadre there.

RAM organizers (Stan Daniels and myself) while attending the national NAACP convention in Chicago as Philadelphia youth delegates, sponsored by Philadelphia NAACP president Cecil B. Moore met with some of the Amistad Society group made up of John Bracey, Jr., Don Sykes and Tom Higginbottom. After discussions about the contradictions of the convention and its featured speakers, the Amistad Society participated with the RAM organizers in demonstrations against Chicago Mayor Daley and Rev. Jackson of the National Baptist Convention.

In Chicago there was general discussion of what had been started in Philadelphia and then the discussion centered on what could be done in Chicago. Someone mentioned that Mayor Daley and Rev. Jackson the head of the Baptist convention, who had publicly denounced Dr. Martin Luther King, Jr., and the civil rights demonstrations, were going to speak at the NAACP rally that Saturday.[24]

It was decided that the cadre would organize community support to protest against Daley. Daniels and I would organize the youth inside the NAACP convention. We stopped a NAACP youth dance.

We called for support of the upcoming demonstration. NAACP officials became alarmed and stopped us from speaking. The Chicago cadre, in the meantime, contacted activists and others in the community about the demonstration scheduled for July 4th. Leaflets were handed out on the streets, subways and buses.

The NAACP rally proceeded as planned, with top NAACP people in attendance. To keep the NAACP youth from participating in the demonstrations, the top brass had all the youth delegates sit on stage with them. Mayor Daley was introduced. Demonstrators marching from the back of the park began booing Daley. The booing was so loud that Daley could not finish speaking; he became angry and left. Then Rev. Jackson was announced as the next speaker. As Jackson approached the podium, the demonstrators began to chant, "Uncle Toms Must Go!"[25] The audience picked up the chant. Demonstrators charged the stage. Twenty-five thousand people became enraged and a full-scale riot broke out as the masses chased Jackson off the stage into a waiting car that sped him off to safety.

It was decided by the cadre to get Daniels and me out of town immediately because the city might bring inciting-to-riot charges against us—we had charges against us already from the May 27, 1963 construction site demonstration in Philadelphia. Daniels was sent back to Philadelphia and I to check on UHURU in Detroit to help them get things going. I met with UHURU and told them what had happened in Chicago.

A black prostitute named Cynthia Scott had been shot in the back and killed by a white policeman the previous weekend. UHURU decided to hold a rally and protest demonstration in front of the precinct of the guilty cop. UHURU approached the Group On Advanced Leadership (GOAL), a black nationalist civil rights group, for help in the demonstration. Within two weeks, marches were organized against the precinct with thousands in the community participating. I returned to Cleveland and reported what was developing in Detroit. From Cleveland I returned to Philadelphia.

THE BLACK VANGUARD CONFERENCE: CLEVELAND, OHIO, SUMMER 1963

By mid-July, 1963, local grass-roots activist groups were talking about marching on Washington and bringing the capital to a standstill. Freeman decided the time had come to call the various revolutionary nationalist cadres together in what was called a black vanguard conference. The black vanguard conference was to be a secret, all-black, all-male conference to draft strategy for the proposed march on Washington and the direction of the movement. The conference was held in early August in Cleveland, Ohio. Activists attended from Chicago, New York, Philadelphia and Cleveland. Detroit was barred because of a security leak in the cadre there.

Freeman presided over the conference. Discussion centered on changing the existing rights movement into a revolutionary nationalist movement. It was discussed that the cadre could achieve this by infiltrating the existing civil rights groups (CORE, SNCC, NAACP, SCLC). The march on Washington was also discussed. It was decided that an organizer would be sent into Washington prior to the march to decide what kind of strategy the cadre should take during the march.

During the discussion of what form the coalition of activists should take, the beginnings of an ideological split emerged. Chicago and New York favored using the name RAM since RAM had established a mass breakthrough of developing community support. Those advocating this position wanted a tight-knit structure based on disciplined cells, with rules and organization based on democratic centralism. Freeman argued against this position and advocated a loose coalition called the black liberation front. Philadelphia voted with Freeman, because Freeman had more experience than most of the activists there. The rest voted on calling the gathering the Black Liberation Front (BLF). Chicago also raised the question of whether the BLF should be a Marxist-Leninist formation, but there was no consensus or agreement, so it was decided that the BLF would be revolutionary nationalist.

March on Washington: August 27, 1963

At the march on Washington, the cadre met again. The BLF organizer who had been sent to Washington reported that the march did not have support from the majority of the local African-American community there. From his conversations with people on the street, many did not know a march was being planned for D.C. It was also observed that the army was posted at strategic places in the city and was on alert to move in case of trouble. On the basis of the report, it was decided just to participate in the march and observe.

By chance, while cadres were handing out leaflets in the community, they ran into Donald Warden, who was then chairman of the Afro-American Association (AAA), a nationalist organization based in Oakland, California. A meeting was set up with Warden, who explained what the AAA was about for about 2 hours. After the meeting, it was decided that the cadre would stay in touch with Warden, but Freeman concluded that Warden was a bourgeois nationalist. It was decided that the cadre would go back to their respective locales and build bases.

After the march on Washington, several events occurred which shaped the civil rights movement and later the black liberation movement. One was the bombing of four African-American girls in a church in Birmingham, Alabama. The news of this both angered the African-American community and sent waves of demoralization inside the civil rights movement. It was like a mortal blow after the march on Washington.

> RAM organizers occasionally went south either to attempt to organize, learn organizing techniques, or to make contacts. In the fall of 1963, I went to Atlanta and visited the SNCC office. I met Willie Peacock of the Mississippi Field Staff, who was based in Greenwood. We had discussions and he drove me into Greenwood and introduced me to people in the community. He said he would prepare for me to come back into Greenwood the following year. I got a ride with SNCC people going back into Atlanta and left Atlanta going back to Philadelphia. When I returned to Philadelphia, Azelle (Ethel Johnson) showed me a Progressive Labor (PL) newspaper story of young brothers with guns in trees in Monroe, NC. She said that one was only fourteen years old. Azelle said she had received word from "Rob" Williams that he wanted her to return to Monroe to counteract PL's influence there and to keep the young brothers from getting killed. Azelle said that before she would leave, she would turn us over to a new mentor. That mentor was none other than Queen Mother Audley Moore.[26]

Azelle took me to see Queen Mother and it was agreed that she would become our new mentor. I was still afraid of Queen Mother, because I knew she had been a member of the Community Party and I still had a fledgling degree of anti-communism in my thinking that communists could brainwash you. Queen Mother said that she would send books and pamphlets over to the RAM core collective house where some of us were staying. The required reading included, *Wage, Price, Profit,* by Karl Marx; *The Communist Manifesto,* by Karl Marx and Frederick Engels; *What is to be Done?, State and Revolution, Imperialism: The Highest Stage of Capitalism, and Two Tactics,* by V.I. Lenin; as well as *On Practice, On Contradiction, On Art and Literature,* and *On Protracted War* by Mao Tse Tung. The book Queen Mother had us read was James S. Allen's, *Reconstruction: The Battle for Democracy, 1865–1876.* She said Allen's book was simple and easy reading and we could read W.E.B. Dubois' book, *Black Reconstruction* at a later date, because it would take time due to being very detailed and complicated. We also had to read Harry Haywood's *Negro Liberation.*

Then came the assassination of John F. Kennedy, President of the United States. Many African-Americans across the country felt they had lost a friend. To the RAM cadre the ultra-right had made a move. Don Freeman came through Philadelphia and told the RAM cadre that fascism was coming and to go underground.

Malcolm X, speaking the Sunday after the assassination, made reference to the Kennedy assassination as "chickens coming home to roost." Elijah Muhammad, head of the Nation of Islam, suspended Malcolm from speaking for 90 days and later extended the suspension indefinitely.

In Philadelphia, a coalition of African-American radical groups held mass rallies to protest police brutality. After one of the rallies, African-American teenagers began small-scale rioting. Members of RAM, observing the riot, began to theorize about the potential of this kind of activity:

> RAM began to think about these questions as far back as November 1963. In November of that year a brother named Willie Philaw, who was a black epileptic, got in an argument with a White store owner in North Philadelphia and was shot in the back of the head by a White cop and killed. We started a coalition, a black united front, which lead some demonstrations and rallies against police brutality. One night when Playthell Benjamin was speaking at a street rally, the young brothers and sisters broke-out in one of the first, at least to our knowledge, spontaneous rebellions in the north. A month earlier, October, in a civil rights demonstration in Jacksonville, Florida when the police entered the black community the youth attacked them with rocks and

bottles. When Playthell spoke and the youth started breaking out windows in stores we realized that a mini-rebellion had jumped off. We recognized that black youth constituted a potential revolutionary force that was not being galvanized. We began to theorize about the concept of the street force as the leadership of the black liberation movement.[27]

The coalition led mass marches on the cop's police station (17th and Montgomery Street) only to be met by machine guns staring them in the face. The coalition decided it had gone as far as it could go without getting innocent people hurt. Freeman traveled to Philadelphia to talk to the RAM cadre. He told the cadre to cease all public activity and said that the ultra-right was preparing to crush the movement. The word was "go underground."

How Queen Mother Audley Moore Became RAM's Second Mother

Wanda Marshall and I had been afraid of Queen Mother, because of anti-communism red-baiting against progressive people. Though I read some Marx, Lenin, and a little of Trotsky, I still had the sting of anti-communism in me. Wanda would say, "you know communists can brainwash you." When the RAM cadre along with others would go over to Queen Mother's house, attending "Free Mae Mallory" meetings, we would be in the hall talking before breaking up. Queen Mother would interrupt the discussion, point at me, and would say, "you, darling, you're the one I want." This would scare the "living daylights" out of me, and I would promptly leave. Queen Mother would say to me before I left, "if you ever want to come by, the front window of my study is open; just raise it and come on in."

One Friday afternoon, while travelling from North Philly to West Philly, I found myself walking right past Queen Mother's house, and something said, "why don't you go in." I went up on the porch of the house and opened the window and went into the study. What I found in the study amazed me. In the study, Queen Mother had rare books, but beyond that, on the floor of the study, Queen Mother had collected news clippings of the movement from the 1930s to the 1960s. I guess I was in the study an hour or two reading the news clippings when Queen Mother came into the study and said in a joking tone, "oh, what do we have here." She said, "take your time; I'm going upstairs to fix us something to eat." When dinner was ready, Queen Mother called me upstairs. As she began to talk, she made more sense to me than anyone in life—except Robert F. Williams, Ethel Johnson, and Malcolm X, all of whom she was in agreement with.

After dinner, she showed me how to pull out a cot in the study and gave me a wash cloth and towel. I already knew where the bathroom was from previous meetings. I slept and studied in the study all weekend long, interrupting Queen Mother with questions and listening to her responses and additional teachings. Without me knowing it, the RAM cadre from North Philly had called her trying to find out where I was, and she told them I was there and was alright. When I went back over to North Philly, the RAM cadre told me, never to do that again, i.e., disappear without notifying anyone where I was. I felt bad about not telling them where I was, but I relayed to them how much I had learned, how much knowledge I had acquired. From that point on, Queen Mother became the advisor to RAM.

RAM's Impact on the Civil Rights Movement

The year 1964 was a year of transition for the civil rights movement and a year of ideological development for black radicals. In January, Brooklyn CORE, led by Isaiah Bronson, planned the Stall-in at the World's Fair to protest discrimination being practiced there. The purpose of the Stall-in was to stop or slow down traffic in the streets and subways, to bring New York City to a standstill.

Isaiah Bronson from Brooklyn CORE, who was also a member of RAM, organized a "stall-in." This tactic raised an ideological question in the civil rights movement. Brooklyn CORE decided to disrupt the World's Fair because African-Americans were not being hired in even the most menial positions at the Fair. Brooklyn CORE decided to disrupt the city of New York in January 1964. The leadership of CORE came out against Brooklyn CORE. James Farmer of the national leadership of CORE and Roy Wilkins of the NAACP came out against Brooklyn CORE. But SNCC came out in support of Brooklyn CORE. For the first time the question of African-Americans disrupting the system was advanced in the civil rights movement. This tactic of African-Americans disrupting the economy, or a city or the government was a different kind of tool. The stall-in was not successful because it had been publicized in advance and the police were waiting. But it raised a critical fact—African-Americans were in a strategic position to disrupt this system. To disrupt the function of a city was a new tactical use of civil disobedience.[28] While the Stall-in was not successful, it raised the questions of the possibility of the movement disrupting the functioning of the system.[29]

Two events occurred in March 1964 that changed the direction[30] of the black liberation movement. Malcolm X announced his independence from the Nation of Islam and Robert F. Williams' article "Revolution Without Violence?" in the February 1964 issue of *The Crusader* reached the United States. Williams's article raised many eyebrows. In it he described how many African-Americans could bring the U.S. to a standstill through urban rebellions and urban guerrilla warfare. This went beyond the concept of armed self-defense.

Almost every activist was watching Malcolm's development to see in what direction he was heading. Freeman from the BLF had attended Malcolm's press conference and encouraged him to proceed in a more radical direction. Freeman decided it was time to challenge SNCC concerning the concepts of armed self-defense and black nationalism on its own home grounds, the south. After organizing a protest demonstration in coalition with other groups in front of the Philadelphia City Hall and the U.S. Federal Building demanding that Ohio Governor Rhodes not send Mae Mallory back to North Carolina and demanding her freedom, I wrote Don Freeman a letter requesting to come to Cleveland to rest. Freeman sent me bus fare to Cleveland. After I arrived, Freeman gave me instructions to organize an all African-American student conference in the South. The BLF, of which RAM was a part, had connections to revolutionary nationalists, who were inside of local SNCC groups. One particular group was the African-American Student Movement (ASM) at Fisk University in Nashville, Tennessee led by Michele Paul and Betty Rush.

I was sent to Detroit to raise money for the conference. While fund-raising, I went to see James and Grace Lee Boggs, then two leading theoreticians of the black liberation struggle. In discussions with Grace Boggs, she described the problems that had emerged in the Michigan Freedom Now Party, as lessons to avoid in organizing. Grace asked me if I had seen Robert Williams' February, 1964 issue of *The Crusader*, and I said, "no." She gave me a copy, which I read earnestly. After reading it, we discussed his analysis, which we both agreed on, and I described our RAM activities from the year before (1963).

I showed her a mimeographed copy of *Black America* and some leaflets from our organizing efforts. Grace (Lee Boggs) asked if she could see other copies, so I called the RAM cadre in Philly and asked that they send a whole set to Detroit. I think there were about six or seven issues.

Mae Mallory was incarcerated in Cleveland awaiting extradition to Monroe, North Carolina, because she was accused of aiding, supposedly, the kidnapping of a white couple during racial disturbances there in the summer of 1961. Robert F. Williams and his family escaped the frame-up by fleeing to Canada and eventually to Cuba.

The *Black America* issues were sent via airmail special delivery, and they arrived in a few days. After reading them and other RAM material, Grace said, "this is the highest level to come out of the civil rights movement." I was stunned, because it was hard for me to assume we were doing that kind of work.

Boggs asked me to write an article on RAM, which she later printed in *Correspondence*, a bi-monthly periodical that was published in Michigan. From Detroit, I went to Chicago, where I wrote Malcolm telling him of the upcoming student conference he had discussed with Freeman. From there I went south to the annual spring SNCC conference to recruit SNCC field workers, especially from Mississippi, who were responsive to an all-African-American student conference. In the south, RAM had built a small but significant following at Fisk University, the training ground for many leading SNCC activists.[31]

Writing to Michele that I was on the way to Nashville, she secured a place for me to stay. We discussed the conference and a place to hold it. Michele said that a Dean at Fisk University was favorable to student activists. I put on a sport coat to look as respectable as I could when I went to see the Dean. In the conversation with the Dean, I mentioned how studies showed that students who were involved in the movement were the most studious and that we were about increasing the intelligence and intellectual abilities of students. The Dean allowed ASM to use Fisk facilities for the conference.

While organizing and propagandizing for the conference, I went to Atlanta spreading word of the conference. At one point, the SNCC staff was going to set up a debate at their retreat on non-violence vs. self-defense, but later declined. I was stressing SNCC should hook up with Malcolm and the Pan-African Student Organization of the Americas (PASOA). This is when I met the charismatic Willie Ricks, who would give impromptu speeches to brothers and sisters on the street corners of Atlanta. From the SNCC retreat and circulating in SNCC circles, I recruited some of the SNCC field staff (particularly) from Mississippi to attend the conference.

From May 1st, to the 4th, 1964, the first Afro-American Student Conference on Black Nationalism was held at Fisk University. It was the first time since 1960 that African-American activists from the north and south sat down to discuss Black Nationalism. The conference was the ideological catalyst that eventually shifted the civil rights movement into the black power movement. Don Freeman in his article in the fall 1964 issue of *Black America* described that the first session of the conference evaluated the efforts of civil rights organizations, such as CORE, SNCC and NAACP as being bourgeois reformism. The conference went on record of substantiating Dr. W. E. B. Dubois' conviction that "capitalism cannot reform itself; a system that enslaves you cannot free you." The Conference went on to examine the impotence of traditional or "bourgeois" nationalism. Conference delegates agreed that the traditional nationalist approach of rhetoric rather than action was ineffectual because it posed no pragmatic alternative to bourgeois reformist civil rights activities. The young revolutionary nationalists said that bourgeois nationalist's demands for an autonomous African-American economy were termed bourgeois due to failure to differentiate such an economy from capitalism and was unfeasible because it was the intention of white and Jewish capitalists to continue their "suburban colonialism" form of exploitation of the African-American community. The consensus of the conferees was that African-Americans needed to control their own neighborhoods, similar to what Malcolm X was teaching at the time, but they also stated they realized that the contemporary reality necessitated the use of a strategy of chaos that was advocated by Reverend Albert Cleage which would involve a more devastating civil disobedience than the kind undertaken by the established civil rights reformist groups.

The young revolutionary nationalists asserted that they were the vanguard of a black revolution in America but they had to create:

"1) An organizational apparatus to 'translate' Nationalist ideology into effective action; this requires Black financing to insure Black control; 2) dedicated, disciplined, and decisive youth cadres willing to make the supreme sacrifices to build and sustain a dynamic Nationalist Movement."[32]

The conference stated that African-American radicals were the vanguard of revolution in this country, supported Minister Malcolm's efforts to take the case of Afro-Americans to the U.N., called for a black cultural revolution, and discussed Pan-Africanism. The conference drafted 13 points of implementation. The 13 points were:

1. Development of a permanent secretariat to carry out plans.
2. To push the bourgeois reformists as far "up temp" as fast as possible, while at the same time laying a base for an underground movement.
3. The Conference united with the African, Asian and Latin American Revolution (Attempt to get financial help from friendly forces).
4. Adopt Robert F. Williams as leader in exile.
5. The achievement of Afro-American solidarity with Africa (to push the Restoration of the Revolutionary Spirit to Pan-Africanism).
6. Conference philosophy—Pan-African Socialism.
7. The establishment of an Internal Bulletin for the Conference.
8. Construction of a Pan-African Student Conference.
9. Secretariat contact all student liberation organizations around the world to develop rapport and coordination.
10. National public organ name: *Black America.*
11. Charge genocide against U.S. Imperialism before the United Nations.
12. Secretariat develop program for Revolutionary Black Nationalists.
13. Develop two Revolutionary Centers.[33]

From the conference, BLF-RAM organizers went into the south to work with SNCC. With the permission of SNCC chairman John Lewis, an experimental black nationalist self-defense project was started in Greenwood, Mississippi.

> In discussion with the Mississippi field staff of SNCC, BLF-RAM organizers found the staff was prepared to establish a statewide-armed self-defense system. They were also prepared to move in an all-black nationalist direction. All that was needed was money to finance the project. In the meantime, Monthly Review published an article titled "The Colonial War at Home," which included most of [Max] Stanford's Correspondence article, "Toward a Revolutionary Action Movement," edited with some of Malcolm's remarks, and excerpts from Robert Williams' "Revolution Without Violence."[34]

The majority of the SNCC field staff discussed the article. SNCC split between left and right and between African-American and white organizers; between taking a pro integrationist, reformist or a revolutionary nationalist direction. Most of the African-Americans of the Mississippi SNCC field staff thought that the majority of the African-American people in Mississippi were beyond concentration on the voter registration stage. In the ensuing battle between the forces, the integrationist reformist faction eventually won in the organizational split because they controlled the economic resources of the field staff and had connections with the foundations.

SNCC began to involve large numbers of white students in the movement in the summer of 1964. Their involvement led to their radicalization, which later they developed, into the anti-war student movement. The crucial milestone of SNCC's road to radicalism was the Freedom Summer of 1964. Freedom Summer grew out of a remarkable mock election sponsored by SNCC in the autumn of 1963. Because the mass of Mississippi's African-American population could not legally participate in choosing the state's governor that year, Robert Moses conceived of a freedom election to protest mass disenfranchisement and to educate Mississippi's African-Americans to the mechanics of the political process. The Council of Federated Organizations (COFO), organized a new party called the Mississippi Freedom Democrats, printed its own ballots, and in October conducted its own poll. Overwhelming the regular party candidates, Aaron Henry, head of the state NAACP and the Freedom Democratic nominee for governor, received 70,000 votes, a tremendous protest against the denial of equal political rights. One reason for the success of the project was the presence in the state of 100 Yale and Stanford University students, who worked for two weeks with SNCC on the election. SNCC was sufficiently impressed by the student contribution to consider inviting hundreds more to spend an entire summer in Mississippi. Sponsors of this plan hoped not only for workers but also for publicity that might at last focus national attention on Mississippi. By the winter of 1963–64, however, rising militancy in SNCC had begun to take on overtones of black nationalism, and some of the membership resisted the summer project on the grounds that most of the volunteers would be white.[35]

During the Freedom Summer sponsored by COFO in Mississippi, six people were killed, eighty beaten, thirty-five churches burned and thirty other buildings bombed.[36]

The MFDP went to Atlantic City to challenge the Mississippi regulars. Northern liberals tried to work out a compromise that would appease the MFDP and at the same time keep the bulk of the Southern delegations in the convention. President Johnson's proposal was to seat all the Mississippi regulars who pledged loyalty to the party and not to grant the MFDP voting rights but to let them sit on the floor of the convention.[37]

The MFDP refused this proposal and Johnson sent Senator Hubert Humphrey to draw a compromise. Humphrey offered to permit two MFDP delegates to sit in the convention with full voting rights if he could choose the delegates. The Mississippi white regulars walked out and the MFDP, led by Mrs. Fannie Lou Hamer, decided not to accept the compromise.

Development of RAM into a National Organization

The failure of the MFDP to be seated led SNCC to attempt organizing an all African-American independent political party a year later.

From the May 1st to May 4th, 1964 Conference on Black Nationalism at Fisk university, Freeman instructed Askia Muhammad Ture (Rolland Snellings) and myself to build a base in the South. Willie Peacock, who was in attendance at the Conference, said we could build a base in Greenwood, Mississippi. He said he would try to get us put on the SNCC field staff. Willie had smuggled me into Greenwood in 1963, introduced me to people, and told them I would be back in 1964. We went from Nashville to Atlanta, where we met with John Lewis, Chairman of SNCC. Lewis agreed to put us on staff, even though he didn't agree then with our premises, but felt we had the right to see if our ideas would work. We went by car (Willie Peacock, Askia Ture, two SNCC workers, and me) first to Jackson, Mississippi, the SNCC Mississippi headquarters.

As we went into the SNCC office, we noticed the call for the May 1st–4th Conference had been posted on the bulletin board by some white SNCC staffers with an arrow pointing to it saying "the Enemy." We said the Klan was the enemy, but not us.

I saw a brother whom I knew from traveling with SNCC workers, and he looked like he saw a ghost when he looked at me. I asked him what was wrong? He asked me if I had seen the latest issue of the *Monthly Review*. I said, "no, I haven't." He went and got it for me. The feature article/editorial was called, "The Colonial War at Home." He told me to sit down and read the article. I read it with great alarm. Here I was in Mississippi and this article suggested that I was calling for guerrilla warfare. The brothers told me that the Klan had sent word that whenever I was ready, to "come on."

As time passed, events occurred with great rapidity. We went into Greenwood, conducted voter registration and established a freedom school in which Askia taught African and African-American history, and I taught political science. We attended the Mississippi state-wide SNCC retreat in Greenville, Mississippi and challenged the white leftist SNCC staff to go either back north or in southern white communities to fight against racism there. Bob Moses summoned Askia and me to a conference in the back of a building outside to discuss our differences. At that time, Moses was relying on some white liberals in Congress, whom he saw as friends of African-Americans. We (Askia and I) told him we did not have faith in the present structure of the government. Even though he (Moses), at that time, disagreed with us, he arranged to have me speak at a meeting of the Mississippi Freedom Democratic Party where Miss Fannie Lou Hamer was presenting on the importance of the work the MFDP was doing.

The Klan was bombing churches up and down Mississippi in the spring/summer of 1964. On at least one occasion, SNCC workers tried to respond self-defense-wise. A meeting was called at Ameize Moore's house where the militant African-American leadership of the Mississippi field staff stated they were ready to engage in armed self defense—all they needed was money and equipment. SNCC in Greenwood began to shoot back when the Klan would ride by at night and shoot into its office. Robert (Rob) F. Williams sent me a telegram to get out of Mississipi immediately, but I had already left.[38]

I called an emergency organizational meeting in Detroit in the summer of 1964 of BLF cadres, James and Grace Boggs, and other supporters. I gave a report on the conditions within the Mississippi field staff that was ready to move into armed self-defense. It was discussed that a national centralized organization was needed to coordinate the new movement. The Revolutionary Action Movement (RAM) was the name chosen for the new movement. After much discussion, it was decided that the movement should be structured on three levels: the first would be of tight-knit cells in cities that would build political bases and financial support for roving field organizers, who would work full-time like SNCC field organizers in the community and at the same time act as a national liberation front, coordinating a broad coalition of black nationalist groups. The second level was made up of local chapters and the third of secret members who would financially support the organization's work.

Ideological contradictions were present from the start. Political debate centered on the status of people and strategy for liberation. The nationalists stated that African-American people were an internal colony, a nation within a nation whose national territory was the African-American black belt south. They said that in the process of liberation through an African-American socialist revolution the African-American nation could separate from the United States.

The socialists, on the other hand, represented by James and Grace Boggs, asked the question: what would happen to the rest of the country? Could the white left be given the responsibility to govern? What would guarantee that they would be any less racist than those presently in power? After much discussion a compromise was drafted. The position was that African-American revolutionaries would have to seize power in a socialist revolution in the United States, maintaining a black dictatorship over the U.S., with the south being an autonomous region. Grace and James Boggs presented the argument that African-American migration was moving towards cities and that by 1970 African-Americans would constitute the majority of inner cities in the ten major urban areas. Their position was that the organization should place emphasis on building African-American political power in the cities.[39]

A committee read and discussed a twelve-point program drafted by the conference. The program included:

1. Development of a national black student organization/movement.

2. Development of ideology (Freedom) schools.

3. Development of Rifle Clubs.

4. Development of Liberation Army (Guerrilla Youth Force).

5. Development of Propaganda, training centers and a national organization.

6. Development of Underground Vanguard.

7. Development of black workers "liberation unions."

8. Development of block organizations (cells).

9. Development of the nation within nation concept, government in exile.

10. Development of War Fund (Political Economy).

11. Development of black farmer coops.

12. Development of Army of black unemployed.

Officers of the movement were elected.

International Spokesman	Malcolm X[40]
International Chairman	Robert F. Williams
National Field Chairman	Max Stanford
Executive Chairman	Don Freeman
Ideological Chairman	James Boggs
Executive Secretary	Grace Boggs
Treasurer	Milton Henry/ Paul Brooks[41]

RAM's activities during this period helped radicalize both Malcolm and SNCC. RAM organizers in New York would consult with Malcolm daily and wherever Malcolm went in the country, his strongest supporters and also his harshest critics were members of RAM. As opposed to those tendencies that built upon Malcolm's statements on revolution as a struggle for land-based self-determination or focused on black revolution and African liberation, there appeared in the latter '60s revolutionary African-American nationalism rooted in industrial workers and street people. This new group thought that black liberation required a fundamental and basic change in U.S. society. Publicly, organizationally, the Black Panther Party, and the League of Revolutionary Black Workers both represented this revolutionary nationalism. These organizations had direct links to the speeches and organizing efforts of Malcolm X in the spring of 1964, when he said to activists:

> You and I in America are not faced with a segregationist conspiracy, we're faced with a government conspiracy...it is the government itself, the government of America, that is responsible for the oppression and exploitation and degradation of Black people in this country...This government has failed the Negro.[42]

Malcolm's awareness of developments in the movement moved him in a more activist direction. After breaking from the Nation of Islam, Malcolm successively progressed from revolutionary Pan Africanism to one of Third World internationalism. At the time of his death, he was moving to a position of revolutionary socialism.[43]

Malcolm agreed to become the spokesman of RAM but felt his role should remain secret because the United States intelligence apparatus would become alarmed about his connection with Robert Williams, who was in exile in Cuba.

Malcolm was preparing to develop a public mass organization, which he intended would be instrumental in leading the broad mass movement and would serve as a united front. He asked that RAM organizers help in forming that organization and also infiltrate it to develop a security section. He knew the Muslim Mosque, Inc. was infiltrated by police agents and did not know whom he could trust. Malcolm had just returned from his first trip to Africa. He was in the process of attempting to get African nations to endorse his proposal to take the U.S. to the United Nations for its violations of the

Human Rights charter in its crimes against African-Americans.

Both Malcolm and RAM saw that the internationalization of the African-American struggle was necessary to win allies and to isolate the U.S. government. In the organizational discussions that were held daily for a month, various aspects of the struggle were analyzed.

While many writers have discussed Malcolm's change in philosophy and outlook, few trace Malcolm's evolutionary development. Malcolm's celebrated statement concerning some white people not being racists after he made the Hajj did not represent the end of his development on the question. While Malcolm was embracing socialism and ideologically evolving outside of the confines of traditional or fundamentalist Islamic thought before the time of his death, he still maintained a position of organizing the African-American community independently for national liberation.

His Hajj statement was released in April of 1964 after he made his first trip to Africa and the Middle East. While Malcolm saw an eventual alliance between the African-American movement and revolutionary whites, he constantly said, "There can't be any workers' solidarity until there is first black unity."[44]

I asked Malcolm about his statements on white people being in Mecca and his feeling that some could be worked with. I stated that I felt Malcolm would lose his black nationalist following which was his base of support. Malcolm stated that while in Algeria, an Algerian revolutionary showed him a picture of himself that looked as dark as Marcus Garvey, and the statements under the picture made it appear that Malcolm was advocating the superiority of people based on skin pigmentation, i.e., that darker-skinned Africans were superior to lighter-skinned Africans. The United States Information Agency (USIA) had circulated the publication. The Algerian revolutionary convinced Malcolm that if this kind of propaganda had confused him and was isolating Malcolm on the continent of Africa, then, the racists must have been successful in isolating Malcolm from the broad masses of African-Americans. The Algerian revolutionary discussed the concept of the mass line with Malcolm. Malcolm felt that there would always be black nationalists in America but that he had to reach the masses of African-American people who had not become black nationalists yet. He had also been under pressure from the Arabs to practice "true Islam." So he felt it was best that he tone down his line.

It was decided that Malcolm would infiltrate the civil rights movement and later transform it into a revolution. In order to do this, RAM and others would make preparations for Malcolm to go south. Malcolm would eventually join demonstrations utilizing the right of self-defense. He would be the mass spokesman for armed defense units that would be centered around him and a black united front. Malcolm then set about creating the mass organizational form. Malcolm's hard core wanted to call the organization the National Liberation Front (NLF) but it was decided that a public NLF was premature and would frighten most people. Malcolm asked the organizers to come up with a name for the organization. The next week the Organization of Afro-American Unity (OAAU) was chosen. A program for the OAAU was drafted and presented at Malcolm's Sunday mass rallies at the Audubon Ballroom in New York City.

Malcolm and I, as the field chairman of RAM, during the month of June, worked out plans for developing an international revolutionary black nationalist movement. From daily discussions on the political perspective of RAM, Malcolm would incorporate the ideas in his Sunday speeches. The OAAU was to be the broad front organization and RAM the underground Black Liberation Front of the U.S.A. I would periodically meet with Queen Mother Audley Moore, who had taught Malcolm along with her sister, Eloise, earlier (1959) about the importance of Africa and Pan-Africanism. She was perturbed with Malcolm for not calling our people African-Americans, but he told her that he didn't think our people were prepared then (1964) to consider themselves as African, so he used the term "Afro-American."

During his second trip to Africa, Malcolm was to try to find places for eventual political asylum and political/military training for cadres. While Malcolm was in Africa, I was to go to Cuba to report the level of progress to Robert F. Williams. As Malcolm prepared Africa to support the African-American struggle, "Rob" (Robert F. Williams) would prepare Latin America and Asia. During this period, Malcolm began to emphasize that African-Americans could not achieve freedom under the capitalist system. He also described guerrilla warfare as a possible tactic to be used in the black liberation struggle in the United States. His slogan, "*Freedom by any means necessary,*" has remained in the movement to this day.

Malcolm left for Africa in July and I, the RAM field chairman, left for Cuba at the end of July. While Malcolm was in Africa, Harlem exploded. The para-military in Malcolm's organization decided to join the rebellion and participated in armed self-defense actions against racist oppressive forces. Masses of African-Americans exploded in Rochester, New York. The revolutionary Muslims (Malcolmites) engaged in armed struggle against the repressive forces there. Brooklyn CORE held a demonstration to protest police brutality in New York. The demonstration precipitated a mass rebellion. The Brooklyn RAM cadre went into revolutionary action.

While in Africa, Malcolm was poisoned. He also received news of a split within his organization created by police agents.[45] In Cuba, Robert Williams told me that the movement was too out in the open, that it was being set up to be destroyed. He felt Malcolm's press statements exposed too much prematurely, that he was functioning as if he had a force, which he had not developed yet. In retrospect, Malcolm felt a sense of urgency because he knew he was a marked man and would be killed soon.

Also, while in Africa, Malcolm met with John Lewis and others of SNCC. Malcolm had a tremendous impact on African leaders and had an explosive effect on masses of Africans. One incident occurred while he was in Nigeria speaking at a university. During the question and answer period, a Negro from America working with a U.S. government program there, made some remarks defending the U.S. government. After Malcolm answered him, the Nigerian students were so angry that they chased the Negro out of the auditorium to a field and were going to hang him on a flagpole. The Negro would have been hung if Professor Essien Udom had not intervened and saved the Negro's life. This incident gives some indication of the impact that Malcolm had on Africa.[46]

Malcolm's importance as an international spokesman has been recorded but not fully understood by African-Americans. From the program of the OAAU we get an understanding of some of his basic objectives.

> The Organization of Afro-American Unity will develop in the Afro-American people a keen awareness of our relationship with the world at large and clarify our roles, rights and responsibilities as human beings. We can accomplish this goal by becoming well informed concerning world affairs and understanding that our struggle is part of a larger world struggle of oppressed peoples against all forms of oppression.[47]

In Africa and the Middle East, Malcolm met with heads of state in an attempt to solicit support for his proposed indictment of the U.S. at the United Nations. Among his avid supporters was Ahmed Ben Bella, President of Algeria, and Kwame Nkrumah, President of Ghana.

From government documents published in 1964 on Malcolm, the U.S. government estimated that Malcolm had set U.S. foreign policy in Africa back ten years. Malcolm became a prime target of the U.S. government's intelligence apparatus—FBI, Army Intelligence and CIA. Other cities also exploded during the summer of 1964 and the repressive forces were blaming it on Malcolm rather than on the conditions that caused the rebellions.

> In a domestic context, Washington saw Malcolm as a long-range threat: He was widely popular with the black masses, but plagued by organizational and recruiting problems that reduced his political effectiveness. But in foreign affairs Malcolm was an imminent and serious danger; more than any other single factor he was responsible for the growing suspicion and fear with which many African countries viewed Washington's intentions. Washington did not accept this threat to its Third World relations with equanimity. Malcolm X had become a marked man.[48]

When Malcolm returned from Africa in November 1964, he described his experiences in Africa and the Middle East and began to talk more about socialism in the Third World.

> Almost every one of the countries that has gotten independence has devised some kind of socialist system...None of them are adopting the capitalist system because they realize they can't operate a capitalistic system unless you are vulturistic: you have to have someone else's blood to suck to be a capitalist.[49]

But Malcolm's organization and his personal life were in shambles. The pressure from the repressive forces was taking its toll on him. Malcolm tried to regroup. He set up a liberation school within the OAAU. He returned to Africa to consolidate support for his petition to the U.N. Malcolm had opened up avenues for African-Americans who were Muslims to go to the University of AL-Azhar in Cairo, Egypt, and other places in the world for guerrilla training. RAM published its periodical *Black America*. Malcolm in his speeches in Africa would say, "This is my publication."[50]

Malcolm returned from Africa and began to have mass meetings in January 1965. At the same time he began to lay out a perspective for the black revolution. But before he could lay out and develop his perspective, the CIA, FBI, New York police noose began to tighten around him.

Malcolm had achieved part one of his objectives, the internationalizing of the African-American struggle. Branches of the OAAU had been established in England, France, and Ghana. Now was time to expand the OAAU nationally. Right before his death, Malcolm had entered into phase two of his program of direct action. He went to Mississippi and Selma, Alabama to speak and was preparing to begin to lead the civil rights movement to the proposed transition to human rights.

Malcolm's military wing was to have eventually moved into the south to provide security for demonstrations and develop community self-defense groups.

Early in February, Kaliel Said, a member of RAM who had been sent into Malcolm's organization to develop a security wing, was arrested on the Statue of Liberty bomb plot. Inside the Muslim Mosque, Inc. and OAAU, Kaliel's arrest upset Malcolm's internal security. It also set the public climate the intelligence forces wanted for conspiracy.

At this point, the U.S. government plot went into action. Malcolm was expelled from France, his house was fire bombed and he was assassinated on February 21, 1965.

> At the end of 1964, SNCC extended invitations to Malcolm X to come to speak and visit their operations in Greenwood, Mississippi and Selma, Alabama. According to Ahmed, this was the beginning of the implementation of the strategy in which Malcolm X was to be the "mass spokesman for armed defense units that would be centered around him and a Black united front." The assassination of Malcolm X disrupted the meshing of Malcolm's own efforts with students and those related efforts of the RAM cadre.[51]

The first mass spokesman for revolutionary black nationalism had been shot down just as the movement was developing. The revolutionary nationalist movement was under attack.[52]

During the summer of 1964, RAM concentrated on building secret political cells in different parts of the country. These cells were to remain underground and to develop an underground movement. They were to be the support apparatus for field organizers who were openly trying to transform the civil rights movement into a revolutionary black nationalist movement. These cells were to finance the activities of the field organizers and the liberation army, once developed, to hide the organizers when forced underground, to provide the liberation forces with supplies and intelligence information on the activities of the racist governmental apparatus.

RAM received repression and investigation from the U.S. government and the local Cleveland police intelligence units soon after Malcolm X's assassination. In Cleveland, Don Freeman on February 27, 1965 was fired from his job as a social studies teacher at Kennard Jr. High School. In New York, several RAM members from San Francisco, Detroit and New York who had traveled to Cuba in the summer of 1964 were subpoenaed by the Federal Grand Jury investigating the so-called Statue of Liberty bomb plot.[53]

Interviews with ex-RAM members disclosed that the class composition of RAM varied. For the most part in the early beginnings in early 1963 and 1964 the organization consisted of students and intellectuals. According to Brother A., a former RAM member, the class composition of the RAM membership in New York during the 1963–64 period consisted mainly of intellectuals, writers, poets, and artists, some of whom came out of the UMBRA (black literary collective), others were recruited from the Brooklyn chapter of CORE. In Philadelphia, the class composition changed also. Stan Daniels, Wanda Marshall and myself, who were students, constituted the local RAM leadership. By fall of 1963, Jomo L. M. X. (ex-Korean war veteran), Mable Holloway and William Woodley, grass roots community worker/activists, had emerged in the Philadelphia RAM leadership.

As the RAM leadership began to change in class composition, the membership of the organization began to grow. In an interview with Sister Y., recruited from the Communist Party in Chicago, she describes the method of organizational growth in her area.

Field organizers traveled in and out of the city to organize local chapters, teach ideology and help train cadre. Local chapters were responsible for developing local membership, had to raise its own funds. Some funds went to national.[54]

RAM would organize demonstrations around local issues but never used the name RAM. In Chicago, RAM worked through a coalition demanding quality education for African-American students. Eric Perkins describes his recruitment into RAM and the radical political socialization process of the 1960s;

> As we entered high school, we became more and more interested in some kind of organizational affiliation. In 1964 at the local black book store is where I first met John Bracey. All the kids found him a charismatic sort of figure and we all wanted to be just like John at the time. At this time, John had just finished at Howard and had come to Chicago to go to graduate school and was very active as a member of local Chicago organizations. He took a number of us, me, John Higginson and a few others under his wing. We sort of became his youth cadre and he became our mentor.[55]

RAM would have educational and ideological study groups under its name. RAM was a secret cell type of organization. Sister Y. was asked the question, what type of organization was RAM? She responded: If you were part of the study group or part of the cell, that's all you would know.[56] All recruitment into the organization was made by personal contact. There were no RAM offices after 1964 and one could not join the organization by mail. The recruiter was responsible for new recruits. All new recruits had to first be involved in a RAM front and were evaluated on their work within the front activities. If they were approved, they had to submit a written and verbal report and pass orientation one before being considered a RAM member. There were three levels of membership in the organization: those who were professional, 'full-time' field organizers; members having completed orientation two, paid dues, met the standards for the "main criteria of cadre" and were considered active members; and secret members who gave the organization financial support. The RAM organization had three different types of cells or units. Area units were established in a community with members living in the same area where the unit was established. The area unit tried to gain as much influence as possible in its community by organizing around local community issues. Work units were set up in factories, job sites or industries. They organized the League of Black Workers. Political units were organized to actively infiltrate the civil rights movement and lead the black liberation movement.

There was a strict code for RAM cadres.

Code of Cadres

1. Absolute loyalty to the movement and its leadership.

2. High revolutionary spirit.

3. Constant advanced training in Revolutionary Black Internationalism.

4. Strict observation of movement discipline.

5. Direct connection with the masses.

6. Strict observance of the rules of the safekeeping of secrets.

7. Ability to work independently (very important in time of revolution).

8. Willingness to work. Unselfishness.

Rules for the Safekeeping of Secrets

1. Making absolutely no mention of secrets, which should not be mentioned.

2. Making no attempt to find out secrets that should not be known.

3. Taking definitely no look at the secrets, which should not be looked at.

4. Mentioning absolutely no secrets in private correspondence.

5. Recording no secret matters in private notebooks.

6. Discussing no secrets in places not advantageous to security.

7. Keeping a careful custody of classified documents carried on a tour and making sure that they will not be lost.

8. Waging a resolute struggle when discovering violations

of security system and acts of losing and disclosing secrets and reporting immediately to the superior.[57]

Punishment for violation of the code of cadres took different forms depending on the seriousness of the violations. A RAM member always had the right to appeal any charges brought against him/her and had a right to a trial. If the charges were of a treasonous nature, the military affairs committee or the defense minister was instructed to handle the matter.

RAM was governed by a secret central committee, which was called the soul circle. Few officers of RAM were ever known. The RAM organization was based on collective leadership and democratic centralism was its internal organizational principle. The RAM organization had a youth section called the Black Guards. The role of the Black Guards was to protect RAM leadership and to purge the African-American community of counter-revolutionaries. The Black Guards were to be the forerunner of the Black Liberation Army.

RAM also established rifle clubs in various northern communities. Many times followers of Malcolm X were part of an alliance inside these rifle clubs.

RAM infiltrated the Congress of Racial Equality (CORE) in several cities: Chicago, Cleveland, Brooklyn, and Philadelphia. RAM members also were members of northern SNCC chapters and Deacons for Defense members. RAM's strategy was "to push the bourgeois reformers as far up tempo as fast as possible," while at the same time laying a foundation for an underground movement.

RAM organized black nationalist-oriented student groups on campuses in the south and predominately white universities in the north. These groups had various names at different times. One such student group was the Afro-American Student Movement based in Nashville, Tennessee.

The Afro-American Student Movement sponsored a National Afro-American Student Conference on Afro youth in Nashville, Tennessee, October 30–November 1, 1964. Gang members attended this conference from Chicago and students from other areas of the country. The conference was entitled, "The Black Revolution's Relationship to the Banding World."

RAM also established contact with gangs on the west side of

Chicago. "Doug" Andrews of the West Side organization was a leading RAM ex-gang leader.

CHICAGO, ILLINOIS

Eric Perkins was asked the questions, how old were you when you were recruited and did you join any particular organization? He answered:

> I was fourteen or fifteen if I remember correctly...John as a member of SNCC (Student Non-Violent Coordinating Committee) and they had a youth wing and I immediately joined that becoming very active. All of us fashioned ourselves as black nationalists all on the order of Malcolm X. But when King came to Chicago for the open-housing campaign we wanted to establish a paramilitary group to neutralize the violence that came down. This was called the Gage Park incident. This was a major turn in King's Northern campaign. It is what drove him back to the south to reconsolidate and utilize all his energies in the south.[58]

Then Eric Perkins was asked "what was the most important event that led to your development as a youth?" He stated:

> What catapulted all the urban youth in the Northeast, Midwest and the West was the Watts, LA, rebellion of 1965. There's no question that the summer of 1965 was critical in all of our political evolution. We took leaps and bounds in the growth of our political consciousness. This is what we finally could see, the relationship of state power to everyday people and the way this unfolded and the mechanisms that everyday people utilized to respond to it. We decided then that we had to put together a more serious political apparatus to support the response that the masses wanted to take.[59]

CLEVELAND, OHIO

In Cleveland, a youth group of ex-gang members was formed.[60] Cleveland developed early around united front efforts that were all inclusive. The United Freedom Movement (UFM), a coalition of civil rights organizations, ministers and nationalists formed in May 1963. The UFM began picketing a school construction site over school segregation and busing in the Italian neighborhood of Murray Hill in January of 1964. Violence was threatened and implemented against activists and by-standers:

134

In February of 1964, CORE along with the Hazeldell Parents Association and the United Freedom Movement planned a school boycott to demand that black children bused to white schools be integrated with the white students. These groups, along with the NAACP, also picketed an elementary school construction site in Glenville, charging that the site would promote segregation and demanding a moratorium on school construction.[61]

As a result of threats to demonstrators, Louis Robinson of the Freedom Fighters convened the Medgar Evers Rifle Club April 7, 1964.

Tension mounted at a school in Lakeview, where construction work had been undertaken by the Board of Education. UFM wanted construction stopped, and in the heat of emotions, several members from the UFM picket line laid down in front of the cement trucks. Bruce Klunder laid down behind a bulldozer. The driver of the bulldozer was not aware of this and backed up the bulldozer. Reverend Klunder was killed immediately.[62]

A mini rebellion occurred after news of Reverend Klunder's death spread.

Dr. Katrina Hazzard recalls that many youth were recruited through parties and socials held at the JFK (Jomo Freedom Kenyatta) house from 1963 to 1965.

"The JFK house would have meetings where they recruited some women and the brothers would show up."[63]

Harrell Jones recalls how prominent African-Americans verbally attacked the JFK house and how he recruited Fred Ahmed Evans. Leo Jackson was a councilman in the Glenville area who attacked the JFK house. The youth of the JFK house picketed his house. On the way back,

"I was carrying the kids from the JFK House and the police just pulled up and said this is not a demonstration, this is a riot. They maced all of our little kids of the JFK House and that's when this tall astrologer Ahmed Evans who didn't understand why this was happening and why the police were attacking us came up to me. I talked to him and brought him into the movement at that time."[64]

The JFK house was part of or sponsored by the United Black Brotherhood (a local black nationalist united front) that rented a hall where they had periodic meetings, guest speakers and discussions. After the murder of Reverend Bruce Klunder, the UFM (United Freedom Movement) called a boycott of schools on April 20, 1964. The UFM held alternative freedom schools and awarded diplomas.

In May 1964, the rifle club was given the use of a large farm owned by Walter Wills, Sr., a wealthy black undertaker. By November of that year the rifle club had expanded into a youth center called Jomo "Freedom" Kenyatta House. The purpose of JFK House was to prevent delinquency and foster constructive experiences for black youth in the eastern end of Hough. The trustees named were Harrell Jones, also known as Harrell X, and later leader of the Afro Set, Albert Ware, a disabled war veteran; and Robinson himself. Robinson also served a director. The program included table tennis, dancing, games and other such activities for young people.[65]

In July of 1966 a spontaneous rebellion broke out in the Hough area. Police later searched for and hunted community activists. In the period of 1966–1967 with the absence of the indigenous hardcore leadership, the united front between street force community activists began to disintegrate. Two factions began to develop. One around Harrell Jones, prime minister of the Afro-Set who temporarily became influenced by Maulana Ron Karenga of the US organization of Los Angeles, and the other formed around Fred "Ahmed" Evans, prime minister of the Federation of New Libya. Evans who was originally recruited into RAM by Harrell Jones when Evans wondered why the black nationalists were demonstrating; in return he recruited Ali Khan and a hard core street organization called "six tray" (61 to 63 and Quincy Streets) and other youth gangs into the Federation of New Libya. Katrina Hazzard estimates there was approximately a core of a hundred young black nationalists in Ahmed Evans' faction of New Libya.[66]

Though the division among the Cleveland revolutionary black nationalists remained throughout the remainder of the era, they all united in an all class effort to register people to vote and to elect Carl B. Stokes, the first African-American mayor of a major city in 1967. Tensions between the police and Fred Ahmed Evans forced him to close his Afro Culture Shop and continued until they cumulated into a shoot out, July 23, 1968. On July 23, 1968, the racists in Cleveland's police force fired on the apartment house where Ahmed was staying. A gun battle occurred, killing seven African-American freedom fighters and wounding fifteen police.[67]

RAM propagated its anti-imperialist ideology to the African-American community through a quarterly magazine it published called *Black America*. RAM also popularized its writings through feature writers Roland Snellings and me in the popular nationalist monthly *Liberator* magazine edited by Daniel Watts in New York. RAM on the west coast published a quarterly called *Soulbook*. RAM was the first black organization in the 1960s to oppose the United States government imperialist aggression in Vietnam. In the fall 1964 issue of *Black America*, RAM stated,

> On this Fourth of July, 1964 when white America celebrates its Declaration of Independence from foreign domination one hundred and eighty-eight years ago, we of the Revolutionary Action Movement (RAM) congratulate the Vietnamese Front of National Liberation for their inspiring victories against U.S. imperialism in South Vietnam and thereby declare our independence from the policies of the U.S. government abroad and at home.[68]

In 1964, Grace Boggs and Rev. Albert Cleage were instrumental in developing a strong statewide Freedom Now Party. Some members of UHURU were organizers for FNP.

Also, in 1964, UHURU members went to Cuba where they met Robert F. Williams, Fidel Castro, Che Guevara and Muhammad Babu. Some joined RAM. In 1965, they regrouped and formed a chapter of the Afro-American Student Movement in Detroit, which put out a theoretical journal called *Black Vanguard*, edited by John Watson. *Black Vanguard* was distributed to African-American workers in the plants but was too theoretical and thick for a positive response from workers.

In January of 1965, RAM experienced its first organizational crisis. James and Grace Boggs resigned from their positions in the movement. This left only two public officers, Freeman and Stanford. Through correspondence, both decided to resign their positions in the organization. An emergency meeting was convened in Cleveland, where it was decided that new leadership should be elected. Discussing the analysis of Robert F. Williams, who emphasized that the movement should be underground, the new leadership decided it was best to remain secret. From that point on in

January 1965 all leadership in RAM was secret, and all materials written for RAM publications would be anonymous. The political perspective of RAM changed. The concept of a black dictatorship of the U.S., while still being maintained, began to take a secondary position to the African-American nation in the South.

In response to the U.S. increasing involvement in the Vietnam War and U.S. troops invading Panama, RAM issued an appeal to U.S. troops to turn on their imperialist enemies.[69]

NORTHERN CALIFORNIA

In Northern California, RAM grew primarily out of the Afro-American Association. Founded by Donald Warden in 1962, the Afro-American Association consisted of students from the University of California at Berkeley and Merritt College—many of whom, such as Leslie and Jim Lacy, Cedric Robinson, Ernie Allen and Huey Newton, would go on to play important roles as radical activists/intellectuals. In Los Angeles, the president of the Afro-American Association was a young man named Ron Everett, who later changed his name to Ron Karenga and went on to found the US Organization. The Afro-American Association quickly developed a reputation as a group of militant intellectuals willing to debate anyone. By challenging professors, debating groups such as the Young Socialist Alliance, and giving public lectures on black history and culture, these young men left a deep impression on fellow students as well as the African-American community. In the East Bay, where the tradition of soapbox speakers died in the 1930s, save individual campaigns led by the communist-led Civil Rights Congress during the early 1950s, the Afro-American Association was walking and talking proof that a vibrant, highly visible militant intellectual culture could exist.

In theory, the Afro-American Association was open to people representing a variety of ideological positions, but in reality Warden did not get along with the black left nationalists. By 1963, Warden quietly purged the Association of its left presence, leaving a dynamic group of African-American radicals in search of an organizational alternative. Meanwhile, the Progressive Labor Movement (PL) had begun sponsoring trips to Cuba and recruited several radical African-American students in the East Bay to go along. Among them was Ernie Allen, a U. C. Berkeley transfer student from Merritt College who had been forced out of the Afro-American Association.

A working class youth from Oakland, Allen was part of a generation of African-American radicals whose dissatisfaction with the civil rights movement's strategy of non-violent passive resistance drew them closer to Malcolm X and Third World liberation movements. Not surprisingly, through his trip to Cuba in 1964 he found the Revolutionary Action Movement.

The trip was historic: Allen's travel companions included a contingent of African-American militants from Detroit: Luke Tripp, Charles ("Mao") Johnson, Charles Simmons, and General Baker. All were members of the student group UHURU, and all went on to play key roles in the formation of the Dodge Revolutionary Union Movement and the League of Revolutionary Black Workers. Incredibly, I was already on the island visiting Robert Williams. When it was time to go back to the states, Allen and the Detroit group were committed to building RAM. Allen stopped in Cleveland to meet with RAM members on his cross-country bus trip back to Oakland. Armed with copies of Robert Williams' *Crusader* magazine and related RAM material, Allen returned to Oakland intent on establishing RAM's presence in the East Bay. Never more than a handful of people, folks such as Isaac Moore, Kenneth Freeman (Mamadou Lumumba), Zolli Ndele, Bobby Seale (future founder of the Black Panther Party) and Doug Allen (Ernie's brother) established a base at Merritt College through the Soul Students Advisory Council. The group's intellectual and cultural presence, however, was broadly felt. Allen, Freeman, and others founded a journal called *Soulbook* that published prose and poetry that is best described as left black nationalist in orientation. Freeman, in particular, was highly respected among RAM activists and widely read. He constantly pushed his members to think about black struggle in a global context. The editors of *Soulbook* also developed ties with old left African-American radicals; the most famous was former communist Harry Haywood whose work they published in an early issue.

Although RAM as a movement never received the glory or publicity bestowed on groups like the Black Panther Party, its influence far exceeded its numbers—not unlike the African Blood Brotherhood (ABB) four decades earlier. Indeed, like the ABB, RAM remained largely an underground organization.[70]

In 1965, after Dr. King got out of jail, he announced that he would lead a march from Selma to Montgomery. His assistants convinced him not to lead the march in the beginning. Instead, Hosea Williams of SCLC and John Lewis of SNCC led the march of about 525 people. After the marchers crossed Pettus Bridge going to U.S. Highway 80 a battalion of state troopers confronted them. After an exchange of words the troopers attacked. After the attack, Dr. King announced he would continue the march. Suffering setbacks at the beginning, the march was finally successful.

The civil rights movement though was entering a crisis. For many civil rights activists, segregation was crumbling too slowly. The impact of revolutionary black nationalism began to penetrate the ranks of SNCC and it began to re-evaluate its integrationist outlook in 1965.

During 1965, SNCC began discussing how to form an African-American student movement. The Northern Student Movement (NSM) began to organize Afro-American student groups of African-American students on white campuses in the North while SNCC focused on African-American students in the South.

In New York, either in late 1965 or early 1966, my wife Ahada, (aka Helen Brane) and I visited Mary (Yuri) and Bill Kochiyama. We discussed Malcolm and how we wanted to complete his work. Yuri said that if I wanted to do that, then she would introduce me to some youth who had been around her and her sons and daughters doing SNCC support work. I told her I would be working with Jesse Gray (Harlem—1960—rent strike leader) in the summer of 1966 and would have time to try to politicize them.

RAM AND THE DEACONS FOR DEFENSE

Several events took place in 1965 that affected the civil rights movement. The Deacons for Defense, an all African-American community self-defense organization, developed in Louisiana, Mississippi and Alabama. The Deacons provided civil rights marches in Louisiana with armed protection. They also had shootouts with the KKK and on several occasions, with Louisiana policemen. RAM and other black nationalists formed northern Deacons for Defense support groups. RAM and the Deacons developed an alliance. Both groups helped one another organizationally.

Sister Dara (Virginia) Collins relayed through a RAM cadre that the Deacons were not concerned with revolution. I sent a message back that we, in the RAM leadership, would look into it. Sometime in mid-spring 1965, I went to Louisiana in a car with Albert Haynes and John Anderson and their two girlfriends. John wanted to stop in Montgomery, if I'm not mistaken, where he and the young ladies were from; the young ladies would serve as cover also, because it looked life a family taking a trip. We drove from New York to Louisiana and met with Ernest (Chui) Thomas of the Deacons.

In 1965 in meetings in New York, Louisiana and Detroit, an alliance was established between RAM (Revolutionary Action Movement) and the Deacons for Defense. Ernest Thomas ("Chui") of the Deacons met with me and stated that Deacons would take care of the armed self-defense aspect of the movement while RAM could concentrate on the political guidance and development of the movement.[71]

In August 1965, the Los Angeles African-American community exploded. Revolutionary nationalists engaged in armed struggle against the racist repressive forces. RAM organizers from New Jersey went to Watts, L.A. where they found strong revolutionary black nationalist cells.[72] In New York, RAM members began meeting with African-American youth discussing the formation of a black liberation army.

Revolutionary nationalists around the country studied the August mass rebellion in Watts. They saw that spontaneous mass rebellions would be the next phase of the protest movement and began discussing how they could give these rebellions political direction.

RAM was also active in helping LeRoi Jones develop the Black Arts Movement. The Black Arts Movement was originally to be the cultural wing of RAM.[73] RAM, though a secret movement, was gaining popularity and influence in northern African-American communities. On the international level, Robert Williams, RAM's chairman in exile, issued an appeal for world support and spoke at international conferences in Asia and Cuba. The Communist Party of Cuba disagreed with his black nationalist analysis and began to sabotage the movement's influence in international circles. This produced a crisis for the movement as avenues of potential support were cut off.[74]

In the United States, the American Communist Party disagreed with RAM's race and class analysis, and its conclusion that the African-American people were a colonized nation in the U.S. The CP consequently organized against RAM.

RAM AND OPPOSITION TO U.S. INTERVENTION IN VIETNAM

In 1965, several movement activists were drafted into the army. Some decided to go, while others decided to start a black anti-draft movement. Those who went into the army were immediately isolated from other soldiers by army intelligence.

In Detroit, General G. Baker, Jr. received his draft notice. He wrote a political letter to the draft board denouncing U.S. imperialism. Detroit ASM decided to protest Baker's induction. They put out leaflets and press announcements stating that 50,000 African-Americans would show up at the Wayne County Induction Center when Baker had to report. Only eight demonstrators were there but the threat of mass action had convinced the U.S. Army to find Baker unsuitable for service.

Different members of the Detroit cadre began to go in different occupational directions. Watson and Williams became students at Wayne State and General Baker, Jr. worked in the auto factories. In 1965, Glanton Dowdell came into the cadre. Glanton's street experience added valuable skills to the cadre.

> A dropout from the 5th grade, he was put into a home for mentally retarded at the age of 13. In prison on and off since he was 16, he was finally incarcerated on a murder and robbery charge in Jackson. There he organized a strike of black prisoners against discrimination by forming a selected cadre. In prison he read voraciously, learned to paint and after 17 years was released through the intervention of a black probation officer who recognized his genius.[75]

On the West Coast, Ernie Allen held a news conference announcing his refusal to participate in the U.S. Army because of its racist practices.

> I had a press conference and announced that I was not going into the Army and I forgot what I said but I remember being scared to death.[76]

Allen's younger brother recalls his impression:

> By the spring of 1966, I had enrolled at a local community college and was working as a reporter for the college newspaper. One morning I covered a press conference on campus. It was conducted by my older brother, with whom I worked in the area's Black-militant political movement. In front of a crowd of students, reporters and television cameras, he spoke against U.S. involvement in Vietnam. "These

are my induction papers," my brother said. It was then that I learned he had been drafted. "I am a Black man," he continued. "I am not the white man's tool. I will not fight his racist war. There is no power on earth great enough to make me fight for something I don't believe in," he said. "And I don't intend to go to jail." I wanted to stop being a reporter and just be a proud younger brother. I didn't see my brother again for a year.[77]

Douglas Allen decided to follow his older brothers' example:

By 1968 I was working full-time in the struggle and had almost forgotten about the threat of being drafted—when my own papers arrived in the mail. My parents promised their support for whatever I decided to do. (Although they never tried to influence my brother or me one way or other. I later learned that they were deeply opposed to the war. My father and mother had simply raised all their children to think for themselves. It was the greatest of all their gifts to us). I decided not to go.[78]

SNCC began to undergo a policy change. Its staff decided to organize an all-black party in Lowndes County, Alabama. When RAM leadership received news of this, it decided to closely study these developments.

Various activists were called together in the spring of 1965 in Detroit, Michigan. The meeting included James and Grace Boggs, Nahouse Rodgers from Chicago, Julius Hobson from D.C., Bill Strickland of the Northern Student Movement, Don Freeman from Cleveland and Jesse Gray, a Harlem rent strike leader, and other activists from around the country. The conference formed the Organization for Black Power (OBP). The purpose was to raise the position that the struggle for black power was a struggle for black state power and not just for black independent political power. The conference stated that if the black liberation movement was going to be successful the African-American people would have to think about seizing control, one way or another, over the state and other forms of government. OBP was conceived as a coalition of organizations that would organize the African-American people to politically take over large metropolitan areas in the 1970s. The Organization for Black Power was a short-lived group because of ideological splits.

During the winter months of 1965, the RAM leadership developed an ideological perspective into a political document entitled,

143

"The Struggle for Black State Power in the U.S." The document described the difference between a riot and a revolution and outlined what RAM felt was the future direction of the black revolution in the U.S. This document was widely circulated among movement activists. It called for raising the question of black power within the movement. In Detroit, the RAM cadre published a periodical in the automobile plants titled *Black Vanguard*. In New York: RAM began working with a youth gang called the Five Per Centers. After having been radicalized through political education classes, some ex-members of the Five Per Centers formed themselves into the Black Panther Athletic and Social Club.[79]

The radicalizing year for SNCC was 1965. The Atlanta project based in Vine City led by a collective of Bill Ware, Mike Simmons, Don Stone, Roland Snellings and Dwight Williams started a black consciousness movement inside of SNCC. The movement also addressed itself to purging whites out of SNCC. The Atlanta project was also instrumental in changing SNCC policy in foreign affairs. It started the first anti-draft demonstrations in the country, which consequently led to SNCC publicly denouncing the war in Vietnam. At one point there was near gunplay between James Forman and his supporters and the Atlanta project over the question of black nationalism.[80]

In the early part of 1966, RAM decided that many of the African-American revolutionaries across the country who were engaging in armed struggle were isolated and needed a public organization from which to operate legally.

When the shift towards black power occurred in SNCC, RAM decided to develop a public mass black political party. RAM began having a series of meetings with local nationalist organizers in Harlem, along with Harlem representatives of SNCC.[81] These meetings, which were a coalition of activists, decided to set up an independent black political party which would be a northern support apparatus of the Lowndes County Freedom Organization, whose symbol was the Black Panther. It was decided to call the party the Black Panther Party.[82] I wrote Carmichael asking if it was all right to use the name Black Panther. Through the New York SNCC office the word came back, "OK, go ahead." Queen Mother Audley Moore on July 13, 1966, began organizing weekly Black Nationalist Action Forums at the YMCA in Harlem. These meetings were recruiting sessions for the Black Panther Party.[83]

In about June 1966, I started working with Jesse Gray at a program designed to train youth in Harlem how to inspect apartment buildings for violations in the building codes. Yuri Kochyana arranged a meeting at her apartment, where I met some youth who had worked with her with SNCC in New York: I met Shelton Duncan (who had been named Alkamal—the Camel) as a youth through Malcolm himself. Alkamal's father had been in the Nation of Islam (Temple No. 7) with Malcolm. Both he and his wife (Mrs. Duncan) were very supportive in our effort to complete Malcolm's work. Both said they would give me their son to help guide. I felt it a great honor that they would offer their son's life. I did not know at the time, but found out soon, that Alkamal had sickle cell anemia. Alkamal was a true soldier and had a crew (unit) of brothers that he led in the housing projects in mid-Manhattan.

I would have political education classes with them going over Mao Tse Tung's writings and RAM documents in addition to providing physical workouts. Collectively, they chose the name the Black Panther Social and Athletic Club. This was before news broke on the Loundes County Freedom Organization, which had chosen the Black Panther as its symbol. When that news broke at Queen Mother's weekly Black Nationalist forums held on Friday nights at the YWCA, young revolutionary nationalists began discussing forming an independent black political party.

The Black Panther Party was established in New York in August 1966. Stokely Carmichael went to New York and met with the Black Panther Party. Discussions centered on ideology, direction and national expansion of the Party. It was decided that the Party would be a coalition of SNCC, RAM and other organizations.[84] The Black Panther Social and Athletic Club joined with the New York Black Panther Party and became the Black Guards inside the Party (the ideological and physical security wing).

One of the aims of RAM was to take the spontaneous motion of the Civil Rights movement and urban rebellions and transform them into a revolutionary cadre organization through mass direct action. This is why RAM united with SNCC in helping to form the Black Panther Party in the north and worked on forming student, youth, and worker organizations.

Through the organizational structure, a directive was sent to RAM cadres to form public coalitions with community activists to develop the Black Panther Party.

> We saw that the purpose of the Black Panther Party was to offer black people a radical political alternative to the political structure of this country. We did not see the Black Panther Party as waging armed struggle but of moving the masses of our people to that political position and thereby to another stage of struggle. Even though armed struggle was being waged at this time we needed a political and ideological forum that moved our people through struggle against the system, to that point. The purpose of the Black Panther Party was to exhaust the legal avenues of struggle within the system.[85]

According to Alkamal Ahmed Muhammad (Shelton Duncan), an ex-member of the New York Black Panther Party, the Black Panther Party was part of a city-wide network. The Black Panther Party had reached a broad stratum of people. Approximately 300 people attended weekly Black Panther Party meetings from July to October 1966. The BPP, with community groups, called a boycott of two elementary schools in Harlem on September 12, 1966, to protest the absence of black history reading materials in the New York school system. This was the beginning of the community control of schools movement.[86]

Black Panther Parties were established in Detroit, Cleveland, Chicago, San Francisco, Los Angeles and eventually Oakland, California. Within the Black Panther Party there was discussion of organizing African-American workers.

> For Black Panthers to be meaningful it must deal with the question of economic power as related to the political system. This means Black Panthers must develop an overall program. The question of economics presents the development of black union organizations as part of the party to seize economic power in both the urban and rural south. In the urban north it would pose the fight against job discrimination...and white union discrimination especially on federal supported projects and in the rural south it would deal with "people's" ownership of the land.[87]

In New York, Black Women Enraged (a revolutionary black nationalist women's group) began picketing against U.S. army recruiting offices. They were protesting the U.S. government drafting

African-American men (particularly SNCC activists in Atlanta) into the racist U.S. army to fight in a racist and imperialist war. In early 1966, the Atlanta project held demonstrations at the local draft office in Atlanta, trying to stop the drafting of Mike Simmons.

Mass spontaneous rebellions occurred in more northern inner cities in the summer of 1966. House-to-house fighting occurred between the liberation forces and the racist repressive forces in Cleveland, Ohio. During the early months of 1967, the RAM leadership's analysis was that because of the vast amounts of poverty, unemployment and police brutality in the African-American community, the summer of 1967 was going to be one of mass rebellions. RAM decided to give the forthcoming mass rebellions a political direction and arm the community for defense against racist attacks. It proposed to develop African-American militias and organize African-American youth into a youth army called Black Guards, the forerunner of a Black Liberation Army. The Black Guards were to be a defense army and also the political cadre that would aid the vanguard, RAM, in leading the world black revolution.

RAM saw African-American youth as being the most revolutionary sector of black America. RAM also analyzed that African-Americans needed to engage in a black cultural revolution to prepare them for a black political revolution. Within the black cultural revolution would also be a black anti-draft movement. The slogans of "America is the Black Man's Battleground," "Unite or Perish" and "Black Power" were raised. RAM described the cultural revolution:

> The purpose of a black cultural revolution would be to destroy the conditioned white oppressive mores, attitudes, ways, customs, philosophies, habits, etc., which the oppressor has taught and trained us to have. This means on a mass scale creating a new revolutionary culture.[88]

RAM called for unity of revolutionary nationalists:

> The first step is for revolutionary nationalists and those who agree on basic principles to unite and form a black liberation front. This does not mean that any group dissolves its autonomy, but rather works in common agreement.[89]

RAM issued its critical analysis of the *Communist Manifesto* and the world Marxist perspective. It published its interpretation of persons of African descent and their relationship to the world socialist revolution in a document entitled, *World Black Revolution*. RAM decided to issue a nation-wide call for armed self-defense and to be active in the mass rebellions.

Along with the mass uprisings in the inner cities, RAM planned student revolts in African-American colleges and among high school students. The Black Guards, RAM youth leagues, were to organize African-Americana history clubs to teach black history. These clubs would lead protests demanding the right to wear "natural" hairdo, African dress, and the right to fly the Red, Black and Green flag in rallies. The college students would demonstrate for more student power with the purpose of turning the Negro colleges into black universities.

Early in 1967, a group of African-American students in Orangeburg, South Carolina began protesting about the firing of a white professor. At Howard University an all African-American student group began discussing its opposition to U.S. involvement in the Vietnam War. They rallied around sociology professor Dr. Nathan Hare at Howard University, Washington, D.C.

> In March 1967, students of the Black Power committee at Howard University demonstrated against General Lewis B. Hershey, Director of the Selective Service system. As he attempted to deliver a speech, they jumped onto the stage shouting, "America is the black man's battleground."[90]
>
> March 22, 1967, they held a press conference announcing the formation of the Black Power Committee. SNCC organizers and student activists from around the country met with the RAM leadership in the spring of 1967. They were told to pick up on developments at Howard. Their activities spread to different African-American universities and eventually to white campuses where they demanded black studies programs. The 1967 Howard protest was the first major African-American student rebellion of the decade directed specifically against a university administration. It inaugurated a series of black student protests against the administrations of both African-American and white institutions of higher education; protests which gathered increasing momentum in 1968–69 and were generally built around the demand for "black studies" programs.[91]

As part of the black cultural revolution, RAM attempted to organize a revolutionary African-American woman's movement and worked with other groups to set up African-American cultural committees. RAM felt:

> The key in this period of the revolutionary nationalist is to develop a popular movement inside Black America. The purpose of creating this popular movement will be an attempt to develop a national united front or Black Liberation Front. This would mean attempting to unite all sectors of Black America under a common slogan led by revolutionary nationalists.[92]

RAM was very active during the year 1967. It was attempting to organize street gangs, students, women's groups, politicize the urban rebellions and develop anti-Vietnam war resistance in the African-American community.

PHILADELPHIA, PA.

In Philadelphia starting in October 1966, the RAM organization went through a restructuring. After a couple months of discussion and recruitment from ex-SNCC and ex-Nation of Islam members a new central committee was established. The new central committee consisted of George Anderson (Hakim Rahman), Booker T. Washington X (Salahadine Muhammad), Ibn Yusef Muhammad and Akbar Muhammad. A plan was drafted for recruiting youth gangs from each area of the city into RAM's youth league, the Black Guards. This recruitment was to run concurrent with anti-Vietnam activities, armed and unarmed self-defense classes, a black cultural revolution and the study of and demand for African, African-American history in the public schools. In February 1967, after RAM organizers had circulated among youth, a meeting was convened in west Philadelphia of ten gang leaders. Because of the bitter cold the meeting had to be canceled. The RAM central committee decided to reconvene the initial recruitment in two months in north Philadelphia. In March RAM held a meeting with thirty gang members explaining the Black Guards' program. Recruits to the organization would endure a three-month basic orientation five days a week basic training. Upon graduation the recruits would receive a green star, the equivalent of a green belt in martial arts. After graduation they would continue their training for a red star then a black star and ultimately a RAM star. They would in this process recruit others for the B.G. From the initial recruitment of thirty the processes of attrition narrowed the first recruitment to ten or two units in three months.

Young recruits of the Black Guards had to memorize Lesson Number One: a five page document of questions and answers about the Black Guards. As part of the political education, the B.G.'s recruits would have to take a pamphlet (usually a Chinese Marxist party article) and RAM or historical materials and write a report on it Their interpretation of the document would have to be written in their own words and the recruit would give an oral presentation of it to other B.G. recruits in a weekly political education meeting.[93] A RAM cadre had written African-American history notes, which were used along with *The Crusader* to form African-American history clubs in the high schools.

May 1967 started the second recruitment of the B.G.'s and July 1967 started the third recruitment. In each recruitment phase the Black Guards organization grew. B.G.'s participated in local demonstrations of the times, organized inside the high schools in the day in the form of African-American history clubs/cultural groups and in bars, pool rooms, on street corners, at dances and at cultural affairs in the evening and weekends. Training included basic calisthenics, jogging 2–3 miles three times a week, martial arts training twice a week, armed practice once a week and political education, once internal and the other external twice a week. The events of mass imprisonment, mass organizing against the board of education and repression, cultural fund-raising for those imprisoned, and the assassination of Dr. Martin Luther King, Jr. on April 4, 1968 led to the rapid mass growth of the Black Guards in the area in 1968.[94]

Washington, D.C.

RAM organizers went into Washington, D.C., working with the New School of Afro-American Thought, organized the Black Guards at Howard University. An African-American sociology professor supported the efforts. Dr. Nathan Hare recalls:

> They fired me on the same day they had arrested RAM... They kept trying to come and get me after I got back to Washington because I stayed gone for a while. After I got back, like I was telling the police they would try to get me to do some violence and then would say plan some violence and I'd let them do the talking and then they would try to say well, well they'd call me. So I'd give them the number and I'd call them first and there wouldn't even be such a

number. Then out of different things I just saw that they were police and they kept on and finally left me alone. They tried for a long time to get me involved in something. They were trying to get militants off the street, that's all.[95]

The state responded by imprisoning RAM organizers "en masse" in the summer of 1967. On the east coast, in Philadelphia and New York, police intelligence units fabricated plots against the RAM organization. There was the Queens, New York 17, Roy Wilkins and Whitney Young assassination case. Herman Ferguson felt that RAM underestimated the state. RAM's lack of sophistication didn't allow RAM to be aware of the counter-insurgency program that the U.S. government had put in place to make sure that a liberation struggle or any kind of movement that threatened the system would not materialize. The counter-insurgency program concentrated on black people. It was called COINTELPRO (Counter Intelligence Program). Through COINTELPRO the government introduced undercover agents into RAM and arrested seventeen of the core leadership of RAM in New York; and charged them with conspiracy to overthrow the government and attempting to assassinate mainstream conservative Negro leaders Roy Wilkins of the NAACP and Whitney Young of the Urban League.[96]

In an interview with Herman Ferguson:

Ferguson was not religious minded and felt that out of all the black nationalists at the time, Malcolm X and the Nation of Islam was the most practical with its program of self-reliance. He did not feel the religious aspect would help towards liberation but felt that if Malcolm X were to ever leave the N.O.I. he would become a part of anything he would set up because Malcolm was a brilliant thinker and felt anything he would set up would be very political and would be based on some kind of revolutionary struggle. So when Malcolm left the N.O.I., Ferguson joined Malcolm's organization, the Muslim Mosque, Inc. Ferguson was the only non-Muslim member of the Muslim Mosque, Inc. When Malcolm came back from Africa and established the Organization of Afro-American Unity (OAAU) Ferguson joined and was chairman of the education committee. Ferguson felt Malcolm X was the sole individual that had the most important impact of his development. Malcolm crystallized his consciousness to evolve from traditional black nationalism to revolutionary black nationalism. But the organization that brought

Ferguson to a higher stage of development was his experience with the Revolutionary Action Movement. Ferguson felt RAM's call for guerrilla warfare and a liberation struggle is what he had been moving towards and looking for all the time.[97]

The concept of self defense, gun clubs, and preparing African-Americans for protracted struggle against the oppressive capitalist, imperialist system was the direction Ferguson felt African-Americans needed to go.

In Detroit, RAM organizers were arrested on riot charges. In Cleveland, there was a manhunt for RAM organizers.[98]

Some of those remaining in the streets were killed in the process of fighting racist police, the National Guard and the U.S. Army. Others continued to organize the street force and mobilized the community for legal defense of incarcerated members.

RAM organizers used direct agitation, leafleting and talking with the street force in bars, schoolyards, pool halls and street corners. Revolutionary nationalist classes were set up, teaching African and African-American history and the organization's line. The national RAM organization that eventually emerged was based on clandestine local cells, with the central leadership forming coalitions with existing African-American organizations to prepare for a national liberation front.

RAM worked with and through many different mass organizations in trying to develop revolutionary consciousness. There is certainly much evidence that their work found a ready response at the grass-roots. RAM guided the Afro-American Student Associations that led the fight for African-American history in the public schools of Philadelphia, Cleveland, Chicago, New York and other cities. In Chicago, for example, RAM cadre, working behind-the-scenes at their 39th St. UMOJA Black Student Center, coordinated the October 1968 high school strike that brought out half of the city's African-American high school students in mass demonstrations. There, the city Afro-American Student Association united recognized student leaders from over twenty African-American high schools. RAM classes discussed guerrilla warfare and socialism with young activists.[99]

From taped interviews with twenty-five ex-RAM and Black Guards (BG) members, it was discovered that there was a great influx or growth in RAM membership between 1966 and 1968. A mass recruitment drive between January 1967 and May 1968 in the organization of the Black Guards was seen as a major reason for United States Government repression against RAM in those years.[100] Most of those interviewed had been recruited through the Black Guards. They felt the BG's were a mass youth movement with revolutionary potential.

Of the twenty-five ex-RAM/Black Guards members interviewed, twenty-three were from working class families and felt their backgrounds had contributed to their becoming involved with the RAM organization.

BOSTON, MASSACHUSETTS

From an interview with Drew King, III on June 15, 2005 it was learned that King, a resident of Shaker Heights and son of a medical doctor (Dr. Drew King, Jr.), became involved in the city-wide Cleveland CORE (Congress of Racial Equality) as a staunch integrationist between the ages of 15 and 16. Cleveland CORE was under the leadership of Ruth Turner. Turner introduced Drew to direct action demonstrations and took him to the Baltimore, Maryland CORE project, called "Target Cities," in the summer of 1964. Drew returned to Cleveland and became involved in a voter registration project, which was Dr. Martin Luther King, Jr.'s Special Projects Committee campaign. Soon afterward, Drew King became involved in the Freedom schools in Cleveland, boycotting the Shaker schools. He began to try to get other students involved through the help of Dr. Clements, a prominent physician in Cleveland. In 1965, when he was 17, Drew met Don Freeman. Drew began reading *Muhammad Speaks*. When he went to church, the Unitarian church at 82nd and Euclid, he met fellow Unitarian, Wilbur Grattan, who began to discretely teach him. Drew was pro-Martin Luther King, Jr., but as he continued to read *Muhammad Speaks*, he found that parts of it made sense and he slowly began to change his views. He became a revolutionary black nationalist. Drew King later went to the JFK. (Jomo Freedom Kenyatta) House where he met Marty Friedman, Harold (Buddy) Mitchell, Ware Bey, and Harlell Jones in 1965. Drew enrolled in Harvard University in September 1965 and began to gravitate to SNCC, meeting Robert Eubanks and Patty Mapp. Drew King met students at Harvard, who were interested in Africa. Robert and JoAnn Eubanks housed SNCC at their home and in 1966 started a paper called *Rebellion News*. Also in 1966, through his association with SNCC, Drew met Mike Simmons and Larry Fox of the Atlanta Project. While on campus, Drew King was active around RAM and began distributing *The Crusader* (Robert F. Williams' newsletter). Through its Civil Rights committee, Drew tried to get 'Negro' history—later called 'Black' history—incorporated into the curriculum at Harvard. As an active member and secretary of the Society of Afro-American Students, King served as editor of its newsletter, *L'Ouverture* (named after Toussaint L'Ouverture) in 1965 and 1966. When Drew would come home to Cleveland for the summer, he would consult with Don Freeman, Wilbur Grattan (now King's mentor), Ahmed Evans, and others at the JFK House. In the summer of 1966, Drew met William Strickland at a conference in Philadelphia, PA. Returning to Harvard University in the fall of 1966, Drew brought Carl B. Stokes (who, in 1967, became the mayor of Cleveland—the first African-American mayor of a major U.S. city) to Harvard to speak on a panel to debate the significance of African-American involvement in traditional electoral politics. Drew soon became involved with the Boston Action Group (BAG) led by Sara and Donald Henshaw. Drew King married Arvetta Joyce Orr in 1967. He began teaching African and African-American history in the prisons along with Robert Hall, continuing for two to three years. In 1967, Drew began working with *Rebellion News* (an African-American internationalist newspaper) writing history and started relating to the Boston inner-city community. He became a distribution manager for the newspaper. When Drew returned home (Cleveland) in the summer of 1967, he worked with Alex Weathers, who had a house for white SDS students, and Ron Lucas. Returning to Harvard in the fall of 1967, he secured a job with the Job Corps screening agency. He also became more active with what was happening in the Boston community and became editor of *Rebellion News*. In 1968, King became more involved in the demand for Black Studies at Harvard. African-American students would meet at Drew's house in Roxbury to plan their activities. The Society of Afro-American Students, led by Jeff Howard (from Chicago) and "Bob" Hall demanded the institution of Black Studies at Harvard. By this time, King was being influenced by Al Haynes (Muhammad Zaid) from New York, Ware Bey from Cleveland, Ohio, and Dawoud As Salaam from Pittsburgh, Pennsylvania and Washington, D.C. all members of RAM. In the fall of 1968, the Society of Afro-American Students engaged in a sit-in and seized a building at Harvard to demand the incorporation of Black Studies in the Harvard curriculum. Lani Guinier was involved with the African-American students, and the Harvard administration chose her father to become the first director of Black Studies at Harvard.[101]

GROWTH OF THE RAM ORGANIZATION

The RAM organization grew rapidly during the 1967–68 period.[102] In Philadelphia in 1967, there were approximately thirty-five RAM members. By 1968, estimates by ex-Black Guards members figure Black Guard's membership to be from 350–500 Black Guards members.[103]

In Cleveland, by 1968, there were 800 to 1,000 members in units of the black nationalist army.[104] The RAM organization and its affiliates were estimated to be 200 in Chicago, 200 in Detroit and 100 in New York. At its highest point of membership, the RAM organization was said to be about 4,000 with 3,000 supporters. The age range of the organization though varied was primarily young. Twenty of the twenty-five ex-RAM/Black Guards members interviewed joined the organization when they were between the ages of 17 and 19.[105]

On November 17, 1967, 4,000 African-American students in Philadelphia marched on the board of education demanding black history classes, a revamping of the curriculum, the wearing of African dress (national dress) to school, and natural hair, and the right to salute the black nation's flag—the red, black and green. The students were attacked by the white racist police force, which framed more than thirty revolutionary black nationalists in a so-called "riot conspiracy" in the summer of '67.[106]

Frank Rizzo, Philadelphia's police commissioner, had the demonstration attacked. Black Guards, unarmed in the demonstration, engaged in hand-to-hand combat with police.

RAM AND THE AFRICAN-AMERICAN STUDENT MOVEMENT

Nathan Hare said in an interview:

> We worked together and did things at Howard to protest an administrative policy to make Howard University into a predominantly black institution. In fact, we put together one night a Black University Manifesto designed to overturn the Negro college and convert it into a black university that would be relevant to the African-American community and its needs. Then with that we began to launch protests.[107]

155

The movement at Howard University ranged from anti-war protests with inviting the People's Champion, Muhammad Ali to campus to calling for a black cultural revolution. The movement spread to other campuses.

In a telephone interview, Veda Harris described the events leading up to the November 17, 1967 demonstration in which 3,500–4,000 African-American high school students marched on the Philadelphia Board of Education to demand the inclusion of African-American history classes.

> A young brother who was very popular with the girls was expelled from school for wearing his hair in an Afro hairstyle. Some of us felt it was in his God-given rights to wear his hair the way he wanted to. So we organized a mass march on the board of education. Word spread and it picked up momentum.[108]

A year later, African-American high school students would demand the inclusion of African-American history in the public educational systems in Newark, NJ, New York, Harrisburg, Lancaster, Erie, York, PA, and Chicago, Illinois as well as other places.[109]

On February 8, 1968, African-American students who were demonstrating against the exclusion of African-Americans at a local bowling alley in Orangeburg, South Carolina were confronted by police on their campus of South Carolina State College. As tense police exploded; shooting into the crowd, killing three and wounding thirty three more; they began beating the terrorized tear-gassed students. The event became known as the Orangeburg Massacre. Cleveland Sellers of SNCC was put under house arrest with an U.S. Army tank lowering its turret in his direction while he was talking on the telephone.[110]

But the African-American student movement began to grow by leaps and bounds. In interviews with Askia Muhammad Ture, the history of black studies begins to emerge: Ture was an activist in the Atlanta project when he received a call from sister Sonia Sanchez in San Francisco in spring 1967 asking Ture would he come out to San Francisco; that Amiri Baraka had been out there early 1967 and would he come out there to help develop a black studies program at San Francisco State. James "Jimmy" Garrett, who was a student at San Francisco State and other activist students coordinated their efforts with Sonia Sanchez in creating black history classes in churches and community centers in the bay area. The Africana studies movement had evolved from the SNCC freedom schools idea in the south.

When the students found out that Ture had been operating freedom schools in Atlanta they asked him to join them. At the time there was an alliance between SNCC and the Panthers. Ture came to San Francisco and began teaching black history classes along with Garrett and Sanchez in churches and community centers there.

Black studies were introduced at San Francisco State when the African-American students from the Black Student League at SFS erupted in a black history class stating, "They were not going to have European teachers teaching them the history of their people." The students took over the building where the classes were being held and would not let anyone go anywhere.

The administration said there were no qualified black teachers to teach black history. Sonia Sanchez was already teaching black literature at SFS. The students called Ture and requested that he teach black history at SFS. Some of the students had been in Ture's classes in the community. Ture met with the administration and a white professor volunteered to sponsor his course.[111]

The requirement of African-American teachers teaching black studies courses was that they needed a white sponsor. Seven African-Americans started their black studies classes at San Francisco State in January 1968. Nathan Hare came to San Francisco State on February 1, 1968 to chair the Black Studies program.

In an interview, Nathan Hare said:

> After Max Stanford and the RAM students were among those arrested in Philadelphia and I escaped the police dragnet, I decided to go back into boxing and I went into training before I was accepted at San Francisco State to run the Black Studies program. The first Black Studies Program in the United States was being started at San Francisco State College.[112]

By 1968 African-American students in places never heard of were seizing school buildings, boycotting classes en masse, up to 30,000 in Chicago. African-American students battled police in New York and Brooklyn over African-American community control of schools. By 1968, the movement had spread to many cities, with African-American students organizing massive boycotts and walkouts demanding African-American history classes.

Eric Perkins, a student activist in the Chicago area in the 1960s recalled:

Black student unions became one of the leading student unions in the country, in 1966, and we linked up with student unions in Northwestern and Columbia. These were the two biggest black student demonstrations, which occurred in May of 1968 when the two campuses were closed at Northwestern and Columbia. The reason for that is that the Columbia black student union was run by Ralph Metcalf, Jr., who was the athlete, Ralph Metcalf's son. He was a good friend. We had grown up together and we had been in touch and did an example in 1967. Victor Goode and I went to a number of campuses here on the East Coast. We went to Cambridge, we went to Columbia, and this is where we cemented ties with other black student organizations. Such that the May event, as it was called, when the most campuses all over the country were closed down that that's how it all came about. We had begun planning for that as early as 1967. It was May 1968. It was all together thirty-four or thirty-five major white campuses closed down at that time. The true history of this episode by the way is only now coming out right at this moment. It is how we all came together and had prepared for this much earlier.[113]

Perkins goes on to explain the impact of revolt among African-American high school students in Chicago:

The same organization worked with a number of high school students starting first at Evanston Township High where they had a tracking program for the black students all the way down to all black high schools. Dunbar, Dusable, Cabral. We worked with a number of student leaders down there and again with John Bracey and others to push these kinds of strikes so that we had the whole base covered. We even wanted to get down to the grammar schools to put black consciousness and black awareness and basic black nationalism all the way down to the sixth grade level. But yes, in 1968, there were a series of major strikes at the black high schools all over the greater Chicago area that caused quite a stir to the authorities. The October 1968 African-American student boycott in Chicago, Illinois, led by UMOJA Black Student Center and the Afro-American Student Association led 30–50,000 students in demonstration.[114]

The revolutionary black nationalist movement became a mass movement in 1968. Thousands of angry African-Americans rose in revolt, burning over one hundred cities protesting the April 4th assassination of Dr. Martin Luther King, Jr.

DISSOLUTION OF RAM

By the summer of 1968, some RAM organizers were back on the streets. RAM and the Black Guards especially had grown into a mass organization. The issue that arose within the ranks was how to survive the pending repression against the movement. Internal contradictions began to become prevalent as arguments over direction occurred and some secondary cadres began striving for personal leadership. Some made themselves generals or regional commanders of the black nationalist army that emerged. How to maintain discipline within an undeveloped mass political force became a preoccupation of the RAM leadership.

In Philadelphia, the RAM and the Black Guard leadership split over the partitioning of 2 million dollars offered by the Black Coalition established secretly through agreement between Frank Rizzo and Jeremiah Shabbaz of the Nation of Islam; and financed by Philadelphia banks.[115] Internal shoot-outs occurred and adventurous confrontations led to the dissolution of the Philadelphia RAM organization.[116]

New forces were simultaneously beginning to emerge and were beginning to eclipse RAM which was having internal organizational discipline problems, legal entanglement of several of its leaders, financial crisis, ideological dis-unity and government repression. The Black Panther Party was expanding into a national organization from its base in Oakland, California. Maulana Ron Karenga, leader of the US organization was clashing with several revolutionary nationalist forces. The Republic of New Africa, then based in Detroit, Michigan was competing with the BPP and US for political dominance.

RAM's leadership felt that the forces the FBI wanted to crush were those who had fought the state and had been advocating urban guerrilla warfare. With many RAM members in jail or just being released from jail and key members under legal indictments or facing long prison terms, notably Glanton Dowdell in Detroit, Michigan, Fred Ahmed Evans in Cleveland, Ohio, Arthur Harris and Herman Ferguson in New York and myself in New York and Philadelphia, the RAM leadership decided to convene a conference to reorganize. RAM called for the formation of a National Black United Front to combat what the organization felt would be the escalation of an FBI conspiracy (later known as COINTELPRO) against the black liberation movement.

RAM reviewed its accomplishments in a six year period; confrontations to increase job opportunities in the construction and auto industry, and corresponding unions; the awakening of a mass revolutionary nationalist consciousness; the organization of African-American student and youth organizations and the increasing mass mobilization of them to demand black and relevant studies in high schools, colleges and universities catalyzing opposition of U.S. imperialism's war against the people of Vietnam; a support of African and other Third World liberation movements. The RAM leadership decided it had exhausted both its human and material resources and had lost the element of surprise. More importantly, the leadership had learned from actual practice, "that the struggles for liberation was protracted and would take many years to achieve."[117]

In October of 1968, the RAM central committee met and decided that they needed to cease to use the name of RAM because right wing journalists and the U.S. intelligence community was using the name RAM as an excuse to attack the movement. It was decided due to the lack of self-discipline of many of its mass troops and growing ideological dis-unity in the ranks over the direction in which the movement should proceed; the organization's best option was to retreat, go underground developing an ideologically developed self-disciplined cadre party that would be based on a scientific day-by-day style of work.

RAM was a serious attempt that failed to build a national revolutionary organization, an African-American version of the Algerian FLN or the July 26th Movement of Cuba that did not sustain itself or survive. It wasn't a "legal," above-ground organization after 1965. It never was a civil rights organization. It was the result of the new message of Robert F. Williams and Malcolm X, trying to put their insights into practice. From the start RAM aimed at socialist revolution. RAM developed into a broad network of revolutionary nationalists, a semi-public organization with clandestine cells and full-time traveling organizers.[118] Probably ninety years premature, RAM was a prototype for future development.

1. *Ebony Pictorial History of Black Americans, Vol. 3* [Chicago, Illinois: Johnson Publishing Company, 1970], p. 2.

2. Freeman voluntarily left the RAM organization after his firing in 1965 as a Cleveland School teacher. Interview with Don Freeman, Cleveland, Ohio, 4/94.

3. Haywood Burns, *The Voices of Negro Protest in America* [New York: Oxford University Press, 1963], p. 42.

4. Howard Zinn, *SNCC* [Boston, Mass.: Beacon Press, 1964], p. 3.

5. Muhammad Ahmad, "A Brief History of the Black Liberation Movement in the 1960's: Focus on RAM," [unpublished speech: Chicago, Illinois: Northeastern University, 7/78], p. 4.

6. Interview with Malcolm X, Shabazz Restaurant, Temple No. 7, 11/62, New York, N.Y.

7. Max Stanford, "Orientation of a Black Mass Movement" [Philadelphia, Pa.: Unpublished RAM documents, 10/62], p. 4.

8. Arthurs C. Willis, *Cecil's City: A History of Blacks in Philadelphia, 1638–1979* [New York: A Hearthstone Book, 1990] p 86

9. Max Stanford (Muhammad Ahmad), Formative Years: Fall, 1962–63 [Unpublished paper, Amherst, Mass., 10/74], p. 1.

10. A Cadre Discussion on RAM [Unpublished paper], p. 3.

11. Editorial, "The Panthers: Communist Guerrillas in the Street," *American Opinion, Vol. XIII, No. 4*, p. 7.

12. Interview with Barbara Montague, 5/02.

13. Interview with John Bracey, Jr., Amherst, Mass., 10/94.

14. Arthur C. Willis, *Cecil's City: A History of Blacks in Philadelphia, 1639-1979* [New York: A Hearthstone Book, 1990] p. 192

15. Ibid, p.193

16. Ibid, p. 101

17. *Op. Cit.* (A Cadre Discussion on RAM), p. 3.

18. *Op. Cit.* (A Cadre Discussion on RAM), p. 4.

19. "Six Injured on School Picket Line Blocks Most Workers," *The Evening Bulletin, May 27, 1963, Vol. __, 117th Year, No. 46*, p. 1.

20. Arthur C. Willis, *Cecil's City: A History of Blacks in Philadelphia, 1639–1979* [New York: A Hearthstone Book, 1990] p.

21. William Sales, Jr., *From Civil Rights to Black Liberations: Malcolm X and the Organization of Afro-American Unity* (Boston, Massachusetts: South End Press, 1994), p. 75.

22. *New York Times Tuesday, July 16, 1963, pp. 1:2 cont. On pp. 15:1, also see New York Times, Tuesday, August 13, 1963, p. 21:1.*

23. *Op. Cit.* (Ahmad), p. 6.

24. Cecil B. Moore, *Conversation in the Philadelphia NAACP Office*, 5/63.

25. Interview with John Bracey, Jr., Amherst, Mass., 1994, p. 23.
26. "Hecklers Cut Daley Talk to NAACP," Chicago Sun-Times, Vol. 16, No. 132, Friday, July 5, 1963, p. 1.
27. Ahmad, "Discussing the Past," p.5
28. *Op. Cit.* (Muhammad Ahmad, A Cadre Discussion), p. 7.
29. "CORE Suspends Chapter for Urging Tie-up at Fair," *New York Times, April 11, 1964*, p.1.
30. Stall-in Leaders Defy Plea to Bar Tie-up Tomorrow" *New York Times, Tuesday, April 21, 1964*, p. 1.
31. Don Freeman: Black Youth and the Afro-American Liberation," *Black America, Fall, 1964*, pp. 15–16.
32 Robin D. G. Kelly and Betty Esch, "Black Like Mao: Notes on Red China and Black Revolution," p. 8.
33 *Ibid.*, pp. 15–16.
34. *Revolutionary Nationalist, Volume 1, November 1, Summer, 1965*, p. 1.
35. William Sales, Jr., *From Civil Rights to Black Liberation: Malcolm X and the Organization of Afro-American Unity* [Boston, Massachusetts: South End Press, 1994], p. 130.
36. Bracey, Meier, Rudwick, etc., ed., Allen J. Matusaw, "From Civil Rights to Black Power: The Case of SNCC, 1960–1966," *Conflict and Competition: Studies in the Recent Black Protest Movement* (Belmont, California:: Wadsworth Publishing Company, 1971), p. 142.
37. *Ibid.*, p. 140.
38. *Ibid.*, p. 143.
39. Discussion with Robert F. Williams in Havana, Cuba, summer 1964.
40. James Boggs, *Racism and the Class Struggle* [New York: Monthly Review Press, 1970], p. 39.
41. It was suggested that Malcolm X would be the spokesman for the movement. I was to go the New York to talk to Malcolm about it. RAM members went back to their communities to organize cells, while others traveled around spreading the movement.
42. *Twelve Point Program of the Revolutionary Action Movement*, 1964. See appendix.
43. Malcolm X, "The Ballot or the Bullet," *Malcolm X Speaks* [New York: Grove Press, 1965], pp. 28–31.
44. George Breitman, *The Last Year of Malcolm X: The Evolution of a Revolutionary* [New York: Schocken Books], p. 35.
45. Interview with Malcolm X, 6/64, Hotel Theresa, New York, New York.

46. Interview with Malcolm X, 1/65, 22 West Restaurant, New York, N.Y.

47. Interview with Malcolm X, 7/64, New York, N.Y.

48. *Op. Cit.* (George Breitman), p. 116.

49. Eric Norden, "The Assassination of Malcolm X," *Hustler, December,* *1978,* p. 98.

50. *Op. Cit.,* (George Breitman), p. 116.

51. Max Stanford, participant-observer observation, Auditorium, Harlem, New York, 12/64.

52. William Sales, Jr. *From Civil Rights to Black Liberation: Malcolm X and the Organization of Afro-American Unity* [Boston, Massachusetts: South End Press, 1994], pp. 130–131.

53. RAM was accused, in New York's newspapers of being responsible for Malcolm's assassination. During this period, RAM published a newspaper, *Afro-World,* with the headlines: "Malcolm Lives."

54. Interview with Donald Freeman; Cleveland, Ohio, 5/94.

55. Taped interview with Sister Y., Chicago, Illinois, October 30, 1978.

56. Interview with Eric Perkins, Philadelphia, Pa., 10/94.

57. *Ibid.*

58. *RAM Organizational Document,* 1965, p. 4.

59. Interview with Eric Perkins, Philadelphia, Pa., 5/94.

60. Interview with Eric Perkins, Philadelphia, Pa., 5/94.

61. Louis G. Robinson, *The Making of a Man,* [Cleveland, Ohio: Green & Sons, 1970], p. 126.

62. Pramb Chatterjee, *Local Leadership in Black Communities* [Cleveland, Ohio: School of Applied Social Sciences, Case Western Reserve University, 1975], p. 74.

63. Ibid., p. 80.

64. Interview with Katrina Hazzard, Philadelphia, Pa., 8/93, p. 8.

65. Interview with Harrell Jones, Cleveland, 5/95, p. 5.

66. *Op. Cit.,* (Pramb Chatterjee, *Local Leadership in Black Communities*), p. 81.

67. Interview with Katrina Hazzard, Philadelphia, Pa., 9/93.

68. Louis H. Masott, Jerome R. Corsi, *Shootout in Cleveland: Black Militants and the Police*: July 23, 1968 [New York: Bantam Books, 1969], p. 23.

69. "Greetings to Our Militant Vietnamese Brothers," *Black America,* Fall, 1964, p. 21.

70. *Appeal to Afro-Americans in the United States Imperialist Armed Forces,* July 4, 1965. See Appendix A.

71. Robin Kelly, D. G. Kelley and Betsy Esch, "Black Like Mao: Notes on Red China and Black Revolution," unpublished paper), pp. 19–22.

72. Interviews with Earnest (Chui) Thomas, organizer of the Deacons for Defense, Louisiana, New York and Detroit, Michigan, 8/65. Also see, Lance Hill, *The Deacons for Defense: Armed Resistance and The Civil Rights Movement*, (Chapel Hill: The University of North Carolina Press) pp. 60, 221

73. Interview with ex-field organizer of RAM, Ozzie (Bill White), Atlanta, Ga., 8/78.

74. Meetings with LeRoi Jones and Max Stanford, Brooklyn, N.Y. 3/65 (Larry Neal was to be the liaison between Jones and Stanford).

75. Robert Carl Cohen, *Black Crusader*: A Biography of Robert Franklin Williams [Seacaucus, New Jersey: Lyle Stuart, Inc., 1972, pp. 291–292. Also see Ruth C. Reitan, *The Rise and Decline of an Alliance: Cuba and African-American Leaders in the 1960's* [unpublished Ph.D. dissertation], p.173.

76. Grace and James Boggs, *Detroit: Birth of a Nation*, Pamphlet, October, 1967, p. 7.

77. Interview with Ernest Allen, Amherst, Mass., 5/74.

78. Jesse Douglas Allen-Taylor, "On Men and War," "Say, Brother," *Essence*, February, 1988, p. 9.

79. Ibid.

80. Max Stanford, Participant-Observer interview, 4/65, New York, N.Y.

81. Interview with Hakim Rahman, Philadelphia, Pa. 8/02.

82. Interview with *Sam Anderson*, New York, 4/94, p. 5.

83. Interview with Eddie Ellis, New York, N.Y., 4/94, p. 4.

84. *Riots, Civil and Criminal Disorders* (Washington, D.C., U.S., Government Printing Office, 1969), p. 4237.

85. "Black Panthers Open Harlem Drive," Amsterdam News, September 31, 1966.

86. Akbar Muhammad Ahmad, "A Brief History of the Black Liberation Movement in the 1960's: Focus on RAM," unpublished, p. 10.

87. Alkamal Ahmed Muhammad, Taped Interview (New York: December 20, 1978).

88. *Op. Cit.*, (Ahmad), p. 12.

89. Revolutionary Action Movement, Internal Document, *Some Questions Concerning the Present Period*, 1967, pp. 2.

90. *Ibid.*, p. 2.

91. Michael W. Miles, *The Radical Probe: The Logic of Student Rebellion*,

(New Jersey: Antheneum Publishers, 1971), pp. 192–193.

92. *Ibid.*, p. 193.

93. Revolutionary Action Movement, Internal Document, "Some Questions Concerning the Present Period," 1967, p. 4.

94. Max Stanford/participant observer report, 3/67.

95. Interview with Hakim Rahman (George Anderson), 5/94, Philadelphia, PA.

96. Interview with Dr. Nathan Hare, 9/00. Also RAM Leader, "Five Teenagers are Held in Jail for Conspiracy to Incite to Riot," *The Evening Bulletin, Monday, July 31, 1967, (Philadelphia)* p. 4.

97. Interview with Herman Ferguson, New York, New York, 5/02, "The Strange Plot to Kill Roy Wilkins," *Sepia, September 1967*, pp. 58–63 and "Police Pick Up First of Three In Bomb Plot" *Evening Bulletin, September 29, 1967.*

98. Ibid (Ferguson)

99. Interview with Albert Forrest, Cleveland, Ohio, 3/71. Also see Arthur C. Willis, *Cecil's City: A History of Blacks in Philadelphia 1638–1979* [New York: A Heatherstone Book: Carlton Press, Inc., p. 141.

100. Etani Kae Sera, False Internationalism: Class Contradictions in the Armed Struggle [Chicago, Illinois: A Seeds Beneath the Snow Publication, 1985] pp. 173–175.

101. Interview with Khalid Muhammad, and Salahdin Muhammad (Booker T. Washington X), Camden, N.J., 7/73.

102. Interview with Drew King, III, Cleveland, Ohio, June 15, 2005.

103. Interviews with activists (ex-Black Guards) in Philadelphia, Pa., 6/78. Interview with Phil White, New York, N.Y. 5/78, p. 2.

104. Ibid., p. 4.

105. Interview with Albert Forrest "Breeze," Cleveland, Ohio, 3/71.

106. Taped interviews with ex-RAM/Black Guards members, 5/77.

107. "Police Rout 3,500 Unruly Pupils at Black Power Protest," *The Philadelphia Inquirer, Saturday Morning, November 18, 1967*, p.1.

108. Interview with Nathan Hare, 9/00.

109. Interview with Veda Harris, telephone, Cleveland to Philadelphia, PA, 10/97.

110. Dwayne C. Wright. Black Pride Day. 1968: High School Student Activism in York, Pennsylvania: *The Journal of African-American History, Volume 88, No. 2, Spring 2003, pp. 151–161. Also see, VP Franklin, "Black High School Student Activism in the 1960s: An Urban Phenomenon?" Journal of Research in Education, Fall 2000, Volume 10, No. 1, pp3–8 See*

Matthew J. Countryman, Civil Rights and Black Power in Philadelphia: 1940–1971, Ph.D. dissertation, University of North Carolina, 1999

111. Jack Bass and Jack Nelson, *The Orangeburg Massacre*, [Mercer University Press, 1984], pp. 60–71. Also telephone conversation with Cleveland Sellers and Max Stanford, from Philadelphia, Pa. And Orangeburg, South Carolina, Spring, 6/68.

112. Interview with Askia Muhammad Ture, 10/5/00, 5/02, Cleveland to Boston.

113. Interview with Nathan Hare, tape, 9/00.

114. Eric Perkins, Interview, Philadelphia, Pa., 1994.

115. Ibid.

116. Conversation with Attorney Cecil B. Moore and Max Stanford, Jr., Philadelphia, Pa., 6/68.

117. Participant-Observer reflections (Muhammad Ahmad), Cleveland, Ohio, 8/97.

118. Max Stanford, Participant-observer, The 3rd National Black Power Conference, Philadelphia, PA, 8/68.

119. *Op. Cit.* (E. Tani & Kae Sera, False Nationalism, False Internationalism), p. 173.

The *Black Panther* newspaper
was widely circulated.

BLACK PANTHER PARTY

The Lowndes County Freedom Organization (LCFO) was founded in late 1965 under the leadership of Stokely Carmichael of SNCC. The LCFO was a black independent electoral party in Alabama using the tactics of armed self-defense. The LCFO chose the Black Panther as its symbol and it became known as the Black Panther Party. The strategy of the BPP was to elect independent candidates in an attempt to control the community in which African-Americans were the majority legally. This was the first development of the BPP.

The second development of the Black Panther Party occurred on the East Coast as SNCC developed an alliance with revolutionary black nationalists in New York.

When the shift toward black power occurred in SNCC, RAM decided to develop a public mass black political party. Meetings were convened in Harlem, New York, with independent nationalists forces to bring together a coalition, which they wanted to call the Black Panther Party. RAM wrote SNCC a letter asking if the party could be called the Black Panther Party.

I wrote Stokely Carmichael asking if it was alright to use the name Black Panther in forming another support branch of the BPP. Through the New York SNCC office the word came back, "Ok, go ahead." Queen Mother Audley Moore on July 13, 1966, began organizing weekly Black Nationalist Action Forums at the YMCA in Harlem. These meetings were recruiting sessions for the Black Panther Party of New York. The object of the BPP was to create an independent multi-class front organization led by revolutionary nationalists and black Marxist-Leninists to increase black political empowerment.

> I came to New York and met with the New York Black Panther Party. Discussions centered on ideology, direction and national expansion of the Party. It was decided that the Party would be a coalition of SNCC, RAM and other organizations.[1]

The New York Black Panther Party was established in June of 1966 and had approximately 250 members from July 1966 to October of 1966. Its purpose was to implement an independent black electoral strategy in order to break African-Americans allegiance with the Democratic and Republican Party and eventually the capitalist system. It worked in unity with the BPP in Lowndes County, Alabama. It also had the support of Congressman Adam Clayton Powell, Jr. Its tactic was one of armed self-defense, but it did not stress it publicly and kept defense units separate or underground from its public organizations.

The Black Panther Party not only concerned itself with electoral politics but also was an activist community organization. One of the first activities the Party engaged itself in was the struggle for quality education of children in Harlem.[2] It participated in demonstrations of school boycotts of two schools and raised the slogan of "community control of schools."

According to Alkamal Ahmed Muhammad (Shelton Duncan), an ex-member of the New York Black Panther party it was part of a citywide network.

> The Black Panther Party had reached a broad stratum of people. Approximately 300 people attended weekly Black Panther Party meetings from July to October 1966. The BPP, with community groups, called a boycott of two elementary schools in Harlem on September 12, 1966, to protest the absence of black history reading materials in the New York school system. This was the beginning of the community control of schools movement.[3]

Reported in an article in the *Amsterdam News*, September 3, 1966 "Black Panthers Open Harlem Drive," described an event which William Epton head of the Harlem branch of the Progressive Labor Party, Stokely Carmichael, chairman of SNCC and Max Stanford, a member of the Black Panther Party spoke at a meeting of two hundred fifty people. The New York Black Panther Party along with other community groups called for a boycott of two schools in Harlem on September 12, 1966.[4]

Through the RAM organizational structure, a directive was sent to RAM cadres to develop a public coalition with community activists to develop the Black Panther Party.[5]

RAM's rationale for entering into an alliance with SNCC to form the Black Panther Party is described in a RAM internal document titled "Steps Towards Organizing a National Movement in the African-American struggle for National Liberation part II":

> The concept of the Black Panther Party and Mississippi Freedom Labor Union has opened up new awareness for the

development of a national movement. Organize, deepen and expand the Black Panther Party "nationally north and south." Revolutionary black nationalists must do this in order to keep from being isolated from the masses of our people and also to seize the initiative in our struggle; to develop a broad mass community organizational base (north and south)...For a Black Panther to be meaningful it must deal with the question of economic power as related to the political system...by developing a national Black Panther Party we can develop our struggle to an even level of consciousness in every black community. We can educate our people to the fact the existing political system is anti-black and break their allegiance with both the democratic and republican parties and also from the capitalist system...6

The purpose of the BPP was to provide a political alternative for black people to the capitalist, racist Democratic and Republican parties and also exhaust the legal political means of protest.

We saw that the purpose of the Black Panther Party was to offer black people a radical political alternative to the political structure of this country. We did not see the Party as waging armed struggle but of moving the masses of our people to that political and ideological form of struggle that moved our people through struggle against the system. The purpose of the Black Panther Party was to exhaust the legal avenues of struggle within the system.7

The New York Black Panther Party had a youth and political ideological section called the Black Guards that were supposed to be the political defense of the leadership of the local central committee. According to activist Sam Anderson self-defense efforts began on the East Coast before on the West Coast. Anderson was active in self-defense efforts of African-American and African students at Lincoln University in Lincoln, PA against the KKK in early 1966. He also said that the New York Black Panther Party had a ten-point program, planned to run candidates for local and state political offices in New York and was planning a city-wide party congress.8

Major divisions occurred in the New York BPP when Larry Neal, Eddie Ellis, and Donald Washington (Hassan) led a coup against Lloyd Weaver then chairman of the New York BPP. The Neal faction wanted to pressure the Harlem gangsters into contributing to fund the party while the Weaver-Haynes faction wanted to concentrate on community organizing. The party was organizing a citywide party congress when the split occurred.

At one mass party meeting the Neal-Washington faction pulled guns on Weaver voting him out of office at gunpoint. Somehow a call was made from the meeting and Black Guards led by Alkamal Ahmed Muhammad (Shelton Duncan) entered the meeting, threatened showdown, surrounded Weaver and took him from the meeting. Such antics discouraged community support. The Harlem community was just recovering from the assassination of Malcolm X and shootouts of the Harlem Black Arts Theater in the year prior. By November of 1966 the N.Y. Black Panther Party had lost much of its dynamism and became defunct by early 1967.[9]

SNCC and RAM sent directives to organize the Black Panther Party across the country. Black Panther Parties with the same strategies formed in Cleveland, Philadelphia, Los Angeles, Detroit and San Francisco. This was the second development of the Black Panther Party.

Responding to RAM directives the Black Panther Party of Northern California was established in San Francisco in August of 1966. The class composition of the first two BPP developments was made up of black workers and revolutionary intellectuals. Within the BPP there was discussion of organizing black workers.

> For Black Panthers to be meaningful it must deal with the question of economic power as related to the political system. This means Black Panthers must develop an overall program. The question of economics presents the development of Black Union organizations as part of the party to seize economic power in both the urban and rural south. In the urban south it would pose the fight against job discrimination...and white union discrimination especially on federal supported projects and in the rural south it would deal with "peoples" ownership of the land.[10]

The third and most famous development of the Black Panther Party occurred on October 15, 1966 when Huey Newton and Bobby Seale drafted the ten-point program of the Black Panther Party for Self Defense in Oakland, California.

Ula T. Taylor and J. Tarika Lewis in describing the history of the Black Panther Party talked about the evolution of Huey P. Newton's activism and his convergence with Bobby Seale. Huey Newton and Bobby Seale attended Merritt College along with a host of other young revolutionary African-American intellectuals. The two met when they became involved in Donald Warden's Afro-American Association that had a storefront across the street from Merritt College in North Oakland. Though Huey was six years Seale's junior, he became Seale's mentor. Newton soon left the Afro-American Association in ideological conflict with Donald Warden's glorification of the African past but refusal to deal with the present. Newton soon attended Marxist groups and attended Progressive Labor Party meetings. Newton read four volumes of writings by the Chairman of the Chinese Communist Party, Mao Zedong. Newton heard Malcolm X speak at a conference sponsored by the Afro-American Association at McClymonds High School in Oakland. He attended the Nation of Islam's mosques in Oakland and San Francisco and became familiar with the Nation of Islam's ten-point program. Bobby Seale joined RAM in the bay area and invited Newton to attend a meeting but Newton became impatient with the group's cautiousness and left. Seale also soon left the organization, because he did not think they were going to do anything. He said, "I became very discouraged about being able to work with them."[11]

After graduating from Merritt College, Newton enrolled in San Francisco Law School. Newton spent six months in jail after an altercation at a party. When Newton got out of jail in 1965 he looked up Bobby Seale.

> Former RAM members organized the Soul Student Advisory Council (SSAC) at Merritt College and the Black Panther Party of Northern California. Huey joined the SSAC central committee, which also included Doug Allen, Bobby Seale, Isaac Moore, Virtual Murrell and Alex Papillion. The SSAC organized a major rally against the draft of black men into the Vietnam War and also led a successful protest to have a black history course added to the curriculum at Merritt College.[12]

Their activities led to the group demanding the creation of an African-American Studies program. Newton and Seale wanted the students to wear guns in front of the school to protest police brutality.

Newton explained later "we did not intend to break any laws but were concerned that the organization start dealing with reality rather than sit around intellectualizing and writing essays about the white man.[13]

But the students rejected their proposal. Newton and Seale were radicalized about the citizen alert patrols that emerged after the Watts 1965 rebellion. The citizen alert patrols were repressed by the Los Angeles Police Department. After an altercation with police over the right of Bobby Seale to read a poem and after a series of cases of police brutality in the bay area, Newton and Seale began a series of discussions.

> Most of these conversations took place at Seale's apartment, close to the campus. Others participated in the discussions that became heated because there were so many issues and so few solutions. They read Frantz Fanon, Mao Zedong, and Che Guevara and studied Malcolm X's writings and speeches. Robert Williams's Negroes with Guns and literature on the Deacons of Defense had a profound affect on the Party's development.[14]

In the spring of 1966 Seale and Newton circulated throughout the black neighborhoods of Oakland, Berkeley, Richmond, and San Francisco talking with community people about their constitutional right to bear arms. Bobby Seale worked for the Antipoverty Center where Huey Newton would study law in the law library. After the summer of 1966 Bobby Seale organized a Negro history fact group, which had a profound influence on some black student unions in some of the local high schools. One afternoon, October 15, 1966, both Seale and Newton went to the government Anti-Poverty Center to review their initial work. Huey Newton began to dictate to Bobby Seale a ten-point program patterned after the Nation of Islam's platforms. As a result the ten-point program was formed for their organization that they called the Black Panther Party for Self-Defense.[15]

> Newton, a pre-law student, had carefully researched California's legal code as it related to guns and the police. At that time the state law allowed people to carry loaded pistols, rifles and shotguns so long as they were not concealed. Newton and some others decided that this loophole in the law could be exploited. The first task was getting weapons. One day they were reading the newspaper about how the famous "little red book," Quotations from Chairman Mao Tse-Tung, had just been published in English. Huey got an idea. They went across the Bay to China Books, where the "little red book" had just gone on sale, bought a bunch, and drove back to Berkeley. Within an hour, hawking the "little red book" at the gate to the University of California campus, they sold all the books they had. With that money they

drove back to China Books, bought the store's whole stock of "little red books," and sold them all to curious Berkeley students. They made enough money to buy two shotguns.[16]

Conflicts over tactics between the San Francisco Black Panther Party and the Oakland Black Panther Party for Self-Defense began to occur. Major differences over strategy and tactics occurred between the two factions of the Black Panther Party in the Bay area.[17]

The basic contradictions that led to the demise of the BPP lay in the ideological arguments in its formation. The Black Panther Party in Northern California (San Francisco) led by Ken Freeman was the original BPP formed in the Bay area. The main dispute that the BPP of Northern California had with the BPP of Self-Defense (Oakland) was Huey Newton's, Bobby

Seale's insistence of testing bourgeois legality of armed self-defense.

Bobby and Huey first tried to take over a student group formed by RAM called the Soul Students Advisory Council at Merritt College. In the midst of the power struggle, it was learned that Bobby and Huey had taken fifty dollars from the student group's treasury without authorization. According to Bobby's account of the situation, after he and Huey were arrested for an altercation with a police officer. Virtual Murrell, a leader of SSAC, gave them $25.00 to get a lawyer.[18] When most of the students did not support them, Bobby and Huey resigned from the student group.

Ernie Allen, an ex-member of the San Francisco Black Panther Party, described Huey P. Newton's personality:

> Huey at that time had a dual personality. A lot of people who were saying that you know he changed in his later life, but Huey didn't change. What happened was that, in other words that dual aspect was always in Huey's life. We were all going to Merritt College for example and Huey would take a few classes and then he'd drop out and he didn't have any kind of sustained stay in Merritt College from my knowledge. But what he did do for example, he would break into cars and steal books and then sell them back to the bookstore. You know he would be talking about this, and naturally it's in his autobiography as well. He would go to banks and do quick change on the tellers and he'd make money that way.[19]

According to Brother D., an ex-member of the Black Panther Party of Northern California, one of the discussions centered on the role of armed struggle. Bobby Seale and Huey P. Newton's position was that the armed vanguard went out and brought down repression on the community. The BPP of Northern California did not have the answer to how to successfully pull off a revolution but knew from the lessons of Nazi Germany that premature repression could also crush a people's movement. Bobby Seale saw a revolution as one gigantic shootout:

> A revolution is when the police is on one side of the street and the revolutionaries line up on the other side of the street. Whoever pulls their pieces first and gets off the rounds and survives wins the revolution.[20]

On January 1, 1967, the Black Panther Party for Self-Defense opened its office at 5624 Grove Street in North Oakland, California and started an armed patrol monitoring police. The Oakland Panthers wore uniforms and openly displayed guns. Huey P. Newton, Minister of Defense challenged police over the right of armed self-defense on several occasions.

> By that fall of 1966, the BPP had recruited its first members, mostly from Huey's neighborhood in Oakland, and had set up a storefront office. It says something about the popular mood that folks could be recruited to join a tiny political group whose members had to publicly face off with the police, while carrying guns. In public face-offs, Panthers refused to hand over their guns to the pigs, insisted loudly that "If you shoot at me, or if you try to take this gun, I'm going to shoot back," and all the while lecturing the gathering New Afrikan crowd about their rights. The first time that happened, in front of the BPP's Grove Street storefront office, a dozen men who had been watching immediately joined up.[21]

The BPP of Northern California felt it was adventurous to be openly carrying guns. They felt it led to premature confrontations with the police and unnecessary repression. But the Oakland Panthers continued to grow. They began to get public attention.

While this appeared revolutionary, the BPP of Northern California felt it was romantic and would bring a pre-mature repression of the military-police complex against the party before it would be able to build a cadre from the masses.

The question of "underground" was the question of whether use of "public military confrontation"—which RAM felt the movement was not prepared for vs. the discrete "behind the scenes, armed self-defense" counter-attacks which the movement had used for years in the south as well as in the north would be successful.

In his essay, "The Correct Handling of a Revolution: July 20, 1967," Huey responded to RAM's criticism that the BPP should not use armed self-defense openly.

> A vanguard party is never underground in the beginning of its existence; that would limit its effectiveness and educational goals. How can you teach people if the people do not know and respect you. The party must exist aboveground as long as the dog power structure will allow and hopefully, when the party is forced to go underground, the party's message will already have been put across to the people.[22]

Sundiata Acoli, a previous member of the BPP, also a political prisoner and member of the New York 21, in an historical reflection assesses mistakes of the BPP.

> "Combined Above and Underground: This was the most serious structural flaw in the BPP Party members who functioned openly in BPP offices, or organized openly in the community, by day they might very well have been the same people who carried out armed operations at night. This provided the police with a convenient excuse to make raids on any and all BPP offices, or members homes, under the pretext that they were looking for suspects, fugitives, weapons, and or explosives. It also sucked the BPP into taking the unwinnable position of making stationary defenses of BPP offices. There should have been a clear separation between the aboveground Party and the underground apparatus. Also small military forces should never adopt, as a general tactic, the position of making stationary defenses of offices, homes, buildings, etc."[23]

The Revolutionary Action Movement had a military alliance with the Deacons for Defense, which had been in existence since 1965. Because of the nature of the U. S. government's plan to destroy the movement, the practical aspects of this alliance remained "secret" within the movement, "known to those who were involved in it." Due to Huey P. Newton and Bobby Seale being younger politically than the Deacons for Defense, SNCC, OAAU and RAM forces disregarded this "successful military experience" that was passed on from real military confrontations with the Southern police and the KKK. So, the question of building an underground military wing came from east-coast, mid-west and southern RAM organizers working with Malcolm X in his formation of the OAAU; with Robert F. Williams, who organized armed black self-defense groups to fight against the KKK in Monroe, N.C. in 1959–60 and confrontations in South Carolina, Louisiana, Alabama and Mississippi with the Deacons for Self Defense. Much of the public open display of arms position was at the time being purported by the bay area section of the Socialist Workers Party who politically influenced Huey's thinking at the time.[24]

In February 1967, armed Panthers marched into the airport and escorted Mrs. Betty Shabbazz (Malcolm X's widow) to an awaiting car.

> Cleaver conceived of a three-day program for February 1967 that would memorialize Malcolm's assassination and serve also as a forum for the resurrection of the OAAU. Malcolm's widow, Betty Shabbazz, would give her blessing to the idea in a keynote speech on the final day of the program. Thus late in January, Cleaver sent out a call to black organizations in the Bay Area asking them to assist in setting up a steering committee to plan for the memorial. Responding to Cleaver's invitation, several organizations came together to form a temporary coalition known as the Bay Area Grassroots Organizations Planning Committee.[25]

Cleaver's planning committee called for a change of the proposed program for the memorial from a three-day event to an entire week. Mrs. Betty Shabbazz was to given the keynote address on the opening night. The Black Panther Party for Self-Defense was asked to be the honor guard for Mrs. Shabbazz.[26] But, what made the Oakland Panthers famous was their march on the state capital to protest California's gun laws.

The Black Panther Party for Self-Defense in Oakland was in constant conflict with the Black Panther Party in San Francisco and Los Angeles. The conflict escalated when Eldridge Cleaver began to rise in the Oakland hierarchy. Gun battles almost occurred between the branches. The Oakland branch began publishing a paper called the *Black Panther* with Cleaver as editor.

The Oakland Black Panther Party for Self-Defense was different from the other BPP's. It was a public para-military party with no separation of military from political strategy.

Huey agreed with Mao Tse Tung that political power grows out of the barrel of a gun but also believed that according to revolutionary principles the gun was a tool to be used in the strategy of teaching African-Americans their right to armed self defense and it was not an end in itself.

With the BPPSD patrolling police, reading people their constitutional rights agitated the police and politically educated the people. The BPPSD had become an armed agit-propaganda team especially after publishing the Black Panther newspaper.[27]

This was in fact not armed defense but a step further without perhaps its participants realizing it. It was a form of legal armed agit-prop. When we say legal the fact that having armed guns in open display were based on the fact that at the time you could do this in California. In most Northern areas of the United States of North America you could not do this. So the BPP for Self Defense was in it's founding a *legal armed agitational-propaganda unit.* Cleaver secretly joined the BPPSD because it would violate his parole to carry guns. The Black Panther Party for Self Defense achieved national notoriety when on May 2, 1967 the BPP led an "armed" delegation of Panthers on the California capital building to oppose the Muliford Act, a bill then being passed taking away the right to carry guns in public.

The New York Times Wednesday, May 3, 1967 issue reported an article titled "Armed Negroes Enter California Assembly in Gun Bill Protest,"

> Sacramento, California, May 2 (AP)—A group of young Negroes armed with loaded rifles, pistols and shotguns entered the Capitol today and barged into the Assembly chamber during a debate. Members of the group said they represented the Black Panther Party of the Oakland Area and had come to protest a bill restricting the carrying of loaded weapons within city limits. One shouted that the bill had been introduced for the "racist" Oakland Police force.[28]

Cleaver accompanied the Panthers to the state capitol on May 2, 1967, but without a gun in order not to violate his parole. He had with him a signed letter stating he was covering the event as a journalist for *Ramparts* magazine.

The Revolutionary Action Movement viewed this as *"left wing adventurism" which would bring a military response from the state.* The RAM organization began to dissolve its chapters of the BPP and its cadres remained underground or operated through other public organizations.

Huey P. Newton was probably the first organizer since Robert Williams developed a defense guard in Monroe, North Carolina, in 1957 to recruit the black street force or lumpen into a public para-military organization.

What made Huey's para-military agit-prop team different was that Huey developed it into a radical organization with a ten-point program and created uniforms for the Black Panther Party for Self-Defense. The famous black leather jacket and black beret came to symbolize membership in or support of the BPP.

The social composition of the third Black Panther Party was different than the first two developments. The social composition of the Black Panther Party for Self-Defense was made up of the "Lumpen" ex-pimps, stick-up men, dope pushers and students. Huey picked up the gun publicly again.[29] The differences between armed self-defense in the south and armed defense in the north need to be investigated.

By placing the primary focus on fighting police, the essence of class struggle against the capitalist system was lost to the concept of vanguard vs. the police (pigs) developed. But Huey Newton developed revolutionary nationalism to a higher level with the BPP ten-point program. The ten-point program raises the question of power and self-determination of the African-American national community. The Black Panther program advanced the line the African-Americans were a kind of colony, which are oppressed for racist and economic reasons by the U.S. government.

> Although black Americans were widely dispersed rather than compressed into a compact territory, the Panther leaders declared that they were, nevertheless, a "subjugated nation" because of bonds due to their psychological makeup, ghetto language, concentrations in congested inner cities or in rural areas, and in economic status similar to colonial peoples.[30]

The year 1967 was a year of rapid growth for the Black Panther Party for Self-Defense (BPPSD). Its public aggressive armed stance in confronting police concerning police brutality electrified the surrounding African-American community particularly the youth.

> In April 1967 the BPP was asked by the family of Denzil Dowell, a 22 year-old youth who although not armed had

been shot six times in cold blood by Richmond police, to help them investigate the killing. Panthers interviewed witnesses and proved that the official police account was a fabrication. Guarded by twenty armed Panthers, Newton and Seale spoke to a street rally of 150 persons in the Dowell family's Richmond neighborhood. Panthers accompanied the family and other New Afrikan residents to meet with the County Sheriff and District Attorney. Three hundred New Afrikans, some as young as twelve years old, applied to join the BPP that month in Richmond.[31]

SNCC was still the center of the movement in 1967. Over the Labor Day weekend, 1967 in Chicago, the National Conference on New Politics convened. The conference was supposed to create a broad coalition to defeat Lyndon Johnson in 1968 elections. The Chicago meeting brought 2,000 delegates from 300 different groups across the nation. There were 600 black delegates who formed a black caucus. James Forman ideologist for SNCC called on black revolutionaries to become black Marxist-Leninists. This was the first time in the movement in the sixties that a major figure had raised the question of Marxism-Leninism as the movement's ideology.

Over the summer months of 1967, the BPPSD drafted Carmichael to serve as Black Panther field marshal for the eastern half of the United States. The BPPSD began to grow in the bay area and northern California and began to expand as other chapters were established in New Jersey. As the Black Panther Party for Self-defense began to grow in numbers of recruits now limited in its ability to carry guns publicly because of the passing of the "Muliford" gun law, it began to draw the resentment of Oakland police because of its monitoring their activity. Bobby Seale was jailed from August until December 1967 as a result of the May 2nd Sacramento incident.

THE POLICE ATTACK ON HUEY NEWTON

On October 27, 1967 at approximately 4 p.m., Huey P. Newton was wounded in a shoot-out with the police. Newton while driving home with a friend after a night of celebrating his release of parole was pulled over by police. Officer Frey, known for his racial attitude towards African-Americans ordered Newton out of his car and to follow him to the back of the police cruiser. Newton was beaten and in the scuffle shots were discharged and officer Frey was killed, the other officer Herbert Heanes wounded, and Newton wounded.[32]

179

With its two top officers in jail, the Minister of Information, Eldridge Cleaver, led the Black Panther Party for Self Defense. Cleaver steered the party on a new course. He initially built supportive alliances with black nationalists, on the one hand, and white radical organizations on the other, despite a strained relationship between the two camps in this period.[33]

The party now had a dilemma of defending its Minister of Defense who was charged with the murder of a police officer. Building Huey's defense:

> Early in January 1968, Cleaver and Seale, who was now out of prison, flew to Washington, D.C., to talk with Carmichael and to invite him to speak at an upcoming rally for Newton in Oakland. The talks with Carmichael were expanded to include other members in the SNCC hierarchy. The upshot was the establishment of an alliance with SNCC. Carmichael was made Honorary Prime Minister of the Panthers, James Forman, Minister of Foreign Affairs and H. Rap Brown, Minister of Justice.[34]

It so happened that the date secured was February 17, which was Huey P. Newton's birthday, so the rally became a planned birthday celebration for Newton at the Oakland auditorium that was in downtown Oakland across the street from the County Jail where Newton was being held. Seale recalls:

> We brought Stokely out a little early to visit Huey. There was a lot of press coverage, and a lot of people realized that it was time to come out for Huey P. Newton.[35]

The February 17, 1968 Free Huey rally was a success. Four thousand people crowded the auditorium. Stokely Carmichael, James Forman and H. Rap Brown of SNCC spoke.

> ...we decided that if they (SNCC leadership) all accepted the ten-point platform and program, we'd make Stokely Carmichael the Honorary Prime Minister, James Forman the Minister of Foreign Affairs, and brother Rap Brown the Minister of Justice of the Black Panther Party. We thought that would give us a good group of black revolutionary leaders to unify the black liberation struggle across the country.[36]

At the rally the SNCC-Panther alliance was announced. Cleaver for whatever reason called the alliance a merger, which was the beginning of tedious relations.

The SNCC-Panther alliance did not last long. SNCC was restructured at a June 1968 conference at which time the proposal for accepting the BPPSD ten-point program was voted down. By mid-July, H. Rap Brown and James Forman resigned their posts in the party. Stokely Carmichael continued his post in the party and was eventually expelled from SNCC. The Panther Party leadership feared Forman as a tactician.

The New York Times, Monday, October 7, 1968 reported that in a rift between members of the Black Panther Party and SNCC, Black Panther members walked into James Forman's office on Fifth Avenue in New York in July. The report, which cites its source coming from Federal authorities, stated one of the Panthers pulled out a pistol and put it into Forman's mouth squeezing the trigger several times. Forman in his book *The Making of Black Revolutionaries* states this report was a complete fabrication. He says while relations between the organizations sometimes came to near gun play this incident never occurred. He called Cleaver describing the need to deny the story but the issue was never resolved. What is important to record is that the mis-information campaign of the F.B.I.'s COINTELPRO program helped dissolve the SNCC-BPP alliance.[37]

The SNCC central committee voted to terminate their alliance with the Panthers a few weeks after the incident. In an interview with Don Stone of SNCC, he said that after the incident with Forman he traveled to Oakland, armed and went to Cleaver's apartment. In a meeting with Cleaver, he told Cleaver that he and others in SNCC had not been intimidated by the KKK and were not intimidated by the Panthers. He indicated that if Forman and other SNCC members were harmed by the BPPSD that SNCC would retaliate. Stone feels that Cleaver realized the implications of the meeting and violence between the two groups was alleviated.[38]

RAM in 1968 criticized the emerging Black Panther Party, for left wing adventurism. RAM stated that the open display of guns was violating the basic principles of people's secrecy. In order for the people's forces to be successful they must have the element of surprise. Huey disagreed with RAM's analysis. In response to the criticism raised against the BPPSD by the west coast branch of the Revolutionary Action Movement (RAM), Newton wrote an essay titled "The Correct Handling of the Revolution." The west coast branch of RAM had criticized the BPPSD for their above ground action—openly displaying weapons and talking about the necessity for the community to arm itself for its own defense. RAM said that they were underground, and saw this was not the correct way to handle a revolution.[39]

The BPPSD hastened to transform the organization for the defense of Newton. It adopted an increasingly contentious position regarding governmental and law enforcement authorities.[40]

For an extended period of time the party would utilize its coalition with white leftists, valued for their administrative machinery and know how for generating publicity and funds.

According to JoNina Abron in a letter to Muhammad Ahmad, the BPP was a revolutionary nationalist organization, dedicated to fighting racism and capitalism. Consequently, Black Panthers worked with individuals and groups of all races and nationalities that shared the party's objectives.[41] To secure masses of demonstrators for Newton's court appearances and to publicize the case in the black community, Panthers conceived the idea that a sound truck would be most helpful. In November of 1967 the organizers of the predominately white Peace and Freedom Party (PFP) appealed to the BPP. According to a former Panther, the eventual coalition with the PFP was the most successful coalition to be established after the imprisonment of Newton. To assist in publicizing the Newton case and the Panther program nationally and abroad, the BPP used a number of available young militants, both black and white. They were used to print, write, and distribute thousands of leaflets, posters, buttons, and other materials, combined with the use of printing equipment and sound trucks. Rallies and speaking tours were tactics used by the BPP in the Free Huey campaign. The scope of this strategy extended for about one year, due to the fact that the prosecution had only reached its first stage, when a jury sent Newton to prison for a non-capital offense or "voluntary manslaughter," on September 8, 1968. Dissension erupted in the Oakland headquarters, after the verdict and subsequent appeal that resulted in a Seale-Hilliard union that commenced a purging of the ranks and at the same time attempted to establish a new course and programs.

From the time of his indictment on murder and other charges, on November 13, 1967, a white lawyer named Charles Garry was hired by the Panthers to represent Newton. A white, anarchist-oriented youth headed one of the first local groups organized to solicit legal defense funds for Newton.[42]

According to Earl Anthony, it was Eldridge's idea to use the Peace and Freedom Party sound truck that first brought about contact between the two groups on December 22, 1967.[43]

After getting out of jail Bobby Seale joined Eldridge Cleaver in forming a coalition with the Peace and Freedom Party in an effort to utilize their resources and to work in their communities in an effort to build a massive defense for Huey Newton, the imprisoned Minister of Defense of the Black Panther Party. Remembering that Newton had always taught that the role of white people should be to work to end racism in their own community; Seale along with Cleaver secured $3,000 for the Free Huey Movement encouraging African-Americans to register to vote as Peace and Freedom Party members. Seale and Cleaver after agreeing to the coalition went to the jail where Newton was being held and got his approval.

Seale recalled:

> We had a number of rallies in the black community, in Hunter's Point, the Fillmore and West Oakland, with the Peace and Freedom Party supplying sound and technical equipment which the Black Panther Party did not, at that time, have at all. With the $3,000, we were able to pay a fair retainer to Charles R. Garry for Huey's defense. In the white community as well as the black, we initiated a broad campaign for increased concern about, the problems of the black community, centered around our leader and Minister of Defense, brother Huey P. Newton.[44]

An editorial in *The Black Panther* of March 16, 1968, explained the party leaders' motives in working with whites, especially the "white radicals" who created the Peace and Freedom Party. With Newton's life at stake, the party saw no excuse for indulging egos, the paper declared, and from the moment of Newton's arrest, the leaders "began a frantic search for building a broad base of support to set him free." In the elections held in November 1968, the PFP had a shortage of signatures to get on the California ballot to propagate its opposition to American military intervention in Vietnam. In exchange for the additional signatures that were essential by a January 1968 deadline that the Panthers could and did procure, the PFP agreed to permit the BPP use of its organization facilities in the Newton defense campaign. However, it was when Cleaver became the

PFP candidate for President of the United States on the ballot in California and other states, that the Newton case received nationwide publicity. The party presented Newton, who was imprisoned at the time, as a contender for the U. S. Congress from the Seventeenth District (Oakland), and Bobby Seale for the California Assembly from the Seventeenth Assembly District (Berkeley); Kathleen Cleaver ran for U. S. Congress in San Francisco. Militant African-Americans challenged the Panthers that they were relying on the "ballot more than the bullet." Panther leaders assured them that the strategy was to help Newton and the organization, and not to win political office in a society that consistently alienated African-Americans.[45]

Party efforts in the 1968 local primaries drew Newton and Seale over 25,000 votes a piece, qualifying them for the general election.

Police raided Cleaver's apartment in January. The Seale's were arrested in their apartment early one morning in February, with the police using the excuse that they were looking for weapons. The police seemed like they were attempting to exhaust the funds raised by the Black Panther Party. It was in this period; on February 28, 1968 after the Newton birthday rally that Cleaver's *Soul On Ice* was published. As events were developing, these leaders were becoming national celebrities.

> Following the raid in the Cleaver and Seale apartment, Newton issued "Executive Mandate 3" on March 1st, ordering all members "to acquire guns" to be able to defend their homes or face expulsion if they failed. Seale recommended that each home have "a shotgun, a .357 magnum, and a .38 pistol."[46]

Differences over strategy, tactics and primary activity began to emerge within the Black Panther Party leadership in early 1968. Eldridge Cleaver "Papa Rage," had a militarist approach to building the party and encouraged, armed adventurism activity among the BPP membership while Bobby Seale, Huey Newton and David Hilliard thought the party should place emphasis on what became known as survival programs.

On April 4, 1968, Dr. Martin Luther King, Jr., was assassinated in Memphis, Tennessee. African-Americans vented their anger spontaneously erupting in urban rebellions in over 100 cities north as well as south. The Black Panther Party for Self Defense working in conjunction with the Oakland police circulated throughout the

Oakland African-American community pleading with African-Americans to remain calm. The Oakland community did not explode.

David Hilliard in *This Side of Glory* describes how enraged and agitated Eldridge Cleaver became over Dr. King's assassination. Feeling that he and the BPP had to prove they were the vanguard, he proposed an ambush of the police on April 6, 1968.

> We got to do something...we got to prove we're the vanguard. Everybody's doing something around the country..."The brothers and sisters are moving and the party's not with them; we must sign our name to what's going on...It's time to intensify the struggle...Now's the time to show people the correct way to do this.[47]

After internal discussion and debate a vote was taken by most Panthers to put Cleaver's plan into action.

On the night of April 6, 1968, Eldridge Cleaver, David Hilliard, John Scott of San Francisco, Wendell Wade and Bobby Hutton were cruising around with two other Panthers cars carrying ten more Panthers following in a caravan. Cleaver halted his car and got out to relieve himself in the street. An approaching police car noticed a ducking figure behind the parked Panther car crouched. The police fired shots at the Panthers but the stories vary. The police opened a barrage of gunshots at the Panthers, and Eldridge Cleaver and Bobby Hutton were held up in a walk in basement under a frame house at 1218 E. 28th Street. The shootout began at 9:07 p.m. and lasted until 10:30 p.m. The other Panthers were quickly rounded up as they scattered; Hilliard made it as far as a bedroom of the house next door, but the residents turned him in.[48]

Caught by surprise the Panthers were scattered. A shootout occurred for 90 minutes between Cleaver, Hutton and the police. Essentially the house began to catch fire as a result of the police volleys.

Cleaver was struck in the chest by a tear gas canister. Cleaver stripped naked to see where he was wounded.[49] Cleaver advised Bobby Hutton to also strip naked and when the two of them walked out of the house naked the police would be shocked and might not kill them. Bobby Hutton is said to have been too shy or had too much pride to strip fully naked. He stripped down bare chest to his waist still wearing his pants. The police tear-gassing of the house forced Cleaver and "Lil" Bobby Hutton out of the house. The police told Bobby Hutton who was stripped down to his waist to run and shot him in the back as he ran. Cleaver was arrested and charged with violation of parole. The April 6th incident further propelled the Black Panther Party into the news media. Many celebrities came in the open to support the BPP. The BPP gained mass support in Northern California and its influence soon spread throughout the state of California and across the country. Eldridge Cleaver was released from prison on $50,000 bail on June 12, 1968, six days after the assassination of Robert Kennedy (John Kennedy's brother was a leading Presidential candidate in the Democratic Party primary). Cleaver being the presidential candidate of the PFP became a cause.[50]

GROWTH INTO A NATIONAL ORGANIZATION

The Black Panther Party for Self-Defense (Oakland) grew rapidly. Huey P. Newton said "it grew much too rapidly."[51] It grew from approximately 31 members as of May 2, 1967 to approximately 5,000 members by December 1968. By the end of 1969 dropping the title for Self-Defense, the Black Panther Party had approximately 10,000 members.

By the summer of 1969, the BPP was a national organization with over 32 chapters and branches throughout the United States.[52]

According to Huey P. Newton, the Black Panther Party in the 1967–1968 period had a membership of 10,000 with 50,000 supporters and at the time of his trial for the murder of a prostitute, estimated membership of the BPP was 200.[53]

The Black Panther Party emerged in the latter '60s as clearly the largest public African-American revolutionary organization. By estimates of previous members it was estimated that 30,000 African-Americans had joined the BPP between 1966 and 1978 when it closed it's doors.[54]

The Black Panther Party began to expand into a national organization in April 1968, when the national headquarters in Oakland began granting official recognition to local Black Panther Party chapters around the country. During the spring of 1968, Bobby Seale and David Hilliard, representing the central committee of the BPP, began granting charters to groups calling themselves Black Panthers in various cities. The groups certified as Black Panther Party chapters had to agree to meet qualifications established by the national office. Members who wanted to lead new chapters were required to come to Panther national headquarters in Oakland for six weeks training.

Potential Panther leaders came to Oakland, sold *The Black Panther* (the Black Panther Party newspaper), memorized the rules and platform of the Party and attended political education classes. From January to June 1968, a dozen new Panther chapters were established throughout the nation. By April 1968, the Black Panther Party had chapters in Los Angeles, New York, Chicago and Seattle. In the month of June, alone a thousand new members were recruited in the party.

According to U. S. government accounts the Black Panther Party grew from October 15, 1966 as a local organization to a national organization of from 1,500 to 2,000 members scattered in 25 chapters across the country in 1968. It (the U. S. Government) estimates the BPP reached its peak in membership by December of 1968.[55]

Most of the BPP chapters were established after January 1, 1968. The Black Panther Party at one time or another since its founding, October 15, 1966 until early 1971, had official chapters in at least 61 cities in 26 states and in the District of Columbia.

Police reports indicate fifteen BPP chapters were organized in 1968, thirteen more in 1969; giving twenty more chapters in 1969 and ten chapters in 1970. Eight chapters became defunct in 1969 and six in 1970. According to local law enforcement agencies there were 77 cities in 32 states where the Black Panther Party was reported to have been active.[56] Most of the chapters functioned in large urban centers outside of the South. By winter of 1970, there was Black Panther activity in 35 cities in 19 states and the District of Columbia. This activity was conducted under the supervision of 13 Black Panther chapters and five branches, 20 National Committees to Combat Fascism and two community information centers.[57]

Party members were not encouraged to work but to live in Panther collectives, working full-time for the Party (BPP), receiving revenue from sales of the party newspapers. As the party expanded so did their efforts to transform the party from an organization protesting police brutality into a political organization.

Throughout its development the Black Panther Party attempted to further politically develop its membership, sophisticate its organization and refine its program.

The Black Panther Party was based on collective leadership. By April of 1968 it had established a national central committee of eleven, 10 men and 1 woman, which later expanded to 13, 12 men and 1 woman. The method of making policy in the BPP prior to April of 1968 was democratically decided by a vote of Panther Party membership in the Oakland area, not exceeding 50.

The majority of Panthers were male and between the ages of sixteen and twenty-five.[58]

There was a six-week political education for party members divided into three parts: community, leadership, and cadre.

> The National Headquarters (Oakland) created a standard format, under the direction of George Murray, minister of education and sent weekly lessons to chapters. Party members read books such as Franz Fanon's *Wretched of the Earth*, Mao Tse Tung's *Little Red Book (Quotations of Chairman Mao Tse Tung)*, *The Autobiography of Malcolm X* and Kwame Nkrumah's *I Speak of Freedom*.[59]

At times in political education classes' members of the BPP would have to read a paragraph of a document and explain it.

In the initiation process Party members had to read and discuss material in local newspapers and in the Black Panther newspaper. They also had to memorize the Ten-point program and party rules. Members were encouraged to write essays, reports and poetry and to contribute to the Party's newspaper. New members also learned the duties of the Panther positions.

> Captains were the highest-ranking officers of rank-and-file membership. They linked the ministries and foot soldiers; then negotiated on behalf of both groups. New recruits had to take a pass/fail test. The new recruits were then sectioned into cadres (five to six members), which in many ways functioned like extended families. Cadres studied and worked together and watched each other's backs. Many cadres would eventually live together in the same apartment or house. Some of the volunteer duties that Panthers performed included cleaning up, security, officer of the day, secretarial, distribution and sale of newspapers, cooking, answering phones, enlisting donations, distributing, announcing community activities, passing out leaflets and posters, transportation, sales of buttons and posters.[60]

In the final stage of the initiation process Panthers were taught respect for weapons, how to clean and assemble artillery, technical and military training. In some cases, Panthers were secret members in order to safeguard their personal employment.

In the initial period, the BPP operated as a three-tiered structure to accommodate its rapid expansion.

> At the highest level, the party's governing body, the Central Committee, comprised BPP founders Huey P. Newton as Minister of Defense and Bobby Seale as Chairman along with Minister of Information Eldridge Cleaver, Deputy Minister of Information Frank Jones, and Chief of Staff David Hilliard. The Central Committee was always based at national headquarters in the Bay area. The intermediate level was formed by the state regional chapters such as Illinois, Maryland, and New York. The leaders of these chapters were chosen or if self-selected, confirmed by Chairman Seale or a representative of national headquarters. Local franchises represented the BPP at the ground level.[61]

The rank-and-file members would report to branch or chapter leaders depending on Party organization development in a specific geographic area.

Assata Shakur describes the strength and weakness of the BPP political education program.

There were three different political education classes: Community classes, classes for BPP cadre and PE classes for Panther leadership.[62] Shakur says that the BPP had no systematic approach to political education and she feels this was the main reason many Party members underestimated the need to unite with other black organizations and to struggle around various community issues. Assata felt the party had some of the most politically conscious sisters and brothers but failed to spread that consciousness to the general cadre and failed to teach them organizing and mobilizing techniques.

Shakur analyzed two major points that hindered this. She, Newton and others said that the Party grew too fast and almost from its inception, the BPP was under attack from the U. S. government. These two factors did not allow the BPP enough time to develop a step-by-step approach to Party building and consolidation of mass support.

> Assata says, "I am convinced that a systematic program for political education, ranging from the simplest to the highest level, is imperative for any successful organization or movement for Black Liberation in this country.[63]

The party grew tremendously in 1968. First with its initial alliance with SNCC, chapters were established and a national framework for a national organization was created. Then through the network and grapevine of various left or Marxist groups who saw the BPP as a positive development; the influence of the BPP grew significantly among African-American College students particularly on white college campuses.

THE LOS ANGELES CHAPTER OF THE BPP:

The Los Angeles chapter of the Black Panther Party was established by early march, 1968 under the initial leadership of Bunchy Apprentice Carter. Starting with an initial cadre of 20 the L. A. Chapter grew to approximately 200 and during the summer of 1968 its' membership grew to over four hundred. Bunchy Carter was appointed Deputy Minister of Defense for Southern California of the BPP.[64]

As early as mid-March or early April 1968 antagonisms between the L. A. Chapter of the Black Panther Party and Ron Karenga's U. S. (United Slaves) organization had emerged including minor shootouts. Since the release of F.B.I. COINTELPRO documents it has been revealed that the F.B.I. and/or police agents who served as agent provocateurs infiltrated both groups. Earl Anthony an F.B.I. informant and agent provocateur in the BPP has documented some of his treacherous activity in his book *Spitting In The Wind*. At the height of its development the L. A. Chapter of the Black Panther Party using James Forman's 10 by 10 by 10 plan, could sell 6,000 *Black Panther* newspapers in three days.[65]

Though 1968 was the year of national expansion of the BPP, by 1969 the BPP was receiving repression from police seemingly across the country. According to Abdul Qahhar, the BPP sold 30,000 copies of the Black Panther newspaper on a weekly basis in Chicago and 35,000 copies a week in New York.[66]

According to Rashad Byrdsong, many Panthers were committing offenses to secure means of survival because revenues from the newspaper were not enough for an income.[67]

THE FOUNDING OF THE NEW YORK CHAPTER

According to Sundiata Acoli, the Black Panther Party was organized in New York in the summer of 1968:

> In the summer of '68, David Brothers established a BPP branch in Brooklyn, New York and a few months later Lumumba Shakur set up a branch in Harlem, New York.[68]

Cleaver arrived first in the New York City area on October 11, 1968, and he gave two speeches on the same day.

In the afternoon, he was driven with a Panther escort to a little Christian Brothers men's liberal arts school in New Rochelle called Iona College. While he was there local police, a state police investigator, and an FBI agent James Gorgan, all of who later described the events to the Internal Security Subcommittee for the Senate Judiciary Committee, headed by conservative James O. Eastland of Mississippi, attended his speech.[69] Several cadre of the New York Chapter of the second Black Panther Party (Oakland) came out of high school struggles waged by African-American students. Students like Lumumba Shakur, Zayd Malik Shakur, Matula Shakur and Bila Sunni Ali were members of the African-American Student Association that had close contact with the African-American Teachers Association. The African-American Teachers Association had been organized around the defense of Herman Ferguson (RAM) Revolutionary Action Movement member framed in the infamous 1967 Queens "17" Assassination plot. Lumumba Shakur had experienced gang fighting in Philly, New York City, and Atlantic City. In all the cities, he felt the phenomenon was the same, that is, the animosity (alienation) and hostility of African-Americans, created by hundreds of years of white repression were directed against each other instead of against the system that created the repression and hostilities.[70] He also felt:

> If the street gang brothers and sisters were ever politicized to the point where they knew who their real enemy was, the American system would be in danger of collapse.[71]

The young students had waged a yearlong battle in the New York public school system for the incorporation of African-American history in the curriculum. As RAM ceased agitational activity, the young students either joined the Republic of New Africa or the efforts to rebuild the Black Panther Party in the New York area. The New York chapter of the BPP became one of the largest if not the largest chapter of the Black Panther Party.

> Though the membership of the New York City chapter of the Black Panther Party fluctuated at times, its membership could be as high as five hundred members.[72]

There were ideological differences between the Oakland BPP and the New York BPP from the beginning. The New York BPP tended not to see the contradictions between them and cultural nationalists as contradictory and felt the two positions could be synthesized. Also there were various ideological positions held by members of the New York BPP that did not surface until 1971.

In Cleo Silver's interview, she states that she was recruited out of the health workers and hospital workers movement in New York. When Eldridge Cleaver initiated the line that the lumpen proletariat was the vanguard of the black revolution, Cleo held an internal meeting with Zaid Shakur and Lumumba Shakur of the New York BPP and said she disagreed that the lumpen proletariat was the vanguard. She raised the question inside the BPP in 1968 that the black working class was the vanguard of the black revolution. They were sympathetic to her position, but felt that impending repression was going to occur and did not feel it was timely that they engage in internal ideological debate. They took her to the eastside of Harlem for her to work with the Young Lords Party who at the time was doing work with workers. She joined the Young Lords Party and eventually helped organize the Revolutionary Health Workers Union Movement, eventually going to Detroit and joining the League of Revolutionary Black Workers working in the plants as an industrial worker.[73]

Many demonstrations were held across the country as the "Free Huey" movement grew. On July 1968 more than 6,000 protestors came out in support of Huey Newton on the steps of the Almeda County Courthouse in Oakland. The Brown Berets (Mexican-American) organization patterning itself after the BPP made their first public appearance. Later an Asian American organization called the Red Guards, a Puerto Rican organization called the Young Lords party and a poor white American group called the Young Patriots and the White Panther Party would appear. A mass movement built momentum to free Huey Newton in 1968. Panthers particularly on the West Coast were sporadically arrested or assassinated by police in a variety of circumstances. In its rapid growth process the BPP exhausted it's alliance with SNCC, between June-July, 1968, developed hostile relations with Ron Karenga's US (United Slaves) organization and because of its alliance with the mainly all-white Peace and Freedom Party and Students for a Democratic Society (SDS) alienated a good portion of the African-American community. Eldridge Cleaver was nominated presidential candidate for the PFP on August 3, 1968. Cleaver received 36,000 votes for president as the

Peace and Freedom Party candidate in 1968.[74] Bobby Seale, chairman of the BPP and Captain David Hilliard spoke to 5,000 antiwar anti-establishment demonstrators at the National Democratic Convention. The demonstrators were eventually attacked by the Chicago police in what is on record as a "police riot," Bobby Seale was eventually indicted for conspiracy to riot along with seven others who were known as the Chicago Eight. On August 28, 1968 Stokely Carmichael, prime minister of the BPP was expelled from SNCC (the Student Non-Violent Coordinating Committee). In September of 1968, George Murray who was Minister of Culture of the BPP was expelled as a teacher at San Francisco State College. The Black Students Union of SFSC called a campus wide strike.

On September 8–12, 1968, Newton was convicted of voluntary manslaughter. This was considered a compromise for the BPP because it was felt that Huey would have gotten the electric chair had he been found guilty of murder. The BPP felt the verdict was a tactical temporary victory and that the mass mobilization techniques had been effective. The University of California (Berkeley) offered Eldridge Cleaver a non-credit lectureship. Governor Ronald Reagan opposed his hiring and sought to cut off UC (Berkeley's) funds if Cleaver was not fired. UC students responded by staging a sit-in at the administration building. On September 28, 1968, Huey P. Newton was sentenced to 2 to 15 years in state prison. Drunken Oakland police shot up the Panther office. Cleaver was ordered to return to jail and his parole revoked in 60 days.[75]

David Hilliard, Chief of Staff, took command of the BPP with Newton's absence. On October 9, 1968, Eldridge Cleaver began his first lecture on the UC Berkeley campus. He led approximately 5,000 students in a chorus of "Fuck Ronald Reagan" on the steps of Sproul Hall. On November 6th students and some staff at San Francisco State College began a major strike.

On November 24th Eldridge Cleaver disappeared three days before he was scheduled to turn himself in to serve the remainder of the thirteen-year sentence for a 1958 rape conviction. Having fled the United States in 1968 to avoid prosecution for the April 26 shootout he secretly traveled by way of Canada to Cuba where he came into conflict with Cuban authorities about his supposedly sexual behavior. At the bequest of the Cubans, the Algerians gave Cleaver exile status where he established the international section of the

BPP. Cleaver described its main tasks as: internationally publicizing the Panther "struggle"; making alliances with other movements; receiving assistance from other groups; and laying proposals before the U.N. in the future.[76] Carmichael and his faction within the Panthers were purged from the party in 1969.

Panthers on the East Coast (New York) were involved in the Ocean-Hill Brownsville alternative quality education movement to establish a community-controlled school. They provided some of the foot soldiers, demonstrators and security for the parents and students.[77]

On the West Coast, on December 4, 1968, more than five hundred members of the community went to San Francisco State campus to support the strikers. Confrontation between strikers and police resulted in a number of arrests. Throughout 1968 Panther offices were raided and Panthers arrested.

From a very anarchistic and adventurous beginning the national leadership led by Huey Newton and Bobby Seale and David Hilliard in 1969 began to develop a disciplined organization.

In 1969, 348 Black Panther Party members were arrested for a series of offenses. This phenomenon escalated to such a degree that chairman Bobby Seale began reorganizing the party. There was a general reorganization of the BPP, both nationally and locally in 1968 and 1969. In the January 4, 1969 issue of the *Black Panther*, 26 rules of the Black Panther Party drafted by Bobby Seale appeared along with a press conference statement by the central committee of the BPP stating that the BPP was going to purge provocateur agents, kooks and avaricious fools who had joined the party.

In this period the BPP engaged in an organizational and ideological purge.[78] Not only did the BPP undergo a purge of agent provocateurs but also underwent an ideological purge. There were standing differences between Carmichael, who advocated an all class united front of African-Americans and Pan Africanism and Cleaver who advocated a multi-cultural unity of various allies, red, black, brown, yellow and white emphasizing class struggle against the capitalist class and the black petty bourgeoisie and cultural nationalist. The debate came out into the open at a Pan African Festival held in Algeria in 1969. Cleaver, the Panther Minister of Information at that time still held considerable weight on the BPP national central committee. The Panther 26 rules of discipline were published in the

Black Panther newspaper, January 4, 1969.

The Party's decision to close ranks further contributed to the increased opportunities for women to fill nontraditional female roles. Party leaders in January 1969 prohibited infiltration by police informants. Consequently, a greater reliance was placed upon the current membership rather than new recruits to implement Party programs. Concurrently, the national leadership initiated the expulsion of suspected police informers and insubordinate Party members.

During this period of organization flux, women in the party emerged as national and local party members.[79]

Beginning in late 1968 and early 1969, community services programs, such as the free breakfast for children and free health clinic projects as well as liberation schools and community political education classes, were implemented nationally (with varying degrees of success). Prior to initiating the official "survival" programs, Panther chapters had already been involved in local community struggles for decent housing, welfare rights, citizens' police review panels, black history classes, and traffic lights on dangerous intersections in African-American neighborhoods.

The development of an overt and public dialogue within the Party about male chauvinism also intensified in late 1968 and continued throughout 1969. Each of these events influenced the ideological and practical development of the BPP.

In January of 1969, the BPP started its most successful survival program, the Free Breakfast for Children Program. The FBCP was designed for poor children to give them breakfast before attending school. It was first initiated at St. Augustine's Church in Oakland. Huey P. Newton and Bobby Seale said the program followed the BPP's principles that were to "serve the people." While the Panthers on the East Coast worked with political and cultural nationalists, on the West Coast tensions between them then developed into assassinations. On January 17, 1969 in a conflict over who was going to be chosen as Black Studies Director at UCLA, two Panthers were ambushed and shot to death by two members of Ron Karenga's US (United Slaves) organization. John Huggins and Alprentice "Bunchy" Carter, key figures in the Los Angeles BPP were those gunned down.[80]

On February 13, 1969, in Berkeley, 37 student strikers were arrested in the UCLA Berkeley third world strike. On March 14, 1969 in Los Angeles following a student strike meeting at Victory

Baptist Church, an altercation ensued in the parking lot between Panthers and members of the US organization. Ronald Freeman, a Panther was wounded in the chest and groin. BPP members, Bobby Seale and Massi Hewitt toured Scandinavian countries, Denmark, Norway, Sweden and Finland. They established BPP support committees. On April 1, 1969, twenty-one key members of the New York BPP were arrested for conspiring to blow up New York subways and other supposedly targets. On April 10, 1969, New York high school students held a demonstration at Long Island City High School to demand freedom for the Panther Twenty-One.

Carmichael and wife, South African singer, Miriam Makeba moved to Conakry Guinea. Carmichael announced that this move to Guinea was to study with Kwame Nkrumah (deposed president of Ghana) and Sekou Toure, President of Guinea.

Difference in leadership style and ideology, which had been suppressed in efforts to build support for Huey Newton's defense, began to surface after Newton was convicted of manslaughter in September of 1968 for the October 1967 shoot out. The first major difference was Eldridge Cleaver's insistence of creating armed confrontations with the police that resulted in the April 6, 1968 killing of Bobby Hutton.

In 1969, the exiled Cleaver called Panthers to hold and defend their offices. Cleaver resurfaced in April 1969 in Algiers, Algeria. Numerous shootouts occurred with many Panthers going to jail. This strategy also targeted the Party for destruction because the police and F.B.I. through informants, agents, and electronic surveillance were aware of most of the planning of these extra legal activities before they occurred. Huey Newton from prison was stressing more emphasis on service programs which he called survival programs. Cleaver also alienated the African-American nationalist community because he was seeking monetary resources from the white left needed for Newton's defense. Newton seemed to have temporarily tolerated this. Differences between Carmichael and Cleaver surfaced by 1969 but the two had been battling inside the BPP since Carmichael was drafted as Prime Minister of the BPP in 1968. Carmichael saw the need for an all-class African-American united front before concentrating on efforts to solidify alliances with the Euro-American left.

Carmichael and his faction had been under attack for having

a Pan-African cultural nationalist line in the Party. His faction was being purged within the Party. Carmichael and Cleaver met at the Pan African Cultural Arts Festival held in Algeria with Cleaver favoring an Alliance of various ethnic groups inside the U.S., which Fred Hampton Chairman of the Illinois BPP called the "Rainbow Coalition."

Carmichael denounced the BPP for its concentration of building alliances with the white left. Thirteen members of the New York Black Panther Party were purged with their names published in *The Black Panther* on April 27, 1969. The Free Breakfast program proved to be a success with thousands of children being fed throughout the Bay area.

On May 1, 1969, more than 1,000 people participated in a mass "Free Huey" rally at San Francisco Federal Court. On May 4, 1969, the New Jersey Black Panther Party chapter expelled nineteen members. "Free Huey" rallies were held in twenty major cities at U. S. Federal District courts.[81] On May 21st in New Haven, Connecticut, Panther Alex Rackley was viciously tortured and murdered by Panthers who suspected him of being an agent. Agent jacketing spreading rumors that key Panther members of the party were police agents was one of the tactics that police agents used to destroy the party. This was an effective tool of the F.B.I.'s C.O.I.N.T.E.L.P.R.O. program. Panther George Sams eventually pleaded guilty to a second-degree murder charge. The New Haven, Connecticut, Panther office was raided by police and Panthers were arrested on conspiracy to commit murder on May 22nd.[82] On May 23, 1969, in San Diego, California, US organization members murdered Panther, John Savage.[83] On June 4th Detroit police raided the BPP office, looking for suspects in the New Haven murder of Alex Rackley. Twenty thousand dollars worth of damage was done to the office and bail was set at $4,000 each. Charges on all Panthers arrested were dropped.[84] On June 5, 1969 in Denver, Colorado, Roy Hithe and Landon Williams were arrested with no bail and charged with conspiracy in connection with the New York 21 and Connecticut 8 as well as unlawful flight to avoid prosecution.[85] On June 6, 1969, in Salt Lake City, Missouri, Lonnie McLucas was arrested in connection with the New Haven murder.[86] On June 7th the Chicago, Illinois BPP office was raided in search of Panther member George Sams. Eight Panthers were arrested and charged with harboring a fugitive. Bail was set at

$1,000 each member; eventually all charges were dropped.[87] On June 15, 1969 a Panther "Free Health Clinic" in Berkeley, California opened. On June 21st Panther William Brent hijacked a plane to Cuba.[88] Fred Hampton, a young Chicago Black Panther leader had signed a unity pact with the Blackstone Rangers (Chicago's largest street gang), poor whites and SDS chapters in the summer of 1969. This coalition was called the Rainbow Coalition.[89]

On July 2, 1969 a Panther liberation school opened in San Francisco. In New Haven, Connecticut on July 17th, the BPP initiated lead poisoning testing because the state had the worst lead poisoning record in the country. The BPP convened a "United Front Against Fascism" conference in Oakland, California July 18, 1969 to galvanize supporters from all communities to work for community control of police. A Panther liberation school with ninety children opened in Queens, New York. On July 22nd Eldridge Cleaver officially opened the Afro-American Information Center in Algiers, Algeria. A delegation of Panthers joined him in attending the twelve-day Pan-African Cultural Festival. The international section of the Black Panther Party was established.[90] The BPP office in Chicago was raided on July 31, 1969. Police destroyed food and took five hundred dollars in cash. Pete Hayman, a Panther was charged with attempted murder and was beaten so severely that he had to be hospitalized.[91] On August 2nd, the police raided the BPP office in Richmond, California.[92] In San Diego, Panther Sylvester Bell was shot and killed by US members on August 15, 1969.[93] On August 16th, Kansas City, Indiana, Staten Island and Philadelphia BPP chapters expelled members.[94] On August 19th Bobby Seale was arrested in Berkeley after leaving the wedding of Masi Hewitt and Shirley Neely. He was taken to San Francisco and charged with initiating the riots at the 1968 Democratic Party National Convention in Chicago and the New Haven murder of Alex Rackley.[95] On August 20th Bobby Seale was released on twenty-five thousand dollar bond, rearrested and secretly extradited to stand trial in Chicago.[96] In Los Angeles Panther Nathaniel Clark was murdered on September 12, 1969.

In a speech on September 22, 1969, during a trip to North Korea, Cleaver acknowledged that his comrades at home did not necessarily share his view on the need for immediate assumption of armed hostilities in the United States.[97]

Police and F.B.I. raided the Philadelphia BPP office on September 24th. The FBI took files, records and petitions for community control of police. On October 4, 1969, the Chicago BPP office was raided and seven Panthers were charged with attempted murder. Bail ranged from $10,000 to $20,000 each.[98]

In October, Bobby Seale went to trial on the Chicago Eight case. The Los Angeles metro squad in broad daylight murdered Panther Walter "toute" Pope on October 18th as he dropped off BPP newspapers at a store. On November 6th, the Seattle, Washington BPP chapter opened a free medical clinic.[99] In November 1969, at a Vietnam Mobilization Day rally in San Francisco Golden Gate Park, David Hilliard Chief of Staff of the BPP spoke and in his remarks attacked President Richard Nixon. He was arrested two weeks later for threatening the life of the President.

On November 12th in Los Angeles, police raided the BPP office while the BPP was holding a community meeting with leaders and doctors and nurses to establish a Bunchy Carter Free Medical Clinic. Police were forced to retreat because of the broad representation of the community present at the office. On November 22, 1969, 5,000 demonstrators marched and converged at the state courthouse in New Haven Connecticut in support of BPP members charged with the murder of Alex Rackeley. In Chicago on November 25, 1969, 13 Panthers were held in "preventive detention" on $100,000 bail for conspiracy charges to blow up various locations. On November 28th while in custody, Bobby Seale was beaten by prison guards and subjected to inhumane treatment.[100] On December 4, 1969 in Chicago, police raided Fred Hampton's apartment at 4:00 a.m. in the morning murdering Hampton and Mark Clark in their sleep, shooting eighty-two bullets into the apartment during the raid.[101] According to John Bracey, Jr. and Louis Randall (Randy) both members of RAM, talked to Fred Hampton of the Illinois Black Panther Party before his assassination warning him of the location of his building; how he was vulnerable to attack from the police, military logistics wise. They also tried to persuade him to tighten up his own security because they had "community" or "grape vine" information that the Illinois chapter of the Black Panther Party was deeply infiltrated.[102]

There were 29 raids and other confrontations by police against the Black Panther Party between July 28, 1968 and December 4,

1969. On December 8, 1969 in Los Angeles, the police attacked the Southern California BPP.[103] In a pre-dawn raid at two separate locations, 400 officers had a four-hour shootout and arrested Party members and children. The Los Angeles community responded with massive support and the establishment of a Friends of Panthers coalition.[104] The year 1969 was one of great repression against the Black Panther Party, one in which there was a coordinated effort to arrest the expansion and development of the BPP. In 1969, 348 Black Panther Party members were arrested for a series of offenses.[105] In 1970, while violent physical repression continued at a slower rate there was an increase in psychological counter-insurgency (genocide) against the BPP.

On January 9, 1970, Lee Berry, one of the New York Panther 21 was beaten severely in a Chicago jail and he had an epileptic seizure. After emergency surgery, he was listed in critical condition.[106] On January 19th Philadelphia police set fire to the BPP office but it was put out in time.[107] In February 1970, the Panther warehouse in San Francisco was set on fire burning all past issues of the Black Panther newspaper. On February 15, 1970, Huey Newton birthday benefits were held in Berkeley, New York City, New Haven, Connecticut and Seattle, Washington.[108] On March 10th in Algeria, six Panthers were expelled from the international section. On April 4, 1970 in New Haven, Connecticut, David Hilliard and Emory Douglas were jailed for contempt of court, both received six-month sentences and bail was denied them.[109] On April 12th in New York, the Panther 21 defense office was burned destroying legal papers.[110]

On April 17, 1970, in Oakland, Panther Randy Williams and three other Panthers were arrested on assault with intent to commit murder and a deadly weapon charge. Williams was severely beaten while in custody.[111] On April 18th in Frankfurt, West Germany, the solidarity committees of France, Britain, Denmark, Netherlands, West Germany and Sweden meet to discuss the repression against the Black Panther Party in the U.S.[112] On May 1, 1970, in New Haven, more than 25,000 people gathered in support of Panthers Lonnie McLucas, Bobby Seale, and Erica Huggins. At Yale University on May 16th a black student revolutionary conference was held.[113] On May 4th at Kent State University, Kent, Ohio, National Guardsman killed four unarmed white students and wounded nine at an anti-Vietnam war demonstration.[114] In Detroit and Philadelphia BPP chapters expelled members. On May 29th the California Court of Appeals reversed Huey P. Newton's manslaughter conviction. The court though denied Newton bail pending, the prosecutions appeal.[115] On May 31st the BPP in Boston opened a Free Health Clinic.[116]

On June 19th in Cleveland, Ohio, Winston Salem, North Carolina and Seattle, Washington, the BPP expelled members. One hundred police carried out a military assault on the BPP office in Cleveland, Ohio on July 1, 1970[117]; Los Angeles police raided the BPP office. In New Bedford, Massachusetts on July 31, 1970, police raided the Panther office and arrested 21 Panther members on charges of conspiracy to commit anarchy, inciting to riot and unlawful assembly. Bail totaled two million, three hundred and fifty thousand dollars. July 1970 Cleaver visited North Vietnam.

On August 3, 1970 in Philadelphia police and FBI go on a search and destroy mission to destroy three information centers. They stole money, destroyed clothes, and force Panthers to strip naked in the streets. Fifteen Panthers were arrested and their initial bail set at $100,000 each. Later bail was reduced to $1,500.

> As legal difficulties of national and chapter leaders increased in late 1968 and 1969, supporters staffed fundraising committees with such names as the Los Angeles Friends of the Panthers, Legal Defense Committee of the New York Panther Party, and later the New York Committee to defend the Panthers. An appeal for legal defense and local funds was also the purpose of an Emergency Conference to Defend the Right of the Black Panther Party to Exist, held March 7 and 8, 1970, in Chicago. Officials of the CPUSA, despite their theoretical differences, with the Panthers, were among the participants in the affair that led to the creation of a continuations committee to carry on the cause.[118]

Many small contributions as well as some substantial gifts from individual donors proved to be vital sources of funds that were applied toward the $50,000 bail needed for Newton's release from prison.

The turning point in the national organization of the BPP occurred in August of 1970. On August 5, 1970, Huey P. Newton was set free on bail.[119] According to Safiya Bukhari many of the rank and file across the country were dissatisfied with the national leadership and favoritism seemingly parted to a chosen few. Huey Newton was expected to rectify these grievances upon his release. The release of Newton seemed to be the hopes of all those in dispute.

Particularly, venom had been directed against chief of staff David Hilliard. Madalynn Rucker said the accusations against David Hilliard were unjust because he lived in a commune and did work like everyone else, receiving no special privileges.[120]

In hindsight, the sixty-seven agents the F.B.I. had infiltrated into the Party may have fostered much of this discord. Whether the rank and file had written Newton is not commonly known at this point but the F.B.I. did. By the time Newton was released he did not trust hardly anyone particularly Hilliard, a life long friend, or Cleaver whom he had strategic differences with.

What most Panther members and the general public did not know was that the F.B.I. for years had been initiating plans of disruption of the Black Panther Party.

> On August 13, 1970, the Philadelphia Field Office had an informant distribute a fictitious BPP directive to Philadelphia Panthers, questioning Newton's leadership ability. The Philadelphia Office informed FBI headquarters that the directive stresses the leadership and strength of David Hilliard and Eldridge Cleaver while Huey Newton is only useful as a drawing card. It is recommended this directive... be mailed personally to Huey Newton with a short anonymous note. The note would indicate the writer, a community worker in Philadelphia for the BPP, was incensed over the suggestion Huey was only being used by the Party after founding it, and wanted no part of the Chapter if it was slandering its leaders in private. Headquarters approved this plan...[121]

Ten thousand supporters greeted Huey Newton upon his release on bail. Hilliard was there for guidance, comradery, and protection.[122]

On August 7, 1970, in a Marin County courthouse in San Rafael, California, Jonathan Jackson, the younger brother of George Jackson, a Soledad brother, entered the courthouse in San Rafael, California kidnapping a judge, the prosecutor and three women jurors in an attempt to secure the release of his brother and other Soledad brothers.[123] The attempted escape was part of young Jackson's plan to be coordinated with backup from Panther security in the area. The head of Panther security for the area was Melvin "Cotton" Smith, a police informant.[124] According to Louis Tackwood in *The Glasshouse Tapes*, California police intelligence authorities knew about the plan beforehand and allowed for it to occur. For whatever reason, "Cotton" Smith decided not to provide reinforcements but Jonathan decided to act anyway. Whether Newton knew of the plan beforehand is speculation but police informants spread the rumor after the incident that Newton had vetoed the action. This caused dissension within the ranks of the BPP and the greater social movement particularly in California as well as across the country. During the incident James McClain, William Christmas and Ruchell McGee convicted felons in the courtroom-assisted young Jackson and all but McGee were killed in the shootout that resulted. The judge was also killed.[125]

Newton while in prison had studied and had time to think or strategize. Realizing that the BPP was under siege from all forces of the state, Newton planned a strategic retreat from his original position of confrontation with guns. When released he was planning his protracted emphasis on survival programs. This caused a division between him and those emphasizing immediate confrontation.

Because Newton was arrested for the murder of a police officer in Oakland, California in October 1967, and was subsequently convicted of manslaughter in September 1968 and released from prison August 1970 he had in three years become an international symbol of African-American resistance in America for equality.

The F.B.I. through its infiltration of the BPP knew there were differences in the Panther leadership since 1968. Using its illegal tactics the F.B.I. focused on creating a split in the BPP when Newton was released. When Newton was released he worked to get Bobby Seale, Chairman of the BPP who was imprisoned, released.

According to Madalynn Rucker, Newton began to place more emphasis on community programs than verbal self-defense because many African-Americans in the community were also repressed, harassed for supporting the party and were becoming afraid to support it.[126]

At this time Eldridge Cleaver was in exile in Algeria heading the International Section of the BPP. Newton and Cleaver, two of the Party's most prominent members and leaders of the central committee, increasingly differed on strategy and tactics. Newton downplayed self-defense and police confrontation. Cleaver, however, advocated violent revolution and urban guerrilla warfare. Cleaver failed to recognize that the emphasis on military action isolated the BPP from the community thereby reinforcing its image as a gang of (super) revolutionaries. On the other hand, Newton was unprepared and overwhelmed by a national organization, built largely in his name. In the late 1970s, he toured the country speaking at major political events and visiting Panther chapters.

Bobby Seale was released from prison on bail and he and Newton attended the funeral of Jonathan Jackson. Huey Newton gave the eulogy. On August 19, 1970 in San Francisco, a national demonstration and mass rally to free all political prisoners took place. On August 27th, Philadelphia police raided the Panther Information Center.

Though he felt that Eldridge Cleaver's idea of convening a Revolutionary People's Plenary Session was grandiose and impractical, Newton gave a major address at its plenary session in Philadelphia at Temple University on September 5, 1970.[127] More than 10,000 were in attendance. Many were disappointed at Newton's academic abstract philosophical method of presentation. Unlike Bobby Seale, Eldridge Cleaver, Fred Hampton, Michael Tabor or a Richard "Dhruba" Moore, Newton was not a fiery speaker.

Newton was not appealing to audiences and this greatly disappointed his followers. He proved to be a philosophical lecturer rather than a charismatic speaker. This contributed to being a real let down to the rising expectations "by the New York chapter that Newton would solve many of the BPP's contradictions." Not known to many at the time Newton had contracted a cocaine habit from his increasing socializing with Hollywood celebrities. Later David Hilliard, Chief of Staff of the BPP, would introduce them to "crack" "freebasing" cocaine. From studies of COINTELPRO, the F.B.I. and other intelligence agencies knew of Newton's cocaine habit and allowed it if not fostered it to increase Newton's developing paranoia. There were other issues at hand that were the cause of the eventual split in the BPP in 1971.

Newton felt the Party was too militaristic and should de-emphasize armed struggle and he felt Eldridge Cleaver had a fixation with armed struggle.[128]

> ...the Minister of Defense had several traits that first exploded in his conflict with Eldridge and later with other, mostly eastern, Panthers. In his earliest years of adolescence, Huey fought hard, mostly against his fellows in the neighborhood, and suspected anyone who he didn't know was friend to be his enemy. Can we say that this formative experience

and youthful inclination simply disappeared when he created the party as a young, angry man? It appears that this deep, instinctual way of knowing, or of fearing the unknown, may have been a powerful factor in Huey's relationships with other Panthers.[129]

Newton like Robert Williams realized in this period that a successful revolution had to have the support of the majority of the people and therefore a "minority revolution" was impossible; even a minority led revolution was impossible unless it had the overwhelming support of the majority, in the case of the United States, white Americans. In his new political insight of this theoretical proposition in November 1970 and the fact that the state was bent on destroying the party, the BPP shifted its goal of achieving self-determination to obtaining self-determination through socialist revolution. Newton therefore began to place more emphasis on survival programs.

The decision by Huey P. Newton to concentrate on survival programs and electoral politics was a retreat from confrontation with the police; out of necessity and a return to the original posture of earlier Black Panther Party development.

In Algiers, Algeria, in September 1970, Eldridge Cleaver presided at the opening of a new international section of the Black Panther Party. The Algerian government gave the BPP official recognition as a liberation organization, a Villa and, $30,000 a year stipend.

On October 3, 1970, a Panther delegation including Elaine Brown and Eldridge and Kathleen Cleaver visited North Korea, North Vietnam and Peking, China. Eldridge Cleaver announced while in Moscow that there were differences within the Black Panther Party. He said he represented the militant wing of the party.

On October 13, 1970, Angela Davis who was accused of buying guns and helping Jonathan Jackson in the August 5th San Rafael shootout in California was captured in New York by law enforcement agencies.

On October 16, 1970 Julio Rolden, a Young Lord's Party leader, was found murdered in his cell at Riker's Island Prison in New York. In Detroit, six hundred police with two tanks and automatic weapons raided the Panther office.

On November 13, 1970, in Algeria, the international section of the BPP hosted visitors from South Africa's African National Congress and Ambassadors from China, North Korea, and Ethiopia. As

Cleaver traveled and established sub-chapters of the BPP, his view of revolutionary African politics waned.

In November 1970 the BPP planned to convene the People's Revolutionary Constitutional Convention that was scheduled for Howard University.

> Two months later we hold the second meeting of the convention in D.C. The weekend is a disaster. After promising Kathleen will come, Eldridge keeps her in Algeria; meanwhile Howard University backs out and refuses to give us space, and the only people who show up are already converted white movement types. In six months the massive popular appeal of the antiwar and radical movement has vanished. Kent State has scared away the thousands who last spring seemed ready to be revolutionaries.[130]

On January 23, 1971, Huey Newton expelled Los Angeles Panthers Elmer "Geronimo" and Sandra Pratt. Newton had become paranoid as a result of the F.B.I.'s COINTELPRO program and his use of cocaine. The rank and file of the BPP responded to Geronimo's expulsion. The New York 21 wrote a public open letter criticizing the leadership of the BPP demanding the expulsion of David Hilliard, chief of staff of the BPP.

Huey Newton centralized BPP money and personnel and closed most chapters around the nation.

> Newton formed Stronghold, a legal entity that would allow the Black Panther Party to receive revenues from sales of his first, soon to be published book, *To Die for the People*, as well as from other artistic and business activities. He announced the formation of an Ideological Institute and summoned representatives from Panther chapters across the country to attend bi-monthly, two-day learning sessions that he taught on esoteric philosophical questions like free will and determination.[131]

Newton went to New Haven to support Bobby Seale and Ericka Huggins in the trial concerning the death of Alex Rackley. Michael Tabor and Richard "Dhruba" Moore, two of the New York 21, which had been accused in spring of 1969 of conspiring to blow up department stores, police stations, and commuter railways violated the conditions of their bail, (not to leave New York state) in order to discuss the ideological differences in the rank and file and also the leadership of the Black Panther Party.

> The meeting of Tabor and Moore with Newton did not go
> well. The two immediately resigned from the party, as did
> Newton's secretary, Connie Matthews, who had married
> Tabor.[132]

Tabor and Moore jumped bail and immediately disappeared. Tabor's wife, Connie Matthews, who was Newton's secretary, also disappeared taking with her a number of Newton's important papers. When Judge John Murtaugh learned Tabor and Moore had violated their bail arrangements he revoked their bail. The Weathermen, a white radical underground faction who had split off from (SDS) Students for a Democratic Society bombed Murtaugh's house in show of support of the BPP. Members of the New York 21 issued a public statement praising the Weathermen saying they were the vanguard, criticized Newton and demanded David Hilliard's BPP chief of staff's expulsion.

Safiya Bukhari said the conflict was not one of east and west coast but one of a rank and file undercurrent, which wanted more representation and equality in terms of life styles for the Party.[133]

New York Panthers noted that the lack of chapter representation on the central committee hampered their local organizing efforts. Moreover, African-American nationalism was very strong among New York Panthers exemplified by adoption of African names, the display of the red, black, and green flag, symbolizing the black nation, and frequent participation in black cultural events.

Newton responded by expelling all of the New York 21 from the Black Panther Party. Also as part of the ideological split, the Cleavers, living in Africa, had become more nationalistic while national headquarters was emphasizing class over race, the New York Panthers were saying that you had to synthesize race with class.

Michael Tabor and Connie Matthews surfaced later in Algiers with Eldridge Cleaver.

> To publicize an upcoming Intercommunal Day of Solidarity
> on March 5, 1971, in Oakland, which was also to serve as a cel-
> ebration of Newton's birthday, Newton agreed to appear on a
> local radio program. He then suggested that Cleaver also
> appear on the program via international telephone hookup.[134]

While on the San Francisco talk show via international telephone hookup, Cleaver began to criticize Newton for his policies. He questioned Newton's housing in a penthouse apartment and attacked his position of the co-existence of both a Palestinian and Israeli state. Cleaver also questioned Newton on expelling of Geronimo Pratt and the New York 21. He put the demands of the open letter in his own words and demanded the demotion of David Hilliard as chief of staff. After the program Newton expelled Cleaver and the entire international section of the Black Panther Party from the BPP. Cleaver in turn, expelled Newton and the Oakland leadership and said that the Black Panther Party would be run from Algiers and New York. On March 5, 1971, in a nationally televised broadcast from Algiers, Eldridge Cleaver announced there was a split in the Black Panther Party. The FBI's COINTELPRO program which had been successful since the early 1960s from the Nation of Islam to the BPP was finally successful in destroying the national organization of the BPP. The Black Panther Party continued to exist but from the public announcements of its leaders it was never again a viable national force. It mainly became a regional and local political party whose character was transformed. We will investigate that transformation in the next section.

With announcements of the mutual expulsions the black radical movement known as the black liberation movement was grossly affected. Panthers George Jackson, Ericka Huggins and Bobby Seale sided with Huey Newton with Huggins and Seale moving to Oakland once freed of charges against them in the New Haven case.

While the majority of the chapters remained loyal to Newton, the majority of members in all the East Coast chapters, the San Francisco and half of the Los Angeles chapter pledged loyalty to Cleaver. What followed was part of a design that was created by the FBI and police departments through their covert involvement in implementing internal warfare between the factions of the BPP.

Newton supporters shot a Cleaver supporter, Robert Webb to death in Harlem, New York. Newton supporter Sam Napier who was in charge of distribution of the Black Panther Party newspaper in Queens, New York, was murdered in the BPP newspaper office and the office set on fire by Cleaver supporters in retaliation for the Webb assassination. As murders from internal warfare continued, approximately thirty percent of the members of the BPP left the party or went into hiding.[135] Of those remaining above ground still in the BPP went with Newton.

On May 19, 1971, the New York Panther 21 were acquitted of

conspiracy charges. On May 24th, Bobby Seale and Ericka Huggins were acquitted on all charges in the Alex Rackley murder case. Both returned to Oakland with Huggins becoming editor of the *Black Panther* newspaper. In July, David Hilliard was convicted for his participation in the April 6, 1968 shootout. Newton who was paranoid by this time expelled Hilliard from the Party, while he was serving his prison term. Newton appointed Elaine Brown of the Los Angeles chapter the new Minister of Information. Brown lived in a collective with other Panthers and her daughter Ericka was cared for in one of the Party collectives.

On August 21, 1971, George Jackson one of the Soledad brothers; older brother of Jonathan Jackson was assassinated. He was shot in the back by prison guards during a prison disturbance, which was said to be an attempted prison break.

George Jackson was leader of most African-American prisoners in the state of California. He had built a statewide prison organization that eventually became known as the Black Guerrilla Family. Jackson had issued a call for all his men to protect Huey Newton when Newton was imprisoned.

Jackson through the grapevine requested to join the Black Panther Party and his request was granted. Jackson was made a member of the People's Revolutionary Army and given the rank of General and Field Marshal. For three years Jackson and Newton were in constant communication through various carriers, transmitting messages on paper and tape. Jackson became a Panther theoretician writing for *The Black Panther* newspaper.[136]

When Jackson planned his escape Panthers imprisoned at the same prison, San Quentin were supposed to create minor disturbances to throw off the prison security. For whatever reason, Newton supposedly told Panthers to "freeze" on the idea.

Bobby Seale was released from prison on bail of the New Haven murder conspiracy. He and Newton attended the funeral of George Jackson. Huey Newton gave the eulogy. But the Black Guerrilla Family never forgave Newton for Jackson's death. This would haunt Newton years later.

In October of 1971, the Oakland Community Learning Center, which had originally started as a school for Panther children opened its doors as an independent alternative school in a former church facility in East Oakland.

On December 15, 1971, Huey Newton was freed after the third mistrial stemming from the October 27, 1967 incident in which officer John Frey died. One central weakness of the Black Panther Party was around Huey Newton. Power within the organization had been centralized within one individual who had supreme power within the central committee. As Newton increased his cocaine addiction his actions became more irrational which led to the destruction of the BPP from within. The collective leadership failed to give constructive criticism and discipline its leadership. Bobby Seale was put in charge of the party's survival programs by Newton after a dispute on the Panther newspaper with Elaine Brown. Under Seale's supervision in Oakland, the BPP organized extensive food giveaways. In this period, the BPP survival programs included testing for sickle-cell anemia in its clinics. The BPP bought a shoe factory and gave away shoes. Both Rashad Brydsong and Kalid Muhammad stated that the BPP should have charged a minimum price for the shoes and other items so the BPP could have become independent, "self-reliant."[137]

Huey Newton decided to build a model base for the BPP in Oakland. Newton called all the Panthers to relocate to Oakland. Bobby Seale disagreed with Newton. While Seale agreed to build a base in Oakland, he did not believe that all of the other chapters should be shut down. Newton began to withdraw from Panther activities but still made rational political decisions. But his social behavior became more bizarre.

Before Nixon was invited to China, the Chinese invited Huey Newton and a delegation of Black Panthers to visit. Newton, his bodyguard Robert Bay and Elaine Brown went to China. While in China, Newton met with representatives of FRELIMO, an African liberation organization, who were at that time fighting to liberate Mozambique from the Portuguese. Part of FRELIMO's program was to create alternative institutions in the liberated territories inside of Mozambique. These provided for an institutional basis for the economically self-reliant communities. Feeling this was the successful way to go and witnessing both FRELIMO's and the Chinese full equality of women in their societies, convinced Newton to institute a two-prong program. He was more assured that survival programs were the correct paths instead of immediate armed resistance. Newton decided to recognize the status of women as equal to that of men in all levels of the party. After the China trip Newton elected Elaine Brown to the central committee of the BPP and officially recognized the full equality of female members.[138]

THE ELECTORAL POLITICAL AND ACTIVITIES OF THE BLACK PANTHER PARTY 1971–1974

> The 1972–73 centralization of the party in Oakland had another impact that was, perhaps, unforeseen by the Central Committee: it communicated to many common people that the Party was in decline. Why else, people wondered, would the Panthers close down their community programs? Therefore, the centralization contributed to the Party's own demise.[139]

In his decision to develop a political base in Oakland, Newton decided the BPP chairman, Bobby Seale, should run for Mayor of Oakland and Elaine Brown for City Council in the April 1973 election. Bobby Seale and Elaine Brown announced their candidacies for local political office in the city on May 13, 1972.

> To mobilize resources for the campaign Seale issued a directive that ordered its members to cease operations in their local chapters and report to Oakland, while all of the Party affiliates did not close immediately, the transfer of members to Oakland enhanced female participation in the BPP.[140]

Much of the BPP's political strategy was the thinking of one man—Huey P. Newton. The BPP's critical error was the allowing of the centralizing of all organizational power in the hands of one individual. A strategic mistake that Newton made in an attempt to build a base for the party in Oakland was to attack an organization of the African-American middle class that was well established and had a good track record of positive achievements. From earlier accounts in this chapter Huey had always had a pathological violent streak and walked on the edge from his days as a student at Merritt College. Now after release from prison Newton exercised or abused his authoritarian power through political intimidation. Later it would erupt to "insane" political murders with the covert plan to control the drug traffic in the bay area.

An African-American coalition of African-American liquor store and club owners in California, called Cal-Pak which by 1971 had been responsible for the creation of nearly 500 jobs for African-Americans in the beverage industry; became the target of political pressure by the BPP. In May 1971, Huey went to the president of Cal-Pak in Oakland, Bill Boyette asking for cash donations.

> ...Boyette stated that Newton approached him during the last week of May and requested that each of the twenty-two local members of Cal-Pak pay the Black Panthers $5 per member per week. Later that same week, Newton visited Boyette again, raising the requested amount to $10 per member per week. Acting on behalf of the entire association, Boyette refused both requests.[141]

On July 21, 1971 Bobby Seale attended a Cal-Pak meeting representing the Black Panther Party. He reiterated Newton's demands and said if it was not forthcoming that the BPP would close each business of every member of the association in Oakland. Cal-Pak responded by sending a letter on July 29th to Huey Newton offering to donate 75 gallons of milk, 500 loaves of bread, 60 pounds of meat, 30 dozen eggs and two cases of cereal to the Black Panther free breakfast program for children. On July 30th, Newton answered saying the cash demand stood and that if Boyette didn't comply the BPP would attempt to close Boyette's businesses. Cal-Pak was an organization that had a consistent record of contributing to community causes. It had a scholarship program as well as helped to secure 230 jobs for African-Americans in the area in the previous six months.

On July 31, 1971, approximately fifty Panthers began picketing Boyette convenience/liquor store at 5350 Grove Street. The demonstrators carried signs stating that he should contribute to people's survival programs. Ex-Panther, Austin Allen, felt this was a huge error because it polarized the African-American community when the Party needed the support of a united black community.[142]

The party announced in its newspaper it was rejecting CAL-PAK's offer for food because it was a one-time deal. To make matters more complicated the BPP stated that CAL-PAK had sought the support of the BPP in boycotting Mayfair's, a supermarket in North Oakland. CAL-PAK said it had launched the boycott at Mayfairs market but that the BPP had joined in without an invitation from the association.

As the boycott dragged on against Boyette's business, his sales dropped off 98 percent basically because patrons were scared to cross BPP picket lines. Some two hundred African-American business people in the Oakland area, owners of small retail establishments, real estate sales offices, law practices, funeral homes, beauty shops and medical services organized to support Boyette by forming the ad hoc committee to preserve black business in Oakland. The committee held a meeting with the BPP. At the meeting, Boyette again made his offer to donate food rather than cash to the Panthers. Huey Newton pounded a desk three times saying the offer was unacceptable threatening to make Boyette a poor man. Needless to say, this erratic behavior left a bad taste in the mouths of many of the local black establishment.

The boycott dragged on until January 1971, when newly elected Congressman Ron Dellums, nephew of C. L. Dellums, stepped in to negotiate a settlement. The compromise agreement called for the formation of an umbrella organization of black businessmen called the United Fund of the Bay Area, which would donate food or money to a wide variety of black charitable causes at their own discretion. Among those programs were to be those to the Black Panthers. Donations to the Panthers were to be made through Saint Augustine's Episcopal, the church of the party's spiritual advisor, Father Earl Neil.

Huey said:

> During the latter part of June 1971, the Black Panther Party held a series of meetings with CAL-PAK package Store and Tavern Owners Association and asked their continuing voluntary, self-determined (in terms of amount) support of survival programs. After a series of meetings CAL-PAK was steadfast in a single offer of bread, milk, meat and eggs for the free breakfast program. They said they would not contribute on a continuing basis. They wanted to make a payoff, which was rejected. We are not extortionists.[143]

Newton stated that a continuing trickle of support is more important to the community than a large, once-only hush-mouth gift. He said as long as there was one hungry child, one barefoot person, one medically neglected individual, or one brother or sister without a winter coat, the Black Panther Party would not be paid off and would not be quiet. In essence, by time of the compromise there was a "win to win" situation for both the African-American businesses concerned and the Black Panther Party.

On December 15, 1971, Huey went to court for the third time

for the shooting of officer John Frey and it ended in mistrial. This freed Huey Newton of any criminal proceedings. On March 29, 1972, Huey Newton redrafted the Black Panther Party 10-point program. In June 1972 in Los Angeles, Elmer "Geronimo" Pratt was convicted of murder and sentenced to life in prison. Newton refused to offer him any support.

Nineteen seventy-three was a decisive year for the BPP. This was the year that members of the Black Panther Party who had migrated from other areas in the country put out an all out effort to win community support for the BPP candidates, Bobby Seale and Elaine Brown. At the same time, Huey Newton's behavior at the Lamp Post (a night club run by the BPP) and other places was becoming more erratic due to substance abuse.

Austin Allen, previous member of the Newton faction of the BPP, estimates that there were approximately 500 members of the BPP in Oakland from 1971–1975. Allen said that Seale and other members of the central committee would give political education classes for Black Panther Party members on a bi-monthly basis but Newton was seldom seen.[144]

The BPP advanced a very practical platform,

> Among the planks in their platform were calls for an International Trade Center, a program to safely escort senior citizens living in dangerous neighborhoods, and a preventative medicine screening program for the citizens of the city. Seale also called for two hours paid leave from jobs so Oakland citizens could vote.[145]

While the Panthers registered some 30,000 residents, violent anti-social behavior by Newton and his squad (a tight knit group of bodyguards) seemed to run in contradiction. Though Seale and Brown lost their election bids both made a good showing.

In October 1973, Oakland's BPP youth institute moved into a larger building and was renamed the Oakland Community Learning Center. It grew as an educational institution and became a role model for alternative schools, enrolling approximately 150 children. Newton due to cocaine use and increasingly drinking cognac became more paranoid. He expelled David Hilliard while Hilliard was serving his sentence for the shootout that led to Bobby Hutton's murder. Newton also expelled June Hilliard and Pat Hilliard, David's wife. Also Masai Hewitt was beaten and expelled. As beatings of party members increased and knowledge of Newton's cocaine use and abuses against the people by him and the squad increased, party members started leaving the party. The year 1974 marked the beginning of the end of the party. The existence of the party was prolonged by the stability of the women in Huey's absence. The average age of a Panther was about 25 in 1974 and its' membership had dropped to approximately 150.

Madalynn Rucker remembers,

> A lot of good work was going on, establishing links with labor, registering people and political campaigns led by Bobby and his section. But there was the parallel more sort of underground drug stuff with Huey and the goon squad and with these folks on the other side. There was a lot of negative stuff that began to happen then around the life style of Huey and the penthouse. There were a lot of things happening in terms of Huey's relationship to the community. A lot of the drug pushers and pimps he was going up against were black, so there was a lot of black on black violence going on in the community.[146]

It became common knowledge the drug use and prostitution were occurring at the Lamp Post. Probably the most devastating occurrence to party members was the brutalization of Bobby Seale co-founder of the BPP by Huey Newton who also expelled him from the party. The event was precipitated during a political argument. Huey then appointed Elaine Brown, chairman of the Black Panther Party, who was there when it occurred in the penthouse.[147]

Bobby Seale in *A Lonely Rage* said he had begun to develop the desire to own his own house and raise a family like everyday African-American workers. He said this desire that began to come to his conscious mind; he realized was the main reason he decided not to run for mayor of Oakland again. Seale felt that a mistake had been made in breaking down the national structure of the BPP to having only about a hundred members in the Oakland headquarters and a North Carolina chapter. He also felt that the maintaining of bodyguards was distorting reality.[148] He was also critical of Huey Newton's attempt to take over the drug traffic in the Bay Area. He mentions this on the video "All Power to the People." Whatever is historical accuracy or combination Seale left Oakland abruptly with his lady friend to reside in Philadelphia, Pennsylvania.

Newton continued to get involved in a series of events that would be attributed to irrational or modified behavior. During the summer of 1974 Newton was arrested after ordering his bodyguard to shoot a plains clothes police officer. After making bail in less than a week later, Newton was accused of the August 5, 1974 shooting of 17 year old prostitute Kathleen Smith who had yelled out "Hey, baby" as Newton's car was cruising down a street in Oakland. Within days Newton was reported to have beaten a staff member, a woman with a pistol at the Lamp Post (the Party's bar) and beat two women customers at the Lamp Post. To make things worst, Newton pistol-whipped Preston Collins, a tailor who he had invited to his penthouse to make him a custom tailor made suit. In the process of negotiations and conversation with Newton, the tailor made the reference to Newton "Oh, don't feel that way, baby." [149]

For whatever reason, either from abuse while in prison, a hated street name of "Baby Huey," police harassment, behavior modification and or a combination of all, the word "baby" in reference to Newton triggered a violent reaction. That and a combination of paranoia to strong African-American male figures within this own organization and a display of arrogance, uncontrollable violence towards people and an abuse of power all signaled the beginning of the end of one of the most dynamic organizations built in the late 1960s.

After posting bail for the pistol-whipping of Collins and shooting Kathleen Smith, Newton on the advice of family and friends jumped bail and went with his girlfriend Gwen into exile in Cuba. A brief period of stabilization came to the party (three years) with Newton's absence. Under the leadership of Elaine Brown as chairperson of the party, the women of the party concentrated on building survival programs and alternative institutions. The Black Panther Party in December of 1975 filed a $100 million dollar lawsuit against the FBI.

WOMEN IN THE BPP:

While often barely noted or in fact invisible in the history of participation in community based political movements, African-American women have long played significant roles. This was the case for women in the BPP from February 1967 to its dissolution in the 1980s. The primary focus of media coverage was on the principal male leadership but Panther women held positions in leadership at the local and national levels. Panther women participated in the community survival programs that provided free clothing, food, health services, and other essentials.[150]

Contrary to popular belief the organization was not just composed of politically active black men: two-thirds of the Black Panther Party consisted of women. Panther women held positions in the party's leadership at both local and national levels, in addition to giving speeches at Panther rallies and participating in the community survival programs.[151]

According to Seale in February 1967, Tarika Lewis (also known as Joan Lewis or Matilaba) is recognized as the first women to officially join the Black Panther Party. After graduating from Oakland Tech High School, Lewis joined the BPP. As a Panther, Lewis recalled that her "duty was to open the eyes of people to give them hope, courage, understanding; to teach, guide, and pull the cover off what was going on and what should be done about it.[152] In 1967 many women followed Lewis' lead, and joined the BPP. No women received special treatment because they were females. Everyone, male and female had to participate in physical training, and political education classes.

Both male and female Panthers said that "...women were always there doing the work," which is what was the foundation for maintaining the organization so well during the span of the program.[153]

In October 1967, when Huey Newton was shot, arrested and charged with the murder of a white Oakland cop, the BPP was converted into a national political movement. The party expanded from a small Oakland based organization to a national organization as black youth in 48 states formed chapters of the party. In addition, Black Panther coalition and support groups began to spring up internationally, in Japan, China, France, England, Germany, Sweden, Mozambique, South Africa, Zimbabwe, Uruguay, and also Israel.

Kathleen Cleaver was the most prominent and influential woman during the formative stages of the BPP. She joined the party in November 1967, shortly after moving to California to live with her new fiancée, BPP minister of information Eldridge Cleaver. She was instrumental in the free Huey campaign and served as assistant editor of the party's newspaper. Cleaver would become the first woman to sit on the organization's central committee.[154]

According to Rashad Byrdsong, African-American women had equal responsibility in the administration of the BPP. Returning home from Vietnam, he decided to join the BPP. He went to his hometown office of the BPP (Seattle, WA). He said that when he walked into the Panther Party office in 1969, a young African-American woman was the officer of the day, commanding the office. He asked her how he could join the BPP and questioned her about the program of the party and fronted her off on her ability to defend herself. She had a revolver on the desk and in the confrontation which was motivated by his then sexism toward women, she put the nozzle of the revolver in his face and said that if he came closer to her she would kill him. This convinced Byrdsong of the female Panther's ability; it ended his sexism toward women, and he joined the party.[155]

Angela Brown's research indicated that the experience of the women in the party differed according to where there were located. Ms. Brown states that she thinks many people preferred to work away from the national headquarters after 1972. According to her interviews, numerous women felt less confined when they were at chapters other than the national office in Oakland where things were more rigid, prior to this period. This attitude can be attributed to the leadership at the time and the fact that there was a notable favorite group in Oakland. Since everyone was no longer necessarily working with the people they were used to working with, the previously established rapport along with issues that had been resolved in one place in some cases had to be reworked.[156]

The incarceration of so many of the party's members, especially the men helped to create the opportunity for Panther women to achieve positions of power. In chapters like New York and Chicago, police targeted the men because they thought the men were the only leaders and if they (the men) were eliminated the organization would crumble. This chauvinistic perspective by the police was the fallacy that enabled the women and the few remaining men to keep the party functioning.

Women who were involved in revolutionary activities in countries like, China, Cuba, Vietnam, and Africa influenced Panther women. This aided them in addressing and assessing what they were experiencing internally and helped to define their roles as revolutionary black women.

From 1967 until the dissolution of the party, Panther women faced male chauvinism within the Panther community. Although gender-based discrimination was not a condoned policy through its gender blind doctrine, Panther women experienced the assignment of gender-specific tasks and sexism.[157]

But Jonia Abron dispels this general conclusion. She said in an interview that the BPP tried to put into practice the position of equality for female members. When Ms. Abron and other African-American female members arrived in Oakland in 1974, they were told by a central committee member that the women did not have to sleep with anyone they did not want to and if they were sexually harassed to report it and it would be dealt with.

The party's Minister of Information, Eldridge Cleaver expressed reproach about this subject when women in the party began to voice their dissatisfaction of the BPP at party meetings and in *The Black Panther*, yet at the same time, their procurement of leadership positions increased and their involvement in community activities expanded.

Besides the many different survival programs the BPP had created; another positive contribution of the BPP was its avocation and practice of equality for women throughout all levels of the organization and in society itself. This occurred at a time when most black nationalist organizations were demanding that the woman's role be in the home and/or one step behind the black man, and at a time when the whole country was going through a great debate on the woman's liberation issue. This is not to say that there were not sexual inequalities within the party, or that some of the men did not have male chauvinistic attitudes. According to female members of the party, the level of sexism was much less than any other organization at that time. Location also played a key role in regards to sexism, gender discrimination, and internal problems. It seemed to have been worse in Oakland at the central committee.

According to Angela Brown's interview with Kathleen Cleaver, Cleaver said she did not experience any sexism. The reason for that was because:

> She came into the party when the party was on the verge of collapse, which was November 1967. There were only about six or seven panthers at that time. It was just she and Eldridge Cleaver, they had their San Francisco apartment,

and she did her press contact jobs out of her apartment. So she admits that part of the reason that she didn't experience it was because she was isolated and wasn't living in the same kinds of situations that other women were. She also joined Eldridge Cleaver when he went into exile in late '68. So she was physically removed.[158]

According to Ericka Huggins, "There were some men who could (not) have cared less about what women thought about anything and there were some who were on the right page."[159]

Cleo Silver joined the BPP in New York, 1968. She was mostly attracted to the ten-point program. Silver admits that joining the BPP was one of the finest things that ever happened to her in her life. Shortly after being in the party, the New York 21 was arrested. Two women, Joan Bird and Afeni Shakur, were among the Panther New York 21 arrested in April, 1969, on conspiracy charges to bomb police stations, the Bronx Botanical Gardens, a city commuter train and five department stores.

Silver stated in a videotaped interview that the BPP was the most revolutionary, dedicated, courageous, and most principled organization that ever existed. She never experienced any direct sexism or sexual abuse. To Silver, BPP men were very polite and never hit on her. The women were also extremely kind, encouraging, and there was a lot of unity, caring, and mutual concern especially for women who had children. Silver was analogous to everyone else in the party, dedicated all of her time to the movement. Auspiciously that did not interfere with Panther women on the East Coast parenting their children. According to Silver, their children accompanied them to work; they were with them all the time. BPP members were like aunts and uncles. Members would have them at the office or at a Panther house or with them doing their activities. Men as well as women participated in baby-sitting the children.

Cleo Silver left the party in 1969, because she disagreed with Eldridge Cleaver that the lumpen proletariat was the vanguard of the black revolution. She had ideological discussions with Zaid and Lumumba Shakur in the New York BPP who agreed with her.[160]

Women like Elaine Brown who was appointed Chairman of the BPP in 1974 still rose to power despite negative attitudes by many members that brandished the idea that it was a violation of some black power principle of a black woman assuming a role of leadership. She was said to be eroding black manhood, to be hindering the progress of the black race. She was an enemy of black people.[161]

Brown and other women in positions of accountability in the BPP did not shrink from the challenge of the sexist attitudes that existed. They believed in the party's objectives and felt that they could help the party realize its goals because they believed in them.[162]

Some of the other women that Elaine Brown named to key positions of accountability were: Joan Kelly, administrator of Survival Program and legal matters, Norma Armour, coordinated finances, and Erika Huggins began administering over the school and its related programs. The assignment of these women and others cause ample discontent among the men of the party, however, men remained in control of the newspaper and military affairs.[163]

With Brown at the head of the BPP, more of its activities were legitimate. Although there was still underground activity, Ms. Brown and the BPP were proving to be highly effective community leaders and organizers.[164]

Becoming affiliated with the party generated questions of female sexuality and motherhood plagued some women, who complained of being pressured into engaging in sexual activity. Reproduction and birth control were also issues. There were difficulties of rearing a child and being a full-time political activist.

Male party members except when they wanted sexual favors considered women sexless. According to Elaine Brown "there was a clear signal that the words "Panther" and "comrade" had taken on gender connotations, devoting an inferiority in the female half of us...driving a wedge between Sisters and Brothers...attacking the very foundation of the party."[165]

While the opportunity to develop political organizing skills was one of the many reasons that women joined the BPP, other reasons include backing the party's goals, and to support a spouse or significant other already involved in the party.

Panther women had to confront the issue of police surveillance and harassment, which were equally problematic for women and men; so female members were forced to face both internal and external pressures.[166]

Panther women administered and staffed many of the community programs despite the incessant lack of finances. These programs thrived and included: Seniors Against a Fearful Environment

(SAFE), free breakfasts for schoolchildren, child care centers, child development centers, legal aid and advice services, teen peer counseling, free music classes, dance and martial arts classes, free transportation to and from prison (for people wanting to visit incarcerated loved ones), GED classes, political education classes, voter registration, free food giveaways, petition campaigns for community oversight of the police, and free medical care (testing for sickle cell anemia), and many others.[167]

Madalynn Rucker joined the BPP in San Francisco, transferred to San Jose, then back to San Francisco, then finally to Oakland where she stayed for 3 years. In 1968 at eighteen years of age Rucker worked in the party, but did not officially join until 1969 at the age of nineteen. Rucker first heard of the BPP in 1967 when Huey was arrested. She joined the party because she agreed with the right to defend herself. She did not think that the M.L.K., non-violence approach was working. Rucker admits that sexist behavior went on, but it occurred a lot less than in the general public. Due to the fact that the party was under continuous attack from police, FBI and COINTELPRO, it didn't allow much contemplation for sexism. The FBI denounced the party itself as a group of communist outlaws bent on over-throwing the U.S. government.[168] There had been every kind of assault imaginable on the party's social programs and destruction of party property; from police raiders who smashed breakfast program food on the floors of churches, and crushed party free clinic supplies, to those who caused the destruction of batches of the party's newspapers. In addition, intimidation and other such tactics were being employed to undermine the party's support, and to break the spirit and commitment of party members, party supporters, and family members. Focus went from protecting themselves from police, to protecting themselves from each other.

Nevertheless, the party survived and continued to build its survival programs, which came to include not only the free breakfast program and free clinics, but also grocery giveaways, the manufacture and distribution of free shoes, school and education programs, senior transport and service programs, free busing to prisons and prisoner support and legal aid programs.

In 1971 the last couple of years as a member of the BPP, Rucker worked at the Lamp Post located in Oakland, California. The Lamp Post was the bar and restaurant Newton bought taking it over from a distant cousin. Rucker worked with Huey personally at the Lamp Post. She described him as having a volatile personality. Rucker conceived a child that year which was placed in BPP child development center for two years, along with other BPP children. They were raised in a collective. BPP mothers on the West Coast were not as fortunate as the mothers on the East Coast in regards to being with their children on a day-to-day basis. Madalynn Rucker left the party in 1974, because she was asked to do illegal activities while working at the Lamp Post.

The Black Panther Party continued to build its programs and move its agenda, as it began to consolidate its efforts in its home base of Oakland, California:

> The party decision to close ranks contributed to the increase opportunities for women to fill nontraditional female roles. During the state of organizational flux, women in the party emerged as national and local party leaders. Both Kathleen Cleaver and Patricia Hilliard held influential positions at the national levels. In Panther affiliates throughout the nation, Elaine Brown, Erica Huggins, Barbara Shankey, Ann Campbell, Afeni Shakur, Yvonne King and Audrea Jones were among many women who became influential leaders in their respective chapters during the Revolutionary phase of the BPP.[169]

In 1971, Elaine Brown was appointed Chairman of the Los Angeles BPP branch. Despite the negative attitude, sexism, and gender discrimination she endured from the men in the party.

A woman attempting the role of leadership was said to be making an alliance with "counter-revolutionary, man hating, lesbian, feminist white bitches."[170]

Brown as well as her sisters in the struggle Joan, Ericka, Evon Carter, and Gwen Goodloe refused to play an inferior role to the brothers in the revolution. Because of their strong beliefs in gender equality they were labeled as "the clique." The men believed they all had bad attitudes. The reputation of the clique "smart bitches" was known throughout the party.

Elaine Brown states that she would not reward any brother with her body, in the bedroom or in the kitchen, but not everyone in the party shared Brown's and her clique beliefs. Some women encouraged the use of their bodies as a reward to the BPP men. Up north a 15-year-old girl named Marsha told Elaine at Bobby's request:

> "First of all, a brother's got to be righteous. He's got to be a
> Panther. He's got to be able to recite the 10-point program,
> and be ready to off the pigs and die for the people..."Can't
> no motherfucker get no pussy from me unless he can get
> down with the party,..." A sister has to learn to shoot as well
> as cook and be ready to back up the brothers. "A sister has to
> give up the pussy when the brother is on his job and hold
> back when he's not. "Cause sisters got pussy power."[171]

In March 1970, Elaine Brown gave birth to a baby girl Ericka
Brown. Due to her overwhelming responsibility to the party, she
found it difficult to be a real mother. Ericka was with other women
in the party or with Elaine's mother, while she took care of the party
responsibilities.

In 1974 Elaine Brown took over the national chairmanship of the
party during those three years that Newton was in exile in Cuba. The
more women became coordinators of programs, the longer those
programs lasted, and the more efficient and effective they were. The
party gained much more respect from the local Oakland community after it had centralized under Elaine Brown's leadership, when
they were developing all of the programs. The school received a com-
mendation from the California state legislature for being one of the
most effective alternative educational institutions. Initially the school
was just for the Black Panther Party members' children. But around
1973 it opened up to the larger Oakland community.[172]

Elaine Brown recalls; only months after Huey returned from
exile in Cuba, "I felt something very damaging was occurring inside
the party ranks."[173]

Women stayed dedicated to the party until the very end. Jonia
Abron in an interview said one of the issues for many of the women
in the party over a period of time; those who had children wanted
to spend more time with their children and their work would not
allow it.[174]

Women were responsible for a few remaining community programs. According to Angela Brown women stayed loyal mainly for
two reasons: one, because of their love and devotion to the children, the other reason was because too many women felt as though
the party was their entire life. Ericka Huggins, and Jonia Abron were
among the few remaining women.

Ericka Huggins, the most prominent female member remaining in the party after Elaine Brown's resignation, served as the Oakland Community School director until 1981. She was a thirteen-year member, (1968–1981) of the organization. Huggins attributed her decision to remain a Panther, in spite of Newton's erratic and criminal behavior, to her commitment of the OCS students. Huggins attributes her eventual resignation from the party to Newton's increasing drug problems Another Panther still active during the final phase of the BPP was Jonia Abron. A nine-year BPP veteran, she originally joined the Detroit Branch in 1972, after earning a Master of Arts degree in communication from Purdue University.[175] The most momentous thing about the Black Panther Party was that the Panthers put their lives on the line for creating change. They sacrificed themselves for the cause. The Black Panther Party's members were loyal and remarkably dedicated to the struggle. They demanded equal rights regardless of race, gender, and class.

CORRUPTION AND DECLINE

Newton from exile continued to run the party. He would call Elaine Brown and issue directions through courier and Brown and other Panthers would visit him. Under Elaine Brown's administration, led by the squad, the Black Panther Party continued its clandestine operations of extortion of the pimps and drug pushers in the Oakland area. Brown had maneuvered through good management and public relations her way within the Democratic Party machine in Northern California. Through the Oakland Community Learning Center run by Ericka Huggins, the party received respectability of creating a model alternative school. In 1975, Brown ran again for City Council losing her election bid but receiving 44 percent of the vote.[176] Brown became a broker in democratic politics. She attended the 1976 Democratic Party National Convention as a delegate for California Governor Jerry Brown. Under Elaine Brown's influence, sixty Panthers actively campaigned to help elect John George Alameda County supervisor from the fifth supervisory district. As a result, several Panthers were placed in key administrative positions and Brown herself was appointed to the powerful Oakland Council for Economic Development (OCED) at the insistence of Governor Jerry Brown. Entering into alliance with Representative Ron Dellums and key establishment personalities, Brown endorsed

Superior Court Judge Lionel Wilson in becoming the first African-American mayor of Oakland. Organizing the approximately one hundred remaining but well disciplined Panthers left; the party registered thousands of new voters and mobilizing many poor Oakland residents to vote for Wilson. After Wilson's election victory, Newton decided to return to the United States from Cuba on July 3, 1977.

With Newton's return, tensions began to resurface in the party and the community. Citing all his legal troubles were the cause of the FBI and the CIA, Newton won temporary community support. A two-story house was purchased for him. Newton was reported to have been seen in after-hour clubs, high on coke, intimidating people with his elite squad members for backup, while he beat up on men, taking their women. The final beginning of loss of community support came in October of 1977 when an aborted assassination attempt on Crystal Gray, witness for the prosecuting attorney of the Kathleen Smith case went foul. Nelson Malloy, (a member of the squad), who had been shot in a shootout with Crystal Gray's landlady and then taken to the Nevada desert and shot and left for dead turned state's evidence. Elaine Brown is rumored to have confronted Newton on the party's negative publicity and to have been beaten badly by Newton.[177] Whether beaten or rumor of such, Brown immediately disappeared and left the party.[178]

After news reports of Brown's beating appeared in the press along with a series of negative articles on the party, public officials began to distance themselves from the Panthers. An investigation began of the Panther Oakland Community Learning Center. The investigation exposed the fact of misappropriation of funds with funds being used for Newton's squad. Funds began to slow down and wither away coming into the party. By 1978, the party had dwindled to a couple of dozen of dedicated cadre. Newton was arrested on charges of assault and parole violation of illegal gun possession. Newton beat his charges of having murdered a prostitute resulting in two trials, which resulted in a hung jury with the majority voting for acquittal. Out of bail, Newton received a Ph.D. degree from the University of California at Santa Cruz in the history consciousness for his writing of "War Against the Panther: A Study of Repression in America." On June 15, 1980 he became Dr. Huey P. Newton.

But Newton was thoroughly addicted to cocaine, alcohol, and cigarettes by this time and his behavior was so erratic that he was unemployable except in criminal life.

Between 1980 and 1982 Newton continuously used the Panthers resources for his and the squad's personal use. In 1981, Ericka Huggins resigned as principal of the Oakland Learning Center over the issue. In 1982, the Oakland Learning Center and the Youth Institute being the Panther's last survival programs closed its door's due to lack of funds.

Between 1982 and 1989 was one of rapid deterioration of Huey Newton, co-founder of the Black Panther Party. The Lamp Post closed. *The Black Panther* newspaper shut down for lack of funds and other party members left. In and out of jail for minor offenses; now a thoroughly addicted crack cocaine addict, Newton spent a large part of his time demanding free crack cocaine or sticking up dope pushers for their crack. In 1987, Newton was convicted of illegal gun possession and served several months in prison. In 1987, Newton was ordered to prison for the 1978 pistol-whipping of Preston Collins; having lost his case after appeals of having illegal weapons. After serving six weeks for parole violation, Newton demanded the release of Elmer "Geronimo" Pratt, an imprisoned ex-Panther. After Newton was released he continued to degenerate pressuring crack dealers to supply him with free crack. Newton did not pay much attention to the rumors of a contract for a hit on him ordered by the Black Guerilla family (BGF), previously organized by George Jackson and now a full-time black mafia unit as well as disgruntled ex-Black Panthers, many who were still in prison. On August 22, 1989, Huey Newton was shot and killed by a drug pusher, member of the BGF.

Jonia M. Abron, former editor of the *Black Panther Intercommunal News Service* in a letter to Muhammad Ahmad dated June 17, 1999 stated,

> Ultimately, Huey Newton was a casualty of war—the relentless war waged by the U. S. government to crush the Black Liberation movement. The Black Panther Party, arguably, was the most influential group of the movement, and therefore, bore the brunt of the government's war.[179]

David Hilliard, former BPP chief of staff delivered an insightful assessment of Huey's problems at the funeral of his life long friend,

> I want to say that Huey's problem with chemical dependency represents all our weaknesses here in America. To focus on his chemical dependency really doesn't allow us to

see him in proper context. We get blinded to the programs and ideals that he was about. So our correct focus is to deal with the solution—not only Huey's problem, but to America's problem: drugs and alcohol. Because Huey's problem was not a problem unique to Huey. It's a societal ill.[180]

1. Interview with Kwame Ture (Stokely Carmichael), Oberlin, Ohio, 5/96.

2. Interview with Eddie Ellis, New York, N.Y., 8/14/93.

3. Alkamal Ahmed Muhammad (Shelton Duncan), taped interview, New York: 12/78.

4. *Amsterdam News*, September 3, 1966.

5. Interview with Kenneth Freeman, Washington, D.C., 8/68.

6. "Steps Toward Organizing a National Movement in the African-American Struggle for National Liberation Part 2," (N.Y. BPP position paper), pp. 1 (8/66).

7. Akbar Muhammad Ahmad "A Brief History of the Black Liberation Movement in the 1960s: Focus on RAM," unpublished, p. 10.

8. Interview with Sam Anderson, Harlem, N.Y., 9/93.

9. *Op. Cit.*, Interview with Alkmal Ahmed Muhammad (Shelton Duncan). Also, see *Amsterdam News*, September 3, 1966 and *The New York Times*, September 13, 1966.

10. *Op. Cit.*, Steps Toward Organizing a National Movement in the African-American Struggle for National Liberation Part I, p. 3.

10. Bobby Seale, *Seize the Time: The Story of the Black Panther Party and Huey P. Newton,* [New York: Random House, 1970], p. 23.

11. Mario Van Peebles, Ula Y. Taylor, J. Tarika Lewis, *PANTHER, A Pictorial History of the Black Panthers and The Story Behind the Film,* [New York: New Market Press, 1995], p. 23.

12. Huey P. Newton, *Revolutionary Suicide,* [New York: Writers and Readers Publishing, Inc., 1973], pp. 108–109.

13. Ibid, p. 24.

14. Bobby Seale, *Seize the Time,* [New York: Random House, 1990], p. 60.

15. E. Tani and Kae Sera, *False Nationalism, False Internationalism: Class Contradictions in the Armed Struggle,* [Chicago, Illinois: A Seeds Beneath the Snow Publication, 1985] p. 187.

16. Earl Anthony, *Picking Up the Gun,* [New York: Dial Press, 1971], pp. 37–39.

17. Bobby Seale, *Seize the Time,* [New York: Random House, 1970], pp. 28–29.

18. Interview with Ernie Allen, Amherst, Mass., 1994.

19. Interview with Brother D., ex-member of the BPP of Northern California, Amherst, Mass., 1978.

20. *Op. Cit.*, (*False Nationalism, False Internationalism*), p. 187.

21. Huey P. Newton, Toni Morrison (ed.) *To Die For The People: Selected Writings and Speeches,* [New York: Writers and Readers Publishing, Inc., 1973], p. 16. Also see Huey P. Newton *Revolutionary Suicide*, p. 117. Also see John T. McCartney, *Black Power Ideologies: An Essay in African-American Political Thought,* [Philadelphia: Temple University Press, 1992], p. 146

22. Sundiata Acoli, "A Brief History of the Black Panther Party and It's Place In The Black Liberation Movement," p. 3.

23. Interview with Kenneth Freeman (telephone), May 3, 1967, Philadelphia, PA/San Francisco, California

*Historical Note: RAM was organized as an on-campus organization in 1962 and expanded or reorganized as a community organization in Philadelphia, PA in 1963 by founder mentor/senior central committee member, Mrs. Ethel "Azelle" Johnson who had been a co-worker of Robert Williams in Monroe, N.C. since 1957. RAM organizers met with Williams in Havana, Cuba in 1964, where he accepted the position of international chairman of RAM. Some RAM members had worked with Williams as individuals as members of other formations such as the Fair Play for Cuba Committee and the Monroe Defense Committee.

24. Robert H. Brisbane, *Black Activism: Racial Revolution in the United States 1954–1970,* [Valley Force: Judson Press, 1974], p. 202.

25. Earl Anthony, *Picking Up the Gun,* [New York: Pyramid Books, 1971], p. 16. Also see, *Spitting in the Wind* [Malibu, California: Roundtable Publishing Company], p. 23.

26. *Op. Cit.*, (*False Nationalism, False Internationalism*), p. 188.

27. *New York Times*, Wednesday, May 3, 1967, p. 3.

28. Historical Note: The classical definition of lumpen proletariat and the intentions or definitions of Huey P. Newton, Bobby Seale and Eldridge Cleaver are a matter of ideological dispute. It is suggested to read *The Black Panther Party: Reconsidered,* [Baltimore: Black Classic Press, 1998], especially pages 43–47.

29. G. Louis Heath, *Off The Pigs: The History and Literature of the Black Panther Party,* [Metuchen, N.J.: The Scarecrow Press, Inc. 1976], p. 21.

30. *Op. Cit.*, E. Tani and Kae Sera, *False Nationalism, False Internationalism,* [Chicago, Illinois: A Seed's Beneath The Snow

Publication, 1985], pp. 187, 188.

31. *Op. Cit.*, [E. Tani and Kae Sera], p. 190.

32. *Op. Cit.*, John T. McCartney, *Black Power Ideologies*, p. 147.

33. Robert H. Brisbane, *Black Activism: Racial Revolution in the United States*, [Valley Forge: Judson Press, 1974], p. 209.

34. Bobby Seale, *Op. Cit.*, p. 219.36

35. Bobby Seale, Ibid, p. 221.

36. James Forman, *The Making of Black Revolutionaries*, [Seattle, WA: Opened Hand Publishing, Inc., 1985], pp. 522–523.

37. Interview with Don Stone, Atlanta, Georgia, 1994.

38. Huey P. Newton, *To Die for the People: The Writings of Huey P. Newton* (Toni Morrison (ed.)), [New York: Writers and Readers Publishing, Inc., 1995], pp. 14–19.

39. *Op. Cit.*, G. Louis Heath, p. 49.

40. Letter from Jonia Abron to Muhammad Ahmad 6/17/99. Historial Note: RAM considered itself a revolutionary nationalist organization. RAM cooperated and worked with various white left groups since 1963 but was critical of them.

41. Jim Haskins, *Power To The People: The Rise and Fall of the Black Panther Party*, [New York: Simon & Schuster Books for Young Readers, 1997], p. 61.

42. Earl Anthony, *Picking Up the Gun* [New York: Dial press, 1971], p. 81. Also, *The Black Panther Party: Reconsidered*, [Baltimore: Black Classic Press, 1998], p. 31.

43. Bobby Seale, *Seize The Time: The Story of the Black Panther Party and Huey P. Newton*, [New York: Random House, 1968], p. 208.

44. G. Lewis Heath, *Off the Pig! The History and Literature of the Black Panther Party*, [Meuchen, N.J.: The Scarecrow Press, Inc., 1976], p. 50.

45. Kathleen Rout, *Eldridge Cleaver*, [Boston: Twayne Publishers, 1991], p. 63.

46. David Hilliard and Lewis Cole, *This Side of Glory: The Autobiography of David Hilliard and the Story of the Black Panther Party*, [Boston: Little, Brown and Company, 1993], p. 183.

47. Jim Haskins, *Power to the People: The Rise and Fall of the Black Panther Party*, [New York: Simon & Schuster Books for Young Readers, 1997], pp. 44–48.

48. *Op. Cit.*, (Kathleen Rout, *Eldridge Cleaver*), pp. 70–71.

49. Ibid. p. 72.

50. Interview with Huey Newton in "Eyes on the Prize" video.

51. Kirt Kim Holder, *The History of the Black Panther Party 1966–1972: A Curriculum Tool for African-American Studies*: unpublished dissertation, p. 122.

52. Video Power to the People.

53. Interview with Bila Sunni Ali, Amherst, Mass., 1975.

54. House of Representatives, Ninety-Second Congress, Report by the Committee on Internal Security, *Gun-Barrel Politics: The Black Panther Party, 1966–1971*. Washington, D. C., U. S. Government Printing Office, 1971, p. 69.

55. *Black Panther Party Part 4 National Office Operations and Investigation of Activities in Des Moines, Iowa and Omaha, Nebr./Hearings before the Committee on Internal Security* House of Representatives Ninety-First Congress Second Session Appendix A, p. 4977.

56. *Op. Cit., Gun Barrel Politics*, p. 69.

57. Mario Van Peebles, Ula Y. Taylor and J. Tarika Lewis, *Panther: A Pictorial History of the Black Panthers and the Story Behind the Film*, [New York: New Market Press, 1995], p. 67.

58. Ibid, *Panther*, p. 70.

59. Ibid, *Panther*, p. 71.

60. Ollie A. Johnson III, "Explaining the Demise of the Black Panther Party: The Role of Internal Factors" in Charles E. Jones (ed.) *The Black Panther Party: Reconsidered* (Baltimore Black Classic Press, 1998), p. 398.

61. Assata Shakur, *Assata: An Autobiography*, (Chicago, Illinois, Lawrence Hill, 1987), p. 221.

62. Ibid, (A. Shakur), p. 222.

63. Earl Anthony, *Picking Up the Gun*, [New York: Pyramid Books, 1971], p. 100.

64. *Op. Cit., Picking Up The Gun*, p. 107.

65. Interview with Abdul Quhar (Ben Simmons), Cleveland, Ohio 1997.

66. Interview with Rashad Byrdsong, Cleveland, Ohio, 1998.

67. Sundiata Acoli, "A Brief History of the Black Panther Party and Its Place in the Black Liberation Movement," April 2, 1985, p. 1.

68. *Op. Cit.*, Kathleen Rout, *Eldridge Cleaver* (Boston: Twayne Publishers, 1991), p. 83.

69. Kuwasi Ballagoon, Joan Bird, Cetewayo, Robert Collier, Dharuba, Richard Harris, Ali Bey Hassan, Jamal, Abayama Katara, Kwando Kinshasa, Baba Odiga, Shaba Ogun Om, Curtis Powell, Afeni Shakur, Lumumba Shakur, and Clark Squire, *Look for Me in the Whirlwind: The Collective Autobiography of the New York 21*, [New York: Random House, 1971] p. 148

70. Ibid, p. 150

71. Interview with Safiya Bukhari 6/6/98. Cleveland to New York, Telephone Interview.

72. Video Interview with Cleo Silver (1999) New York to Cleveland, Ohio.

73. Kathleen Rout, *Eldridge Cleaver*, [Boston: Twayne Publishers, 1991], p. 136.

74. Ibid, (Kathleen Rout), p.71.

75. *Op. Cit.*, Rout, p. 72.

76. Eyes on the Prize Power! Video (1966–1968).

77. Bobby Seale, Seize The Time [New York: Random House, 1970] p. 370.

78. Charles Jones, (ed.) *The Black Panther Party Reconsidered*, [Black Classic Press, 1998], p. 130.

79. Elaine Brown, *A Taste of Power* [New York: Pantheon Books, 1992], pp. 156–160.

80. Mario Van Peebles, Ula Y. Taylor and J. Tarika Lewis, *Panther*, [New York: New Market Press, 1995], p. 182.

81. *Gun Barrel Politics: The Black Panther Party, 1966–1971*, [Washington, D.C.: U.S. House of Representatives, 197], p. 54.

82. Mario Van Peebles, Ula Y. Taylor and J. Tarika Lewis, *Panther: A Pictorial History of the Black Panthers and the Story Behind the Film*, [New York: New Market Press, 1995], p. 182.

83. Ibid, p. 182.

84. *Op. Cit.*, p. 182.

85. Ibid, p. 182.

86. *Op. Cit.*, p. 182.

87. William Lee Brent, *Long Time Gone*, [New York: Times Books, 1996], pp. 133–142.

88. Charles E. Jones (ed.), *The Black Panther Party [Reconsidered]*, [Baltimore: Black Classic Press, 1998], pp. 370–372.

89. Ibid. pp. 220–224.

90. Mario Van Peebles, Ula Y. Taylor and Jitarika Lewis, *Panther*, [New York: New Market Press, 1995], p. 183.

91. Ibid., p. 183.

92. Jim Fletcher, Tanaquil Jones and Sylvere Latringer, *Still Black, Still Strong*, [New York: Semiotext (e), 1993], p. 232.

93. *Op. Cit.*, p. 183.

94. Bobby Seale, *Seize the Time*, [New York: Random House, 1970], pp. 289–296.

95. Ibid., pp. 296–314.

96. Ibid., *Gun Barrel Politics*, p. 100.

97. *Op. Cit.*, (Fletcher, Jones, Tatringer), p. 232.

98. *Op. Cit.*, (Van Peebles), p. 184.

99. Ibid., p. 184.

100. Ward Churchill and Jim Vander Wall, *Agents of Repression* [Boston, MA: South End Press, 1990], pp. 64–77.

101. Interview with John Bracey, Jr., Amherst, Mass. , 1993, Interview with Louis Randall, Amherst, Mass., 1975.

102. *Op. Cit.* (Mario Van Peebles, *Panther*), p. 184.

103. Ibid., p. 184.

104. Kenneth O'Reilly, *Racial Matters: The F.B.I.'s Secret File on Black America, 1960–1972*, [New York: The Free Press, 1989], p. 297.

105. *Op. Cit.*, (Mario Van Peebles), p. 184.

106. *Op. Cit.* (Mario Van Peebles, *Panther*), p. 184.

107. Ibid., p. 105.

108. David Hilliard and Lewis Cole, *This Side of Glory*, [Boston, MA: Little, Brown & Company, 1993], pp. 290–294.

109. *Op. Cit.*, (Fletcher, Jones, Latringer), pp. 234–235.

110. *Op. Cit.* (Mario Van Peebles), p. 185.

111. Ibid., p. 185.

112. Yohuru Williams, *Black Politics/White Power*, [New York: Brandywine Press, 2000], pp. 152–154.

113. Scott L. Bills, *Kent State/May 4*, [Kent, Ohio: The Kent State University Press, 1988], pp. 16–18.

114. Huey P. Newton, *Revolutionary Suicide*, [New York: Writers and Readers Publishing, Inc., 1973], pp. 265–267.

115. Charles E. Jones, *The Black Panther Party (Reconsidered)*, [Baltimore: Black Classic Press, 1998], p. 184.

116. *Op. Cit.* (Mario Van Peebles), p. 186.

117. G. Louis Heath, *Off the Pigs!: The History and Literature of the Black Panther Party*, [Methuchen, J.J.: The Scarecrow Press, Inc., 1976], p. 139.

118. Huey P. Newton, *Revolutionary Suicide*, [New York: Writers and Readers Publishing, Inc., 1973], pp. 267–292.

119. Interview with Madalynn Rucker, 1998. 8/23/98.

120. David Hilliard & Lewis Cole, *This Side of Glory: The Autobiography of David Hilliard and the Story of the Black Panther Party*, [Boston: Little, Brown and Company, 1993], p. 307.

121. Jim Haskins, *Power To The People*, [New York: Simon & Schuster Books for Young Readers, 1997], pp. 75–76.

122. *Op. Cit.* (Ward Churchill and Jim Vander Wall), pp. 95–96.

123. *Op. Cit.* (Ward Churchill), p. 86.

124. Jim Haskins, *Power to the People: The Rise and Fall of the Black Panther Party*, [New York: Simon and Schuster Books for Young Readers, 1997], p. 79. Also see, Louis E. Jackwood, *The Glass House Tapes*, [New York: Avon Books, 1973].

125. Interview with Madalynn Rucker, 8/23/98, Cleveland, Ohio to Sacramento, California, Telephone Interview.

126. David Hilliard and Lewis Cole, *This Side of Glory! The Autobiography of David Hilliard and the Story of the Black Panther Party*, [Boston: Little Brown and Company, 1998], pp. 312–313.

127. *Op. Cit.*, (Hilliard, *This Side of Glory*), p. 306.

128. Mumia Abu-Jamal, *We Want Freedom: A Life in the Black Panther Party* [Cambridge, Massachusetts: South End Press 2004] p. 220

129. Ibid., (Hilliard, *This Side of Glory!*), p. 314.

130. Jim Haskins, *The Rise and the Fall of the Black Panther Party*, [New York: Simon & Schuster Books for Young Readers, 1997], p. 80.

131. Ibid., p. 81.

132. Interview with Safiya Bukhari, 6/6/98: Cleveland, Ohio to New York, Telephone Interview.

133. *Op. Cit.*, (Haskins), p. 82.

134. Bobby Seale interview (video), All Power to The People: The Black Panther Party and Beyond.

135. Huey P. Newton, *Revolutionary Suicide*, [New York: Writers and Readers Publication, Inc., 1995], pp. 306–307.

136. Interview with Rashad Byrdsong, Cleveland, Ohio, 1997, and Interview with Kalied Abdul Raheem Muhammad, Chicago, Illinois, 3/20/98.

137. Interview with Austin Allen, Cleveland, Ohio, 11/19/93.

138. Mumia Abu-Jamal, *We Want Freedom: A Life in the Black Panther Party*, [Cambridge, Massachusetts: South End Press] p. 224

139. Ibid. (Byrdsong) 5/30/98.

140. Hugh Pearson, *The Shadow of the Panther: Huey Newton and the Price of Black Power*, [Reading, Massachusetts: Addison-Wesley Publishing Company, 1994], p. 241.

141. Interview with Austin Allen, Cleveland, Ohio 11/19/93. Historical Note: This in no way implies that Dr. Austin Allen felt the boycott was an act of extortion. He basically felt it was ill timed or planned.

142. Huey P. Newton, *To Die For The People: Selected Writings and*

Speeches, [New York: Writers and Readers Publishing, Inc., 1995], p. 111.

143. Interview with Austin Allen, Cleveland, Ohio, 11/19/93.

144. *Op. Cit.,* (Pearson, *The Shadow of the Panther*), p. 259.

145. Interview with Madalynn Rucker, 8/23/98.

146. *Op. Cit.,* Elaine Brown, *A Taste of Power: A Black Woman's Story*, pp. 348–353.

147. Bobby Seale, *A Lonely Rage: The Autobiography of Bobby Seale*, [New York: New York Times Books, 1978], pp. 228–238.

148. *Op. Cit.* (Pearson, *The Shadow of the Panther*), p. 267.

149. Karl Krapper, "Women and the Black Panther Party, Introduction," *Socialist Review, Vol. 26, No. 1 & 2, 1996*, p. 27.

150. Interview with Angela Brown," *Socialist Review, Vol. 26, No. 1 & 2, 1996*, p. 27.

151. Angela D. LaBlanc-Ernst, "The Most Qualified Person to handle the Job, Black Panther Party Women 1966–1982," in Charles E. Jones (ed.) *The Black Panther Party; Reconsidered*, [Baltimore: Black Classic Press, 1998], p. 307.

152. *Op. Cit.* (Angela Brown), p. 35.

153. *Op. Cit.* (Angela D. LeBlanc-Ernest-Black Panther Party [Reconsidered]), p. 308.

154. Interview with Rashad Byrdsong, Cleveland State University, Cleveland, Ohio, 5/30/98.

155. Karl Krapper, "Women and the Black Panther Party: An Interview with Angela Brown," *Socialist Review, Vol. 26, Nos. 1 & 2, 1996*, p. 40.

156. Telephone interview with Jonia Abron, Cleveland, Ohio, Kalamazoo, Michigan, January 17, 1999.

157. *Op. Cit.,* (an interview with Angela Brown), p. 43.

158. Ibid., pp. 41–42.

159. Cleo Silver, videotaped interview in New York, 1998.

160. Karl Knapper, "Women and the Black Panther Party: an Interview with Angela Brown," *Socialist Review, Vol 26, Nos. 1 & 2, 1996*, p. 46.

161. Cleo Silver, taped interview, 1998.

162. Jim Haskins, *Power to the People: The Rise and Fall of the Black Panther Party*, [New York: Simon & Schuster Books for Young Readers, 1997], pp. 97–98.

163. *The African-American Almanac*, [Detroit, Michigan, 1997], p. 346.

164. Elaine Brown, *Taste of Power: A Black Woman's Story*, [New York: Pantheon Books], p. 445.

165. Regina Jennings, "Why I Joined the Party: An African Womanist

Reflection" in Charles E. Jones, *The Black Panther Party [Reconsidered]*, [Baltimore: Black Classic Press, 1998], pp. 262–264.

166. *The Black Panther Party Reconsidered*, [Baltimore: Black Classic Press, 1998], p. 263.

167. Madalynn Rucker, audio taped interview, 1998. 8/23/98.

168. Charles E. Jones (ed.), *The Black Panther Party Reconsidered*, [Baltimore: Black Classic Press, 1998], p. 310.v

169. Elaine Brown, *A Taste of Power: A Black Woman's Story*, [New York: Doubleday, 1992], p. 357.

170. Elaine Brown, *A Taste of Power: A Black Woman's Story*, [New York: Doubleday, 1992], p. 189.

171. *Op. Cit.*, (Karl Knapper, "Women and the Black Panther Party: An Interview with Angela Brown, *Socialist Review, Vol. 26, Nos. 1 & 2, 1996)*, p. 38.

172. Elaine Brown, *A Taste of Power: A Black Woman's Story*, [New York: Doubleday, 1992], p. 445.

173. Interview with Jonia Abron, January 17, 1999.

174. Charles E. Jones, *The Black Panther Party (Reconsidered)*, [Baltimore: Black Press, 1998], p. 324.

175. *Op. Cit.*, (Brown, *A Taste of Power: A Black Woman's Story*), p. 375.

176. *Op. Cit.*, (Pearson, *The Shadow of the Panther*), p. 281.

177. *Op. Cit.*, (Brown, *A Taste of Power*), p. 448.

178. Jonia M. Abron, Letter to Muhammad Ahmad, June 17, 1999, p. 11. Also see Kenneth O'Reilly "*Racial Matters: The FBI's Secret File on Black America. 1960–1972*, [New York: The Free Press, 1989], pp. 293–324.

179. David Hilliard and Lewis Cole, *This Side of Glory: The Autobiography of David Hilliard and the Story of the Black Panther Party*, [Boston: Little, Brown and Company, 1993], p. 436.

LEAGUE OF REVOLUTIONARY BLACK WORKERS

This chapter focuses on the League of Revolutionary Black Workers, the only African-American radical organization to emerge in the period 1960–1975 whose primary concentration was organizing black workers at their work places (at the point of production). Any study of the League of Revolutionary Black Workers would not be comprehensive if it did not include an interview with General Gordon Baker, Jr.; it's central founder and organizer. But to include an interview with Baker in full text would be too long for this study. The chapter is based on an extensive interview with Baker, but also includes excerpts of other primary interviews from LRBW members.

INTRODUCTION

To approach a study of the League of Revolutionary Black Workers (LRBW), an independent black radical workers' formation in Detroit, a branch of the black liberation movement, several questions should be answered. We should ask ourselves what is the history of black workers' relations in white unions? Also, is there any particular phenomenon that contributed to the League emerging in Detroit rather than in any other city?

African-American workers' involvement in large numbers began during the first imperialist war, when there was a shortage of laborers and Detroit was becoming the center of the auto industry. In 1910, there were only 569 African-Americans out of 105,759 autoworkers.

The southern whites who migrated to Detroit brought with them racist attitudes. The large Polish minority who were immigrants from Europe made up a large portion of the work force in the auto plants began to display the same prejudice against African-American workers after the southerners came. The auto industry was one of the last major industries in the United States to hire large numbers of African-American workers. African-Americans were excluded from regular jobs in most auto plants. Until 1935 only the Ford River Rouge plant hired African-American workers in large numbers. African-American workers who did work in auto plants were confined to janitorial work or to the unpleasant, backbreaking foundry jobs that white men did not want. Except in the Rouge plant, they were barred from the skilled work.

> Approximately one half of the Negroes in the industry were employed by the Ford Motor Company and 99 percent of these in the huge River Rouge plant. The Negro employees of General Motors and Chrysler were also concentrated in a few plants: Buick No. 70 in Flint, Pontiac Foundry in Pontiac, Chevrolet Forge in Detroit, and Chevrolet Grey-Iron Foundry in Saginaw—all of General Motors; and Main Dodge of Chrysler in a Detroit suburb. Few Negroes were employed in automobile plants outside of Michigan.[1]

Of the auto manufacturers, Ford developed a policy of hiring ten percent African-Americans in his work force at the River Rouge plant. The story goes that at the beginning of the 1921 depression, African-American workers employed at River Rouge and African-American middle-class leaders from Detroit approached Ford and talked about his racist bias in layoffs. Ford is then said to have changed his hiring policy at River Rouge. He placed African-American workers in all departments and occupations in the plant. But he did not extend this policy beyond River Rouge. Ford assembly plants in the South only employed African-American workers as janitors and porters. However, Ford's employment policy won him loyalty of the African-American community, particularly the African-American church. Ford made financial contributions to selected African-American churches; he would then use the ministers as employment agents. African-American workers were hired when they presented a written recommendation from their minister to company officials. African-American ministers loved Ford's assistance because it increased church attendance, helped the church financially and strengthened their community leadership position. Thus once receiving Ford's approval, a minister would willingly follow Ford's anti-labor position.

> When A. Philip Randolph, head of the Brotherhood of Sleeping Car Porters, was invited in 1938 to speak at a Negro church, those of its members who were employed at Ford were threatened with firing. After Randolph spoke, some were actually dismissed and frankly told that Randolph's speech was the reason.[2]

Mordecai Johnson, president of Howard University, made a pro-union speech at an African-American church and three months later he was denied a second appearance.

Prior to 1929 the American Federation of Labor (AFL) was primarily made up of craft unions. The AFL discriminated against African-American workers. African-American membership in the AFL in 1930 was estimated to be about 50,000, but thousands of African-American craftsmen were ignored by the AFL while others were in segregated unions. One exception can be noted for lack of racial discrimination was the United Mine Workers (UMW) under the leadership of John L. Lewis. With the depression, the militant rank and file of the AFL began to push for unionization of unskilled (industrial) workers. A Committee for Industrial Organization was established. In 1937 the committee was expelled from the AFL and became the Congress of Industrial Organizations (CIO). The CIO recognized that if it was going to be successful it had to have the support of African-American workers. African-Americans and the Communist Party were instrumental in helping to build the CIO. The National Negro Congress, formed in 1936 with 500 African-American organizations in its membership, was a left-wing worker-oriented organization. It supported the CIO vigorously. Led by A. Philip Randolph until African-American cadres of the Communist Party began to direct its line according to Russia's foreign policy; it helped radicalize the African-American community. An African-American/CIO alliance began to develop.[3]

But African-American workers were not too receptive at first to the idea of becoming involved in labor activism. This probably stemmed from years of racial discrimination by labor and their precarious position at the point of production. When large sit-down strikes broke out in 1936 and 1937, few African-American workers participated.[4] Most stayed at home, but they did not serve as scabs either. In some plants there had been racial clashes in the plants prior to the strikes. The last plant to be organized in Detroit by the CIO was the River Rouge plant, where African-American workers resisted efforts at unionization until convinced by the CIO that it was on their side. By 1942 the Ford River Rouge plant was unionized after the majority of African-American workers had walked out on strike.[5]

As progressive as the CIO was, African-American trade unionists still had to fight against racial discrimination within it. During the World War II, the Communists emerged as the extreme right wing in the labor movement. They advocated sacrificing the rights of African-Americans to the interests of the war. So when A. Philip Randolph proposed an African-American March on Washington to protest job discrimination, he was opposed and openly attacked by the Communist Party. Roosevelt established the Fair Employment Practices Committee (FEPC) as a result of the proposed march. During the war, African-American workers were in constant struggles to get skilled jobs in the war industry. The auto plants were converted to war production. When an African-American worker was upgraded, often white workers would walk off the job. The federal government and the UAW had to apply constant pressure to stop racist work stoppages by white workers. When the war ended, old discrimination patterns in hiring reappeared. Thousands of African-American workers lost their jobs. In the 1950s the labor movement purged the Communists. McCarthyism was the mad rage of the country. Even in a period of political hysteria, A. Philip Randolph constantly attacked racism within the CIO. In 1955, the AFL and CIO reunited. Right before the merger, African-American unionists met to secure the election of African-Americans to the AFL-CIO Executive Council and to get the federation to adopt a strong civil rights position. After the merger, African-American labor organized in major cities to fight for the interests of African-American workers.

> One of these organizations was the Trade Union Leadership Conference (TULC), formed by a group of Detroit Negro unionists in 1957. Most of the founders were from the UAW but in 1960 there were about as many Negroes from the other unions in the TULC as from the UAW.[6]

Many African-American trade unionists attacked the TULC for racism in reverse. They feared the TULC and similar organizations would divide the labor movement. The TULC attacked these critics as labor uncle toms of the AFL-CIO convention. George Meany verbally attacked A. Philip Randolph. The TULC wrote a letter to Meany denouncing Meany's outburst and told Meany they objected to attacks on the NAACP by Charles Zimmerman. The TULC endorsed the NAACP's memorandum of December 4, 1958, charging racial discrimination and segregation by unions affiliated with the AFL-CIO.

The TULC's 2500 members (in 1961) in the Detroit area had engaged in political action; contributed financially to various civil rights activities and to political candidates; worked to improve Detroit public schools; established contacts in the Polish, Jewish, and Spanish-speaking communities; helped Negroes in the Hod Carriers and Common Laborers local union replace "unfriendly" white officers with Negroes and more sympathetic whites; and served as a model for the Negro-American Labor Council and similar organizations in other Northern cities.[7]

So while the TULC was no longer considered militant as it was surpassed by the impact of the civil rights activity in Detroit, it had set the precedent for the emergence of the Dodge Revolutionary Union Movement (DRUM).

BACKGROUND TO THE BUILDING OF THE DETROIT CADRE:

To properly evaluate the history of the League of Revolutionary Black Workers, it would be necessary to investigate the overall development of the black movement in Detroit. Another factor that should be taken into consideration is the concentration of industry in Detroit. Most of the key organizers of the LRBW were from Detroit (born) and raised in Detroit and were second-generation children of autoworkers. Many were students or ex-students at Wayne State University, an urban university where they became exposed to a radical tradition. Detroit was also unique in having an active post World War II, African-American organized radical leadership, which nurtured these young progressives.

More African-American workers were hired in the auto plants between the end of World War II and 1960. The African-American community for a large part relied on the liberal-labor coalition. There were adult African-American labor leadership as well as prominent African-American radicals in the community. Detroit's inner city was also the midwestern center of African-American nationalism. It is probably important to mention that the Socialist Workers Party had a strong base in Detroit. Their influence was felt in the African-American community in the early sixties.

Of the various groups in Detroit, GOAL (Group On Advanced Leadership) led by Richard and Milton Henry was representative of adult involvement in the movement. GOAL was a black nationalist, civil rights group. Reverend Albert Cleage was considered

GOAL's ideological leader. James and Grace Boggs, who split with the "Facing Reality" group of C.L.R. James, played an instrumental role in providing a synthesis between Black Nationalism and socialism. The loose linkage of the Henrys, Cleage, and the Boggs' provided young African-American radicals with an adult black radical leadership, which could be their resource base.

General Baker, later a founder of the League of Revolutionary Black Workers, entered Detroit's Black Left through participation in the Detroit Robert F. Williams Defense Committee in 1962. He recalls reading *The Crusader* and hearing "Radio Free Dixie" while attending Wayne State University, where he helped to form UHURU, one of Detroit's first Black Nationalist collectives.[8]

The Boggs' were important to young African-American radicals because they had a wealth of information, constantly wrote and published a newsletter called *Correspondence*, helped organize the Grassroots Leadership Conference in 1963 and the Freedom Now Party in 1964. Discussion sessions were held at the Boggs' home which provided young African-American radicals with insight on concepts, goals, strategy and tactics of socialism and revolution.

Whether one disagrees either partially or substantially with the politics of these organizations or individuals is quite beside the point; what should not be overlooked is that collectively they functioned as ongoing radical institutions which preserved and transmitted historical information and revolutionary values to a fresh generation of Detroit activists.[9]

Early in 1963, African-American students at Wayne State University formed a revolutionary black nationalist/socialist action cadre called UHURU. UHURU was more militant than GOAL, Rev. Cleage and the Boggs' but maintained close relations with them. Luke Tripp, John Williams, John Watson, Charles Johnson, General G. Baker, Jr., and Gwen Kemp led UHURU. UHURU members studied Marx, Lenin, Mao, Fanon, Malcolm X, Robert F. Williams, Che Guerara and many others. They attended Socialist Workers Party weekly forums, listened to members of the Communist Party and followers of C.L.R. James. The UHURU cadre considered themselves black Marxist-Leninists and was inspired by the Cuban and Chinese revolutions.

Several of the UHURU cadre and many of those who later joined DRUM were among the first generation of African-American workers hired in the plants in the 1960s who were raised in the north.[10]

In 1965, at this time, I am at the Dodge Main Plant and I am working with the African-American Student Movement. We had published a couple of publications. We started printing a publication called *Razor*, which was a publication for the African-American Student Movement in Detroit, and we circulated it at Wayne State Campus and Highland Park Community College campus. We also printed this thing called *Black Vanguard* that was a publication for black workers in the various shops around the city.[11]

In 1964, when Grace Boggs and Rev. Albert Cleage were instrumental in developing a strong statewide Freedom Now Party, some members of UHURU were organizers for it. Also in 1964, UHURU members went to Cuba, where they met Robert F. Williams, Fidel Castro, Che Guevara and Muhammad Babu. Some joined the Revolutionary Action Movement (RAM). In 1965 they regrouped and formed the Afro-American Student Movement (ASM), which put out a theoretical journal called *Black Vanguard*, edited by John Watson. *Black Vanguard* was distributed to African-American workers in the plants but was too theoretical and thick for a positive workers' response.

The Afro-American Student Movement (ASM) was an attempt by RAM to build an all African-American student movement in urban areas. Watson felt V. I. Lenin's "Where to Begin?" was a model theoretical treatise towards building a state-wide black Marxist-Leninist party around a newspaper expanding across the state of Michigan and eventually into a national party building process state by state.[12]

SEPTEMBER 10TH MOVEMENT

General G. Baker, Jr. received his draft notice in June 1965. He wrote a political letter to the draft board denouncing U.S. imperialism. ASM decided to protest Baker's induction. At this point we should discuss some aspects of Baker's background.

General Gordon Baker, Jr. was born in Detroit, Michigan on September 6, 1941 to Clara Dixon Baker and General Gordon Baker, Sr. Baker, Jr. was raised in a family of three sisters and one nephew who was raised like a brother. The Baker family were sharecroppers from Georgia, who migrated to Detroit in the early forties seeking work in the auto factories. Baker's father worked as a welder in the Midland Ross steel mill plant in Detroit and was a member of the UAW. The plant had a militant local and Baker, Sr. was an active

243

member of the local. Baker, Sr. was a supporter of the Democrats and hated the Republicans. Baker, Jr. first began to develop a political consciousness when as a child he would hear of union (UAW) politics while attending family picnics or Labor Day parades.

Baker, Jr. attended Southwestern High School and graduated in June 1958. Baker played football and basketball in high school. In 1959, General Baker, Jr. enrolled in Highland Park Junior College. Baker was outraged because he had not been taught black history and knew nothing of the black Muslims, Malcolm X or Elijah Muhammad though they were being highlighted in the media at the time. ASM put out leaflets and press announcements stating that 50,000 African-Americans would show up at the Wayne County Induction Center when Baker had to report. Only eight demonstrators were there, but the threat of mass action had convinced the U.S. Army to find Baker "unsuitable" for service.

> What we did was organize what we called a September 10th Movement. The September 10th Movement was a movement that was, basically, an attempt to try to destroy the draft. We leafleted all the plants in the city of Detroit, most of the campuses and some of the high schools in terms of building resistance against the draft with the general agitation around the slogan of "no Vietnamese ever called me a Nigger," and that "we need to fight the discrimination here at home."[13]

Different members of the group began to go in different occupational directions. Watson and Williams became students at Wayne State and Baker worked in the auto factories. In 1965 Glanton Dowdell came into the cadre. Dowdell's street experience added valuable skills to the organization.

> A dropout from the 5th grade, he was put into a home for mentally retarded at the age of 13. In prison on and off since he was 16, he was finally incarcerated on a murder and robbery charge in Jackson. There he organized a strike of black prisoners against discrimination by forming a selected cadre. In prison he read voraciously, learned to paint and after 17 years was released through the intervention of a black probation officer who recognized his genius.[14]

In 1966, Dowdell, Baker and Rufus Griffin helped form the Black Panther Party in Detroit. A mini-rebellion broke out on the east side and the police picked up the three and charged them with carrying concealed weapons. Baker and Dowdell were convicted and placed on five years' probation. Early in 1967, Dowdell was given a suspended sentence. During the winter months of that year, RAM organized the Black Guards and self-defense community militias in Detroit. "Join the Black Guards" slogans were on walls all over Detroit. On July 23, 1967 the largest insurrection in the history of the United States raged as African-Americans in the thousands took to the streets and fought the police, National Guard and the U.S. Army for five days.

Dowdell and Baker were picked up on July 24th. They were later released on $50,000 bond. The Detroit Rebellion raised the national consciousness of African-American workers. It started an air of militancy for most African-Americans.

While being detained (preventive detention), arrested and incarcerated during the Detroit rebellion, Baker observed that many of the participants arrested for suspected activity in the rebellion were fellow co-workers who worked in the auto plants. "There in the same cell block was half of the assembly line of my job."[15] From his participant-observer studies Baker summarized that many young African-American workers in Detroit had a developing revolutionary consciousness.[16]

Dowdell was elected the vice chairman of the City-wide Citizens Action Committee (CCAC), a coalition which attempted to organize the African-American community after the rebellion. At times over 2,000 African-Americans would attend the CCAC meetings. Baker returned to work in the plants. There he began to see that the consciousness of African-American workers was much higher than before the rebellion.

> Other forces were able to take advantage of rebellions in other cities, but our critical position was that we had the RAM connection, local connections with the black liberation movement and Black Panther Party. We talked about building a network of people that would be put up in the best position to take tactical advantage of the rebellion.[17]

In September 1967, John Watson, Mike Hamlin, Luke Tripp, Ken Cockrel, General Baker and others organized an African-American radical newspaper called *The Inner City Voice* (ICV), which addressed itself particularly to the oppressive conditions of African-American workers and called them to organize.

Mike Hamlin, John Watson, and Ken Cockrel began discussing

What Is To Be Done? by V. I. Lenin on their job at the Detroit News. They all agreed with Lenin's proposition of how a newspaper could initiate, generate or serve as a center for working class activity and organization. Hamlin and Watson decided to start a monthly radical African-American newspaper. Mike Hamlin borrowed money on his credit card. He and Watson created a monthly African-American newspaper named *The Inner City Voice* and opened an office.

They brought Ken Cockrel onto the staff of the newspaper. *The Inner City Voice* staff represented a coalition of African-American Marxist Leninists and cultural nationalists. The cultural nationalists, a group of twelve writer supporters, objected to *The Inner City Voice* printing articles or works by Ho Chi Minh and "Che" Guevara because they were not "black."

To mediate the dispute Watson and Hamlin brought General Baker in the *Inner City Voice* group. Baker, large in physical size and known for not negotiating with vacillating political positions, was originally brought in because the cultural nationalist community respected him and also his presence would have an intimidating effect.

Baker recalls,

> "Within one month of the Detroit rebellion, The *Inner City Voice* newspaper sponsored Rap Brown's visit to Detroit at the old theater on Dexter Avenue that was packed. So many people came that we had standing room only and had to put loud speakers on the street. It was there these kinds of activities that opened up and allowed for us to take real advantage of."[18]

In an interview with Chuck Wooten, July 14, 2002, he gives a description of "worker's self-organization" and the role of cadre in relation to that becomes crystal clear.

Charles "Chuck" Wooten began working at Dodge Main–Hamtramick assembly plant August 13, 1964. This was his first industrial plant job. Wooten experienced racial discrimination in the plant. Wooten worked in the 9110 department, which was at the time the body assembly plant that puts the car together. The plant had hundreds of African-Americans working the assembly line who were scheduled for the hardest work while whites received light work.

Wooten's consciousness began to sharpen as he realized there were no avenues for advancement in the skill trades and better jobs. The turning point in Wooten's life was the Detroit rebellion of July 23, 1967. Wooten became a black nationalist as he began to realize

African-Americans' struggle for equality was also a struggle for power. In late 1967, after the Detroit rebellion, Wooten started meeting with Ron March and other workers from the plant at a bar and outside the back of the bar, and began discussing about the conditions inside the plant and what needed to be done about them.

Around February 1968 General G. Baker, Jr., known affectionately by his friends as "Gen," started holding discussions first with one of the African-American worker leaders in the plant at the *Inner City Voice* office. Baker stressed the idea of organizing African-American workers at the plant to fight for better working conditions and more representation in the union.

In April 1968, Ron March who knew Baker from the afternoon shift brought Baker to the workers discussions.

Baker suggested to the informal workers discussion group of starting a black workers weekly newsletter inside the plant. The group decided to call itself the Dodge Revolutionary Union Movement (DRUM). The newsletter was named after the plant to give workers identification of where they worked.[19]

In its formation in May 1968, DRUM consisted of eight Chrysler workers who constituted an editorial board that met formally every Sunday in the *Inner City Voice* offices.[20]

Baker recalls,

> We had a little formation called the Black People's Liberation Party, which included myself, John Watson, John Williams, Kenny Cockrel, Marian Kramer, Orion Hatch, Kyle Gregory and a few other people. They were coming together to form a black people's liberation party. The combination of us represented, Marian Kramer, the community people or the West Central Organization. Cockrel and most of the rest of them still represented students. Kyle Gregory represented some level of professors and I represented some workers input from the shops. So we had a little network that we were working with and developed. We all supported the development of the *Inner City Voice* newspaper that began to play a real critical role after the rebellion.[21]

THE FOUNDING OF DRUM

On May 2, 1968, a walkout of 4,000 workers occurred at the Hamtramick Assembly Plant that stemmed from a gradual speedup of the production line. The facts show production soared from

49 units to 58 units an hour within the short period of a week. The mobility of the worker was retarded to the extent that it was difficult to keep pace. As a result of the walkout, picket lines were set up around the gates and individual workers began to mass. This situation occurred on the afternoon shift of which General Baker worked and carried over into the first shift. During the initial picketing, the company sent out photographers who photographed some of the pickets. The pictures were used as evidence against some of the pickets and were instrumental in the discharge and disciplining of certain workers who took part in the walkout and picketing.

Most of the overall administration of punishment, including discharges and disciplinary action taken against the pickets, was overwhelmingly applied to the African-American workers. They were held responsible for the walkout, which was directly caused by company indifference towards working conditions. Three African-American workers were fired; ten were given from one to five days off. Seven persons (five African-American and two white) were fired, but all except two—General Baker and Bennie Tate, both African-American and DRUM (Dodge Revolutionary Union Movement) leaders—were eventually rehired.

Chuck Wooten, one of nine workers who founded DRUM, describes how DRUM came into being.

> During the wildcat strike of May 1968, upon coming to work...there were picket lines established...manned by all white workers at the time and as a result of this the black workers received the harshest disciplinary actions. A few workers and I went across the street and sat in a bar...It was here that we decided we would do something about organizing black workers to fight the racial discrimination inside the plants and the overall oppression of black workers...And this was the beginning of DRUM.[22]

Prior to the wildcat strike at Dodge Main, General Baker began to pull together a group of eight African-American workers. They would meet in the offices of the *Inner City Voice*.

> Black workers who were either dismissed or penalized moved to organize the workers at Dodge Main by using a weekly Newsletter (DRUM) as an organizing tool. The contents of the Newsletter dealt with very specific cases of racism and tomism on the job and stressed the necessity of

united action on part of black workers to abolish the racial aspects of exploitation and degradation at the plant.[23]

The first issues of the DRUM newsletter dealt with the May 2nd wildcat strike.

The African-American workers enthusiastically accepted the first issue of the weekly DRUM newsletter. They were somewhat astounded to see accurate reporting of conditions they were experiencing inside the plant.[24]

The second issue carried an "expose" on several African-Americans in the plant whom DRUM considered to be "uncle toms." The issue also outlined the DRUM program.

> DRUM is an organization of oppressed and exploited black workers. It realizes that black workers are the victims of inhumane slavery at the expense of white racist plant managers. It also realizes that black workers comprise 60% and upwards of the entire work force at the Hamtramick Assembly Plant, and therefore hold exclusive power. We members of DRUM had no other alternative but to form an organization and to present a platform. The Union has consistently and systematically failed us time and time again. We have attempted to address our grievances to the U.A.W.'s procedures, but to no avail; its hands are just as bloody as the white racist management of this corporation. We black workers feel that if skilled trades can negotiate directly with the company and hold a separate contract, then black workers have more justification for moving independently of the U.A.W.[25]

The third issue of DRUM dealt with charges and documentation of racist conditions in the plant and also attacked the UAW for endorsing the annual Detroit Police field day. It also listed a number of deaths attributed to the police department. After the third week, African-American workers in the plant began to ask how to go about joining DRUM. Members of DRUM working in the plant proselytized and recruited African-American workers on the job. The strength and influence of DRUM grew tremendously.

> Around the sixth week the more militant workers wanted to go for some concrete action against Chrysler and the UAW. At this point the editors of DRUM decided to test their strength. They called for a one-week boycott of two bars outside the gate that were patronized by a large number of brothers. The bars didn't hire blacks and practiced racism in other subtle ways. DRUM received about 95% cooperation.

This was achieved without the use of pickets or picket signs. As a further test of strength DRUM called for an extension of the boycott. Again DRUM received solid support so they decided to get down.[26]

Seeing that the boycott was a success, DRUM decided to test its strength by showing Chrysler and the UAW it could shut down the plant. The ninth issue of the DRUM newsletter carried a list of 14 demands. The newsletter prepared the workers for the proposed strike. DRUM demands:

1. DRUM demands 50 black foremen.

2. DRUM demands 10 black general foremen immediately.

3. DRUM demands 3 black superintendents.

4. DRUM demands a black plant manager.

5. DRUM demands that the majority of the employment office personnel be black.

6. DRUM demands all black doctors and 50% black nurses in the medical centers at this plant.

7. DRUM demands that the medical policy at this plant be changed entirely.

8. DRUM demands that 50% of all plant protection guards be black, and that every time a black worker is removed from plant premises that he be led by a black brother.

9. DRUM demands that all black workers immediately stop paying union dues.

10. DRUM demands that two hours pay that goes into union dues be levied to the black community to aid in self-determination for black people.

11. DRUM demands that the double standard be eliminated and that a committee of the black rank and file be set up to investigate all grievances against the corp., to find out what type of discipline is to be taken against the corporation and also to find out what type of discipline is to be taken against Chrysler Corporation employees.

12. DRUM demands that all black workers who have been fired on trumped up racist charges be brought back with all lost pay.

13. DRUM demands that our fellow black brothers in South Africa working for Chrysler Corporation, and its subsidiaries be paid at an equal scale as white racist co-workers.

14. DRUM also demands that a black brother be appointed as head of the board of directors of Chrysler Corporation.

The power base for these demands will be as follows:

1. Legal demonstration at Local 3 and Solidarity House.

2. Legal demonstration at Highland Park (Chrysler Corp. headquarters).

3. Legal shut down of Hamtramick Assembly.[27]

In the ninth week of its existence, DRUM moved. On Thursday, July 7, 1968, DRUM held a rally in the parking lot across from the factory, which attracted over 300 workers. After speeches from DRUM leaders, African-American workers, along with a number of African-American community groups and a Congo band, formed a line and marched to the UAW Local 3 headquarters two blocks away. DRUM had carefully planned the picketing to coincide with the union executive board meeting. When the workers arrived at the local, they proceeded into the building.

The panic-stricken executive board immediately canceled their meeting and opened the union auditorium to listen to criticisms aimed at the company and the union. DRUM leaders described how the union worked hand-in-glove with the corporation, the union's failure to address itself to the workers' grievances, and DRUM's demands. Unsatisfied with the defense of the union's pro-capitalist line by Ed Liska, president of UAW Local 3, and Vice President Charles Brooks, DRUM stated it would close Dodge Main in defiance of the union contract.

On Friday, July 8, 1968, DRUM and supporting groups arrived at the plant gates at 5 A.M. in order to be there when workers began arriving for the 6 A.M. shift.

> Picket lines were set up and manned entirely by students, intellectuals, and community people. Workers were excluded. White workers were allowed to enter the factory without interference but all Blacks were stopped. No force was applied but verbal persuasion was sufficient to keep an estimated 70 percent of the Black workers out of the plant.[28]

While the majority of white workers entered the factory, many honored the picket line and went home. Some 3,000 African-American workers stood outside the factory gates as production came almost to a halt.

DRUM leaders talked to workers one hundred yards from the picketers because the Chrysler Corporation had obtained a court injunction hindering DRUM members from being in any struggle in the plant in violation of the union contract or face arrest.

About noon, six DRUM members went to Local 3 and met with Liska and other union officials. DRUM presented their grievances again.

About this time the police arrived, massing across the street from the workers. They began putting on tear gas masks and got into riot formation. A detective then came forward and ordered the workers to disperse. DRUM dispersed most of the strikers after organizing at least 250 workers into car pools. The car pool drove five miles to Chrysler headquarters. The Highland Park police arrived with gas warfare gear. Many of the demonstrators had gas masks. A group of DRUM representatives went into the Chrysler building and demanded to see the policy makers. They refused to meet with DRUM. The DRUM representatives returned to the demonstration and said the company had refused to meet. Satisfied with having achieved it's immediate objectives, DRUM transported the demonstrators back to their homes.

On Sunday twelve DRUM members were invited to the regular citywide meeting of African-American UAW representatives. The African-American UAW officials said they would support specific DRUM demands but DRUM felt the officials did not represent the African-American rank and file of the union, had not stepped forward before DRUM began demonstrations and the meeting ended with no real consensus.[29]

On Monday, the following day, DRUM again demonstrated at the plant. The Hamtramick police served John Doe injunctions on the demonstrators. The police proceeded to break up the demonstration. DRUM activists, feeling they had been successful, tore up their injunctions and either went to work or went home. The wildcat lasted for three days with Chrysler losing the production of approximately 1900 cars and no one was fired as a result of the action.

The wildcat strike forced the leaders of Local 3 to act on the cases of the workers who had been fired in May. The Local 3 leaders however accepted a package deal offered by Chrysler in which five of the seven were to be rehired except General Baker and Bennie Tate who remained fired. DRUM still viewed the July wildcat walkout an overwhelming success because it was a test of what an African-American radical workers organization could do.[30]

In August an African-American organization made an attempt to usurp DRUM. The group was made up of African-American trade union men and a Chrysler professional employee who was pretending he had been fired from the company. The group filed incorporation papers in the name of DRUM—the Detroit Revolutionary Union Movement. They called a meeting between the original DRUM—Dodge Revolutionary Union Movement—and themselves. The Detroit DRUM said they thought the original DRUM leadership was incompetent and needed direction. The meeting didn't lead to positive results because the original DRUM criticized them for not having a base and also incorrect style of work.

But DRUM learned that in order not to be co-opted or misrepresented, it had to move immediately to formalize its structure and tighten up the organization.

> Originally in May, DRUM consisted of eight Chrysler workers who constituted an editorial board which met formally every Sunday. In September, DRUM had developed into a fairly large organization whose form was for the most part amorphous. In the middle of September DRUM submitted its constitution and theoretical structure for acceptance at a general meeting. Both the constitution and structure were accepted unanimously.[31]

A trustee in the UAW Local 3 died and a special election was scheduled for September 3, 1968 to choose his successor.

> DRUM leadership was divided as to whether they should run a candidate. Those opposed believed that participation

in union electoral politics would: (1) appear to be compromising with a "corrupt" UAW; (2) might create the potential for opportunism in some DRUM members; and (3) the election might be lost. Those in favor argued that the election could: (1) demonstrate Black solidarity; (2) demonstrate DRUM's leadership; (3) serve as a vehicle for political education; and (4) aid DRUM's membership drive.[32]

DRUM chose Ron March, a DRUM member, to run for the post of union steward, and presented a platform for the upcoming election:

1. The complete accountability to the black majority of the entire membership.

2. All union decisions will coincide directly with the wishes of that majority.

3. Advocating a revolutionary change in the UAW (including a referendum vote and revive the grievance procedure).

4. Public denouncement of the racial practices within the UAW.

5. A refusal to be dictated to by the international staff of the UAW.

6 Total involvement in policy by the workers as opposed to dictatorship by the executive board.[33]

The election campaign was organized primarily as a tool for political education while also attempting to elect Ron March. March led the balloting in the election with 563 votes to 521 for his nearest competitor.

The Hamtramick police attacked some African-American workers near some bars the same night that the election returns were announced. Chuck Wooten, a member of DRUM, described forms of harassment:

> The Hamtramick police department began to move in a much more open way. They gave us tickets on our cars and just generally harassed us. One day about fifty of us were in the union hall, which is right across from the police station. The mayor of the city and the chief of police came in with guns in their hands. They told us to stop making trouble, and we said all we wanted was to win the election. We asked

them why they weren't harassing the others. While we were talking, a squad of police came through the door swinging axe handles and throwing Mace around.[34]

Between the time of the first election and the runoff, the union sent letters to retired workers appealing to them to participate in the election. While African-Americans made up 63 percent of the active work force in UAW Local 3, white (primarily Polish-Americans) made up the overwhelming majority of the retired workers.

On October 3, 1968, Ron March was defeated in the runoff by a vote of 2,091 to 1,386. With negative publicity from the established and union press and repression from police forces, DRUM felt that Ron's pulling forty percent of the vote under those conditions was a good showing. After running in two additional elections and receiving similar results, DRUM decided to terminate its direct participation in union electoral politics. Instead it supported African-American candidates who were not identified as DRUM members but who were progressive.

As DRUM expanded its operations, it had to address itself to how it was going to raise funds to carry out operations. The two main sources of finances were dues from DRUM members and contributions from workers. But these weren't enough to sustain the organization.

DRUM organized parties, demonstrations, and rallies that were attended by workers, students and people from church and neighborhood groups. DRUM also organized a picket line outside of Solidarity House to publicize its demands. DRUM decided to engage in fund-raising activity that would at the same time raise the consciousness of the workers and also informed the African-American community of DRUM's existence. With the help of the African-American clergy, DRUM was able to secure a church to hold a mass rally. DRUM sold raffle tickets prior to the rally, which served as both a fund-raiser and a publicity drive. First prize was a M-1 rifle, second prize a shotgun, and third prize a bag of groceries. The rally, which was held on November 17, 1968, had a large community turnout.

Marion Kramer, who worked as an organizer for the City-Wide Welfare Rights Organization typed and justified the DRUM newsletter; when in 1967 she was asked to come to a meeting to form a black people's liberation party.

At the meeting it was discussed, what direction to take. Kramer and her husband at the time (Dave Kramer) were frustrated with the rate of social change in the United States and were going to tour Europe. She said she was convinced "to get that out of your mind," by General Baker, Mike Hamlin, John Watson, John Williams and others. They said the purpose of the session was to plan and pull together an organization to serve the interests of African-Americans.

Kramer said the meeting was a turning point in her life because she decided to go deeper in her understanding of what was happening in the United States. Edna Watson and Dorothy Duberry had been invited to the meeting along with Kramer but Kramer was the only woman who showed up of the women invited to attend.

> One of the struggles that even started to develop then was the whole question of the relationship between the struggle taking place in the community and the struggle at the point of production.[35]

Kramer said she was beginning to understand how important workers were to the government.

REVOLUTIONARY UNION MOVEMENTS FORMED IN OTHER FACTORIES

The example set by DRUM inspired African-American workers in other plants to establish DRUM-type organizations at other factories. Workers from other plants began calling the DRUM office at Oakland and Owens. Brothers and sisters would attend DRUM meetings to learn the techniques of organizing and to discuss the situation at the plants all across the state, from which African-American workers would come to help in launching chapters of DRUM. The strike at the Hamtramick plant called by DRUM stimulated the creation of ELRUM (Eldon Avenue Revolutionary Union Movement) and FRUM (Ford Revolutionary Union Movement). Both of these RUM's had their own newsletters. ELRUM was organized on November 10, 1968.

The development of ELRUM was especially significant because the Eldon Avenue plant was Chrysler's only gear and axle plant. ELRUM led a demonstration in front of the UAW Local 961 in its eight-week of its existence. A meeting resulted between the UAW local representatives and members of ELRUM. It lasted so long that 300 workers missed their afternoon shift starting time at work. When they returned to work the next day, 66 of the 300 were immediately punished and more were later on. Punishments ranged from five days to a month off without pay. To protest this punishment ELRUM called for a wildcat strike on January 21, 1969. At the same time RUM's (Revolutionary Union Movements) were growing everywhere in the city, so on the eve of the ELRUM strike we called for the formation of the League of Revolutionary Black Workers (LRBW).[36]

In the Eldon Avenue strike, a higher proportion of African-American workers participated and production was completely halted because African-Americans comprised a larger portion of the total labor force than had been the case at Hamtramick Assembly plant. Later the ELRUM cadres analyzed that the strike had been premature, because 22 strikers were fired despite the fact that picket lines were manned by support cadres. *

On May 27, 1970, the Eldon Safety Committee and the League of Revolutionary Black Workers set up picket lines to protest the death of Gary Thompson who had been buried under five tons of steel when his faulty jiney tipped over on May 26, 1970 at the Eldon Gear and Axle plant. While the second wildcat strike called by ELRUM was not as successful as the first, it did cost Chrysler 2,174 axles over a two-day period.

ELRUM in its early development had to deal with the fact that most of its cadres were thrown out of the plant and had to address itself to the sustenance of the families of the brothers who were fired.

Soon after the Eldon Avenue Revolutionary Union Movement (ELRUM) was established (FRUM) Ford, Jefferson Avenue (JARUM), Mack Avenue (MARUM) and General Motors (GRUM) soon followed it. Each Revolutionary Union Movement had a nucleus of from ten to fifteen workers in each plant that produced their plant weekly newsletters and would give them to other cadre who would distribute them throughout the plant.

As RUM's sprang up in factories across Detroit and in other cities, DRUM and its support cadres felt the need for a centralizing organization.

According to Marion Kramer in an interview July 5, 2002:

> The League of Revolutionary Black Workers came together from the RUM's movement as a result of the women rebelling and calling for a more systematic approach to organization.[37]

The women, Marion Kramer, Gracie Wooten, Arlene Baker, Mary Baker, Cas Smith, Jeanette Baker, Helen Jones and others were doing the typing, participating in demonstrations, handing out leaflets, organizing in the community; doing just about everything but they were not represented in the leadership of the collective. So the women who were involved in the revolutionary union movement effort in Detroit developed a strong sense of unity; that is "they stuck together."

During the period of multiple RUM's, 68–69, the Detroit RUM collective had organized the Black Student United Front, various RUM's in the plants and hospitals; in the social workers community and the international black appeal. The collective had gone through the New Bethel incident and was the main force getting people set free. It had been a force behind the organizing drive to save Judge Crockett who had come to the defense of the New Bethel detainees.

General Baker had gone underground at this time because Chrysler had made moves to arrest him. Even with Baker off of the scene the RUM collective's roots were so embedded among the Detroit African-American working class that when the UAW held its national convention in Detroit; cadre from the RUM's and community people held massive demonstrations in front of the UAW convention. The RUM collective had mobilized thousands of people including an effort to stop the taking of attorney Ken Cockrel's license. The RUM collective had also been involved in defending an African-American worker; James Johnson who had killed his foreman and two others at the plant and the collective had successfully defended him with Johnson winning his case. The women were "sick and tired" of doing all of the work for the sections (RUMs) and not being part of the decision making process while there was no organizational process that had any plans. The women had formed the black women's committee and knew of ensuing internal struggles. Young sisters from the Black Students United Front now joined them. So as the black women's committee they decided to take some stands.

The women worked around the *Inner City Voice* as well as helping to develop various newsletters of the RUMs plus help train the workers of the RUM to edit and print their own RUM newsletters. The women got tired of being "dumped upon" and started to say, "we need an organization."[38] Through the women spearheading and leading the motion to call an organizational meeting, a group of over a hundred people involved convened on January 21, 1969 and formed the League of Revolutionary Black Workers.[39]

THE LEAGUE OF REVOLUTIONARY BLACK WORKERS ORGANIZED

An important factor in the League's development is the fact that it came into existence as a reaction to the spontaneous self-organizing of African-American workers. The national (race) consciousness of African-American workers was at the high point as a result of the July 1967 rebellion. This carried into the plants, where young African-American workers were more determined than ever to do something about the inhumane working conditions.

Though DRUM was in its formative stages as an in-plant study and action group, the May 3, 1968 wildcat strike at Hamtramick Assembly plant was the catalyst that made DRUM into a viable in-plant African-American workers' organization. Organization and structure did not come into existence until two months after DRUM's development. Reacting to the spontaneous actions of the workers proved to be a contradiction that was never fully solved within the League. Sustaining activity and the interest of the workers became major problems for the in-plant organizers of the League. The concept of a League of Revolutionary Black Workers had been in the minds of activists General Baker, John Watson, John Williams and Luke Tripp for years. In 1964 and 1965 they had put out a theoretical journal called *Black Vanguard* which called for a League of Black Workers. Between December 1968 and spring 1969, meetings were held with the cadre collective (a loose coalition of activists who had worked together since the days of UHURU) to discuss the formation of the League of Revolutionary Black Workers.

The contradictions that later emerged within the League were prevalent from its inception. A major aspect of these contradictions occurred between in-plant organizers (workers), community activists and revolutionary intellectuals. General Baker and Chuck Wooten (in-plant DRUM organizers) were the guiding force as far as the rest of the African-American workers were concerned inside the LRBW. J. W. Freeman remembers:

> I remember the meeting where the League of Revolutionary Black Workers was officially formed, and vividly recalled Luke Tripp's assertion that "if you want to know our political position read the *Peking Review*. Kenneth Cockrel chaired the meeting, which took place in a building located

on the corner of Elmhurst and Linwood in Detroit. At the time the building was owned by "Mama and Papa Oden" and is currently used as a drug rehabilitation center, "the Elmhurst House." "Mama Oden" was a profoundly religious women, whose spiritual depth was boundless and responsible for hundreds of young black men being deterred from the path of evil. She literally took me by the hand and several times presented me to the revolutionaries at 179 Cortland. "Papa Oden" was a businessman whose wealth meant nothing if it was not used to up lift the black masses. "Mama and Papa Oden," on more than one occasion helped save my life...and spirit.[40]

Glanton Dowdell, organized most of the community support for DRUM and the League until his forced exile to Sweden in August 1969. Baker and Dowdell had both been members and leading cadre in Detroit RAM and had worked together for years. The incorporation of Ken Cockrel, Mike Hamlin, John Watson and John Williams into the leadership of the League was due to the fact that they had administrative and other technical skills needed to coordinate an expanding semi-spontaneous African-American workers' movement. The League published position papers and a public document titled "Here's Where We're Coming From." In order to develop internal democracy within the League, it was structured into compartments, which had a semi-autonomous character. The compartments were broken down into a membership and circulation committee, an editorial committee, a financial committee, an education committee, a public relations committee, and an intelligence/security committee. All committees were directly responsible to the central committee known as the executive committee. The central staff was a body of League consistent cadres under the executive committee and was responsible for the day-to-day activities of the League.[41] From the beginning, a major contradiction within the League was that the executive committee only included two African-American workers, General Baker and Chuck Wooten. The executive committee was made up of Baker, Ken Cockrel, Mike Hamlin, Luke Tripp, John Watson, John Williams and Wooten.[42] Glanton Dowdell was in charge of intelligence and security. Also, Baker and Dowdell were members of the black people's liberation party (then an underground party) that was a vestige of RAM.[43] While Dowdell was in Detroit, strict discipline was maintained within the League, and the out-of-plant intellectuals—Mike Hamlin, John Watson and Ken Cockrel—didn't dare to buck Baker and Wooten.[44]

The LRBW was legally incorporated in June 1969 and opened its headquarters at 179 Cortland Street in October. The League began its efforts in July 1969 with the *Inner City Voice* as its official organ. For the most part, a citywide African-American student movement developed in the high schools and colleges and affiliated themselves with the League. The high school groups, led by the students at Northern High School, put out a newsletter called *Black Student Voice*. While in Detroit, Dowdell was the students' mentor.

Within a few months after the formation of the League of Revolutionary Black Workers the UAW leadership suddenly stopped the practice of mobilizing opposition to African-American candidates to local elections of unions. African-American workers were elected as presidents of Local 900 (Ford's Wayne plant), Local 47 (Chrysler Detroit Forge), Local 901 (Chrysler Eldon Gear), Local 7 (Chrysler), Local 51 (Plymouth) and Local 1248 (Chrysler Mopar). An African-American was elected vice president of Briggs Local 21 for the first time and in several plants African-American committeemen and shop stewards were chosen.[45]

The Black Economic Development Conference

The National Black Economic Development Conference (BEDC) met in Detroit, April 25–27, 1969. Called by African-American clergy and lay people who planned this conference, has been noted as the turning point for the League.

At the conference, James Forman (formerly of SNCC and the Black Panthers) had drafted a black manifesto dealing with demands for reparations. The black manifesto demanded money from white churches to support things like a black publishing company, a black workers' strike fund and a land bank. Forman did not have much support, and the Republic of New Africa (RNA) saw the manifesto as a watered-down version of reparations. Forman approached John Watson of the LRBW and asked him to support the manifesto. In return he promised to get money for the League. Watson called on the League cadres at the conference to support the manifesto. After much bitter debate with the RNA, the manifesto was passed.

Some members of the League joined the executive committee

of BEDC and demonstrated at white churches with Forman. Forman then requested to become a member of the League and was eventually put on its central staff. Forman's entrance into the League was the beginning of real problems for the League. Through money provided from BEDC, the League was able to establish a print shop (Black Star Press) and a bookstore (Black Star Book Store) and to make a movie, *Finally Got the News*.

But none of this was without strings attached. The agreement on funding Black Star Press was that one of its first projects would be printing Forman's book, *The Political Thought of James Forman*. During this time a debate took place between General Baker and Muhammad Ahmad over letting Forman into the League. The two would consult on a bi-monthly basis on internal development and problems within the League. Ahmad's position was that Forman was a control or destroy organizer (one who either controls an organization or divides it) and that while the money would help the League, it would boost Forman's influence in the League and the League would be split within a year.

The League drafted a manifesto and called for a black worker's congress. According to General Baker and Norman Otis Richmond in-plant leadership felt the League was over extended and had become a professional liberation organization but had lost its focus; a base among African-American workers in the plants. They felt that the priority should be on building strong RUM's (Revolutionary Union Movements) in the factories in Detroit first before expanding to other cities. The RUM's in existence had become weakened by strikes and repression against them. So the question for the in-plant leadership, how do you maintain and develop what you already have and consolidate it, not expand on thin air.[46]

The first beginnings of an ideological split within the executive committee of the League occurred over the question of BEDC. General Baker voiced reservations about BEDC and refused to be on its steering committee. Cockrel, Hamlin and Watson, out-of-plant intellectuals and administrators, dismissed Baker's objections and joined BEDC. Baker also alluded to Forman as being questionable. All agreed to support the idea of establishing an International Black Appeal (IBA) as a tax-exempt charity which would be a self-sustaining fundraising apparatus. John Williams was named IBA director.

The *Inner City Voice* began to run out of funds in September 1968. In October John Watson, who was an irregular student at Wayne State University, ran for editor of Wayne State's student newspaper and was elected editor for the 1968–69 academic year. The coalition of white and black students who supported him were firm supporters of DRUM.

Watson immediately turned the *South End* into a voice for the League. As the *South End* began to feature stories on various revolutions, particularly Palestine, it came under attack from the University administration and the white power structure in Detroit. On February 10, 1969, Joe Weaver, newscaster for conservative WJBK-TV, went to the *South End* offices to get a taped interview with Watson. Watson refused to be interviewed and closed the door to his office. Weaver forced his way into Watson's office. Watson ordered him to leave. Weaver continued to ask Watson questions with TV cameras filming. Other members of the *South End* staff came into the office to block the camera. A rumble (fight) ensued, leaving Weaver with a black eye. Weaver left the office and went to police headquarters, where he filed charges against Watson for assault and battery. Ken Cockrel, the League's lawyer, defended Watson at his jury trial and he was acquitted. While Watson was the *South End* editor he helped build student support for the League.

While the *South End* was an excellent vehicle for the LRBW it could not relate to African-American workers in the same way as the *Inner City Voice*, which had ceased publication for lack of funds. The *Inner City Voice* was written specially for African-American workers while the *South End* was written for students. In retrospect, at this point the LRBW should have taken assessment, withdrew and concentrated on continuing the *Inner City Voice*.[47]

A dispute within the *South End* staff over collective decision-making resulted in Watson and DRUM losing control of the *South End* the following school year.

ACTIVITIES OF THE LEAGUE IN THE COMMUNITY AND RELATIONS WITH OTHER GROUPS

The primary focus of the League's activity up to 1970 was concentrated on organizing African-American workers at the point of production. All other activities were viewed as secondary with the intent of stimulating support for the RUM's. But as soon as the League received publicity, particularly exposure by parts of the American and European left, the out-of-plant intellectuals—Cockrel, Hamlin and Watson—began to project themselves as the leaders or spokesmen for the League and eventually lost all touch with the workers in the organization.

> ...the primary concern of General Baker and Chuck Wooten was...that of plant organizing; that of Watson/Cockrel/ Hamlin was more visionary, in the sense of advocating a greater political involvement of the LRBW in the larger Detroit community as well as beyond; and that of Luke Tripp and John Williams as steering a cautious middle course between these two positions.[48]

From the League's conception, it had a fraternal organization relationship with the RNA. On March 29th, 1969 the Detroit police attacked the RNA during its meeting at New Bethel Baptist Church after a shootout between RNA security guards and police. One policeman was killed and another other wounded. Police surrounded the church as they laid an armed siege. The police raided the church, arrested one hundred fifty people, and held them incommunicado.

African-American State Representative James Del Rio contacted Judge George Crockett, an African-American judge. Judge Crockett came to the police station where RNA citizens were being held and found that no charges had been brought against anyone. He set up court in the station and released about fifty. Wayne County Prosecutor William L. Cahalan stopped him, but his actions had caused concern over violation of civil rights and the police released most of the RNA citizens the next day.

Judge Crockett immediately came under attack from the white establishment and white press. A Black United Front was formed to support Judge Crockett. Some sixty organizations were in the Front, ranging from the NAACP and the Guardians (an African-American policemen's organization) to the RNA and DRUM.

> On April 3, 1969, the Black United Front called for demonstrations in support of Crockett, and some three thousand people responded.[49]

The formation of the Black United Front and the demonstration threatened to polarize Detroit. Within a matter of weeks, the

Detroit Commission on Community Relations issued a report favorable to Crockett. The *Detroit Free Press* published an editorial apologizing for previously publishing racist articles against Crockett. The Michigan Bar Association and spokesmen for the UAW and New Detroit defended Judge Crockett's legal positions.

John Watson of the LRBW was appointed director of the West Central Organization (WCO) after it had received a $30,000 grant from BEDC. During this period the Detroit Board for Education announced a plan to decentralize control. WCO called a conference attended by 300 representatives from seventy organizations to deal with the decentralization plan. The conference formed a coalition called Parents and Students for Community Control (PASCC). PASCC addressed itself to community control of schools and a number of community issues. The League had influence on African-American high school students in particular and some African-American college students. A high school cadre began to form in Northern High. Their first advisor was Glanton Dowdell and later Mike Hamlin. Their newsletter, *Black Student Voice*, called for student control of the schools:

> The summer is over and we are back in the same old bag; white teachers, books, and heroes are still hanging on the walls of our schools. It is about time that the students and non-students stand up and be black men and women, and tell the teachers, principals, and administration, and uncle tom students that you are sick and tired of this white bullshit that is going on in our black schools. What about our Black Heroes; Malcolm X, Stokely Carmichael, Rap Brown, Nat Turner, Robert Williams, Huey Newton, and many others which your racist uncle tom teachers refuse to tell you about. All black students should join or support any black student organization working towards an effective change, and making the school more relevant to black students. These racist ass honkeys must stop controlling our black schools. The students should be making the decisions on who is going to teach and govern the schools period, not some racist white honkey from the suburbs.[50]

While the LRBW was generally sympathetic to the revolutionary stand of the Oakland-based Black Panther Party (BPP) uniting with them on many issues, particularly with those who identified themselves as Marxist-Leninists, they believed the Black Panther Party was moving in the wrong direction by concentrating on organizing lumpen elements of the African-American community. The LRBW believed the BPP was engaging in self-defeating adventurist activities based on their romantic orientation toward the lumpen rather than a more realistic one toward workers. The LRBW did not believe that a successful movement could be based upon the lumpen as they lack a potential source of power. The LRBW believed that African-American workers had the most promising base for a successful African-American liberation movement because of the potential power derived from their ability to disrupt industrial production.

The LRBW emphasized that the working class is the vanguard of the major force within the revolutionary struggle, and that the lumpen proletariat is in and of itself a class that is unstable. The LRBW believed that whole sections of the lumpen proletariat are totally undisciplined and have a "Go for yourself" mentality regardless of the political situation. The LRBW believed though there are some sections of the lumpen proletariat, which can become revolutionary.[51]

The relationship between the League and the Panthers soon broke down, as the national office in Oakland purged Luke Tripp and others in 1969. There were serious ideological differences.

The DRUM forces felt that it was wise to keep their membership in low profile as much as possible. DRUM felt those involved in military operations should be underground having little identity with public political activity. DRUM felt it was an unrealistic approach presenting oneself as a super revolutionary to the community exposing it to unnecessary excessive repression; one that the community would be afraid to engage itself in. DRUM felt that the key to mobilizing the community was organizing a "realistic" day-to-day style of organizing that recruits, trains cadre and preserves them through the protracted class war of liberation.[52]

While the League was getting more involved in the community and becoming recognized across the country as an African-American revolutionary workers' organization, it was beginning to lose its base among African-American workers within the plants. The operations the League continued to be set up that began to draw its personnel further and further away from its focus of organizing the plants. Also, a bureaucratic structure began to replace its once-flexible modus operandi. The ideological division, which burst into the open, was centered on tactical concerns.

THE IDEOLOGICAL SPLIT IN THE LEAGUE:
THE A GROUP AND THE B GROUP

As the League expanded its base in Detroit, questions over direction became more prominent within the leadership. RUM's spread among hospital and newspaper workers. Also, RUM's developed in steel and other industries in other cities. The League had become the inspiration of African-American workers' caucuses around the country.

To address itself to questions of a national African-American workers' organization, the League leadership decided to form a Black Workers Congress which would coordinate the various RUM's and African-American workers' caucuses in the nation. The BWC would be an American version of a soviet workers congress making decisions concerning their own liberation. But at this point of development, the League began to split into two factions which were divided between the in-plant revolutionary black nationalist workers and the out-of-plant, Marxist-Leninist intellectuals.

The split in the League raged for a year, starting openly in 1970 and culminating on June 12, 1971 with John Watson, Ken Cockrel and Mike Hamlin resigning to go with the Black Workers Congress. The ideological differences were over different conceptual frameworks, issues, where priority of the organization should be, national consciousness, cooperation with white radicals, social relations, scope and the direction of the struggle. The League had become a bureaucratic structure with people working full-time in various projects. The RUMs, which came into existence because of the rise of national consciousness that the Detroit rebellion developed in African-American workers, was becoming more difficult to sustain. The in-plant organizers addressed themselves to the problem of maintaining high morale among the workers. Most of the RUMs developed from semi-spontaneous actions (wildcats) over grievances. But how to maintain an ongoing organization in the plants was becoming an increasing problem. Cultural affairs were organized by the League to provide members with social activities. These affairs were to allow League members to get to know one another and develop further cohesion among members. At one point there was a discussion of establishing a workers' supermarket to develop economic self-reliance.

In an interview with Ernie Mkalimoto Allen he said the LRBW

(referred to as the League) leadership in the plants had become isolated.

> They had with the Wildcats strikes and that sort of thing, had out-skirted both the union and management. The retaliation came in the form of firings of the organizers, economic reprisals. In terms of the intelligence of these operations of these various plants, they passed the word on. So the co-called troublemakers, in other words the leadership was isolated and fired and of course the union wasn't paying them any benefits or supporting them and so the League had to do that. So basically that movement never was able to revive itself in that particular period. The League was going to have tremendous reverberations elsewhere I think mostly in the South like Atlanta, Georgia and of course down in Newark with the Mahwah Group and the plant and so forth. But they were never able to recoup.

> Basically what happened was that when the League came together it was formed from a coalition of people. They had different kinds of purposes, different kinds of directions. Some had worked together before and they had fallen out with one another and they came back together because they needed each other and each others skills, and for the summer rebellion in Detroit in '67. There were actually three different groups in there. The first group was formed with Mike Hamlin, Ken Cockrel, John Watson. They considered themselves I think to be Marxist-Leninists. That was true of the second group which was formed of Luke Tripp and John Williams who considered themselves to be Marxist-Leninists as well.

> But the third group which in terms of leadership there was probably was General Baker and Chuck Wooten were more nationalist oriented, well versed in terms of having read as much literature as everybody else, in terms of Marxist literature and so forth. There were some who advocated a kind of a slow policy. In terms of General Baker and Chuck Wooten, they wanted to concentrate on the plants, it said energy and resources have to be put into the plants. Hamlin, Cockrel and Watson on the other hand were more towards branching out, what they wanted to do was to expand the League organization outside of Detroit.[53]

The out of plant intellectuals wanted to form the League of Revolutionary Black Workers in other cities as well, to start expanding the organization immediately. Luke Tripp and John Williams, Allen remembers, were a little bit more cautious and were for expansion but not as fast as the Hamlin, Cockrel, Watson group.

There were various issues and they split in various ways. One of the most important points Allen thought in terms of the liabilities of the organization were that the support aspects of the organization, the whole infrastructure that had been built to support the plant takeovers and plant organizations began to become entities in themselves. That's what happens when an organization sometimes grows too fast. Initially, the League needed money to put out the newspaper; when there were strikes or people lost their jobs they lost the ability to support people economically. To that end, the League's printing plant began to develop the film, "Finally Got The News." These sorts of ventures started to become entities in themselves.

There was a Control, Conflict and Change book club, which was for basically liberal and left leaning whites where it was supposed to raise money. There would be members of the League who sold books, and give lectures to whites. Allen felt that, while that was an amenable sort of thing, it was hard to see how this figured politically in terms of the schemes of things; it did not have anything to do with plant organizing. Middle class whites basically were being organized in this. It did not make money, in other words, from a political standpoint it did not make too much sense. The film making measure got kind of crazy. After finishing "Finally Got The News," John Watson who was really the main person behind the film venture was talking about making a film about Rosa Luxenberg and getting Jane Fonda to star in it, and a film about Lenin. The League started moving away from its roots. The kind of central focus that the League had for a short period of time was no longer there, and when the film was finished, "Finally Got The News," the League as it was portrayed in the film no longer existed. A lot of people got fired up watching it, but that was not the situation in Detroit anymore. The League effectively had been blocked in the plants.[54]

While the League had a community-wide apparatus, it could no longer mobilize large numbers of African-American workers. Watson, Cockrel, Hamlin, and Forman began to travel more and more outside of Detroit, making press statements and giving interviews for white radical newspapers. Ernie Mkalimoto Allen describes the situation:

...there was the "Cortland office," main center for worker organizing; the "Linwood office," whose Parents and Students for Community Control as well as International Black Appeal were housed; the "Dequindre office," where the Black Star Bookstore and an abortive community organizing project were launched; the "Fenkell office," headquarters for the Black Star Printing operation. There were also geographically separate offices for Black Star Film Productions, the Labor Defense Coalition, and UNICOM, a community-organizing center. To outsiders the operation appeared quite impressive; rank-and-file insiders often saw it as an organizational and bureaucratic nightmare.[55]

Another major contradiction was th inability of the out-of-plant leaders to relate their theory to African-American workers' reality; failure on their part to listen to and learn from the workers and to treat them as equals. One weekend while General Baker was in New York, he convinced Ernie Mkalimoto Allen (an anti-war activist and organizer of the Black Panther Party of Northern California) to move to Detroit and work with the League. Mkalimoto left New York. His involvement in the League helped polarize the contradictions within the leadership. He developed good rapport with the workers and was viewed as a threat by the out-of-plant leadership—Cockrel, Watson, Hamlin.

The League was racked with a serious problem of uneven political development among its members. Political education (P.E.) classes were set up for all League members. There were on the average anywhere from forty-five to fifty workers in the political education class.

Luke Tripp first taught the classes on the basics of Marxism-Leninism. Tripp, not knowing how to break theory down into everyday language, would bore the workers, who often went to sleep in class. Mkalimoto was asked to teach class.

In an interview with Ernie Mklaimoto Allen he reflected on the problems of political education.

Question:

You became a member of the executive board?

Answer:

Allen: No, I was part of the second line of leadership. It was called the central staff. As I look back on it now, I don't think anybody really knew how to put together an organizational structure. It was not well thought out. It was very, very strange. I was brought in to teach the political education courses. The problem with political education courses in the past had been they had been taught too much from the perspective of using materials developed by the Chinese. You know we had Chinese and Vietnamese materials, and so forth and so on. That became the staples of political education in the League. The problem was that what you needed and what we didn't have at the time in which we still don't really have adequately, was a literature that reflected the experience of black workers. That would bring the theory in but at the same time the historical examples would be that of black workers themselves so they could see themselves in it as well as learn about their own historical experiences.[56]

Allen broke it down plain and the workers enjoyed going to political education. It should be noted that most of the workers were revolutionary nationalists. They were not anti-Marxist. Marxism-Leninism was something new to them and if it had been presented to them gradually and in terms they understood, they would have eventually accepted it. But the relations the workers had with those purported Marxist-Leninists and their life styles alienated the workers. John Watson thought that the League should become a black Marxist-Leninist political party. Watson called his faction, representing himself, Cockrel, Hamlin and Forman, the "B group," meaning Bolsheviks, and a faction represented by General Baker, Chuck Wooten, Ernie Mkalimoto Allen, Dedan, Waistline, Mitch, Jalali and little AK as the "A group," meaning Akbar or nationalist faction. Before dealing with differences in the conceptual frameworks of both factions, we should deal with social contradictions.

Male chauvinism was rampant in the League. Though women's equality was the official position of the League of Revolutionary Black Workers, sexism like that in the Black Panther Party was often practiced. Sisters would be asked to "give it up" sometimes when coming to the Cortland office. Discipline began to break down in the ranks after Dowdell left. Some workers had serious drinking problems.

While attempting to address themselves with the deterioration of self-discipline among the members of the LRBW and supporters around the A group; including aggressive sexual harassment toward African-American women members and supporters of the LRBW, the B faction had its own internal weaknesses. The two political models; revolutionary nationalist; of seeing African-Americans in a national democratic colonial revolution seeking self-determination and the other seeing African-American workers the vanguard of socialist revolution of the U.S. in which African-Americans would be integrated into a socialist society, were often seen as opposing paradigms, rather than consciously attempting to creatively apply social science and develop a synthesis of the paradigms. The arguments were often reflected in contradictory life styles. Both A and B group males were womanizers. Some of the B group were smoking marijuana and some secretly snorting cocaine. The A group had for the most part become an undisciplined group and some had become alcoholics. The B group was organizing broad support among the white left while some African-American males sexually abused the white women on the left.

The B group tried to address some of these problems but their internationalist (inter-racial) socializing caused cultural problems or contradictions within the League, which often were used as an excuse to cloud the real underlying contradictions.

Hamlin spent a lot of time organizing League input in the "Control, Conflict and Change" book club organized by the Motor City Labor League. Less than two percent of the approximately 700 members were African-American.

Hamlin in an interview September 27, 1999 said one of his main reasons for organizing white supporters in the form of the Motor City Labor League and other formations was because of his fear that the LRBW would soon be isolated and attacked by the power structure; i.e., the police and the FBI. He said, he and Baker had been confronted and stopped in the streets by the FBI. Hamlin also felt there needed to be a vehicle to harness the support of white workers and intellectuals.[57]

Forman was attacked by the A group for having left an African-American wife for a white wife. He denied ever having been married to an African-American woman. Hamlin and Cockrel lived in the same house with their white female friends. Watson, though he was married, would "jam" white women at League parties and would openly admit he had a "Jones" for white women. African-American female members of the League would watch the B group in disgust.[58] The B group in fact was acting out revolutionary integrationism, something that many Panthers were doing in the same period. Things began to get out of hand, but General Baker refused to fight for his principles against his old friends.

In an interview with Ernie Mkalimoto Allen, he was asked what was the turning point in the LRBW? Ernie Mkalimoto Allen was put on the central staff (second line leadership). Allen was working with General Baker to get the League back on tract; that is organizing African-American workers in the plants. Allen was trying to promote change inside the League along with others but without splitting the organization. The purpose for the formation of the central staff was to give more people inside the organization more responsibilities for day-to-day operations. The purpose for the organization would function without having to wait for the executive board to meet. In the latter part of 1970 there was a meeting between the central staff and executive board; confrontation and confusion occurred. It was then realized that the leadership had underestimated the organizational problems. Many felt the executive board was almost an organization of itself. The executive board had the information, made the decisions and basically the organization as a whole; the rank and file may or may not have been informed by what decision was made. With that type of situation there was no opportunity for the second line leadership to develop. Because the executive board felt there was political backwardness in the organization it called for an organizational retreat of the executive board and central staff. At the retreat a proposal was put forward, that the executive board disband and reconstitute itself with everyone on it having a specific function and a specific responsibility. The majority of the executive board became paranoid. The central staff pushed for a second meeting of the central staff seeking clarity on the organizational structure of how it really ran. The executive board said the central staff could not have a second meeting. The central staff decided and went on and had a second meeting anyway. At that point, the executive board started a purge of the organization in April of 1971.

Among those purged were Ernie Allen, Shola Akentalia, Akai, Ballerene Hiamen and Sunny Hiamen. They and then their spouses were put out of the organization because they were considered to be a security risk. Allen felt this was the incident that started the LRBW on its decline because most of the LRBW leadership on the executive board rarely came into contact with the rank and file. To make matters worse, the leadership of the League of Revolutionary Black Workers began having meetings once a week and started berating people. The executive board would use Marxist political-theoretical concepts to brow beat the supporters of those expelled. The executive board appeared arrogant to them.

> The political disagreements between the League leaders began to feed personal antagonisms. The in-plant people charged that the BWC wing like to be with "bourgeois" people and with white folks more than they liked to be with Black workers. Cockrel was cited for having what was termed an arrogant and authoritarian attitude toward comrades. Watson was charged with having become a dreamer who let transoceanic trips and film-making fantasies replace his former vision of a worker-led American revolution. Hamlin was said to be so enamored of the idea of a national organization that he had lost his common sense. As for James Forman, who had entered the League through BEDC, he was the wrecker and splitter Baker had suspected him of being all along.[59]

General dissatisfaction emerged in the central staff. Ernie Mkalimoto and some of his supporters were purged from the League in April 1971 for purportedly attempting a coup d-etat under the guise of ultra-democracy. The battle continued to rage until June, when the central staff demanded more voice in decisions of the League, resulting in Watson, Hamlin, Cockrel and Forman resigning. The ideological differences between the A group and the B group were over what James A. Gerschwender calls the capitalist exploitation model and the colonial model. The B Group (Cockrel, Hamlin, Watson and Forman) felt the League should be turned into a black Marxist-Leninist party. Essentially they viewed African-American people as an oppressed minority exploited on both a race and a class basis. Their essential worldview was that the African-American worker was the most significant element in bringing about a revolution in this country. They felt that national oppression (race) would be eliminated through a socialist revolution. They believed in an integrated society after a socialist revolution.

The A group also believed that African-American people are oppressed on a race and a class basis. They believed that 200 years of slavery had developed Africans in America into a nation. The national culture and institutions of the African-American nation became entrenched during the hundred years of racial prejudice after the reconstruction period. The A group felt that the African-American nation's national historical territory was the black belt South. They envisaged an African-American-led socialist revolution in which there would be several independent socialist states cooperating with one another but maintaining political independence. The A group published two pamphlets which explained their position. *Revolutionary Nationalism and Class Struggle* by Ernie Mkalimoto and *World Black Revolution*.

J. W. Freeman (synonym for a cadre of the LRBW) wrote in an unpublished manuscript, *The Revolutionary Way Out*:

> The break up of the "League of Revolutionary Black Workers" has been called a split between the industrial workers and students, and the "small capitalistic minded" revolutionaries. General Baker, Chuck Wooten and John Williams emerged as leaders on one wing; with Kenneth Cockrel, Mike Hamlin and John Watson representing the other. (Actually, there were originally three centers of power). "Workers versus small capitalist minded revolutionaries" was never my point of view. Nor did I subscribe to the definition that workers and students were backward and reactionary black nationalist in opposition to the "Revolutionary Internationalist." Rather, in retrospect, it is my contention that the "League" split based on questions facing the black masses in Detroit in the early 1970s: questions of what direction to transform Detroit's political structure; where to invest the organizations resources and which individuals would merge as the primary leaders. Ethnic and cultural specific organizations are of course here to stay. The League of Revolutionary Black Workers was, in fact, an association of black revolutionaries that did not perceive a necessity to justify its existence.[60]

The third position which has not received much publicity was that of Luke Tripp and John Williams who agreed partially with the in-plant leadership that the LRBW had to maintain or rebuild it's base in the plants; but to be a viable force it must be involved also in the community as well as being a part of a national organization.

So a principled question was, where do we put our emphasis, struggling against national or class oppression? But these were not the real issues. According to Mike Hamlin the primary issue which cause the split in the executive board of the League of Revolutionary

Black Workers was not necessarily the issue of wanting to expand into a national organization: Black Workers Congress (BWC) versus wanting to consolidate the organization locally. That was the official story given to the general public including the membership of the LRBW.

The central issue was with the Baker faction over lack of discipline, liberalism, internal corruption and disintegration within the ranks and crimes against the people committed by workers associated with the Baker faction. One incident involved an African-American worker who identified himself with the LRBW, cornered an African-American female (LRBW) volunteer and raped her inside the Highland Park office. For lack of information we do not know if anything happened to the worker or charges were ever brought against him. It is presumed that nothing was done about the incident since it was a real cause for the split. Another incident involved a 41-year-old African-American man from Chicago who was married to a 27-year-old African-American woman in the League of Revolutionary Black Workers. They attended a youth dance sponsored by the Black Student Union which was closely affiliated the LRBW. A serious physical altercation resulted involving the husband and no known reprimand occurred.[61]

With nothing resolved within the leadership of the organization, those who tended to be more theoretical, intellectual and more amenable to mass media went into the Black Workers Congress and most of the workers recruited through organizing the Revolutionary Union Movements (RUMS), stayed with the LRBW until General Baker went into the Communist League.

Some of the problems of rapid development, uneven levels of political (understanding) consciousness, ideological direction which occurred in the League of Revolutionary Black Workers (LRBW) have resurfaced within various African-American organizations since 1971 (i.e., Black Workers Congress (BWC), African Liberation Support Committee (ALSC), Black Political Assembly (BPA), Congress of African People (CAP), National Black Independent Political Party (N.B.I.P.P.) and the African People's Party (APP).

The question of lack of strong moral (humanist) ethics has not been a well-discussed issue but is one to have been at the cutting edge of both the success and failure of the LRBW. It seems as though some of the issues which African-American radical organizers such as those who organized the LRBW needed to address are:

1. Choosing the correct method of relating to, advancing forward and sustaining the progressive spontaneous development of the masses towards expanding the parameters of democracy. This would include lull (slow), periods as well as high tides (intense, rapid), periods of mass activity.

2. What is the role of an organized cadre in relation to that development?

3. Should primary finances come from self-reliance or from external sources?

4. What is the role and relationship of radical intellectuals to the rank and file members of the organization and visa versa?

5. How to synthesize a comprehensive conceptual framework that is relevant to the daily living reality of the African-American working class?

6. Having a life style and moral or spiritual cultural way of life that the masses respect and learn to emulate in building a new society. The process of selflessness, transformation of oneself to becoming the humanistic new socialist man or woman. Every successful revolution has had this humanist code of ethics at its core.

In the period between the end of reconstruction to the present two eras stand out in contrast to others in terms of mass activity related to African-Americans. The two eras—the 1920s and the 1960s—were ones of huge spontaneous self-organization of the African-American working class. On a local level the role of an initial group of political revolutionaries who tried a series of organizational attempts to harness mass activity of African-Americans, is what this study is about. The organizational development of the League of Revolutionary Black Workers was from 1963–1971, an eight-year period of time.

The study is too short to discuss in particular the role of Ken Cockrel. Cockrel left the LRBW with John Watson and Mike Hamlin to continue in the Black Workers Congress. But Cockrel continued after leaving BWC to run for city council and to work with another local formation, the Detroit Alliance for a Rational Economy (DARE).

Cockrel's role as a revolutionary lawyer with the LRBW is also important to look at. His successful defense of defendants in the New Bethel incident and of James Johnson; the distraught African-American autoworker who killed three people after being dismissed from his job, are case studies within themselves.[62]

It is the writer's estimate that Cockrel's knowledge of the law and his review of the legal infractions within the ranks of the LRBW and the implications for the leadership of the LRBW is what may have prompted Cockrel's faction to seek a serious resolve of the issues.

As the concluding chapter will show, in the case of the LRBW as in all the major African-American radical organizations (1960–1975), the initial grouping consisted of African-American college/university students, full-time or part-time, and elements of the intellectual proletariat (musicians, artists, writers, poets, teachers, etc.).

The League of Revolutionary Black Workers was a logical outgrowth in the north of intensified efforts to desegregate the south led by the Student Non-Violent Coordinating Committee (SNCC). SNCC's efforts emerged from self-organizing of African-American students to resolve aspects of national oppression in the south which had culminated from the successful effort initiated by an African-American worker years before in Montgomery, Alabama; Mrs. Rosa Parks in 1955. SNCC like the Southern Christian Leadership Conference (SCLC) emerged from these self-organizing efforts of African-American working class.

But it should not be forgotten that in all instances as was the case of DRUM-LRBW that an initial cadre of intellectual proletariat existed within the area. So it might be stated that without the presence of or emergence from mass activity of a cadre; depending how one judges the historical circumstances, to lead and further accentuate mass activity, the mass movement of the 1960s in Detroit wouldn't have progressed as far as it did. This study attempted to show how a local young political collective developed. Also important in this study was pointing out the over extension of the collective (cadre) in terms of growth and unpreparedness of the cadre to the system giving in to it's demands. It is my estimation that reliance on external funding in the case of the LRBW was counter productive.

The contradictions that surfaced within the LRBW are related to the questions of social responsibility, sexism and humanism;

questions which have not adequately been addressed in the African-American community yet.

It should be noted that the political cadre that was generating around *ICV* (Inner City Voice) which DRUM spun off from was trying to relate to and advance the spontaneous character of the African-American struggle for parity and democracy in Detroit. But the League of Revolutionary Black Workers would not have come into existence if the urban rebellion of July 1967 had not occurred. Also very important was the fact that Detroit was traditionally a single industry city and most of the participants of the LRBW were second-generation autoworkers who were raised in the North.

The urban rebellion heightened the "national consciousness" or race awareness of African-American workers in the auto plants, making them more receptive to organizing outside of the UAW. The centrality of industry around the auto industry in Detroit with a large entry of young African-American workers from 1964 to 1967 was unique. In his interview, General Baker noted that a worker could look down the assembly line and see someone he had grown up with or gone to school with as a youth. Congregated in large numbers in similar oppressive conditions that one could witness with naked vision, was a potent sociological phenomenon. This combined with national, international events but most important of all with a local African-American radical tradition that spanned two generations, made Detroit unique. The fact that there was an embryonic cadre to give the wildcat strikes at the auto plants organizational form is an essential factor that led to the development of DRUM, other RUMS and the LRBW. The importance of a cadre in advancing a mass movement and transforming it into a social revolution cannot be underestimated. In social revolutions, a cadre's role in the development of a mass movement has usually been the determining factor in that movement's success or failure. Students, worker intellectuals, street people, professionals who develop a political orientation, can all be part of a proletarian intelligentsia. During the 1960s many of these elements in Detroit united around Mao Tse-Tung's theory of how correct ideas are processed. The concept of actual testing one's theoretical premise was held paramount. A very broad loose collective of twenty of more young African-American activists in Detroit united around the concept of practice, theory and practice.

That is that political theory is learned and refined through actual social practice; the act of organizing the people. So the methodology which can be learned from the LRBW experience is practice, theory, practice=praxis.

One decisive factor we can learn from the League experience is the role of finances. In this case, I have attempted to show how finances coming from external sources re-directed the League from its focus of purpose: organizing at the point of production. The question of building independent economic resources based on self-reliance, which may take many years to do, or receiving funds from foundations, etc., was and is a problem for the black liberation movement. Financial resources from forces outside of the African-American community thwarted development of SCLC, SNCC, the Black Panther Party as well as the LRBW.

Again, one comes to the question of the role of the intellectuals who are not in the center of activity and their role with the masses. In the League there arose an arrogant, self-righteous unconscious commandism on the part of the intellectuals in directing the mass organization. There seems to be a crucial problem in America—the inability of intellectuals to be willing to listen to the masses, take their suggestions, learn from the masses, and share in leadership with the masses. The ego-centrism created in intellectuals in the American educational system seems to make most so self-centered that they refuse to be flexible when working with people. Many of these intellectuals—who many times use Marxism-Leninism, Mao Tse-Tung thought, as a dogma rather than a method of achieving empirical truth—unconsciously become the "scientific" saviors of the "heathen" masses.

The problem of university-trained intellectuals is often they harbor an elitist petty bourgeoisie superiority mentality when interacting with working class people. Workers and university intellectuals have different life experiences, which often lead them to view the world differently. While all African-Americans share racial and class oppression on a dual basis, African-American workers reality is more intense. African-American workers usually view abstract ideas as irrelevant and tend to be more subjective. Therefore, African-American workers are usually more likely to have different conceptual and theoretical frames of reference than intellectuals. This was the case for the LRBW.

What the intellectuals or B group failed to do was to relate to the subjectivity of the in-plant workers in order to broaden their subjective paradigm and reform their behavior.

Queen Mother Audley Moore's famous saying is appropriate at this point:

> If you are subjective about the subjective, you will be subjective about the objective. But if you are objective about the subjective, you will be objective about the objective.[63]

Having dual conceptual frameworks and not realizing it, led organizers of the LRBW to build the organization into a mass organization and as a result of this ideological and intra-class stratification led the League to split. The lack of a comprehensive conceptual framework based on empirical data of what "actually exists" within the African-American working class community is still lacking today.

In summation, while I am not condoning or advocating spontaneous activity, the self-organization of the masses plays an important role in the development of a revolutionary mass organization.[64]

Taking the six points raised into consideration, it is important to seriously study the League of Revolutionary Black Workers. It was the most advanced African-American workers organization to emerge in the period of 1960–1975.

AFTERWORD: NOTES FROM A REUNION OF LRBW'S MEMBERS

The LRBW's not only produced worker organizers and agitators, but also produced worker leaders. The LRBW's developed a pedagogy of organic worker leaders (cadres); many LRBW leaders are leaders of their unions today.

Wayne State Community College, as a concept, was born at the DRUM office when a worker read a book by Basil Davidson, who interviewed Amiclar Cabral, in which he said that in 500 years, the Portuguese had only trained two workers. Realizing the significance of this, the idea of a community college for the Detroit area began to ferment. But even with this effort, one of the weaknesses of the LRBW's cadres and other black radical organizations of the time was the failure to continue to organize youth cadres.

Through the Black Student United Front (BSUF), 1969–1971, the LRBW's influenced the lives of hundreds and thousands of Detroit inner city youth. Through the BSUF newsletter, which eventually expanded into a city-wide student newsletter with slogans such as, "Black Youth, the World is Yours, Take it!" and emulating the thinking of Robert F. Williams, who was a local, national, and international hero, the BSUF had a profound influence among the youth in the period 1969–1971 in Detroit. The BSUF called a boycott of the schools calling for a relevant education and went on to establish "Freedom Schools."

One of the weaknesses of the LRBW's was that very few had the insight of giving the BSUF concrete advice on what to do in the future. As a result, the BSUF cadre split following the LRBW's split. Some went into the factories and others went into the colleges and universities in the area taking up the fight for black studies. Of those who went into the factories, many of the women took up the fight inside the plants against sexual harassment, holding collective discussions to get members to run for office in the unions, which was successful.

During the reunion, a cadre stated: "What we are missing today is the wide discussions between young and old people. We don't have a process of a wide collective discussion; without it, we tend to become petty. The question remains of how does one fight for control."

Another cadre said: "We need an intellectual framework, a center, because people don't understand the issues. Revolutionaries must have more than a concept of the destruction of capitalist society and have to have a vision of an alternative new society. People have to know there is another way out."

The question that is asked is, 'what are the steps to empowerment in terms of mobilizing the people?' It was stated by one cadre that one must put forth a new view of society and create as many forms as possible from which indigenous leadership may develop and emerge. Creating a revolutionary culture that nurtures cadre through stages of development, developing an intellectual center that understands the dialectical relation between spontaneity and organization, the building of a youth movement, and having "literacy campaigns" are some of the ideas elder leaders of the LRBW's have today. Their primary objective is to give the youth whatever guidance thy can give them.

The central question and lesson to be learned from the LRBW's, coming from hindsight of the elder leaders of the LRBW's is this:

once the LRBW's won the demands for which they were protesting the question became, what further direction to take; "where do we go from here?" It was also stated that LRBW's cadre had to be void of anger, have a calm and deliberate thinking in order to change society as well as have a sense of responsibility to their personal families and to the community. All in all, the LRBW's elders felt the LRBW's provided organizers with valuable experiences and a new praxis for making a new socialist world. In the words of Wilber Haddock of the United Black Brothers:

> If you really want to get the brothers and sisters; the workers to follow you and to stand, to be there, then you got to consider their feelings.[65]

1. John Bracey, Jr., August Meir, Elliott Rudwick, eds., *Black Workers and Organized Labor* [California: Wadsworth Publishing Company, 1971] p. 56.
2. Irving Howe and B. J. Widick, The U.A.W.: Fights Race Prejudice," *Commentary*, Volume 8, Number 3, September 1949, p. 263.
3. African-American "*On Wheels: Special History Report: The Pivotal Role of Blacks in the UAW Union,*" *Detroit, February/March, 2000,* pg. 32.
4. Fraser M. Ohanelli, *The Communist Part of the United States: From Depression to World War II,* [New Brunswick: Rutgers University Press, 1997], p. 144.
5. *Op. Cit.,* (On Wheels), p. 32.
6. *Op. Cit.* (Bracey, et. al.), p. 212.
7. Ibid., p. 214.
8. Bill V. Mullen, *Afro-Orientalism* [Minneapolis: University of Minnesota Press] p. 8 {Also, see Robert F. Mast, *Detroit Lives,* Philadelphia: Temple University (ed.) Press, p. 306}
9. Ernest Mkalimots Allen, "Detroit: I Do Mind Dying, A Review," *Radical America, Volume II, Number 1, January-February, 1977,* p. 70.
10. Interviews and discussions with General Gordon Baker, Jr. and Darryl Mitchell, 1994 (Detroit, Michigan).
11. Interview with General Gordon Baker, Jr., Cleveland, Ohio, 1994.
12. Meeting, interview and conversation with John Watson, Detroit, Michigan, 1965.
13. Interview with General Gordon Baker, Jr., Cleveland, Ohio, 1994.
14. Grace and James Boggs, *Detroit: Birth of a Nation*, Pamphlet, October 1967, p. 7.
15. Interview with General Gordon Baker, Jr., Detroit, Michigan, 1968.

16. Interview with General Gordon Baker, Jr., Cleveland, Ohio, 1994.

17. Interview with General Gordon Baker, Jr., Cleveland, Ohio, 1994.

18. Interview with General Gordon Baker, Jr., Cleveland, Ohio, 1994.

19. Interview with Charles "Chuck" Wooten, July 14, 2002 (Telephone Cleveland, Ohio to Detroit, Michigan). Also, interview with Mike Hamlin, September 27, 1999, Cleveland, Ohio to Detroit, Michigan, telephone interview.

20. Luke Tripp, "Black Working Class Radicalism, Detroit 1960–1970," Tuesday, October 4, 1994, p. 17 (unpublished paper).

21. Interview with General Gordon Baker, Jr., Cleveland, Ohio 1994.

22. James A. Geschwender, "The League of Revolutionary Black Workers," *The Journal of Ethnic Studies, Volume 2, Number 5, Fall, 1974,* p. 4.

23. Luke Tripp, "DRUM-Vanguard of the Black Revolution," *The South End* (Wayne State University Student Newspaper) *Volume 22, Number 62, Thursday, January 23, 1969,* p. 9.

24. Luke Tripp, *Op. Cit.,* p. 9.

25. *DRUM (Dodge Revolutionary Union Movement) Newsletter, Volume 1, Number 2,* p. 3.

26. *Op. Cit.* (Tripp), p. 9.

27. *DRUM* (Dodge Revolutionary Union Movement) *Newsletter, Volume 1, Number 9,* p. 1.

28. *Op. Cit.* (Geschwender) p. 6.

29. Dan Georgakas and Marvin Surkin, *Detroit: I Do Mind Dying* [New York: St. Martin's Press, 1975], p. 47

30. Phillip S. Foner, *Organized Labor and the Black Worker 1619–1973* [New York: International Publishers, 1974], p. 414.

31. *Op. Cit.,* p. 2.

32. *Op. Cit.* (Greschwender), p. 7.

33. *DRUM Newsletter, Volume 1, Number 13,* p. 1.

34. *Op. Cit.* (Georgakas and Surkin), p. 49.

35. Interview with Marion Kramer, Telephone Detroit, Michigan to Cleveland, Ohio, July 6, 2002.

36. Interview with General Gordon Baker, Cleveland, Ohio [1994].

37. Interview with Marion Kramer, July 5, 2002 (Telephone: Cleveland, Ohio to Detroit, Michigan).

*Eventually all but two of the twenty-two were reinstated. Chrysler refused to reinstate Fred Holsey and another worker whom it accused of having been leaders of the strike. On December 1, 1971, the Michigan Civil Rights Commission upheld a finding by a hearing referee that the

Chrysler Corporation was guilty of unlawful discrimination in discharging Fred Holsey. The commission voted to issue a cease and desist order against Chrysler.

38. Interview with Marion Kramer, July 5, 2002, (Telephone: Cleveland, Ohio to Detroit, Michigan).

39. Interview with General Gordon Baker, Cleveland, Ohio, 1994.

40. J. W. Freeman, *The Revolutionary Way Out, Introduction Revelation*, p. 5 (unpublished manuscript).

41. Interview with General Gordon Baker, Jr., Cleveland, Ohio, 1994.

42. Interview with Chuck Wooten, July 14, 2002 (Telephone: Cleveland, Ohio to Detroit, Michigan).

43. Interview with Marion Kramer, July 5, 2002 (Telephone: Cleveland, Ohio to Detroit, Michigan).

44. Conversation with Glanton Dowdell, November 1969, Windsor, Canada.

45. Phillip S. Forner, *Organized Labor and the Black Worker, 1619–1973* [New York: International Publishers, 1974], p. 917.

46. Interview with General Gordon Baker, Jr. and interview with Norman "Otis" Richmond, 4/21/99, Telephone conversation.

47. Interview with Norman "Otis" Richmond 9/21/99, Toronto, Ontario, Canada to Cleveland, Ohio Telephone Conversation.

48. *Op. Cit.* (Allen), p. 71.

49. *Op. Cit.* (Georgakas and Surkin), p. 69.

50. *Black Student Voice, Volume 1, Number 2, October 1968*, p. 1.

51. Melvin M. Lieman, *The Political Economy of Racism: A History* [London Pluto Press, 1993], p. 229.

52. *Op. Cit.*, Interview with Norman "Otis" Richmond, 9/21/99.

53. Interview with Ernie Mkalimoto Allen, Amherst, Mass., 1993.

54. Ibid.

55. *Op. Cit.* (Allen), pp. 71–72.

56. *Op. Cit.* (Allen interview).

57. Interview with Mike Hamlin, Cleveland, Ohio to Detroit, Michigan (telephone) September 27, 1999.

58. Interview with Michele Jones, Detroit, Michigan, 1973.

59. *Op. Cit.* (Georgakas and Surkin), p. 162.

60. J. W. Freeman, *The Revolutionary Way Out* (unpublished manuscript), p. 5.

61. *Op. Cit.* (Interview with Mike Hamlin).

62. Dan Georgakas and Mavin Surkin, *Detroit: I Do Mind Dying: A*

Study in Urban Revolution Updated Edition [Cambridge, Massachusetts: *South End Press*, 1998], pp. 9–11.

63. Conversation with Queen Mother Audley Moore, Atlanta, GA., 1979.

64. Central premise of C.L.R. James as taught in a series of discussion by James and Grace Lee Boggs in Detroit, Michigan, 1964.

65. Wilbur Haddock interview, *Souls, Volume 2, Number 1, Spring 2000* p. 31

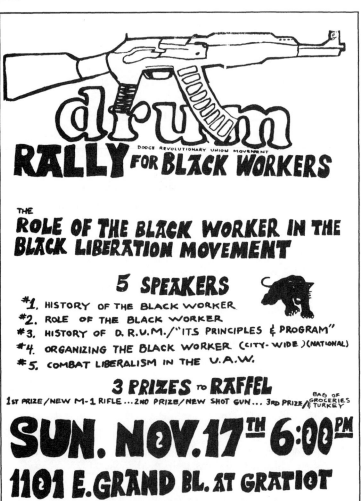

Announcement of a Rally of the Dodge Revolutionary Union Movement, a major force in the League of Revolutionary Black Workers

WHERE DO WE GO FROM HERE?: THE LEGACY OF BLACK RADICAL ORGANIZATIONS, 1960–1975

When summarizing the period 1960–1975 and the role played by black radical organizations I was impressed by the vastness of activity generated by the black radical organizations and the intensity of state response. In the chapters studying each of the organizations, their demise was traumatic, one of dismay, organizational and personal chaos.

To develop a comprehensive approach I had to study the period 1975–2006. While this period is not a subject of the text, a brief historical review is included in an effort to address the question: Where do we go from here?

During the process of summation I came upon an abundance of educational materials on governmental repression from the time period studied 1960–1975 (some of which is included the summation) including the present period 1975–2006. I will attempt to present a synopsis of this activity, presenting legal, institutional, non-legal, and extra legal methods used to politically retard the development of the African-American liberation movement. As a result of this covert (secret) war, African-Americans have not been enabled to the present to successfully regroup and develop dynamic black radical organizations.

Adisa A. Akebulan, in his article, "The FBI's Secret War Against Black America," states,

> The FBI waged a secret war against Black America. It used illegal tactics to cripple and in most cases to destroy African-American leaders and organizations.[1]

The most vivid recent example of the state's use of formal rationality along with covert illegal activities against a people's movement is the techniques used in the FBI's COINTELPRO— Counter-Intelligence-Program. Among the many techniques used by COINTELPRO some of the most widely used were:

1. *Reprint mailings*: The FBI mailed anonymous articles and newspaper clippings targeted group members.
2. *Friendly media*: The FBI gave information or articles to friendly media sources who could be relied on to write pro-Bureau stories and not to reveal Bureau's interests.

3. *Bureau-authored pamphlets and fliers*: The FBI occasionally drafted, printed and distributed its own propaganda to ridicule their targets.

4. *Encouraging violence between rival groups*: The FBI attempted to capitalize on hostility between target groups even when such programs resulted in murder.

5. *Anonymous mailings*: The FBI used anonymous mailings to promote factionalism ranging from the relatively bland mailing of reprints or fliers criticizing a group's leader for living ostentatiously or being ineffective speakers, to reporting a chapter's infractions to the group's headquarters intended to cause censure or disciplinary action.

6. *Interviews*: When the FBI interviewed target group members or supporters, the technique was sometimes used for the covert purpose of disruption.

7. *Using informants to raise controversial issues*: The FBI made extensive flagrant use of informants to take advantage of ideological splits, widen rifts and spread rumors inside of organizations.

8. *Fictitious organizations*: The FBI created three types of fictitious organizations. One type was an organization of which all the members were FBI informants. The other type was a fictitious organization with some unsuspecting (non-informant) members. The third type was a totally fictitious organization with no actual members, which was used as pseudonym for mailing letters or pamphlets.

9. *Labeling targets as informants*: The FBI used the "snitch jacket" technique often when neutralizing a target by labeling him a "snitch" (informant) so that he would no longer be trusted in the organization.

10. *Using hostile third parties against target groups*: The FBI's factionalism techniques were intended to separate individuals or groups, which might otherwise be allies. The FBI often used or manipulated persons and organizations already opposed to the target groups to attack them.

11. *Disseminating derogatory information to family, friends, and associates*: The FBI disseminated personal life information, some of which was gathered expressly for use in its programs to the target's family through an anonymous letter, telephone call or indirectly by giving information to the media.

12. *Contact with employers*: The FBI often tried to get targets fired. This technique was often used against educators. In other instances, the purpose was to either eliminate a source of funds for the target or to have the employer of the target to apply pressure on the target to stop his activities.

13. *Use and cause of government processes*: The FBI used selective law enforcement (Federal, state or local authorities) to arrest, audit, raid, inspect or deport targets. The FBI interfered with judicial proceedings, including lawyers who represented "subversives," interfered with candidates and/or

political appointees; used politicians and investigating committees, sometimes without their knowledge, to take action against targets.

14. *Interference with the judicial process*: The FBI often tampered and manipulated the judicial process to serve its interests. Often the FBI approached a judge, jury or a probation board who a target was to appear before.

15. *Candidates and political appointees*: The FBI targets candidates, it felt should not be elected.

16. *Investigating committees*: The FBI often used state and federal legislative investigating committees to attack a target.

17. *Red baiting of "communist infiltration" of groups*: The FBI often informed groups (civil rights organizations, PTA, Boy Scouts and others) that one or more of its members was a "communist." In cases when the group itself was a COINTELPRO target the information was sent to the media with the intent of linking the group to the communist party.

18. *Organizing, plotting, and executing murder*: The FBI conspired with local and state law enforcement agencies and/or informants to assassinate targets. Though little validation can be made in the many suspected murders alleged to have been executed by the FBI, documented evidence cropped up in the investigations of the assassinations of Fred Hampton and Mark Clark on December 4, 1969 in Chicago of a conspiracy organized by the FBI.

19. *Breaking and entering and burglary*: In many COINTELPRO documents there is recorded evidence, that the FBI on many cases without a search warrant broke into a target's residence illegally searched the premises and often stole documents and other paraphernalia.[2]

The (FBI) concentrated its investigations on black nationalists organizations described as "hate type organizations," with a propensity for violence and civil disorder.

> "Leaders and members of 'Black Nationalist' groups were investigated under the Emergency Detention Program for placement on the FBI's security Index."[3]

Gene Roberts, a bodyguard for Malcolm X later turned up in the Panther 21 case as a police agent.[4] McKinley Welch, an African-Puerto Rican, a BOSS agent in the New York Black Panther Party, confessed to me in 1967 that he had infiltrated Mosque (NOI) Number Seven in New York and had become secretary. When Malcolm X left the Nation of Islam, Welch was ordered by his superiors to infiltrate the OAAU. He said agents from every agency were in the OAAU.[5] From recorded reports of accounts given to *The Herald Tribune*, February 23, 1965, stated that several members of BOSS were present in the audience at the time of Malcolm's assassination.[6]

James Forman in the *Making of Black Revolutionaries* states numerous accounts of how the FBI did nothing to stop attacks against civil rights workers in the South. He also shows how through economic intelligence, using the Bureau of Internal Revenue, the racists attempted to break the back of SNCC.

> The American Government has many ways to fight those opposed to its policies, and one of the most powerful is the Bureau of Internal Revenue. The bureau zeroed in on SNCC in September, 1966—shortly after we began calling for Black Power—and plagued us steadily for two years. Its excuse was that SNCC had not filed an income tax return as an organization, although it had always paid personal income tax on the subsistence pay of staff members. The bureau also demanded that SNCC produce its complete financial records—including the names of people who had made donations to the organization. SNCC's battle against the Bureau of Internal Revenue became time-consuming, expensive and harassing—which was clearly the intention of the bureau, or powers behind it.[7]

SNCC soon began to have financial problems as supporters withdrew support because of unfavorable publicity.

> At the 1964 Democratic National Convention in Atlantic City, New Jersey, the FBI also planted a microphone in the joint headquarters of the Student Non-Violent Coordinating Committee and the Congress on Racial Equality.[8]

The FBI would forward the FBI's "subversive" information concerning individual and/or group activities to the Central Intelligence Agency. In late, semi-monthly summaries of racially motivated activity in urban areas, the reports included: the name of the community; general racial conditions; current evaluation of violence; potential identities of organizations involved in local racial situations; identities of leaders and individuals involved; the identity of leaders and individuals in the civil rights movement, including personal background data. Information on the existence of channels of communication between minority community, the number, character and intensity of demonstrations, and reactions of leaders and members of the white community to the minority demands. These reports concentrated on black nationalist groups.

On March 11, 1968, the Army circulated a classified message to all domestic commands of the Army. The message authorized the Army Security Agency, which intercepts communications for both national and tactical purposes to participate in the Army's Civil Disturbance Collection Plan.

During the time Black Panther Party leader, Huey P. Newton, was brought to trial in Alameda, California, ASA (Army Security Agency) ordered its fixed stations near Warrenton, Virginia and Monterrey, California, to monitor domestic radio communications to determine if there were any groups around the country planning demonstrations in support of Huey. ASA conducted a general search of all amateur radio bands from September 6 through September 10, 1968.[9]

The FBI Ghetto Informant Program begun in 1967 had some 7.402 informants by September 1972.

The ghetto informant originally conceived was to act as a 'listening post", "an individual who lives or works in a ghetto area and has access to information regarding the racial situation and racial activities in his area which he furnishes to the Bureau on a confidential basis."[10]

The role of the ghetto informant was expanded to attend public meetings held by so-called extremists, to identify so-called extremists passing through or locating them into the ghetto area,

> Visited African-American type bookstores for the purpose of determining if militant extremist literature is available therein and, if so, to identify the owners, operators and clientele of such stores.[11]

The FBI's COINTELPRO campaign against black nationalist groups went into full swing in 1967. The Revolutionary Action Movement was active in Philadelphia, Pennsylvania in the summer of 1967. The ASA contacting the Intelligence Unit secured spot check coverage of me by African-American officers as a personal favor after explaining RAM and my position in it to police officials.

> RAM people were arrested and released on bail, but were re-arrested several times until they could no longer make bail.[12]

The Commission also urged that these local units be linked to a national center and clearing-house in the Justice Department. The unstated consequence of these recommendations was that the FBI, having regular liaison with local police, served as the Channel (and supplementary repository) for this intelligence data.

The FBI's most extensive war was the counter-insurgency plan waged against the Black Panther Party. In September 1968, FBI Director J. Edgar Hoover described the Black Panther Party as:

> The greatest threat to the internal security of the country. Schooled in the Marxist-Leninist ideology and the teaching of Chinese Communist Leader Mao Tse-Tung, its members have perpetrated numerous assaults on police officers and have engaged in violent confrontations with police throughout the country. Leaders and representatives of the Black Panther Party travel extensively all over the United States preaching their gospel of hate and violence not only to ghetto residents but to students in colleges, universities and high schools as well.[13]

By July 1969, the Black Panther Party was under constant attack by police and FBI actions coordinated from Washington, D.C.

The BPP was the target of 233 of the total 295 black nationalist COINTELPRO actions.[14] The conspiracy against the Black Panther Party took on mammoth proportions bordering on outright fascist terror tactics. The FBI fostered rivalries between the Black Panthers and Ron Karenga's U.S. organization sending derogatory cartoons and death threats to both groups. The FBI sent an anonymous letter to the leader of the Black Stone Rangers informing him that the Chicago Panthers had a hit on him. In 1969, there were 113 arrests of BPP members in Chicago with only a handful resulting in convictions.

> In the year 1969 alone, 348 Black Panther Party members across the country were arrested for serious crimes including murder, armed robbery, rape, bank robbery, and burglary, the FBI Director informed Congress.[15]

The fact the FBI planned murders of Black Panther leaders is a clear case of genocide/fascism. Roy Wilkens and Ramsey Clark in their book *Search and Destroy: A Report by the Commission of Inquiry Into The Black Panthers and the Police,* (Metropolitan Applied Research Center, Inc., 1973), provide a detailed account of a police raid that was pre-meditated murder on December 4, 1969; police under the pretense of a weapons search raided the Panther's apartment in Chicago at 4:45 a.m. pumping over 80 rounds into the bodies of Fred Hampton and Mark Clark, killing them and wounding four others.

In Los Angeles, murder was committed by both the L.A. Police and the FBI. Steve Bartholomew, Tommy Lewis and Robert Lawrence, of the Black Panthers were sitting in a parked car at a gas station on August 25, 1968, when members of the LAPD's metro squad opened fire, killing them almost instantly.[16]

The intelligence community resorted to all kinds of tactics to destroy the Black Panther Party. Financial supporters of the party were harassed. The FBI contacted newspapers having negative articles written about the party and supporters. The IRS constantly harassed the Party.

The Black Panther paper on February 21, 1970, listing some of the arrests of Panthers on charges ranging from petty theft to criminal conspiracy to commit murder, insisted: "The total amount of money we have paid on bails and fines since the beginning of the Black Panther Party until 1969 is approximately: $5,240,568![17]

Repression of the Panthers by local police reached its peak shortly after the Nixon Administration took office.

From April to December, 1969, police raided Panther headquarters in San Francisco, Chicago, Salt Lake City, Indianapolis, Denver, San Diego, Sacramento and Los Angeles, including four separate raids in Chicago, two in San Diego, and two in Los Angeles.[18]

On several occasions the FBI developed schemes to create friction between the Black Panthers and the Nation of Islam.

The FBI war against the black liberation movement was very extensive. It was proposed that the informants would spread the rumor throughout the black community nationwide.[19]

I have attempted to write a brief but political history of the four major African-American organizations whose goal was empowerment of the African-American people through a radical restructuring of American society. Whether this study will be considered a critical analysis or not will be left to the reader.

Black radical organizations achieved various accomplishments. Varying from voting rights, social service programs such as free breakfast for school children (Head Start), Affirmative Action programs in the skilled trades and in unions to calls for civilian review board of Police and African-American studies among others; many advancements were made. The period 1960–1975 was marked by a rise of national racial consciousness among the African-American minority in the United States. This consciousness and direct action to implement a program that would institutionalize its goals led to a general upsurge of other minorities and a sizeable sector of the white majority of American society to take an anti-establishment position.

The studies of African-American radical organizations 1960–1975 therefore have a direct legacy towards regenerating a progressive multi-national (radical) mass motion forward towards creating a new equalitarian democratic socialist America. Since all four organizations generated from the African-American student movement; it is important to have a theoretical understanding of African-American college/university students relations to an African-American worker and youth alliance and its role in the worker/youth/student alliance. It is also important to understand this alliance's role in preparing the majority of the African-American community to become a vanguard force again towards creating the Rainbow party that will lead an electoral and community struggle for democratic socialism. But before we engage in a legacy for the future, lets try to analyze common denominators of the organizations, strengths and weakness much of which has already been discussed.

The purpose of this study was to show the historical and political evolutionary development of black radical organizations 1960–1975 (SNCC, RAM, BPP and the LRBW). Forty people from the four organizations in the study were interviewed; of which some were quoted in the study. To get a more quantitative analysis, fifty questionnaires with thirty-eight questions were sent to ex-movement African-American activists all of whom had been involved in black radical organizations from 1960–1975. Twenty-three responded (eighteen men and five women). Each filled out the same questionnaire and returned them to me.

The question of state repression and how African-Americans respond to it is an open ended question because the state repression ceased to be a frontal assault approach after 1975 to one that has continued in a qualitatively more intense subtle way. In a study titled *The C.I.A.'s Darkest Secret: How the C.I.A. Dumped Crack in African, Latino and Poor Communities* the premise is documented the C.I.A. in the 1980s sold tons of crack cocaine to street gangs in the south-central Los Angeles and funneled millions in profits to a C.I.A. run contra army in Nicaragua.

This information was substantiated by investigative journalism by writers of *The Mercury News,* a newspaper in Los Angeles in 1996. If these allegations are true then that means the U.S. federal government is waging a chemical war against black America. Many of the recruits of RAM and the Black Panther Party came from street gangs and students. But the drug economy has also affected workers north, east, west, and south. So it has affected the potential base for SNCC and LRBW as well.

The United States has the world's largest market for drugs.

In 1998—the last year studied—people in the United States spent $66 billion on illicit drugs, including $39 billion on cocaine, $12 billion on heroin, $11 billion on marijuana and $2.2 billion on methamphetamines.[20]

As a result of the chemical war of genocide waged against the black community by agencies of the state, the potential recruitment base for revolutionary political activity has dwindled from the years 1975 to the present resulting in an ideological and organizational generation gap between the young hip-hop generation and the "old school" generation of movement leaders. Thus, the efforts to rebuild the black liberation movement from the Black Workers Congress in the 1970s, African Liberation Support Committee, National Black Independent Political Party, National Black United Front in the 1980s; the Million Man/Woman/Youth Marches to the Black Radical Congress in the 1990s all seemed to have become temporarily stagnated or dysfunctional. But an interesting development has been the recent motion around the Millions More Movement. Throughout the organizing for the 10th Anniversary of the Million Man march or what became the Millions More Movement across the country, there was a struggle for this March to have substance and program.

As a million people showed up for the March, there was a clear message supporting HR 40, the John Conyers Reparations Study Bill. The March was attended by thousands of youth: the Hip Hop generation and their political messages from several Hip Hop artists. Minister Louis Farrakhan issued the call for participants to go back to their communities to organize and called for a party of the poor.

With the passing of Mrs. Rosa Parks, mother of the Civil Rights Movement, and Mrs. Coretta Scott King, it becomes evident that the mandate for organizing falls on the younger generation. The movement for reparations from the U.S. government for its involvement in and benefit from slavery, for its allowance of racial abuses and racial discrimination to this very hour; and from companies, corporations, and others who have become unjustly enriched from involvement and support of slavery is becoming a national and international movement and is taking concrete form. African-American youth, in particular, should pay close attention to this movement and become actively involved in it.

The Reparations Movement that currently exists was initiated in 1988 by Imari Obadele and Adjoa Ayetorio and is being led by The National Coalition of Blacks for Reparations in America (N'COBRA). Like the Civil Rights Movement, N'COBRA and others are initiating legislative (legal) challenges that are slowly producing some results.

The movement for reparations has been a long and continuous one. Recently disclosed by Dr. Mary Frances Berry in her book, *My Face Is Black Is True: Callie House and the Struggle for Ex-Slave Reparations*, is the historical revelation that hundreds of thousands of ex-slaves, led by the National Ex-Slave Mutual Relief, Bounty, and Pension Association, petitioned the U.S. Government six times between the years 1898–1913 for pensions as partial restitution for their enslavement. The Association was repressed, and Mrs. House spent a year in prison for the unjust charge of "mail fraud." Movement participants continued their activities up to and including their involvement in the Garvey Movement.

In 1955, Queen Mother Audley Moore founded the Reparations Committee of Descendants of United States Slaves. In 1962, Queen Mother Audley Moore's Reparations Committee filed a claim in California. In 1965, Robert L. Brock, an African-American attorney working along with Queen Mother Moore, filed a brief in federal district court representing the Self-Determination Committee. Queen Mother Audley Moore agitated and educated hundreds of thousands of African-Americans about the importance of reparations, from Elijah Muhammad to Malcolm X, all throughout the 1950s, '60s, '70s, and '80s. In 1969, after being taught the importance of demanding reparations by Queen Mother Audley Moore, James Forman of SNCC demanded that American churches and synagogues pay $500 million in reparations.[21]

The Movement in the early 1980s was led by Omali Yeshitela (Joe

Waller) and the African National Reparations Organization (ANRO), which held Tribunals charging the U.S. of the Crime of Genocide for slavery and the "Stolen Labor" of Africans for 246 years.

On August 21, 1987, Imari Obadele, the president of the RNA, and an avid organizer for reparations, seized the time several weeks prior to the convening of the NCBL (National Conference of Black Lawyers) conference at the urging of Queen Mother Dorothy Benton Lewis, leader of the Black Reparations Commission, and issued a call to more than twenty-five organizations and individuals to come to Washington, D.C. and discuss building support for the armed struggle in Namibia, South Africa, Angola, and Mozambique. Development of a definitive campaign for reparations for N'COBRA was born the next year, 1988.[22]

On November 20, 1989, Congressman John Conyers introduced HR 3745 in congress as a bill asking for a study of slavery to consider whether slavery was a crime against humanity, which affects us today, and whether African-Americans, being descendants of slaves, should receive reparations. He has re-introduced it in the House of Representatives each year since then, most recently as HR 40.[23]

But in the 2000s, reparations continues to come back on the African-American agenda and is beginning to have some concrete breakthroughs. The Reparations Movement had been gathering steam from support declarations from international conferences until being supplanted by 911 and fighting in Afghanistan and Iraq as national issues from the news media dominated by a conservative, imperialist regime.

Groups and individuals have since introduced legislation and law suits against corporations, demanding reparations not until 2000 did a really seemingly breakthrough occur.

In California, a law was passed requiring insurance companies to report slavery profits. Eight companies have thus far disclosed that they sold policies on 614 slaves. Among the companies are Aetna Financial Services, FleetBoston, JP Morgan, and railroad companies CSX and Union Pacific.

On October 2, 2002, Chicago City Alderwoman Dorothy Tillman proposed to the City of Chicago a Slavery Era Disclosure Ordinance that required companies doing business with the City of Chicago to disclose whether they had profited from slavery. The ordinance was passed and signed into law on May 3, 2003.

On May 3, 2005, JP Morgan Chase & Co. admitted that a predecessor company in Louisiana used slaves as loan collateral. Between 1831 and 1865, two predecessor banks of JP Morgan Chase & Co., Citizens Bank and Canal Bank in Louisiana, accepted approximately 13,000 slaves as collateral on loans and took ownership of approximately 1,250 of them when the plantation owners defaulted on the loans.

> Public records in Louisiana indicate that Citizens Bank and Canal Bank, which eventually became Bank One, merged with JP Morgan Chase in 2004. It provided credit to plantation owners and accepted mortgages from them. Records also indicate that both banks often initiated foreclosure on mortgages and took over the property, which usually included enslaved Blacks.[24]

The bank (JP Morgan Chase & Co.) apologized in a letter to its employees. The bank has agreed to establish a $5 million scholarship program called "Smart Start Louisiana," but reparations supporters say that is not enough. Viola Plummer, national co-chair of Millions for Reparations, said, "Every African-American student in Louisiana should be able to attend school for free from pre-school to Ph.D."

> According to lawsuits filed on behalf of all slave descendants, other companies, such as financial institution FleetBoston, insurance companies Aetna and New York Life, railroads Norfolk Southern, Union Pacific, and CSX, tobacco companies R.J. Reynolds and Brown & Williamson, and a textile manufacturer WestPoint Stevens, all have ties to slavery.[25]

On June 1, 2005, the Wachovia Corporation, America's fourth largest bank, revealed that several of its predecessor institutions had profited directly from slavery and had permitted borrowers to use their enslaved African-Americans as collateral for loans. A Chicago ordinance required Wachovia to look through its history for any relationship to slavery. The bank, established in 1781, showed in an investigation that it had connections to hundreds of now-defunct banks, including two that were involved with the slave trade before the Civil War.

> In one instance, the Bank of Charleston, established in 1834, had taken possession of at least 529 slaves on defaulting mortgages and loans from white customers, prior to the Civil War. The Bank of Charleston subsequently became

part of the South Carolina National Corporation, which in 1991 merged into Wachovia.[26]

On February 19, 2004, Council members Reynolds Brown and Wilson Goode, Sr., introduced Bill No. 040133 to the Council of the City of Philadelphia, entitled, "Slavery Era Business/Corporate Insurance Disclosure," which read as follows:

Referred to the
Committee on Finance
AN ORDINANCE
Amending Section 17–104 entitled "Prerequisites to the Execution of City Contracts" by adding a new subsection (2) entitled "Slavery Era Business/Corporate Insurance Disclosure" to promote full and accurate disclosure to the public about any slavery policies sold by any companies or profits from slavery by other industries (or their predecessors) who are doing business with the City of Philadelphia and recodifying Section 17–104 by incorporating various technical changes; all under certain terms and conditions.

THE COUNCIL OF THE CITY OF PHILADELPHIA HEREBY ORDAINS:

SECTION !. Section 17–104 of The Philadelphia Code is hereby amended to read as follows:

§17–104. Prerequisites to the Execution *and Validity* of City Contracts.

[(2) *Prohibited Contracts]*

[(a)] (1) *Definitions.* For the purpose of this subsection, the following definitions shall apply:

([.1]*a*) *Business Entity* Any individual, domestic corporation, foreign corporation, association, syndicated, joint stock company, partnership, joint venture, or unincorporated association, including any parent company, subsidiary, exclusive distributor or company affiliated therewith, engaged in a business or commercial enterprise:

([.2]*b*) *City.* The City of Philadelphia;

([.3]*c*) *City Agency.* The City of Philadelphia, its departments, boards and commissions:

([.4]*d*) *City-related Agency.* All authorities and quasi-public corporations which either:

([i].*1*) receive appropriations from the City; or

([ii].*2*) have entered into continuing contractual or cooperative relationships with the City; or

([iii]].*3*) operate under legal authority granted to them by City ordinance.

([.5]*e*) *Department.* The Procurement Department.

(2) Slavery Era Business/Corporate Insurance Disclosure.

(a) Business, Corporate and Slavery Era Insurance Ordinance. This subsection shall be known and cited as the "Business, Corporate and Slavery Era Insurance Ordinance." The purpose of this subsection is to promote full and accurate disclosure to the public about any slavery policies sold by any companies, or profits from slavery by other industries (or their predecessors) who are doing business with any City Agency or City-related Agency.

(b) Each contractor with whom a City Agency enters into a contract, whether subject to competitive bid or not, within the first 90 days after the contract's execution, shall complete an affidavit verifying that the contractor has searched any and all records of the company or any predecessor company regarding records of investments or profits from slavery or slaveholder insurance policies during the slavery era. The names of any slaves or slaveholders described in those records must be disclosed in the affidavit.

(c) The Department shall make the information contained in the affidavit available to the public, including but not limited to making the information accessible on the City's internet accessible world wide web home page and provide an annual report to the City Council.

(d) Any contract between a City Agency and a contractor which fails to provide the requisite affidavit within ninety (90) days of the contract's execution or which includes material false information on such affidavit shall be rendered null and void.

SECTION 2. This ordinance shall take effect 90 days after final passage.

(e) City Related Agencies. Any contract, lease, grant condition or other agreement entered into by the City with any City-related Agency shall contain a provision requiring the

City-related Agency, in the procurement of goods and services purchased pursuant to such contract, lease, grant condition or other agreement with the City, to abide by the provisions of subsection 17–104(2).

In 2005, the National Coalition of Blacks for Reparations in America (NCOBRA) developed a case statement saying Wachovia directly or indirectly subjected the ancestors of African-Americans to a holocaust of inhumane treatment: kidnapping, murder, slave labor, physical and mental torture, rape, starvation, hangings, and subjected generations of African descendants—African-Americans—to continued effects of these original acts, including, but not limited to: Jim Crow, Klu Klux Klan, race discrimination, affirmative action, and racial disparities in lending and investments.

On December 13, 2005, Mayor John F. Street of the City of Philadelphia signed a bill into law that will make Philadelphia one of the first cities in the United States to demand reparations from banks that have benefited from slavery. The law had been introduced by City Council members Wilson Goode and Blondell Reynold-Brown on February 19, 2004.

Wachovia ties to enslavement of African people in America started with its enabling institution, the Bank of North America, founded in the City of Philadelphia in 1781. Its founders and chief executive officers were Robert Morris and Thomas Swilling, both Philadelphia residents. These two individuals were the renowned slave merchants of Philadelphia in their day. Their mercantile enterprises included trans-Atlantic shipping, railroads, cotton, tobacco, (and) indigo plantation. Both Morris and Swilling served on the Second Continental Congress. Swilling as the Mayor of Philadelphia in 1793, served a term as Justice of the Pennsylvania Supreme Court, and also served as president of the Bank of North America. Robert Morris was Bank of North America' first president. Once the Articles of the new Constitution were ratified, the Congress of the new United States appointed Robert Morris as the Superintendent of Finance. He is the person the term "conflict of interest" was said to be coined after.

According to the historical record, the Bank of North America was founded as a way and a means to finance the American Revolution and get the Continental Congress out of debt at the same time it was financing the slave trade through its various mercantile ventures, such as ships, railroads, plantation, and auctions. After disclosure and apology, Wachovia must take responsibility to repair the damage done to Black people. African-Americans must always equate reparations with restitution.

Ari Merretazon said, "Wachovia financially benefited and inherited huge sums of money and property from its predecessors. In so doing, if furthered the commission of crimes against humanity, crimes against peace, kidnapping, murder, slavery and forced labor, physical and mental abuse, economic conversion and discrimination. Likewise, it should also inherit the debt of the human and social aftermath of its legacy of slavery. It is a matter of corrective moral justice that Wachovia, along with other corporations and other units of government, pay the debt it owes to African descendants."[27]

If N'COBRA and other youth forces are to take on finance capital, it will take a lot of research into the foundations of the global capitalist system. Also, it will take a great "Educate, Agitate, and Organize" campaign to prepare the African-American community and its allies to engage in revolutionary action against the economic and political system that has become unjustly enriched form its oppression.

C.J. Munford, in his article "Reparations: Strategic Considerations for Black Americans," states,:

> Black reparations is a claim on the Western capitalist socioeconomic system. It is not a claim on socialism, communism, or any other non-capitalist "mode of production" or society. Our unpaid forced labor laid the foundations of the western capitalist order, and no other. Our enslavement along enables European civilizations to snare the western hemisphere, appropriate its resources and anchor white wealth and might in the Americas.[28]

> Such a movement will probably necessitate the re-emergence of black radical organizations similar to the ones that existed 1960–1975. African-American students will need a Student National Coordinating Committee (SNCC) to coordinate their actions. There will be a need for a Reparations Action

Movement (RAM) to engage in civil disobedience against an injust economic system and also a form of a trans-community form of a Black Panther Party (BPP) in the form of a People's Party (PP) or Party of the Poor that elects political representatives in the political system that have the courage to demand Reparations for African-Americans and to call for an equalitarian socialist transformation of the system.

Such a movement will need the reorganization on a mass scale of League of Revolutionary Black Workers (LRBW) or a similar form to radicalize the labor movement; to create work stoppages in favor of the reparations demands, and to create new economic forms of survival in the African-American community built around alternative energy (solar) needs.

Amiri Baraka, in his August 15, 2002, web-site statement on "The Essence of Reparations" says:

Reparations is a form of justice, in the philosophical sphere, it is in essence a revolutionary democratic thrust that must force the yet unfinished US democratic revolution, viz. the civil war movements closer to completion.

The fundamental demand for Democracy, as Equal Citizenship rights, which must be coupled with and (are) a confirmation of Afro American Self determination, demands Indemnification for the Slave Trade, The Middle Passage, Chattel Slavery, Capitalist Slavery, National Oppression and Racism, as well as the multiform abuses that have gone with these.[29]

Baraka goes on to say:

Reparations must take the form of Social reconstruction, which is Economical and Political and Cultural at base. For instance, any initial demand must include the demand for free education for the Afro American people, not as affirmative action, but as a constitutional amendment which by law Black Americans obtain education to the highest sectors of the US and other educational institution with charge.[30]

With American having approximately 200 African-American political prisoners and its number one growth industry being the prison-industrial complex, which gets its profit from the criminalization of more than two million plus African-Americans, it has become the number one imperialist, fascist state and enemy of persons of African descent and freedom loving people's in the world.

A revolutionary movement among African-Americans for reparations and self-determination which has the long range goals of uniting with the overwhelming majority of the working class and advancing the movement toward socialism in America should have a revolutionary transitional program, restitution for war crimes of genocide against the African-American people and a re-ordering of the national priorities (resources) of the nation and national government; proportional representation; programs that demand the mass inclusion of African-Americans in the democratic process in all facets of the society that acts as a guide to mass action.

If the present is conducive with objective reality, then the legacy of black radical organizations, 1960 to 1975, reflects the statement, "We Will Return in the Whirlwind."

1. Adisa A. Akebulan, "*The FBI's Secret War Against Black America,*" *Uhuru Fall, 1995*, p. 8.
2. *Supplementary Detailed Staff Reports on Intelligence Activities and the Rights of Americans*; United States Senate Book 3, [Washington, D.C., G.P.O.], pp. 33–62.
3. Ibid, p. 447.
4. Marc Churchill and Jim Vander Veall, *Agents of Repression*, [Boston, Mass.: South End Press, 1958], p. 686.
5. Confession of McKinley Welch to Max Stanford, March 1967, Philadelphia, Pennsylvania.
6. George Brietman, Herman Porter and Baxter Smith, *The Assassination of Malcolm X*, [New York: Pathfinder Press, Inc., 1976], pp. 52–54.
7. James Forman, *The Making of Black Revolutionaries*, [New York: The Macmillan Company, 1972], pp. 471–472.
8. *Suppl. Detailed Staff Reports on Intelligence Activities and the Rights of Americans*, [Washington, D.C., 1976], p. 335.
9. Ibid., pp. 798–801.
10. "The FBI Plot Against Black Leaders" by Iris L. Washington, (*Essence Magazine, October, 1978, Volume 9, Number 6*, p. 70.
11. *Suppl. Detailed Staff Reports on Intelligence Activities and the Rights of Americans, op. Cit.*, p. 253.
12. Counter-Intelligence, Volume One, *National Lawyers Guild Task Force on Counter-Intelligence and the Secret Police*, (Chicago, Illinois, 1978), pp. 53–54.

13. *Suppl. Detailed Staff Reports on Intelligence Activities and the Rights of Americans, Book III*, (Washington, D.C., 1976), p. 494.

14. Ibid., p.494.

15. Louis Heath, Ed., *Off the Pigs*, (Metuchen, New Jersey: Scarecrow Press, Inc., 1976), p. 33.

16. "FBI Plotted to Eliminate BPP Leadership," (*The Black Panther*, Volume XVIII, Number 8, Saturday, March 11, 1978), p. 1.

17. Louis Heath, Ed., *Off the Pigs*, (*Op. Cit.*, p. 137.

18. Robert Justin Goldstein, *Political Repression in Modern America*, [Cambridge, Massachusetts: Schensman Publishing Company, 1978], p. 52.

19. *Counter-Intelligence, Op. Cit.*, p. 58.

20. ONDCP, "What America's Users Spend on Illegal Drugs, 1988–1998," December, 2000, *http://www.whitehouse*drugpolicy.gov/publications/drugfact/american_users_spend/index.htm.

21. Harper's magazine, November 2000, *Does America Owe a Debt t the Descendants of Ex-Slaves?*, pp 103

22. Adajoa A. Ayetorio, "The National Coalition of Blacks for Reparations in America (N'COBRA), It's Creation and Contribution to the Reparations Movement," in Raymond A. Winbush, Ph.D., edited, *Should America Pay?: Slavery and the Raging Debate on Reparations*, [New York: Amistad, 2003] p 211

23. Makebra Anderson, "JP Morgan Chase & Co. Admits Link to Slavery," *The Final Call*, February 8, 2005, p. 4

24. Makebra Anderson, "JP Morgan Chase & Co. Admits Link to Slavery," *The Final Call*, February 8, 2005, p. 4

25. Ibid pp 33

26. Dr. Manning Marable, "Black Reparations: The Caps of Wachovia Bank and Eastman Kodak," Part II of a Two-Part Series, *Along The Color Line*, August 2005, pp 1–2

27. National Coalition of Blacks for Reparations in America (N'COBRA) Press Release, December 28, 2005.

28. Ray L. Brookes (ed.) *When Sorry Isn't Enough* [New York: New York University Press, 1999] p 423

29. Amiri Baraka, "The Essence of Reparations," p.1 [http://webmail.juno.com/.../8?position=4&msgNum=312&folder=Inbox&count=8052&block= 8/15/02

30. Ibid., p2

Linocut flyer for DRUM
(Dodge Revolutionary Union Movement)
from Aaron Pori Pitts' journal,
Black Graphics International (1970)

APPENDIX ONE
RESEARCH METHODOLOGY

Rationale for The Study

In the United States, the 1960s was a period of mass political activism as a divergent set of dispossessed and alienated groups, both singly and collectively, challenged the distribution and exercise of state power. These groups included the anti-war, anti-poverty, Native-American, and the African-American movements. The African-American movement for empowerment, hereafter referred to as the black liberation movement (BLM), was the central catalytic force that served as a source of emulation for practically all of the other groups that were active from 1960 to 1975.

This study focuses on four African-American organizations that were active during this period: the Student Non-Violent Coordinating Committee (SNCC) 1960–1971, the Revolutionary Action Movement (RAM), 1962–1968, the Black Panther Party (BPP) 1966–1978, and the League of Revolutionary Black Workers (LRBW) 1969–1971. All four organizations called for a radical reconstruction of American society and used the term black radical or revolutionary in describing their posture and general orientation to struggle. What does the term black radical mean? The term is usually used to denote a person affiliated with an African American organization, which advocated a form of socialism as a solution to the problem of racial, political, economic and social inequality in the United States. While there are fairly elaborate studies on three of the four organizations, SNCC, BPP and LRBW, there is none that concentrates on the history of all four of the organizations as a joint social force.[1] This study makes a modest contribution toward filling that gap.

In a class-stratified society, radicalism implies the elimination of class distinctions or classes, and by inference, the elimination of most—if not all—private property. The majority of private property would become social, that is owned by the state in which the working class dominates the political decision making process. Black radicalism therefore would refer to those individuals or organizations of African descent advocating a form of socialism or communism in the U.S. and the world at large.

The task of this research is to present a descriptive, qualitative historical and materialist analysis of the four major black radical organizations which were operative during the period of 1960–1975. Inasmuch as all four of these organizations were essentially part of the urban revolutionary movements that evolved in capitalist countries of the Western hemisphere, there was a need to select a conceptual framework or approach that would allow us to understand these movements in both their domestic and international context. The dialectical and historical materialist approach proved to be the best method for this undertaking.[2]

This is a method whereby the researcher approaches the subject matter as a material phenomenon that is constantly changing and is subject to economic and political laws governing human society. The dialectical method begins with the assumption that no phenomenon in nature can be understood in isolation. Phenomena must be considered in connection with the surrounding conditions, and cannot be understood or explained unless considered as inseparably connected to them. No historical force is considered a separate entity, but is rather considered an interconnected force, which affects and is affected by other phenomenon in the world system. In this study of the four organizations, the researcher begins with the assumption that they were characterized by interlocking or overlapping membership and that their tempo and longevity were mutually reinforcing. As activity in one of them changed there were reciprocal responses in the others. In analyzing a formation such as the BLM, relationship of classes in U.S. society and particularly the class structure of the African-American community, historical development of the BLM, and the political climate of the period must be synthesized.

A historical materialist point of view is essentially the extension of the principles of dialectical materialism to the study of social life and the application of the principles of dialectical materialism to the phenomenon of the life of society and its history.

While there is an abundance of research material on Dr. Martin Luther King, Jr. and the civil rights movement (CRM), research materials on black radical organizations are limited. There are approximately twenty books on the Black Panther Party (BPP) (see bibliography), fifteen on the Student Non-Violent Coordinating Committee (SNCC), two on the League of Revolutionary Black

Workers (LRBW) and none on the Revolutionary Action Movement (RAM). There is no definitive research on the four organizations, which proposed radical socialist transformation of the United States. The lack of qualitative autobiographies or written documentation has fostered an inaccurate account of the period from 1960 to 1975. Therefore it is the aim of the researcher to rectify this with oral accounts of the social development process of black radicals and their organizational activities.

The importance of qualitative research: As a participant observer of the described period, my recollection of several important historical developments of the period as well as the recollections of other interviewees were at odds with accounts published by established scholars.

Many of the studies on the BLM in the United States suffer from two major defects. First, they fail to place the BLM in a larger context of being part of a worldwide anti-colonial, third world and socialist revolution, struggling to liberate itself from the world capitalist system. Second, most researchers of the BLM in the U.S.A. usually highlight the role of individuals and their contributions to the race, rather than placing emphasis on the masses as the makers of history. Many researchers fail to concentrate on the mass character of movements that have occurred in the African-American community and when they do, they fail to show the historical continuity from one period of mass struggle to another. Within this context, the vast majority of African-American social scientists fail to understand or show the dialectical relation between racial and class exploitation of African-Americans in the United States.

In order to understand the dialectical nature of racial and class exploitation, it is necessary to develop an analysis of the world capitalist system and the relation of African-Americans to capitalism and slavery as a preeminent factor in the evolution of American capitalism. Understanding the dialectic of race in relation to the dialectic of class requires the development of a new paradigm, a paradigm in which slavery as an economic, social, and political force occupied a central place in the development of capitalism.[3]

A complete analysis of the dialectic of dual oppression, race and class, will not be attempted here but a brief sketch is provided to aid the reader in interpreting the meaning and significance of the black radical and/or black radical organizations 1960 to 1975. What is the rationale for proceeding in this fashion? The rationale is that the leaders and rank and file members of the four organizations were aggressive energetic young people who made non-compromising demands and accelerated the tempo or rising expectations of a generation of oppressed and alienated citizens. They became impatient with the rate of change in the organizations becoming more aggressive in their agitation and posed a potential threat to civil tranquility. Their uncompromising challenge to the status quo forced rapid social change in the social structure, and as a result caused the state apparatus to unleash economic, political, legal and extra-legal repression against the black radical organizations.

STATEMENT OF THE PROBLEM:
THEORY OF BLACK RADICAL ORGANIZATIONS

Black radical organizations investigated in this study did not evolve until the mid 1960s. The only historical precedents for their existence and epistemology were developments in the 1920s with the emergence of the African Blood Brotherhood (A.B.B.) and later in 1941 with the March On Washington Movement (MOWM) organized by A. Phillip Randolph.

The ABB sought to develop a cadre of revolutionary African-Americans and unite them with progressive white workers to bring forth a Marxist-Leninist (socialist) revolution in the United States. The heart of the ABB's ideological perspective was that African-Americans constituted an oppressed nation in the black-belt-south. There is one scant record on the ABB and only a couple of books with a brief history of the organization. The other all-African-American or predominately African-American effort at transforming American society was the March On Washington Movement mobilization effort, which demanded fair access to employment in government jobs. Fear of the effort forced President Franklin D. Roosevelt to issue Executive Order 8802 banning discrimination in federal hiring.

The researcher has chosen the time period from 1960 to 1975. Within this fifteen-year time frame, many of the concepts, terms and theories associated with the elimination of the subjugation of African-Americans to European-American capitalist class domination came to the fore for discussion, debate, and resolution. Thousands of African-American youth participated in four major African-American radical formations. This period of time has been referred to by James Forman as "the high tide of resistance." It is during this period that millions of African-Americans and their allies participated in the form of civil disobedience or non-violent mass demonstrations, or violent rebellions. The time frame 1960 to 1975 represents accumulation of decades of mass protest which has not been witnessed since that time, has not been surpassed in mass mobilization numbers in exception the October 16, 1995, Million Man March, the 1997 Million Women March, and the 2005 Millions More Movement (March).

It was also within this time period (1960 to 1975) that the United States government responded most adamantly and often violently to the activities of African-American radical organizations.

The limitation of the research is due to its being a qualitative analysis that investigates the epistemology of black radical organizations and participants and it does not fully analyze government response. Due to the depth of the research findings the researcher will not be able to investigate extensively the subjects such as the crisis in socialism or the socialist world and how that impacted black radical organizations and participants.

Within the scope of the research is information related to how organizers went about organizing communities and the programs offered by organizations including their shortcomings. The researcher has addressed contemporary questions in the summary, conclusion and recommendations. The research does not address in structural form what to organize in the present or future. In this sense, the research study is limited as a historical study attempting to advance a more comprehensive analysis of the radical or revolutionary tendencies of what became known as the black liberation movement (BLM).

The cultural frame of reference of the research is presented from an "internationalist" or Pan-African perspective in language familiar inside the African-American community. The cultural references have not been slanted to meet the "objective" requirements of European-American academia. The research is a collective qualitative analysis based on subjective experiences. While the researcher is one of the interviewees, a participant-observer, who uses the historical materialist methodological approach, as a valid method of study the research is qualitative and does not pretend to be objective. The research is objective only in the overall analyzing of historical forces. After providing a historical background into the problem, the researcher will not attempt to validate by quantitative statistics whether the black liberation movement's chief adversaries, i.e., the politicized section of local and/or regional police departments and the federal intelligence community, were racist or not.

The context of race that is being discussed played and still plays a major role in American society both institutionally and non-institutionally. So, as black radical organizations became the center of the civil rights/black power movements in the mid-60s, the parameter of racial oppression and mobilization based on racial bloc unity was a central factor.

The question of class and class oppression being the basis of power relations in American and world society had long been established in the political arena by the American Socialist Party and also the American Communist Party. Class oppression was very much adamant in the mid-60s as it is in the present era. Therefore, it too became part of the paradigm of black radical organizations.

Gender oppression, discrimination, and exploitation or domination by men over women have long been issues in American and world society. Often an issue that has been suppressed becomes an issue of focus in the mid-60s to the present. So the historical context was laid by the mid-60s for the formation of an unorthodox or neo-approach of applying the basic tenants of Marxism, Marxism-Leninism, Marxism-Leninism-Mao Tse Tung Thought and Revolutionary Marxism to a racist society based on super ordination and subordination.

Black radical organizations for the most part considering variations (SNCC, RAM, BPP and LRBW) all had a race, class and gender analysis. All after 1966 used a form of what was termed, revolutionary nationalism (unity of lower class, African-Americans, poor) to galvanize the African-American mass radical movement. This is what Cedric J. Robinson called black Marxism and what Rod Bush called black nationalism and class struggle.

Review of Literature with Direct Relevance for the Thesis

One of the critical issues that an analysis of radical black organizations must address is what accounts for their particular evolution. What accounts for their successes and failures? Some commentators focus on the pernicious impact of hostile external forces such as counter-intelligence and state police forces while others place special emphasis on matters internal to the organizations themselves. The issue of ideological orientation is also critical to a study. Were radical black organizations of the period necessarily nationalist and what were the possible relationships between nationalist and Marxist or socialist ideologies? How did the struggles of black radical organizations fit into the world struggle against repression and how, in turn, were radical black organizations influenced by the world system? To what extent were black radical formations also anti-capitalist formations? And, what determined and conditioned strategies for struggle, including armed resistance? Elaborating on these and other questions are essential for understanding the rise and demise of the organizations studied in this study. To set this stage for our analysis, I have chosen to analyze certain selected works to determine what competent researchers and theorists have said on these issues.

Oliver C. Cox's works (as told by Herbert M. Hunter and Sameer Y. Abraham (eds.) in *Race, Class and the World System: The Sociology of Oliver C. Cox*) are important because of the intellectual legacy that his writings provided critical thinkers of the '60s. The intellectual tendency that was called revolutionary nationalist or black internationalist had undercurrents of philosophies of Cox and C. L. R. James.

In the introduction to "The Life and Career of Oliver C. Cox, Hunter and Abraham describe Cox's central thesis. Cox argues that a significant feature of European capitalist societies as early as Venetian capitalism in the thirteenth century was the commercial relations they developed with backward areas in the world system. The editors go on to elaborate that racial antagonisms throughout the world were not the cause of the disillusionment with capitalism, but they were due to the effect of capitalist domination of the less-developed countries. Cox's sociology points out that for a capitalist nation to dominate in the world capitalist system it had to maintain uneven patterns of development. Cox introduced a perspective of a world-system, which is the predecessor of the writings of Immanuel Wallerstein, Samir Amin, and others.

Oliver Cox stated that capitalism was international from its beginnings. He believed it led to underdevelopment of indigenous peoples where it came into contact with them either through slavery, genocide, forced migration, or combinations of various forms of exploitation. Cox believed that racial exploitation and race prejudice developed among Europeans with the rise of capitalism and nationalism, and that because of the worldwide ramifications of capitalism, all racial antagonisms could be traced to the policies and attitudes of the leading capitalist people, the white people of Europe and North America.[4]

Also, in Cox's writings on race relations, he defines the difference between caste and racial prejudice. He writes,

> Caste prejudice is an aspect of culture prejudice, while race prejudice—as distinguished from culture prejudice—is color and physical prejudice. The latter is prejudice marked by visibility, physical distinguish-ability; it is not, however, caused by physical differences.[5]

The importance of the sociology of Oliver C. Cox is that his approach to social theory and analysis was unorthodox or a non-conventional view raising critical thinking in contrast to the Marxist view. Even so, Cox said independent thinkers should be free to draw on anybody of knowledge as long as it proved scientifically sound. He said one need not be a Marxist in order to benefit from Marx's approach.

Marxism for Our Times (Martin Glaberman, ed.) is a collection of C.L.R. James' writings on revolutionary organization. C.L.R James discussed the possibility of the rise of independent Black Nationalist organizations and their relationships with socialist formations. He suggested that African-Americans would develop an independent movement towards socialism and would not be subservient to the Anglo-American movement. That is why he was so highly revered as a theoretician in the 1960s. The collection of essays are a starting point to understanding how young African-Americans were trying to combine nationalism and socialist thought in African-American organizations from 1960 to 1975, the period of this study. The essay "Education, Propaganda, Agitation: Post-War America, Bolshevism," is a discussion of the theory of three layers of organization: The first (top) layer of leadership of the revolutionary organization is the theoretical and political leadership. The second levels are cadre (consistent; reliable) activists who were leaders in their communities, at work, in labor organizations, youth groups, etc., and the third layer consists of a genuine rank and file. James said:

All studies of dialectic, of historical materialism, of political economy, of the history of the working class and of the revolutionary movement are, for the most part, meaningless if they do not concretely contribute to and culminate in the theoretical analysis of party building.[6]

James surmised "no party, no group can grow and develop unless the majority of its members function and functioned intelligently among the workers in industry." He believed the best form of recruitment was "concentration on the personal contact method of making recruits." But even so, James believed this method had its limitations. He believed that personal contact should be augmented by the written word. Revolutionary groups, he argued, should have their own publications. James revealed "the world we live in makes it imperative for us to concentrate all our best energies into making the paper an agent for the training and recruiting of conscious Marxists." James indicated that the revolutionary organization's organ must appeal to and heighten the consciousness of the followers such that the idea should gradually crystallize among thousands of readers and that the organ should become a daily paper. In summing up successful international experiences, he said: "Lenin insisted that the problems of party building should be discussed not only among the leaders and the intellectuals, but in the press before the workers."[7] James focuses his belief on the fact that a viable revolutionary organ of the revolutionary cadre organization must be firmly rooted into the union movement.

Inside the union movement, the American working class is living the intense political life of the times and the American political movement is likely to be tied to the union movement from the very start in an in dissoluble bond. Thus, in the U.S., in particular, our place is in the union movement as the basis for our political action.[8]

C. L. R. James' theories on revolutionary organization are particularly relevant to black radical organizations 1960–1975, because the formations of SNCC, RAM, BPP and LRBW either attempted to create a black mass party, discussed it or were involved in labor struggles. James believed that the foundations of a mass party had to be built from the ground up. This grounding among the masses is what led organizers of the aforementioned organizations to first agitate around issues directly affecting the masses of African-Americans. In this sense, all the organizations developed around practice, theory, practice rather than theory, practice, theory. This essentially meant that the organizations were based on actual practice of organizing around issues with which the African-American masses were concerned. In that sense, recruitment occurred around what the organizations were doing rather than first studying theory.

Functionally, that may have been a structural weakness of black radical organizations since few of its membership had an in-depth understanding of the organizations' ideologies. This is something the study investigates. James addresses this question as one of an "Americanization of Bolshevism." "To Bolshevize America, it is necessary to Americanize Bolshevism." He goes on to state:

> Nothing can be more misleading than the idea that Americanization means seeking historical examples of revolutionary American parties and American heroes of labor with which to "inspire" the American workers and season our journalists. Every great revolution is a truly national revolution in that it represents not only the historic but also the immediate interests of the nation and is recognized as such. But every party which leads such a revolution is also a national party rooted in the economic and social life, history and traditions of the nation. Its own class ideology is cast in the national mold and is an integral part of the national social structure.[9]

C. L. R. James reflecting on Lenin believed the need for American revolutionaries not only to study the great classics of Marxist literature, but also to translate the theory of scientific socialism to the American reality. He wrote about how Lenin had engaged in six years of theoretical work, studying volumes of Capital, Anti-Duhring and other works while in school. By the time he arrived in St. Petersburg in 1894, he was groomed thoroughly in revolutionary theory. James points out that from 1894 to 1914, Lenin's life work was to translate Marxism into Russian terms for the Russian people. Lenin advocated that his party, the Bolshevik party, be rooted in the day-to-day work, in industrial and mass struggles. As a leader, Lenin was an advocate of mass activity and considered his special task to provide those thousands of party leaders, propagandists and agitators with material and method by which they could educate themselves and others. In this way, he also educated himself.

C. L. R. James said the role of propaganda is to discuss the theoretical aspects of the struggle. Agitation, on the other hand, describes conditions and calls for actions or alternatives. James believed for revolutionaries to be meaningful to the American Revolution, theoreticians needed to translate socialist theory to the national condition of the United States.

> Proletarian ideology is not merely a matter of theoretical analysis. It is the weapon and armory with which we must arm and surround the American working class and particularly those who face the enormous tasks confronting us in the present period. Unless it is rooted in the American environment and in such terms as the American worker can grasp, we cannot lift them above the instinctive class struggle, sharp as that will inevitably become. Isn't this what Lenin meant by the socialist consciousness, which the party carries to the working class?[10]

C. L. R. James' theory of revolutionary organization was very relevant for black radical organizations for the period 1960 to 1975. The last of the black radical organizations to evolve, the League of Revolutionary Black Workers, had received direct consultation from James who had returned to the Detroit area in the late '60s, early '70s.

Black Marxism: The Making of the Black Radical Tradition (Cedric J. Robinson) is a good historical, theoretical account of how black radicals had challenged the traditional paradigm of the white left. Cedric J. Robinson discusses black Marxism and states that it is a history of a central theme of many African-American Marxists who from Hubert Harrison, Cyril Briggs, Richard B. Moore to George Padmore, and C. L. R. James; had stated African-Americans would be a significant force towards proletarian revolution in the United States. Robin G. Kelly, in the preface of *Black Marxism: The Making of the Black Radical Tradition*, (Robinson, 1983), states, "*Black Marxism* is a new vision centered on a theory of the cultural corruption of race. Its reach and cross-fertilization of the black radical tradition became evident in the anti-colonial and revolutionary struggles of Africa, the Caribbean and the Americas."[11]

Robinson talks about the contributions of the notable W. E. B. DuBois. He says DuBois in *Black Reconstruction in America* points out how in every instance in the 20th century peasants and agrarian workers had been the primary social bases of rebellion and revolution. While in the case of Russia, the urban proletariat was rebellious and a fraction of the mobilized masses but not the leading force. Robinson goes on to state:

Revolutionary consciousness had formed in the process of anti-imperialist and nationalist struggles, and the beginnings of resistance had often been initiated by ideological constructions remote from the proletarian consciousness that was a presumption of Marx's theory of revolution.[12]

In addition, in Chapter 10, "C. L. R. James and the Black radical tradition," Robinson quotes Cabral on culture and history and alludes to how James carried out the motion of a revolutionary intelligentsia.

...the national liberation of a people is the regaining of the historical personality of that people, its return to history through the destruction of the imperialist domination to which it was subjected.[13]

Robinson said that James defined that collective revolutionary intelligentsia to be the basis for a cadre of professional revolutionists, which were the beginnings of the vanguard party. C. L. R. James analyzed that "the leaders of a revolution are usually those who have been able to profit by the cultural advantages of the system they are attacking."[14]

Finally, *Black Marxism* is an important text to the study of black radical organizations 1960–1975 because it provides both the history of the black radical tradition from which the leadership emerged and also an analysis for its social context.

Rod Bush, We Are Not What We Seem: Black Nationalism and Class Struggle in the American Century, in his comprehensive work dealing with nationalism and class struggle in America addresses the issue of what factors account for the demise of radical black organizations in general and the Black Panther Party (BPP) in particular. He argues that the political history of the nationalist aspects to black radicalism within the United States may not be the reasons why the BPP did not survive. In one chapter, he concerns himself with the study of "The Crisis of U.S. Hegemony and the Transformation from Civil Rights to Black Liberation" (Chapter 7, p. 199). Bush gives a historical and theoretical account of the Black Panther Party (BPP). In other studies some writers attribute the demise of the Black Panther Party to the FBI and police repression as well as the internal degeneration of BPP's national leadership. However, Bush asserts that the social movements reflect both the institutional arrangements existent in their loci of struggle, and the larger social structure of the capitalist world-economy. The BPP concentrated on the permanently unemployed African-American youth often referred to as the lumpen-proletariat, which proved a weakness due to their instability in relation to the world capitalist economy.

Further, Bush describes the development of the League of Revolutionary Black Workers, an organization of young black autoworkers as a more politically mature approach. Bush elaborates on how a schism occurred between in-plant and out-of-plant organizers in the workers organization. Even though he gives a good historical description, Bush's thesis lacks the dimension that I want to address in the area of "ideological underdevelopment within the African-American community." 15 While racism, being a built-in component of historical capitalism, continually thrusts African-Americans forward to advance the parameters of democracy, the movement usually meets defeat from an unexpected place—internal ideological deficiency. This crisis of the African-American revolutionary intelligentsia has yet to be adequately dealt with. Therefore, as Chapter 3 of my study proceeds into black radicalism in the 1970s, it becomes apparent that the various forces that emerge are either dependent on developments in either the Chinese revolution or in Africa. Only Harold Cruse, in The Crisis of the Negro Intellectual, attempts to grapple with this issue.

Liberation, Imagination and the Black Panther Party (Kathleen Cleaver and George Katsiaficas, eds.), is the most comprehensive collection of essays on various issues, which affected the development of the Black Panther Party. Of particular concern for the researcher is the article, "Repression Breeds Resistance: The Black Liberation Army and the Radical Legacy of the Black Panther Party," by Akineyele Omowale Umoja. Umoja's work is the first objective analysis of the BLA and the East Coast Black Panther Party. While the contemporary origins of the BLA go back to young adults who were in alliance with Minister Malcolm X in 1964, Umoja correctly assesses that most of the BLA's activity in the latter '60s, '70s and '80s was associated with the Black Panther Party. Russell Shoats in "Black Fighting Formations: Their Strengths, Weaknesses and Potentialities" alludes to the existence of other fighting formations, but probably due to limited activity and age, Shoats fails to analyze two of the most successful black fighting formations, "the Deacons for Defense, and the Fruit of Islam."

While armed resistance was not the official policy of the Nation of Islam, in various cities, the FOI engaged in resistance. When captured, the combatants had been "expelled" from the NOI and were considered as rebels. Both the rebels and the Deacons had working alliances with other black fighting formations, including the Black Panther Party, throughout the '60s and '70s.

1. Approximate list at end of text in the Bibliography
2. For further reading on dialectical and historical materialism refer to:
   a. Yu A. Kharin, Fundamentals of Dialectics [Moscow: Progress Publishers, 1989].
   b. Berbeshkina, L.Yakovlera, D. Zerkin, *What is Historical Materialism?* [Moscow: Progress Publishers, 1985
3. Eric Williams, Capitalism and Slavery (New York: Capricorn Books, 1996), p.127
4. Herbert M.Hunter & Sameer Y. Abraham (eds.) *Race, Class and the World System: The Sociology of Oliver C.Cox* [New York: Monthly Review Press, 1987] p.51
5. Ibid. , p.61
6. Martin Glaberman (ed.), *Marxism for Our Times* [Jackson: University Press of Mississippi, 1999] p. 3
7. Ibid., p.11
8. Ibid., p.11
8. *Op. Cit.* p. 15
9. Ibid., p. 21
10. Cedric J. Robinson, *Black Maxism: The Making of the Black Radical Traditions* [Chapel Hill & London: University of North Carolina Press, 1983] p.xxxii
11. Ibid, p.240.
12. Amilcar Cabral, *Revolution in Guinea: Selected Texts* [New York and London: Monthly Review Press, 1969] p.102
13. Scott McLemee and Paul LeBlanc (eds), *C.L.R. James: Revolutionary Marxism: Selected Writings of C.L.R. James1939–1949* [New Jersey: Humanities Press, 1994] p.180
14. Rod Bush, *We Are Not What We Seem: Black Nationalism and Class Struggle in the American Century* [New York: New York University Press, 1999] p.244

APPENDIX 2
List of People Interviewed
Interviewees from four Black Radical Organizations

Student Non-violent Coordinating Committee (SNCC)

1. Kwame Ture (Stokely Carmichael)
2. George Ware
3. Muriel Tillinghast
4. Judy Richardson
5. Gloria House
6. Sam Anderson
7. Don Stone
8. Mike Simmons
9. Gwen Patton
10. Cleveland Sellers

Revolutionary Action Movement (RAM)

1. Hakim Rahman (George Anderson)
2. Eric Perkins
3. John Bracey, Jr.
4. Herman Ferguson
5. General Baker, Jr.
6. Donald Freeman
7. Harlell Jones
8. Katrina Hazzard
9. Askia Muhammad (Rolland Snellings)
10. Nathan Hare

Black Panther Party (BPP)

1. Eddie Ellis
2. Bila Sunni Ali
3. Kathleen Cleaver
4. Austin Allen
5. Abdul Quhbar (Ben Simmons)
6. Madalyn Rucker
7. Cleo Silver
8. Rashad Byrdsong
9. Jo Nina Abron
10. Safayia Bukari

League of Revolutionary Black Workers (LRBW)

1. Charles "Chuck" Wooten
2. Norman "Otis" Richmond
3. General Baker, Jr.
4. Mike Hamlin
5. Gracie Wooten
6. Herb Boyd
7. Darrell Mitchell
8. Luke Tripp
9. Ernest Allen
10. Marian Kramer

Linocut flyer for DRUM from
Black Graphics International (1971)

APPENDIX 3

Bibliography

Acoli, Sundiata, *"A Brief History of the Black Panther Party and Its Place In The Black Liberation Movement"*

Allen, Ernest Mkalimoto, *"Detroit: I Do Mind Dying, A Review,"* Radical America, Vol. II, No. 1 (January–February 1977)

Allen, Robert L., *Black Awakening in Capitalist America: An Analytic History,* [Garden City, New York: Anchor Books, 1970]

Allen, Robert L., *Reluctant Reformers* [New York: Anchor Books, 1975]

Allen, Theodore William, *Class Struggle and the Origin of Racial Slavery* [Hoboken, New Jersey: HEP Publishing Company, 1975]

American Opinion, Volume XIII, No. 4

Anthony, Earl, *Picking Up the Gun,* [New York: Pyramid Books, 1971]

Aptheker, Herbert, *Negro Slave Revolts* [New York: International Publishers, 1962]

Banchero, Stephanie, "Hero or Renegade?," *The Charlotte Observer*, Sunday, February 26, 1995

Baron, Harold, "The Demand for Black Labor," *Radical America, Vol. 5, No. 2, March–April, 1971*

Bass, Jackand Nelson, Jack, *The Orangeburg Massacre* [South Carolina: Mercer University Press, 1984]

Beals, Melba Pattillo, *Warriors Don't Cry* [New York: Washington Square Press, 1994]

Belfrage, Sally, *Freedom Summer* [Greenwich Conn.: A Fawcett Crest Book, 1965]

Black Student Voice, Vol. 1, No. 2, October, 1968

Blumberg, Rhoda Lois, *Civil Rights: The 1960's Freedom Struggle* [Boston: TwaynePublishers, 1991]

Boggs, Grace Lee, *Living for Change: An Autobiography* [Minneapolis: University of Minnesota Press, 1998]

Boggs, Grace Lee, "Remembering James Boggs (1919–1993), *Third World Viewpoint, Fall 1993*

Boggs, Grace Lee, "Thinking and Acting Dialectically: C.L.R. James, The American Years," *Monthly Review, October, 1993*

Boggs, Grace and James, *Detroit: Birth of a Nation* (pamphlet), Detroit, 1967

Boggs, James, *Manifesto For A Black Revolutionary Party* [Detroit, Michigan: ADVOCATORS, 1976]

Boggs, James, *Racism and The Class Struggle: Further Pages from a Black Workers Notebook* [New York: Modern Reader, 1970]

Boggs, James, *The American Revolution: Pages from a Negro Workers Notebook* [New York: Monthly Review Press, 1963]

Boggs, James and Grace Lee, *Revolution and Evolution in the Twentieth Century*

[New York: Monthly Review Press, 1974]

Bond, Julian, "SNCC: What We Did," *Monthly Review, Vol. 52, No. 5, October, 2000*

Bracey, John; Meir, August; Rudwick, Elliot (ed.), *Black Nationalism in America* [New York: The Bobbs-Merrill Co., Inc., 1970]

Bracey, John A. Jr.; Meier, August; and Rudwick, Elliot, eds., *Black Workers and Organized Labor, California:* Wadsworth Publishing, Co., 1971

Bracey, John A. Jr.; Meir, August; Rudwick, Elliot (ed.), *Conflict and Competition: Studies in the Recent Black Protest Movement* [Belmont, California: Wadsworth Publishing Company, 1971]

Branch, Taylor, *Parting the Waters: America in the King Years 1954–63* [New York: Simon and Schuster, 1998]

Branch, Taylor, *Pillar of Fire: America in the King Years 1963–65* [New York: Simon and Schuster, 1998]

Brietman, George (ed.), *By Any Means Necessary: Speeches, Interviews and a letter by Malcolm X* [New York: Pathfinder Press, Inc., 1970]

Brietman, George (ed.) *Malcolm X Speaks* [New York: Grove Press, 1965]

Brietman, George (ed.) *The Last Year of Malcolm X: The Evolution of a Revolution* [New York: Schocken Books, 1967]

Brietman, George; Porter, Herman, and Smith, Baxter, *The Assassination of Malcolm X* [New York: Pathfinder Press, Inc., 1994]

Brisbane, Robert H., *Black Activism* [Valley Forge, Pa.: Judson Press, 1974]

Brown, Cynthia Stokes, *Ready From Within: Steptima Clark and the Civil Rights Movement* [Navarro, California: Wild Tree Press, 1986]

Brown, Elaine, *A Taste of Power: A Black Woman's Story* [New York: Pantheon Books, 1992]

Burns, Haywood, *The Voices of Negro Protest in America* [New York: Oxford University Press, 1963]

Bush, Rod, *We Are Not What We Seem* [New York: New York University Press, 1999]

Callinicos, Alex, *Race and Class* [London: Bookmarks, 1993]

Carew, Jan, *Ghosts In Our Blood* [Chicago, Il: Lawrence Hill Books, 1994]

Carmichael, Stokley & Hamilton, Charles V. *Black Power: The Politics of Liberation in America* [New York: Random House, 1967]

Carson, Clayborne, *In Struggle: SNCC and the Black Awakening of the 1960's,* [Cambridge, Massachusetts: Harvard University Press, 1981]

Carson, Clayborne, Gallen Davis (ed.) *Malcolm X: The FBI File* [New York: Carroll & Graf Publishers, Inc., 1991]

Cashman, Sean Dennis, *African-Americans and the Quest for Civil Rights 1900–1900* [New York and London: New York University Press, 1991]

Chafe, William, *Civilities and Civil Rights: Greensboro, North Carolina and the Black Struggle for Freedom* [New York, Oxford University Press, 1981]

Chalmers, David L., *And the Crooked Places Made Straight* (second edition)

[Baltimore: The John Hopkins University Press, 1996]

Chapell, David L. *Inside Agitators: White Southerners in the Civil Rights Movement* [Baltimore and London: The John Hopkins University Press]

Chatterjee, Pramb, *Local Leadership in Black Communities* [Cleveland, Ohio: School of Applied Social Sciences, Case Western Reserve University, 1975]

Clarke, John Henrik (ed) *Malcolm X: The Man and His Times* [Toronto, Canada: Collier Books, 1969]

Cluster, Dick (ed.) *They Should Have Served That Cup of Coffee* [Boston: South End Press, 1979]

Cobb, Charlie, "Black Power" *Emerge Magazine, June 1997, Volume 8, Number 8*

Cockrel, Kenneth V., "From Repression to Revolution," *Radical America, Volume 5, Number 2* (March–April, 1971)

Cohen, Robert Carl, *Black Crusader: A Biography of Robert Franklin Williams* [Secaucus, New Jersey: Lyle Stuart, Inc., 1971]

Cohen, Tom, *Three Who Dared: The True Stories of Three Young Northerners Who Went South to Work in the Civil Rights Movement* [Garden City, New York: Doubleday and Company, Inc., 1969]

Commentary Volume 8, Number 3, September, 1949, The Journal of Ethnic Studies, Volume 2, Number 5, Fall, 1974

Cone, H. Jones, *Martin & Malcolm & America: A \Dream or a Nightmare* [Marylenoll, New York: Orbis Books, 1991]

Couto, Richard A., *Ain't Gonna Let Nobody Turn Me Around: The Pursuit of Racial Justice in the Rural South* [Philadelphia: Temple University Press, 1991]

Crawford, Vicki L., Rouse, Jacqueline Anne, Woods, Barbara (ed.) *Women in the Civil Rights Movement: Trailbrazers and Torchbears 1941–1965* [Bloomington and Indianapolis: Indiana University Press, 1990]

Cruse, Harold, *The Crisis of the Negro Intellectual* [New York: William Morrow & Company, Inc., 1967]

Davis, Angela Y., *Women, Culture and Politics* [New York: Vintage Books, 1990]

Dent, Tom, *Southern Journey: A Return to Civil Rights Movement* [New York: William Morrow and Company, Inc., 1997]

Dittmer, John, *Local People: The Struggle for Civil Rights in Mississippi* [Urbana: University of Illinois Press, 1995]

DRUM (Dodge Revolutionary Union Movement) Newsletter, Detroit, Michigan, Vol. 1, Nos. 2, 9, 13

DuBois, W.E.B., *Black Reconstruction in America, 1860–1880* [New York: Altheneum, 1973]

Ebony Pictorial History of Black Americans, Volume 3 [Chicago, Illinois: Johnson Publishing Company, 1970]

Epps, Archie, *Malcolm X Speeches at Harvard* [New York: Paragon House, 1991]

Evanzz, Karl, *The Judas Factor: The Plot to Kill Malcolm X* [New York: Thunder

Mouth Press, 1992]

Evanzz, Karl, *The Messenger: The Rise and Fall of Elijah Muhammad* [New York: Pantheon Books, 1999]

Fleming, Cynthia Griggs, "Black Women Activists and the Student Non-Violent Coordinating Committee: The Case of Ruby Doris Smith Robinson," *Journal of Women's History, Volume 4, Number 3 (Winter)*

Foner, Philip S., *Organized Labor and the Black Worker* [New York: Praeger, 1974]

Freeman, Don, "Black Youth and the Afro-American Liberation" *Black America, Fall 1964*

Freeman, Jo (ed.) *Social Movements of the Sixties and Seventies* [New York: Longman, 1983]

Freeman, J.W., *The Revolutionary Ways Out* [unpublished manuscript]

Georgakas, Dan and Surkin, Marvin, *Detroit: I Do Mind Dying* [New York: St. Martin's Press, 1975]

Georgakas, Dan and Surkin, Marvin, *Detroit: I Do Mind Dying Updated Edition: A Study in Urban Revolution* [Cambridge, Massachusetts: South End Press, 1998]

Geschwender, James A., *Class, Race and Worker Insurgency* [New York: Cambridge University Press, 1978]

Geschwender, James A., *The Black Revolt* [New Jersey: Prentice-Hall, 1971]

Geschwender, James A., "The League of Revolutionary Black Workers," *The Journal of Ethnic Studies, Vol. 2, No. 3, (Fall, 1974)*

Glaberman, Martin (ed.) *Marxism For Our Times: C.L.R. James on Revolutionary Organization* [Jackson: University Press of Mississippi, 1999)

Goldman, Peter, *The Death and Life of Malcolm X* [Rubana & Chicago, Illinois, University of Illinois Press, 1979]

Grant, Joanne, *Ella Baker: Freedom Bound* [New York: John Wiley & Sons, Inc., 1998]

Grimshaw, Anna (ed.), *The C.L.R. James Reader* [Cambridge, Massachusetts: Blackwell, 1992]

Gross, James A., "Historians and the Literature of the Negro Worker," *Labor History 10 (Spring, 1969)*

Group, Electronic News, All Power To The People: The Black Panther Party and Beyond [video]

Halberstam, David, *The Children* [New York: Random House, 1998]

Hampton, Henry, Fayaer Steve, Flynn, *Voices of Freedom: An Oral History of the Civil Rights Movement From the 1950's through the 1980's* [New York: Bantam Books, 1990]

Haskins, Jim, *Power To The People: The Rise and Fall of the Black Panther Party* [New York: Simon & Schuster Books For Young Readers, 1997]

Heath, G. Louis, *Off the Pigs!: The History and Literature of the Black Panther Party,* (Metuchen, N.J., The Scarecrow Press, Inc., 1976)

Henle, Peter, "Some Reflections on Organized Labor and the New Militants" *Monthly*

Labor Review 92 (July, 1969)

Hill, Herbert, "Racism Within Organized Labor: A Report of Five Years of the AFL-CIO, 1955–1960," Journal of Negro Education 30 (Spring, 1961)

Hilliard, David, This Side of Glory: The Autobiography of David Hilliard and the Story of the Black Panther Party [Boston: Little, Brown and Company, 1993]

Hime, Darlene Clark, Black Women in America, Volume Two M-Z [Bloomington and Indianapolis: Indiana University Press, 1993]

Hime, Darlene Clark (ed.) Black Women in United States History, Volume 6 [Brooklyn, New York: Carlson Publishing, Inc., 1990]

Holder, Kit Kim, The History of the Black Panther Party 1966–1972: A Curriculum Tool for Afrikan American Studies, unpublished dissertation, (University of Massachusetts, School of Education, May, 1990)

Holt, Len, The Summer That Didn't End [New York: William Morrow & Co., 1965]

Howe, Irvin and Widick, B.J., "The U.A.W. Fights Race Prejudice," Commentary, Vol. 8, No. 3 (September, 1949)

Hutchinson, Earl Ofari, Black and Reds: Race and Class in Conflict 1919–1990 [East Lansing: Michigan State University Press, 1995]

Jackson, George, Soledad Brother [New York: Bantam Books, 1970]

Jackson, James E., The Bold Bad 60's [New York: International Publishers, 1992]

Jacobson, Julius, ed., The Negro and the American Labor Movement [New York: Doubleday and Co., Inc., 1968]

Jamal, Hakim A. From the Dead Level: Malcolm X and Me [New York: Random House, 1971]

James, Joy, "Ella Baker: Black Women's Work and Activist Intellectuals," The Black Scholar, Volume 24, No. 4, Fall, 1994

Johnson, Jacqueline, Stokely Carmichael: The Story of Black Power [Englewood Cliffs, N.J.: Silver Burdett Press, Inc., 1990]

Jones, Charles (ed.), Black Panther Party Reconsidered [Baltimore: Black Classic Press, 1996]

Jones, LeRoi, Black Music [New York: William Morrow & Company, Inc., 1970]

Jones, LeRoi, Blues People [New York: Morrow Quill Paperbacks, 1963]

Karim, Benjamin, Remembering Malcolm [New York: Carroll & Graf Publishers, Inc., 1992

Kelly, Robin D.G. and Esch, Betty, "Black Like Mao: Notes on Red China and Black Revolution" Souls, Volume 1, Number 4, Fall, 1999

Killens, John Oliver, "Black Labor and the Black Liberation Movement," The Black Scholar 2 (October, 1970)

King, Mary, Freedom Song [New York: William Morrow, 1987]

Kofsky, Frank, John Coltrane and the Jazz Revolution of the 1960's [New York: Pathfinder, 1998]

Kornhauser, William, "Ideology and Interests: The Determinants of Union Actions,"

Journal of Social Issues 9 (Winter, 1953)

Kornhauser, William, "The Negro Union Official: A Study of Sponsorship and Control," *American Journal of Sociology 57 (March, 1952)*

Lane, James H., *Direct Action and Desegration 1960–1962: Toward a Theory of Rationalization of Protest* [Brooklyn, New York: Carlson Publishing, Inc., 1989]

Leiman, Melvin N., *The Political Economy of Racism: A History* [Boulder, Colorado: Pluto Press, 1993]

Levy, Peter B., *Let Freedom Ring* [New York: Prager, 1992]

Marable, Manning, *How Capitalism Underdeveloped Black America* [Boston, Massachusetts: South End Press, 1983]

Marable, Manning, *On Malcolm X: His Message and Meaning* [Westfield, New Jersey: Open Magazine Pamphlet Series, 1992]

Marable, Manning, *Race, Reform and Rebellion: The Second Reconstruction in Black America, 1945–1982* [Jackson: University Press of Mississippi, 1984]

Marshall, Ray, *The Negro and Organized Labor* [New York: Wile and Sons, 1965]

Mascott, Louis H. and Corsi, Jerome, *Shootout in Cleveland: Black Militants and the Police* [New York: Bantam Books, 1969]

Mast, Robert H. (ed.) *Detroit Lives* [Philadelphia: Temple University Press, 1994]

McAdam, Doug, "Gender as a Mediator of the Activist Experience: The Case of Freedom Summer," *American Journal of Sociology, Volume 97, Number 5, (March, 1992)*

McCartney, John T., *Black Power Ideologies: An Essay in African-American Political Thought* [Philadelphia: Temple University Press, 1992]

McConnell, Darie, "The Father of Black Revolutionaries: While God Lay Sleeping Robert F. Williams Changed Lives," *The Grand Rapid Press, Sunday, February 19, 1995*

McEnvoy, James and Miller, Abraham (ed.), *Black Power and Student Rebellion* [Belmont, California: Wadsworth Publishing Company, Inc., 1969]

McLemee, Scott (ed.), *C.L.R. James On The 'Negro Question'* [Jackson: University Press of Mississippi, 1996]

McLemee, Scott and Le Blanc, Paul (ed.) *C.L.R. James and Revolutionary Marxism: Selected Writings of C.L.R. James 1939–1949* [New Jersey: Humanities Press, 1994]

Meir, August and Rudwick, *CORE: A Study in the Civil Rights Movement 1942–1968* [Chicago: University of Illinois Press, 1975]

Miles, Michael W., *The Radical Probe: The Logic of Student Rebellion* [New Jersey: Antheneum Publishers, 1971]

Mills, Kay, *This Little Light of Mine: The Life of Fannie Lou Hamer* [New York: A Dutton Book, 1993]

Mills, Nicolaus, "Forgotten Greenville: SNCC and the Lessons 1963," *Dissent, Summer, 1990*

Moore, Gilbert, *Rage*, [Carroll & Graf Publishers, Inc., 1993]

Neary, John, *Julian Bond: Black Rebel, A Biography*, [New York: William Morrow and Company, 1971]

Nelson, Britta W., "Ella Baker—A Leader Behind the Scenes," *Focus, Volume 21, No. 8, August, 1983*

Newton, Huey P., *Revolutionary Suicide*, [New York: Writers and Readers Publishing, Inc., 1995]

Newton, Huey P., *To Die for the People: Selected Writings and Speeches* [New York: Writers and Readers Publishing, Inc., 1995]

Newton, Huey Percy, *War Against the Panthers: A Study of Repression in America*, [Ann Arbor, MI: University Microfilms International, 1980] (unpublished doctorate dissertation)

Newton, Michael, *Bitter Grain: Huey Newton and the Black Panther Party* [Los Angeles, CA: Holloway House Publishing Company, 1991]

New York Times, April 11, 1964

New York Times, April 21, 1964

New York Times, May 3, 1967

Norden, Eric, "The Assassination of Malcolm X," *Hustler, December, 1978*

Norrell, Robert J., *Reaping the Whirlwind* [New York: Vintage Books, 1986]

NYCPD Bureau of Special Services: Malcolm X Files [New York: 1993]

Olsen, James S., "Organized Black Leadership and Industrial Unionism: The Racial Response 1936–1945," *Labor History 10 (Summer, 1969)*

Oppenheimer, Martin, *The Sit-In Movement of 1960* [Brooklyn, New York: Carlson Publishing, Inc., 1989]

Ovenden, Kevin, *Malcolm X: Socialism and Black Nationalism* [London: Bookmarks, 1992]

Parks, Rosa, *Rosa* [New York: Dial Press, 1994]

Payne, Charles M., *I've Got the Light of Freedom* [Berkeley: University of California Press, 1995]

Pearson, Hugh, *The Shadow of the Panther: Huey Newton and the Price of Black Power in America* [Reading, Massachusetts: Addison-Wesley Publishing Company, 1994]

Peebles, Mario Van, Taylor, Ula Y & Lewis, S. Tarika, *Panther: A Pictorial History of the Black Panthers and the Story Behind the Film*, [New York: New Market Press, 1995]

Perkins, Eric, "The League of Revolutionary Black Workers and the Coming of Revolution," *Radical America, Volume 5, No. 2 (March-April, 1971)*

Powledge, Fred, *Free At Last?: The Civil Rights Movement and the People Who Made It*, [New York: Harper Perennial, 1991]

Proudfoot, Merrill, *Diary of a Sit-in*, [Urbana and Chicago: University of Illinois Press, 1990]

Reitan, Ruth C., *The Rise and Decline of an Alliance: Cuba and African-American Leaders in the 1960's* [unpublished PhD dissertation]

Review, Socialist, Volume 26, No. 1 and 2, 1996

Rice, J.F., *Up on Madison Down on 75th Street: A History of the Illinois Black Panther Party*, [Evanston, Illinois: The Committee, 1983]

Robinson, Cedric J., *Black Marxism: The Making of the Black Radical Tradition*, [Chapel Hill: The University of North Carolina Press, 1983]

Robinson, Lewis G., *The Making of a Man* [Cleveland, Ohio: Green and Sons, 1970]

Robnett, Belinda, *How Long? How Long? African-American Women in the Struggle for Civil Rights*, [New York: Oxford University Press, 1997]

Rothschild, Mary Aiken, *A Case of Black and White: Northern Volunteers and the Southern Freedom Summers, 1964–1965*, [Westport, Connecticut: Greenwood Press, 1982]

Rout, Kathleen, *Eldridge Cleaver* [Boston: Twayne Publishers, 1991]

Salem, Dorothy (ed.) *African-American Women: A Biographical Dictionary* [New York: Garland Publishing, 1983]

Salem, Dorothy, *Long Journey: History of the African-American Experience* [Dubuque, Iowa: Kendal/Hout Publishing Company, 1997]

Sales, Jr., William W., *From Civil Rights to Black Liberation: Malcolm X and the Organization of Afro-American Unity* [Boston, Massachusetts: South End Press, 1994]

Salzman, Jack, Back, Adina, Sorin, Gretchen Sullivan (ed.), *Bridges and Boundries: African-American and American Jews* [New York: George Brazidler, Inc., 1992]

Samuel, Leah, "A Life Lived for Justice: James Boggs," *Metro Times October 13–19, 1993*

Scheer, Robert (ed.), *Eldridge Cleaver: Post-Prison Writings and Speeches* [New York: Ramparts Book/Random House, 1969]

Seale, Bobby, *A Lonely Rage: The Autobiography of Bobby Seale* [New York: New York Times Books, 1978]

Sellers, Cleveland with Terrell, Robert, *The River of No Return: The Autobiography of a Black Militant and the Life and Death of SNCC* [Jackson: University Press of Mississippi, 1990]

Shaka, Oba T., *The Political Legacy of Malcolm X* [Chicago, Illinois: Third World Press, 1983]

Skakur, Assata, *Assata: An Autobiography* [Chicago, Illinois: Lawrence Hill Books, 1987]

Shyrlee, Dallard, *Ella Baker* [Englewood Cliffs: Burdett Press, 1990]

Smith, Jessie Carney (ed.) *Notable Black American Women* [Detroit: Gale, 1992]

Snodgrass, Kenneth, "James Boggs Lives," *Michigan Chronicle, August 4–10, 1993*

Speaks-Justice, Volume 14, No. 3, "Black Freedom Movement Loses Giant: Robert F. Williams of Monroe, N.C., Succumbs to Cancer"

Spero, Sterling D., and Harris, Abram L., *The Black Worker* [New York: Athenum, 1931]

Spofford, Tim, *Lynch Street: The May 1970 Slayings at Jackson State College*, [Kent, Ohio: The Kent State University Press, 1988]

Starobin, Robert S., *Industrial Slavery in the Old South* [New York: Oxford University Press, 1975]

Stern, Mark, *Calculating Visions: Kennedy, Johnson and Civil Rights* [New Brunswick, New Jersey: Rutgers University Press, 1992]

Stoper, Emily, *The Student Nonviolent Coordinating Committee: The Growth of Radicalism in a Civil Rights Organization* [Brooklyn, New York: Carlson Publishing, Inc., 1989]

Taft, Phillip, *Organized Labor in American History* [New York: Harper and Row, 1964]

Tani, E. And Sera Kae, *False Nationalism, False Internationalism: Class Contradictions in the Armed Struggle* [Chicago, Illinois: A Seeds Beneath the Snow Publication, 1985]

Taylor, Jesse Douglas Allen, "On Men and War," *Essence, February, 1988*

The South End, Volume 22, Number 62, Thursday, January 23, 1969

Thompson, Heather Ann, *Whose Detroit?*, [Ithaca: Cornell University Press, 2001]

Tripp, Luke, "DRUM—Vanguard of the Black Revolution," *The South End (Wayne State University Student Newspaper), Volume 27, No. 62 (January 23, 1969)*

Tung, Mao Tse, *Selected Readings from the Works of Mao Tse Tung* [Peking: Foreign Language Press, 1971]

Tyson, Timothy B., *Radio Free Dixie: Robert F. Williams and the Roots of Black Power* [Chapel Hill: The University of North Carolina Press, 1999]

Tyson, Timothy B., "Robert Franklin Williams: A Warrior for Freedom 1925–1996, *Southern Exposure, Winter, 1996*

United States Government of America, *Black Panther Party Part 4, National Office Operations and Investigation of Activities in Des Moines, Iowa and Omaha, Nebraska/Hearings before the Committee on Internal Security House of Representatives Ninety First Congress Second Session Appendix A* [Washington D. C.: U. S. Government Printing Office, 1971]

United States Government of America, *Gun-Barrel Politics: The Black Panther Party, 1966–1971* [Washington, D.C.: U. S. Government Printing Office, 1971]

United States Government of America, *The Black Panther Party: Its Origin and Development as Reflected in its Official Weekly Newspaper, The Black Panther Black Community News Service,* (Washington, D.C.: U.S. Government Printing Office, 1970)

Wahad, Dhoruba Bin Abu-Jamal, Mamia Shakur, Assata, *Still Black, Still Strong: Survivors of the U.S. War Against Black Revolutionaries* (New York: Semiotext (e), 1993)

Walff, Miles, *Lunch at the 5 & 10* [Chicago: Elephant Books, 1990]

Walton, Hanes, Jr., *Black Political Parties* [New York: The Free Press: London, Collier-McMillan Limited, 1972]

Widick, B.J., *Detroit: City of Race and Class Violence* [Chicago: Quadrangle, 1972]

Williams, Eric, *Capitalism and Slavery* [New York: Capricorn Books, 1966]

Williams, Evelyn, *In Admissible Evidence* [Brooklyn, New York: Lawrence Hill Books, 1993]

Williams, Robert F., *Negroes with Guns* [Chicago, Illinois: Third World Press, 1962]

Willis, Arthur C., *Cecil's City: A History of Blacks in Philadelphia 1638–1979* [New York: A Heartherstones Book: Carlton Press, Inc., 1990]

Wish, Harvey, "American Slave Insurrections Before 1861," *The Journal of Negro History XXII* (July, 1947) Washington, D.C.

Wolfenstein, Eugene Victor, *The Victims of Democracy: Malcolm X and the Black Revolution* [London: Free Association Books, 1989]

Wood, Joe (ed.) *In Our Own Image: Malcolm X* [New York: Grove Press, Inc., 1965]

X, Malcolm, Haley, Alex, *The Autobiography of Malcolm X* [New York: Grove Press, Inc., 1965]

X, Malcolm, *Malcolm X Talks to Young People* [New York: Pathfinder Press, 1991]

X, Malcolm, *On Afro-American History* [New York: Pathfinder Press, 1967]

X, Malcolm, *The Final Speeches* [New York: Pathfinder Press, 1992]

X, Malcolm, *The Last Speeches* [New York: Pathfinder Press, 1994]

X, Malcolm, *Two Speeches by Malcolm X* [New York: Pathfinder Press, 1965]

X, Malcolm, "Zionist Logic," *The Egyptian Gazzette-September 17, 1964*

Zim, Howard, *SNCC: Student Nonviolent Coordinating Committee* [Boston: Beacon Press, 1965]

The writings of Trinidadian revolutionary C.L.R. James were a large influence on U.S. radicals from the 1950s on.

BOOKS TO CHANGE THE WORLD

LUCY PARSONS: Freedom, Equality & Solidarity—Writings & Speeches, 1878-1937, edited & introduced by Gale Ahrens, with an Afterword by Roxanne Dunbar-Ortiz. First-ever anthology of tracts & talks (on anarchism, women, race, class war, the injustice system) by the great anarchist agitator, regarded as "More Dangerous than 1000 rioters"! Includes nearly all of her many IWW writings. Correcting several errors made by earlier writers, it adds much to our knowledge of Lucy and her relevance for freedom struggles today. 191 pages. Illus. $17

THE DEVIL'S SON-IN-LAW: The Story of Peetie Wheatstraw & His Songs by Paul Garon. A study of the great blues singer, song-writer and hobo. Illustrated. 156 pp. With 24-track CD. Cloth $26; Paper $18

BLACK WOBBLY: The Life & Times of Ben Fletcher by Peter Cole. The first book on the legendary African American IWW organizer, with a judicious selection of his speeches and writings. "The audacious radicalism and organizing genius of Ben Fletcher are wonderfully captured in this remarkable collection."—**Dave Roediger.** 152 pp. Paper, $18.00

WHAT'S THE USE OF WALKING IF THERE'S A FREIGHT TRAIN GOING YOUR WAY?—Black Hoboes & their Songs by Paul Garon. "Yet another masterpiece of cultural history by Garon. The stories and songs gathered together in this remarkable book disrupt common notions of what we mean by 'freedom' when it comes to black folk. Hoboes represented a significant segment of the black working class, and their constant movements were both evidence of constraints and acts of freedom. And as Garon so eloquently demonstrates, the men and women who took to the road and their bards have much to teach us about America's 'bottom rail.'"—**Robin D. G. Kelley**, author of *Freedom Dreams*. 288 pages. Illustrated. With 25-track CD. paper, $22

LABOR STRUGGLES IN THE DEEP SOUTH & Other Writings by Covington Hall, edited & introduced by David R. Roediger. Vivid first-hand account of IWW multiracial organizing among timber and dock-workers in Louisiana and Texas in the 1910s. Illustrated. 262 pp. $14.00

Please add $3 postage for the first title, and fifty cents for each additional title.

CHARLES H. KERR PUBLISHING COMPANY
Est. 1886 / 1740 West Greenleaf Avenue, Chicago, Illinois 60626

Other Books from Charles H. Kerr

A HISTORY OF PAN-AFRICAN REVOLT by C. L. R. James. Introduction by Robin D. G. Kelley. The classic account of global black resistance in Africa and the diaspora. *"A mine of ideas advancing far ahead of its time"*—**Walter Rodney**. 160 pp., $14.00

HISTORY AGAINST MISERY, by David Roediger. This collection of 38 articles, covering a wide range of topics—football strikes, the IWW, surrealism, May Day, hiphop, talk-radio, and writers as varied as André Breton, C.L.R. James, and Sterling Brown, focuses on the oppressive late-capitalist ideologies known as "miserabilism." *"A surrealist roadmap to liberated futures .... A book we must keep close to us as we struggle to overthrow misery once and for all"* —**Robin D.G. Kelley.** 184 pp. Profusely illustrated. Paper, $18

DANCIN' IN THE STREETS! Anarchists, IWWs, Surrealists, Situationists & Provos in the 1960s, edited & Introduced by Franklin Rosemont & Charles Radcliffe. Most books on the 1960s focus on ref-rmist politics. *Dancin'* is devoted to the far left of the far left. Multiracial and workingclass, *The Rebel Worker* group were young members of the IWW in Chicago, inspired by the hobo wisdom of their Wobbly elders and also by surrealism. Critics derided them as "the left wing of the Beat Generation," but they were noted for their original revolutionary perspective and class-war humor. 450 pp. Illustrated. Paper $19; Cloth $25

FACING REALITY by C.L.R. James. The celebrated 1950s "underground classic," also known as James's "most anarchist book," with a new introduction by John Bracey, accenting its relevance today. 176 pp. $16.00

THE LESSON OF THE HOUR: Wendell Phillips on Abolition & Strategy, edited & introduced by Noel Ignatiev. Although William Lloyd Garrison was the most widely known of the Abolitionists, Wendell Phillips was the real leader. This volume, the only collection currently available, includes six speeches charting a revolutionary course for abolition, with an introduction establishing their historical context. 160 pages. Cloth, $28.00; paper, $12.00

See our website—www.charleshkerr.net

Please add $3 postage for the first title, and fifty cents for each additional title.

CHARLES H. KERR PUBLISHING COMPANY
Est. 1886 / 1740 West Greenleaf Avenue, Chicago, Illinois 60626